ABOUT THE AUTHOR

Charles Duff (1894–1966) had wide experience in the practical use of Spanish and related modern languages. After serving with the French Army as an interpreter, he was employed for many years as Press Officer by the British Foreign Office. Thereafter, he devoted his time to teaching, writing, and translating. He served as lecturer at the Institute of Education, London University.

Mr. Duff pioneered in developing and applying modern methods of teaching foreign languages, using them in classroom work and as a basis for his popular volumes of self-instruction. He was the author of individual books and editor of a series of books in the field of modern languages, including *French for Beginners, Italian for Beginners, German for Beginners* (with Paul Stamford), and *Russian for Beginners* (with Dmitri Makaroff); *How to Learn a Language;* and the *Basis and Essentials Series.* His articles appeared in many English and American magazines, and he was a contributor to the *Encyclopedia Britannica.*

EVERYDAY HANDBOOKS

S P A N I S H
FOR BEGINNERS

by CHARLES DUFF

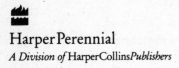
HarperPerennial
A Division of HarperCollins*Publishers*

This revised American edition published by special arrangement with Charles Duff and English Universities Press, Ltd. The original edition entitled *Spanish for Adults* was first issued in Great Britain in 1958.

Library of Congress Number 58-12024

ISBN 0-06-463271-7

99   RRD H   40 39 38 37

INTRODUCING THE COURSE

THIS IS A COMPREHENSIVE course in Spanish. It has been prepared on modern principles, evolved from long experience and practice, and is arranged so that it can be used by adults in several ways, including class instruction. It is *not* intended for children.

Adults who wish to learn Spanish come under these broad headings:

(1) Absolute beginners, many of whom have some knowledge of French or another modern language, and including a number of people who are especially interested in one or more of the Spanish-American countries.

(2) Those who have "picked up" some Spanish, are attracted by the language, and desire to improve their knowledge.

(3) That increasing body of people who are becoming conscious of the fact that Spanish is a most rewarding language from nearly every point of view. Many of them wish to be able to read Spanish or Spanish-American literature in order to enjoy at first hand many excellent books which have not been translated into English.

(4) Those who wish to know the language for some essentially practical purpose such as commerce, travel, amusement, and so forth.

Spanish presents to the linguistic novice many extremely encouraging features. The pronunciation is easy, very easy in comparison with, say, that of French; and the spelling of Spanish is almost phonetically perfect. After a week, the learner can read a simple sentence in Spanish with a pronunciation which at least will be understood. Good and often quite rapid progress is made in the elementary stage in general, because the grammar is straightforward and the exceptions few. A large number of common words are similar in Spanish and English. The order of words is the same as in English, except for adjectives and pronouns, which do not present great difficulties. In even a few weeks the beginner becomes surprised and very pleased with himself because he is able to "make so much" of a newspaper in Spanish or a simple book in the language. But, unfortunately, once the elementary stage has been passed, the easiness has also been passed! It all begins to be more difficult and continues to be difficult—or at least not so easy. This, however, is offset for the persistent student by the fact that he already knows so much and feels so confident that he is encouraged to continue his studies. On the higher plane of literature, Spanish is as easy (or as difficult!) as any other European language. The person whose own language is English and who is unacquainted with Spanish may take it, from those who know it and several other languages, that he will reap a richer reward in a shorter time from Spanish than by the study of any one of the other great languages of the world. I have met few members of the teaching profession who know and teach more than one European language who would challenge this statement.

The course can be used either for self-instruction, for individual study with a teacher, or for class work. It is highly advisable for the self-taught to start with a good pronunciation, and this can rarely be achieved without the help of a native to assist with the whole of Lesson I. Those who from circumstances cannot obtain this preliminary help should remember two things: (a) a bad pronunciation at the start is difficult to eliminate afterwards, and (b) by following the advice given in Lesson I, a quite passable pronunciation can be achieved. All the same, I should like to emphasize the importance of acquiring a good pronunciation from the start, for, as Otto Jespersen has said: "Language cannot be separated from sound; and that is the sum of the matter." But those who intend to learn Spanish for reading purposes only will find here more than enough phonetic and other guidance.

When a teacher is available, everything becomes much easier for the learner. Nothing can replace the good teacher, who is there to correct errors and to solve every little problem. The rest depends on the learner and on the planning and presentation of the lessons.

All students, but more especially the self-taught, should avail themselves of every opportunity of hearing Spanish spoken: whether from radio, Spanish-speaking friends or acquaintances, motion pictures, television, phonograph records, or in any other way.

The course consists of fifteen lessons, each divided into five sections. Each section is intended for a minimum period of one hour's study in class, though it may in certain cases be found that some sections may require more than that. The self-taught will make their own pace throughout, and are advised to devote at least five hours a week to learning new material, and two hours

weekly to review of what has been learned before. Slow progress
need cause no worry so long as one keeps on going.

A word must be said about the method of practice advised until
Situation Material and Continuous Reading and the other items of
reading matter have been reached. Precisely because of the ease in
learning Spanish in the early stage, and the fact that adults and not
children are the learners, I have not provided assigned exercises.
I found some years ago that the adult student likes to make his own
sentences, is far more interested in this form of practice than in
assigned work, and with it makes just as good and often better
progress than in the old way. The intelligent adult student is
always willing to "worry things out"; and this does no harm,
especially if a teacher or native speaker is available to help him.
The self-taught must always work fairly hard, for there need be no
concealing the fact that neither Spanish nor any other language
can be learned entirely "without tears" when there is nobody to
help. Once the Situation Material and the Continuous Reading
have been reached, things become clarified by the translations,
which explain most things and require only that the learner has
assimilated what has gone before.

A word must also be said on an aspect of Spanish which, even
today, causes some misgivings to those who do not know the facts.
It usually arises with some such question as this: "If I learn the
Spanish in this book, shall I be able to get along with the Spanish
spoken in such-and-such a Spanish-American country?" The
answer is: "Yes." The Spanish written everywhere in Spanish
America is Castilian, which is what this book contains. The
spoken language also is the same Spanish with a few variations in
pronunciation. The only differences that matter are in the use of
local words for flora and fauna, perhaps also for some dishes and
drinks, and each country has phrases, turns of speech, and idioms
of its own. To include lists of these for each country would not
only have overburdened a book such as this, but would have confused and perhaps discouraged the learner who could say to himself: "Have I to learn all this?" — to which the answer is: "Certainly not. Learn what is in this book and, if you should go to a
Spanish-American country, note any strange words and phrases
and ask what they mean." For example, **sello** (*postage stamp*) in
Spain is **estampilla** in Spanish America. To convince everybody,
I have included extracts from writers of nine countries — Argentina, Colombia, Cuba, Ecuador, Mexico, Nicaragua, Peru,

Spain, and Uruguay — and if space permitted I could show by extracts from writers of all the other Spanish-American countries that the language of Spain and the language of all those countries have far fewer differences in idiom, structure, vocabulary, and pronunciation than the English of the United States and the English spoken in Britain. But to indicate some of the differences, I have devoted a section to Spanish-American pronunciation, have given some important variants in the use of words, and, where necessary in the reading matter, have drawn attention to other differences.

Grateful acknowledgments are due to the writers and publishers of the extracts included here. Whenever possible the name of the writer is given with the text, but, in a few cases, where newspaper material is used, the writer is anonymous.

For grammar I have relied on the *Gramática de la Lengua Española* of the Spanish Academy. I have found *A Modern Spanish Dictionary* by Margaret H. Raventós (English Universities Press, 1953) of great help because of its up-to-dateness. My final court of appeal for words has been the *Diccionario Manual e Ilustrado de la Lengua Española* of the Real Academia Española (latest edition, Espasa-Calpe, S.A., Madrid, 1950).

I wish to acknowledge the assistance of the Editorial Department of Barnes and Noble, Inc., and of their consulting editor, Dr. Laurence F. Hawkins, for developing the revised form of the Basic Vocabulary and for numerous emendations adapting the original text to the needs of the American reader.

Finally, I wish to thank my Spanish and Spanish-American friends who in various ways have helped me with this book, and especially Enrique Jarero of the University of Birmingham, who kindly read the book in typescript, and Antonio Suelto, who read the proofs. If any errors should still remain, the responsibility for them is mine.

CHARLES DUFF

CONTENTS

INTRODUCING THE COURSE   v
WHY WE LEARN SPANISH xvii
THE SPANISH LANGUAGE, by Emilio Castelar xviii

PART I: FIRST PRINCIPLES

HOW TO STUDY PART I **2**

LESSON I

§ 1. The Spanish Alphabet — Spanish Pronunciation —
     Stress — Vowels — Vowel Combinations — Diph-
     thongs — Triphthongs — Warning **3**
§ 2. Spanish Consonants — Consonants Resembling Eng-
     lish Consonants — Consonants with Sounds Differ-
     ing from Those of Their English Equivalents . . .   **5**
§ 3. Spanish-American Pronunciation **7**
§ 4. Vocabulary and Pronunciation Practice **9**
§ 5. Articles — Nouns; Gender; Agreement of Articles
     and Nouns — Plurals — Contractions **AL, DEL** . .   **11**

LESSON II

§ 1. Some Rules of Gender — Nouns of Nationality . . .   **14**
§ 2. Practicing Pronunciation — Double Letters — Some
     Exceptions to Rules regarding Diphthongs — Punc-
     tuation — Capital Letters — Syllables — Vocabu-
     lary **16**
§ 3. Adjectives — Agreement of Adjectives and Nouns —
     Some Useful Adjectives **19**
§ 4. Adjectives That Lose –**O** before a Noun — **GRAN(DE)**
     — **SAN(TO)** — Two or More Adjectives in Series —
     Vocabulary — Practice **20**
§ 5. Comparison of Adjectives — More Useful Adjectives
     — Adjectives as Nouns **22**

LESSON III

§ 1. The Superlative of Adjectives — Irregular Comparison   **25**
§ 2. Visualization: Thinking in Spanish **26**

§ 3. Personal Pronouns 27

§ 4. **NO** with a Verb — **SER** and **ESTAR** — Position of Pronouns — Vocabulary and Practice — The Orthographic Accent 29

§ 5. The Cardinal Numbers — **-UNO, CIENTO, MIL, MILLÓN** — Learning the Numbers 31

LESSON IV

§ 1. Ordinal Numbers — Differing Usages in Spanish — Measurement 33

§ 2. Practice with Numbers — Some Quantitative Expressions 34

§ 3. Possessive Pronouns — Clarifying Phrases after **SU** — Adjectives as Pronouns 36

§ 4. Vocabulary — Practice Phrases and Sentences 38

§ 5. Relative Pronouns — Interrogative Pronouns — Exclamations — Impersonal Expressions — Telling Age — Practice Sentences — Practice for This Lesson 39

LESSON V

§ 1. Words Common to English and Spanish — Orthographic Differences 44

§ 2. Similar English and Spanish Word Endings — Some Nouns, Adjectives, and Verbs Identical or Similar in Both Languages 45

§ 3. Days of the Week — The Months — The Seasons — Dates — Dating a Letter 48

§ 4. The Time of Day 49

§ 5. Geographical Names — Some Peculiar Regional Names and Nicknames — Reading Practice . . . 50

LESSON VI

§ 1. Demonstrative Adjectives and Pronouns 54

§ 2. Reflexive Pronouns and Reflexive Verbs — **MISMO**. 55

§ 3. Conjunctions 56

§ 4. Interjections and Exclamatory Phrases 58

§ 5. The Adverb — Making Adverbs from Adjectives with **-MENTE** — Position of the Adverb — Invariable Adverbs 59

LESSON VII

§ 1. Prepositions — Simple Prepositions — Some Prepositions Explained 62

§ 2. More Prepositions Explained — Compound Prepositions 64

§ 3. Negative Words and Their Use 66

§ 4. Infinitives in **–AR, –ER, –IR** — Object Pronouns Attached to Infinitives — Present Tense of **COMPRAR, VENDER, VIVIR** — **TENER** and **HABER** — Past Participles — Present Perfect Tense. . . . 69

§ 5. Essential Parts of **SER** and **ESTAR** — The Use of **SER** and **ESTAR** — Essential Parts of **HABER** — Some More Past Participles 71

LESSON VIII

§ 1. The Importance of **–AR** Verbs — Endings of **–AR** Verbs in the Simple Tenses — Progressive Forms with **ESTAR** — Some Common **–AR** Verbs — **GUSTAR** 75

§ 2. The Personal **A** — Practice Reading: Extract from *La Vejez*, by V. Blasco Ibáñez — Literal and Free Translations 77

§ 3. Word Order in Spanish — Position of Pronouns — Position of Adjectives — Position of Adverbs — Position of Negative Words — Word Order in Direct Statements — Word Order in Questions — Variety of Word Order 79

§ 4. Forms of Address — Family Names — Introductions and Polite Expressions 83

§ 5. Words of Relationship — Occupations — Some Personal Titles — A Glance Backwards and Forwards . 85

PART II: FRAMEWORK OF THE LANGUAGE

HOW TO STUDY PART II 90

LESSON IX

§ 1. Introducing Part II — Regular Verbs in **–ER** and **–IR** — Conjugation of Simple and Compound Tenses of **COMPRAR, VENDER,** and **VIVIR** 91

§ 2. Prepositions **A, DE,** and **PARA** after Verbs — Verbs

Not Followed by Prepositions — **DEBER** Followed
by Infinitive — The Infinitive Used as Noun — Situation Material: Greetings   93

§ 3. The Verbs **CONOCER, SABER,** and **PODER** —
Practice with Situation Material — Situation Material: Air Travel   97

§ 4. The Imperative — Polite Requests — Spanish Equivalents of *Let* — **VAMOS, ¡ VIVA!** — **HAY** — Situation Material: Baggage — Reading: Alarcón, **Historia de Mis Libros (1)**   99

§ 5. **PARA** and **POR** — Situation Material: Sea Travel —
Historia de Mis Libros (2)   104

LESSON X

§ 1. How to Use the Table That Follows — Full Conjuga-
tion of **COMPRAR, VENDER, VIVIR** in Simple
Tenses — Situation Material: The Customs; At the
Railway Station — **El Sombrero de Tres Picos (1)** .   110

§ 2. An Introduction to the Subjunctive — Situation Material: Asking the Way; Taxis — **El Sombrero de
Tres Picos (2)**   116

§ 3. The Conditional Mood — Omission of Subject Pronouns — **TÚ** and **VOSOTROS** — Situation Material: Money and Exchange — **El Sombrero de
Tres Picos (3)**   121

§ 4. Orthographic Changes in Verbs — Situation Material:
Hotel and Boarding House — **El Sombrero de Tres
Picos (4)**   126

§ 5. Full Conjugation of **ESTAR** and **HABER** — Uses of
the Present and Future Tenses — Idioms — Situation Material: Getting Up — **El Sombrero de Tres
Picos (5)**   130

LESSON XI

§ 1. Full Conjugation of **SER** — The Passive Voice — Conjugation of **AMAR** in the Passive — Substitutes for
the Passive — Situation Material: The Bathroom
— **El Sombrero de Tres Picos (6)**   138

§ 2. Reflexive Verbs — Situation Material: Going to Bed
— **El Sombrero de Tres Picos (7)**   143

§ 3. Irregular Verbs — Classes of Irregularities — Com-

pounds of Irregular Verbs — Situation Material:
At the Post Office — **El Sombrero de Tres Picos** (8)   147

§ 4. Irregular Verbs with Change of **E** to **IE** — Change of **O**
to **UE** — **ANDAR, DAR, ESTAR, JUGAR** — Situation Material: Drinking — **El Sombrero de Tres
Picos** (9)   152

§ 5. Irregular Verbs with Change of **C** to **ZC** — Some
Common Irregular **-ER** Verbs — Situation Material: Eating (1) — **El Sombrero de Tres Picos**
(10)   157

LESSON XII

§ 1. Irregular **-IR** Verbs — Situation Material: Eating
(2): Breakfast — **Lazarillo de Tormes** (1). . . .   166

§ 2. Irregular Past Participles — Defective Verbs — Impersonal Verbs — Situation Material: Eating (3):
Lunch; Meats — **Lazarillo de Tormes** (2). . . .   173

§ 3. How to Say SOME, ANY, NONE, Etc., in Spanish —
IR and **ANDAR** — Situation Material: Eating (4):
Dinner and Supper; Fowl; Seafood — **Lazarillo
de Tormes** (3)   180

§ 4. Idioms with **HACER, DAR, ECHAR, LLEVAR,
PONER** — Situation Material: Eating (5): Vegetables, Fruits — **Lazarillo de Tormes** (4).   185

§ 5. The Subjunctive: An Outline of Its Uses — Sequence
of Tenses — Situation Material: Eating (6): Desserts; Miscellaneous — **Lazarillo de Tormes** (5). .   193

LISTENING TO RADIO   203

LESSON XIII

§ 1. Compound Nouns — Noun Phrases — Situation Material: At the Barber Shop and Hairdresser's —
Carlos Octavio Bunge: **El Gaucho**   204

§ 2. Compound Adjectives — Adjectival Phrases — Situation Material: At the Bullfight — Bartolomé Mitre:
Bolívar y San Martín.   209

§ 3. Verbs Formed from Nouns and Adjectives — Situation
Material: Photography — Jorge Isaacs: **La Caza
del Tigre**   213

§ 4. Words for Males and Females — Situation Material:
Doctor and Dentist — Ricardo Palma: **Carta.** . . .   218

§ 5. **MACHO** and **HEMBRA** — Nouns with Two Genders
and Two Meanings — Geographical Adjectives —
Situation Material: Clothes; Laundry and Cleaning — Rubén Darío: **Palimpsesto**   223

LESSON XIV
§ 1. Word-building by Derivatives — Augmentatives —
Pejoratives — Situation Material: Motoring —
Amado Nervo: **Las Nubes**   229
§ 2. Diminutives — Situation Material: Theater and
Cinema — Juan Montalvo: **Elogio de la Pobreza.**   234
§ 3. Derivatives with Special Meanings — Nicknames —
Situation Material: Paying Accounts — José Martí:
Un Cuento de Elefantes   239
§ 4. Reference List of Noun and Adjective Suffixes (1) —
José Enrique Rodó: **Mirando Jugar un Niño** . . .   242
§ 5. Reference List of Noun and Adjective Suffixes (2) —
Illustrative List of Derivatives of **Hombre** and
Tierra — Emilio Castelar: **La Lengua Española** .   246

LESSON XV
§ 1. More about the Articles — The Definite Article. . .   252
§ 2. The Indefinite Article — Omission of the Article . .   255
§ 3. **SI,** IF or WHETHER — Newspaper Items.   258
§ 4. Weights and Measures — Spanish and Spanish-American Currencies — Extract from George Borrow, *The
Bible in Spain*, in English and in Spanish Translation.   262
§ 5. Correspondence in Spanish — Some Useful Phrases for
Letter Writing — Two Spanish Book Advertisements   266

THE NEXT STEPS   270
APPENDIX: SUPPLEMENTARY READINGS
I. **Los Gitanos**   273
II. **Literatura en España Durante La Guerra de 1914–18**   275
III. **Españoles y Irlandeses**   275
IV. **El Arte del Traductor**   277
V. **El Pueblo Más Viejo de Europa**   279
VI. **Las Películas de Pablito Calvo por Luis Alberto
Sánchez**   281

BASIC AND SUPPLEMENTARY VOCABULARIES 283

BASIC VOCABULARY 285

SUPPLEMENTARY VOCABULARY 323

INDEX 329

WHY WE LEARN SPANISH

Because:

It is one of the great languages of the world.

It is the easiest of the great world languages for the absolute beginner.

It is spoken by 120 million people as their mother tongue: in Spain and her colonies, in Spanish-American countries, in the Philippines, in scattered communities along the Mexican border of the United States, and by Sephardim in eastern Europe and elsewhere.

It is the same language wherever it is spoken, apart from some local differences.

It opens the door to a rich and interesting variety of cultures and literatures, and is the language in which is written one of the world's greatest books: *Don Quixote*.

It is one of the important "interchange" languages officially recognized by great international bodies such as the United Nations Organization.

It is a very beautiful and most rewarding language, worth learning for itself and for its remarkable adaptability to all purposes of life and civilization.

It is everything that is claimed for it by the Spanish orator and statesman Emilio Castelar in the eloquent passage on the next page

THE SPANISH LANGUAGE*

. . . With several roots interwoven, multiple sounds in harmony, onomatopoeic qualities so musical that they open the sense to divination of the words before knowing them; sweet as the softest melody and resonant as the most brattling thunder; emphatic to the point that only in Spanish is it possible to speak with distinction of supernatural things and informal so that no language has the advantage over it in pleasing manner and the picaresque. It is so nicely proportioned in the distribution of vowels and consonants that there is no need for either the deep-toned solemnities exacted by certain peoples of the South, or the clenched pronunciation required of lips and teeth in the North; free in its syntax, with so many possible combinations that each author can find for himself his own original style without impairing the conjuncture. It is unique in its formation, for on its Latin base with Celtic and Iberian ramifications, the Germanic has introduced some of its expressions, Greek some of its luster, and Hebrew and Arabic such decoration and garlands that they make it without doubt one of the most suitable languages for the natural as for the religious purpose. It is the language which most effectively lends itself to the tones and shades of modern eloquence; the language which has greatest abundance in words with which to respond to the wealth of ideas; the verbal medium of a spirit which glittered in the past and will shine more brightly in the future: for not only will it have this homeland and these our peoples, but beyond the seas vast expanses and free, independent peoples, united with us by affinities of blood and race as by the deeply intimate and spiritual elements of speech and thought, whose virtue would oblige us to continue in the Old and New World a new history worthy of that most glorious history of the past.

EMILIO CASTELAR

* For original Spanish selection, see page 250.

PART I

FIRST PRINCIPLES

> Language cannot be separated from *sound;* and that is the sum of the matter.
>
> *Jespersen*

How to Study Part I

This course is designed for use with or without a teacher. Better and quicker results are achieved with a teacher or with the aid of a Spanish-speaking friend.

Spanish can be learned without the aid of a teacher when the pronunciation is known. But if possible the aid of a native speaker should be enlisted for at least Lesson I, until the pronunciation has been mastered.

Group learning is to be encouraged. Four or five should be the maximum in a group. But, with a teacher, classes of up to fifteen or twenty can use the course.

As much time should be devoted to practice as to study.

Make sure that you know how the grammar *works* before proceeding. Once you know how it works, practice and reading will show it in action and drive it home. As each lesson is finished: (1) go over it again at least once, and (2) go over *all* that has gone before until you feel sure that you know it.

Keep a notebook of those items which seem elusive or which have caused difficulties.

After Lesson V, all learners should try to meet Spanish-speaking people, and they should listen to records or radio programs in Spanish.

LESSON I

§ 1. The Spanish Alphabet — Spanish Pronunciation — Stress — Vowels — Vowel Combinations — Diphthongs — Triphthongs — Warning

THE SPANISH ALPHABET has twenty-eight letters. Twenty-five are the same as those of English; *w* is used only in foreign proper names. In addition to these twenty-five letters, there are **ñ** and **ch** and **ll**, which are regarded as single letters. (Keep this in mind when using a Spanish dictionary; **ñapa** would come after **nutrir, caña** after **canto, chacra** after **cuyo, llama** after **luz.**)

SPANISH PRONUNCIATION follows certain rules that have no exceptions, and it is phonetically simple. When you have mastered this lesson and have had some practice — if possible, with a Spanish-speaking person — you should be able to pronounce Spanish in a way that will be understood. With careful practice an almost perfect enunciation can be achieved by those whose mother tongue is English. What is required is guided imitation. With sufficient of this, no one need despair of achieving a good pronunciation.

IN THIS LESSON, PRONOUNCE ALL SPANISH WORDS ALOUD.

STRESS. (1) Words ending in a vowel (**a, e, i, o, u**), **n**, or **s** have the stress on the next-to-last syllable.

(2) Words ending in any consonant except **n** or **s** are stressed on the last syllable.

(3) Every word that does not follow one of these two rules has the stress indicated by the accent ′, which is placed over the stressed vowel (**á, é, í, ó, ú**) or over the stronger vowel of a diphthong if the stress falls on a diphthong (as **ió, ué**).

EXAMPLES:

(1) **puro, madre, tribu, volumen, antes**
(2) **seguridad, social, esperar**
(3) **ahí, cajón, barítono, boletín, francés, único, huérfano**

VOWELS:

a has the *ah* sound of *a* in *father:* **cama, casa, madre.**

e usually has the sound of *é* in *café:* **Pepe, me.** It is short in a final syllable or in a word of one syllable when a consonant follows, like *e* in *set:* **papel, joven, vale, el, en, mujer.**

3

i has the sound of *i* in *machine:* **Lima, fin, universo.**

o usually has the sound of *o* in *hope:* **poco, vagón,** though somewhat shortened (in duration) at the end of a word. Before **r,** it is somewhat like our *o* in *north:* **corazón, norte.**

u has the sound of *u* in *rule* (never that of *u* in *use*): **un, una, puro, burro, Cuba, bambú.**

y is used as a single vowel (i.e., not in a diphthong or as a consonant) only in the Spanish word **y** (*and*), pronounced *ee.*

See WARNING on page 5.

ALL SPANISH VOWEL SOUNDS MUST BE PURE, CLEAR, AND FULL, ESPECIALLY WHEN STRESSED.

VOWEL COMBINATIONS. When two or three vowels come together in Spanish, each retains its basic sound — the sound indicated above — but one vowel is always pronounced a little more clearly than the others. When two vowel sounds run together to make one sound, this is a *diphthong;* three such vowels make a *triphthong.* These sounds must be mastered.

DIPHTHONGS. These are pronounced as single syllables, but, in the combination of vowels, there is always one vowel stronger (more sonorous) than the other. Strong vowels are **a, o, e.** Weak vowels are **i, y, u.** Spanish diphthongs are never composed of two strong vowels; there is usually a strong plus a weak, but two weak vowels can also form a diphthong. When two strong vowels are found together, each must be given its full sound.

List of Diphthongs

ai, ay:	pronounced like		*ai* in *aisle:* **aire, hay**
au:	"	"	*au* in *sauerkraut:* **caudillo**
ei, ey:	"	"	*ei* in *vein,* *ey* in *they:* **reina, ley**
eu:	"	"	*ey-oo* (stress on *oo*): **deuda**
ia:	"	"	*ia* in *Christian* (i.e., *ya*): **diablo, Sebastián**
ie:	"	"	*yay:* **tiene, bien**
io:	"	"	*yo* in *yoke:* **rubio, Dios**
iu:	"	"	*ee-oo* (stress on *oo*), or *you:* **viuda**
oi, oy:	"	"	*oi* in *coin,* *oy* in *boy:* **oigo, hoy**
ua:	"	"	*ua* in *jaguar,* *wa* in *watch:* **agua, cuarto**
ue:	"	"	*way:* **bueno, fuego** (see note below)
ui, uy:	"	"	*uey* in *gluey:* **ruina, ruido, muy** (see note below)
uo:	"	"	*woe:* **cuota, continuo**

Note: The **u** is silent in **gue** (*gay*), **gui** (*ghee*), **que** (*cay*), and **qui** (*key*): **pague, guiar, quedo, Quito.** But u is pronounced like *w* in **cue** (*cway*), **cui** (*cwee*), **güe** (*gway*), **güi** (*gwee*): **cuerpo, cuidado, agüero, güipil.**

TRIPHTHONGS.   There are only six three-vowel combinations:

iai: pronounced *ee-i*, or *yi*: fiáis
iei: "   *ee-ay*, or *yay:* fiéis
uai, uay: "   *wy:* **La Guaira, Paraguay**
uei, uey: "   *way:* **continuéis, buey**

WARNING.   You must realize that the English equivalents given
above are at best makeshifts and do not represent the true value of
Spanish vowels and vowel combinations.   But, if you do not have
a native teacher who can speak the sounds clearly and correct
mispronunciations, they should help you toward a passable pronunciation.

Furthermore, it must be emphasized that these vowel sounds
are highly important in Spanish, a language of well-sounded, full
vowels which give it much of its beauty.   You will do well to take
this to heart and endeavor to achieve as nearly perfect pronunciation
as possible.

MAKE IT A RULE THROUGHOUT LESSON I TO PRONOUNCE EVERY
SPANISH WORD ALOUD, REPEATING IT A FEW TIMES.

§ 2. *Spanish Consonants — Consonants Resembling English Consonants —
Consonants with Sounds Differing from Those of Their English Equivalents*

SPANISH CONSONANTS.   The attentive learner will have realized
that the Spanish vowels are always pronounced distinctly and without shades.   In this they are unlike English vowels, which are often
so blurred that the foreigner thinks they are nothing but blurs !

Spanish consonants, on the other hand, are softer than those of
English, less distinctly pronounced.   The vowels give Spanish
its fine, robust sonority;   the consonants serve to soften it.   This
is particularly true of Spanish as spoken in Andalusia and in the
Spanish-American countries.

Spanish consonants may be conveniently considered under two
headings: (1) those which in sound closely resemble or approximately resemble their English equivalents;   (2) those which differ
from these equivalents.

CONSONANTS RESEMBLING ENGLISH CONSONANTS:

c before **a, o, u,** or any consonant but **h** is pronounced like
English hard *c* in *can, cold, cut, clan:* **camisa, color. cucaracha,
crema, doctor.**

ch is always pronounced like *ch* in *church:* **cheque, rancho.**

g before **a, o, u,** or a consonant is like English hard *g* in *gay, go, gun, glad:* **gato, hago, águila, grande.**

f, k, l, m, n, p, q, t, and **y** are the same as in English: **flama, kilómetro, página, Quito, yo.** (**Q** appears only in the combinations **que** and **qui** — see note after "Diphthongs," above.)

w (not part of the Spanish alphabet) occurs only in foreign names and is pronounced as in the original language: **Jorge Wáshington, Ricardo Wágner.**

Consonants with Sounds Differing from Those of Their English Equivalents:

b has two sounds in Spanish. At the beginning of a word, after **m** and before **l,** it is an explosive like *b* in *boy, ambition, blend:* **boca, bomba, amable.** In other cases the sound is made by breathing lightly through hardly open lips; thus, **b** in **Habana** sounds almost like *v* in English *Havana.*

Spanish **b** is always softer than ours. Because of the second sound above, in which the lips are not pressed together, it has been said — incorrectly — that Spanish **b** and **v** have the same sound. Many Spaniards treat the two letters as one sound and, to distinguish them in spelling out a word, they say **b de burro** (which means *b, as in burro*) and **v de vaca** (which means *v, as in vaca*).

c before **e** and **i** has, in Castilian, the sound of *th* in *think:* **acera, cinco.** But it is pronounced differently in Spanish America (see § 3, page 7). [*Note:* This sound of **c** in Spanish is the same as the sound of Spanish **z** (see below)].

d is softer than in English, and between vowels is often pronounced like *th* in *though.* Thus, in **dedo** the first **d** is close to English *d*, but the second **d** resembles *th* in *though: day-tho.*

g before **e** and **i** is like English aspirate *h* as in *he:* **gente, página.**

h is always silent; it is retained in Spanish only for philological reasons: **hombre** (*ombre*), **huevo** (*wayvo*).

j is somewhat like a strongly aspirated English *h*, but the true Spanish sound is a guttural, like Scottish *ch* in *loch* or German *ch* in *doch:* **caja, jefe, jota.**

ll in Castilian sounds like *lli* in *million:* **caballo, calle.** But it is pronounced differently in Spanish America (see § 3, page 7).

ñ is like *ni* in *onion, ny* in *canyon:* **señor, caña, cuñado.**

r is much more distinct in Spanish than in English, being always slightly trilled with the tip of the tongue, as Scottish and Irish people trill it: **caro, hora.** When **r** begins a word, the trilling is stronger than when it comes between two vowels: **Ramón, ropa.**

rr is always strongly trilled, or, as some say, rolled: **tierra, horrible.** There must be a difference in pronunciation between **pero** (*but*) and **perro** (*dog*), **caro** (*dear*) and **carro** (*car*). Practice these four words.

s is like English *s* in *so;* it never has the *z* sound of *s* in *rose* (Spanish **rosa** is pronounced *rohssa*). Thus: **así, sala, oso.**

v is often pronounced like English *v* but sometimes like our *b.* You will not be far wrong in pronouncing it like our *v:* **¡Viva! vista.** (*Note:* The Grammar of the Spanish Academy comments that "in the greater part of Spain, as the pronunciation of **b** and **v** are the same," attention must be paid to the spelling of words in which either of these letters occurs.)

x is usually like English *x,* but in **México** and **mexicano** it is pronounced like Spanish **j** (this is a relic of old Spanish, in which we find such spellings as **xefe** for **jefe**). The words **México, mexicano** are written **Méjico, mejicano** in Spain. It would be best to use **x** in Mexico and **j** elsewhere.

Note: In parts of Mexico and in Guatemala you come across words and names of Mayan origin in which **x** is pronounced *sh:* **maxeño** (inhabitant of Chichicastenango), *ma-shane-yo,* **Ixmal,** *Eesh-mahl.* (The sound *sh* does not occur in Spanish, and **x** was given the job of representing it.) In central Mexico, **x** may have the *s* sound in Indian words: **Xochimilco,** *So-chee-meel-co,* **xochitl** (*flower*), *so-cheetl.*

z is, in Castilian, like *th* in *thin:* **zapato, zorro, luz.** But it is pronounced differently in Spanish America (see § 3, below).

§ 3. *Spanish-American Pronunciation*

THE pronunciation of Spanish presented above is that of **castellano,** Castilian, the language of Castile, which is now spoken in most of Spain. Just as American differs from British pronunciation, there are some differences between Spanish and Spanish-American pronunciation. The latter is similar to the speech of Andalusians (the "Southerners" of Spain); it is less clear-cut than Castilian, with many softenings of consonants, though not of vowels.

At this point you should decide whether to learn and use the Castilian pronunciation, which is favored by the schools, or Spanish-

American pronunciation, which is more desirable for those who expect to travel or live in Spanish America. (Many Spanish-Americans consider Castilian pronunciation affected.) If you prefer to learn Castilian, you should be aware of the peculiarities of Spanish-American pronunciation. *Caution:* Do not mix one pronunciation with the other; the effect would be ludicrous.

In Spanish America:

b except before **l** or **r** is generally pronounced like our *v*.

c before **e** and **i** is pronounced like *s in see*. Thus, **cinco** (Castilian *thinco*) is pronounced *sinco*.

d in popular speech is not pronounced between vowels or at the end of a word. Thus, **colorado** becomes *colorao* and **Usted** becomes *Usté*. (See note after **s**.)

ll is like *y* in *beyond*. **Castellano** is pronounced *casteyano*. But in Argentina, Uruguay, and Paraguay **ll** has the sound of *z* in *azure* or, more emphatic, of English *j*. So **caballo** is in Castilian *cabalyo*, in most of Spanish America *cavayo*, and in certain countries named above *cavazho* or *cavajo*. (**Ll** and **y** present a spelling problem for Spanish-Americans.) Learn to pronounce **ll** as *y*.

s, like **d**, tends to disappear in the popular speech of some countries. In Cuba "**se tragan las eses**" (the *s*'s are swallowed), likewise in Chile. **Está** is pronounced *e'tá*.

> *Note:* If you wish to learn Spanish-American pronunciation, do not drop your **d**'s and **s**'s, as these letters *are* pronounced by educated people in most countries. To learn to drop them would be like learning *goin'* for *going* in learning English.

y in Argentina and Uruguay is pronounced as **ll** is pronounced there: *zh* or *j*. Thus **yo** is pronounced *zho* or *jo*.

z is always pronounced like Spanish *s*. Thus, **vez** is in Castilian *veth*, in Spanish-American *ves* (rhymes with *face*).

SUMMARY. To learn Spanish-American pronunciation, learn:

c before **e** and **i** = s

z = s

ll = y

Other pronunciations described above are less important or local.

Each Spanish-American country has many words of Indian origin, most of them names of native plants, animals, foods, etc.;

some local usages of Spanish words (a bus is a **camión** in Mexico, a **camioneta** in Guatemala, though the standard Spanish is **ómnibus** or **autobús**); and its own slang (a bus in Cuba is a **guagua**, pronounced *wawa* — sound of baby crying).

On the whole, however, the Spanish of Spanish America differs much less from the parent Castilian than American and Colonial English differs from British English. In some Spanish-American countries — for example, Colombia — the language spoken is excellent Castilian.

In the text, SA = Spanish-American usage (as regards vocabulary).

§ 4. *Vocabulary and Pronunciation Practice*

You will have noticed that in the preceding sections the meanings of words given as examples of pronunciation were not supplied. That was because there was no need for you to learn two things at the same time — pronunciation and meaning. Now you may do both, using the Spanish words in the vocabulary to practice pronunciation. When in doubt about pronunciation, refer to the rules. Here are the same words (a few omitted for various reasons) in the order in which they appeared and with their meanings. Nouns are preceded by **el** or **la** (*the*) or by **un** or **una** (*a, an*). These words must be memorized, but not all at once — ten words at a time is enough.

PURO, pure
LA MADRE, the mother
LA TRIBU, the tribe
EL VOLUMEN, the volume, size
ANTES, before
LA SEGURIDAD, security
SOCIAL, social
ESPERAR, to expect, hope, wait
AHÍ, there, over there
EL CAJÓN, the case, box
EL BARÍTONO, the baritone
UN BOLETÍN, a bulletin
FRANCÉS, French, Frenchman
ÚNICO, only, unique
EL HUÉRFANO, the orphan (boy)
UNA CAMA, a bed
UNA CASA, a house
PEPE, Joe

ME, me
EL PAPEL, the paper
JOVEN, young, young man
VALE, is worth
EN, in, on
LA MUJER, the woman
EL FIN, the end
EL UNIVERSO, the universe
UN POCO, a little
EL VAGÓN, the (*railroad*) car
EL CORAZÓN, the heart
EL NORTE, the north
EL BURRO, the donkey, burro
EL BAMBÚ, the bamboo
Y, and
EL AIRE, the air
HAY, there is, there are
EL CAUDILLO, the leader

LA REINA, the queen
LA LEY, the law
LA DEUDA, the debt
EL DIABLO, the devil
BIEN, well (*adv.*)
RUBIO, blond
DIOS, God
LA VIUDA, the widow
HOY, today
EL AGUA, the water
EL CUARTO, the room
BUENO, good
EL FUEGO, the fire
LA RUINA, the ruin
EL RUIDO, the noise
MUY, very
LA CUOTA, the quota
CONTINUO, continuous
GUIAR, to guide
EL CUERPO, the body
EL CUIDADO, the care
UN AGÜERO, an omen, a sign
EL BUEY, the ox
LA CAMISA, the shirt
EL COLOR, the color
LA CUCARACHA, the cockroach
LA CREMA, the cream
EL DOCTOR, the doctor
EL CHEQUE, the check
EL GATO, the cat
UN ÁGUILA, an eagle
GRANDE, big, large, great
LA FLAMA, the flame
UN KILÓMETRO, a kilometer
UNA PÁGINA, a page
YO, I
LA BOCA, the mouth
LA BOMBA, the bomb, pump
AMABLE, kind, amiable
LA HABANA, Havana
UNA VACA, a cow
LA ACERA, the sidewalk

CINCO, five
EL DEDO, the finger
LA GENTE, the people
EL HOMBRE, the man
UN HUEVO, an egg
LA CAJA, the box, cash box
EL JEFE, the chief, boss
EL CABALLO, the horse
LA CALLE, the street
EL SEÑOR, the gentleman; **Señor,**
  Mr., Sir
LA CAÑA, the cane
EL CUÑADO, the brother-in-law
CARO, dear, expensive
UNA HORA, an hour
RAMÓN, Raymond
LA ROPA, the clothes
LA TIERRA, the earth, soil
HORRIBLE, horrible
PERO, but
EL PERRO, the dog
UN CARRO, a car
LA ROSA, the rose
ASÍ, thus, so
LA SALA, the hall, (*large*) room
UN OSO, a bear
¡VIVA! Long live! Hurrah!
LA VISTA, the sight, view
MÉJICO, (*Mex.*) **MÉXICO,** Mex-
  ico
MEJICANO, (*Mex.*) **MEXICANO,**
  Mexican
EL ZAPATO, the shoe
UN ZORRO, a fox
LA LUZ, the light
CASTELLANO, Castilian
COLORADO, ruddy, red, colored
USTED, *formal* you (*sing.*)
UNA VEZ, one time, once
EL ÓMNIBUS, *or* **AUTOBÚS,** the
  bus

These words will all have to be learned, with their meanings, but for the moment concentrate on getting the pronunciation right.

You will find that you will remember their meanings after reading them over a few times. Try to get a native speaker to say them over one by one, and imitate his pronunciation as closely as possible.

§ 5. *Articles — Nouns; Gender; Agreement of Articles and Nouns — Plurals — Contractions AL, DEL*

ARTICLES. The words *a*, *an*, and *the* are called *articles;* *a* (or *an*) is the indefinite article, *the* the definite. Whereas *a*, *an*, and *the* never change form in English, the Spanish articles vary according to the gender and number of the following noun.

The Spanish indefinite article is:

UN (*masc.*), UNA (*fem.*), a *or* an; *also* one

as in:

UN MUCHACHO, a boy, one boy
UNA MUCHACHA, a girl, one girl

The plural UNOS (*masc.*), UNAS (*fem.*) means *some:*

UNOS MUCHACHOS,   UNAS MUCHACHAS,
some boys   some girls

The definite article is:

Singular: EL (*masc.*), LA (*fem.*) ⎫
Plural: LOS (*masc.*), LAS (*fem.*) ⎬ the
⎭

Thus:

EL MUCHACHO, the boy   LOS MUCHACHOS, the boys
LA MUCHACHA, the girl   LAS MUCHACHAS, the girls

There is a seldom used neuter article LO, which has no plural. It is used before adjectives (including possessive pronouns and participles) to make them into nouns; for example:

LO ÚTIL, the useful, that which is useful
LO MÍO, that which is mine
LO POSIBLE, the possible, that which is possible
LO DICHO, that which, *or* what, is, *or* was, said

NOUNS; GENDER; AGREEMENT OF ARTICLES AND NOUNS. A noun is the name of a person, thing, or state; *man, table, heat, equality* are nouns. All Spanish nouns are either masculine or feminine. Males are masculine, females are feminine; but in

Spanish, *things* have gender — the sun is masculine, the moon is feminine. Most Spanish nouns end in either –o or –a, and with very few exceptions nouns ending in –o are masculine and those ending in –a are feminine. Thus:

> **EL AMIGO,** the friend (*male or general*), boy friend
> **LA AMIGA,** the friend (*female*), girl friend

Many Spanish nouns do not end in –o or –a. Sometimes the gender is obvious, as in:

> **EL PADRE,** the father   **LA MADRE,** the mother
> **EL SEÑOR,** the gentleman   **LA SEÑORA,** the lady

But often the gender must be learned, and it is best learned by learning the article with the noun:

> **EL DIENTE,** the tooth   **LA CARNE,** (the) meat, flesh

One common word ending in –o is feminine: **LA MANO,** the hand. A common masculine word ending in –a is **EL DÍA,** the day. The word **agua** is feminine but takes **el** before it for euphony: **EL AGUA,** the water (but plural: **LAS AGUAS,** the waters).

PLURALS. In Spanish the plural is usually formed, as in English, by adding –s:

> **EL PADRE,** the father   **LOS PADRES,** the fathers
> **LA MADRE,** the mother   **LAS MADRES,** the mothers
> **LA CASA,** the house   **LAS CASAS,** the houses
> **LA MANO,** the hand   **LAS MANOS,** the hands

EXCEPTIONS:

(1) Nouns ending in –s and family names ending in –s or –z remain unchanged in the plural:

> **EL MARTES,** Tuesday   **LOS MARTES,** Tuesdays
> **LOS FERNÁNDEZ,** the Fernández (family)

(2) Nouns ending in any consonant but –s add –es in the plural:

> **LA CIUDAD,** the city   **LAS CIUDADES,** the cities
> **LA FLOR,** the flower   **LAS FLORES,** the flowers

(3) If a noun ends in –z, the z becomes c in the plural:

> **LA VOZ,** the voice   **LAS VOCES,** the voices

(4) Nouns ending in –ey take the plural ending –es:

> **EL REY,** the king   **LOS REYES,** the kings

The preceding rules govern formation of the plural of nearly all Spanish nouns. The few nouns with exceptional plurals can be learned individually.

Note 1: When a noun takes the plural ending **–es** and thereby gains a syllable, (with only two exceptions) the stressed syllable remains stressed. This some-times requires adding a written accent to, or removing a written accent from, the stressed syllable:

EL JOVEN, the young man   **LOS JÓVENES,** the young men
EL JARDÍN, the garden   **LOS JARDINES,** the gardens

Note 2: Some nouns may, in the plural, mean two or more males, or a male and a female, or a group of males and females. Thus:

LOS AMIGOS, the friends (*male, or male and female*)
LOS PADRES, the fathers, the parents, the father(s) and mother(s)
LOS REYES, the kings, the rulers, the monarchs, the king(s) and queen(s)
LOS JÓVENES, the young men, the young people, the young men and women
LOS MUCHACHOS, the boys, the boys and girls, the children
LOS NIÑOS, the little boys, the (little) children

CONTRACTIONS. The prepositions **a,** *to,* and **de,** *of, from,* when followed by the article **el,** form the following contractions:

a el   (*to the*) becomes **AL**
de el (*of the*) becomes **DEL**

Thus: **AL PADRE DEL JOVEN,** to the father of the young man
Compare: **A LA MADRE DE LA JOVEN,** to the mother of the young woman
A LOS PADRES DE LOS JÓVENES, to the parents of the young people

LESSON II

§ 1. *Some Rules of Gender — Nouns of Nationality.*

SOME RULES OF GENDER. Since all Spanish nouns are either masculine or feminine and many of them are neuter in English, it is necessary for you to acquire the habit of learning each new noun with its article. Instead of learning **pan** (*bread*), learn **el pan;** instead of **sol** (*sun*), learn **el sol;** instead of **luna** (*moon*), **la luna;** instead of **cabeza** (*head*), **la cabeza.** Though the ending of the noun often indicates its gender, there are exceptions; so the safest and best rule is to learn the article with the noun.

It is helpful, however, to know certain rules about gender. The following rules begin with what you have already learned.

(1) With few exceptions nouns in –o are masculine and nouns in –a are feminine. Among the commonest exceptions are **la mano,** *the hand,* and **el día,** *the day.*

(2) Some nouns are masculine or feminine according to whether they refer to a male or a female. Thus:

> **el** *or* **la guía,** the guide
> **el** *or* **la compatriota,** the compatriot
> **el** *or* **la indígena,** the native
> **el** *or* **la artista,** the artist
> **el** *or* **la socialista,** the socialist
> **el** *or* **la mártir,** the martyr
> **el joven,** the young man; **la joven,** the young woman
> **el tigre,** the tiger; **la tigre,** the tigress

And some nouns in –a are necessarily masculine:

> **el cura,** the priest
> **el poeta,** the poet (*fem.:* **poetisa,** poetess)

(3) Some nouns change gender according to meaning:

> **el capital,** the capital (*money*); **la capital,** the capital (*city*)
> **el frente,** the front; **la frente,** the forehead

(4) Certain classes of things are always or usually masculine:

> (a) Days of the week: **el domingo,** Sunday; **el lunes,** Monday; **el martes,** Tuesday

14

(b) The months: **el enero,** January; **el abril,** April; **el diciembre,** December

(c) Countries — if the name does not end in unaccented –**a:** **el Perú, Chile, el Canadá** (the article is used with the names of *some* countries)

(d) Names of trees: **el nogal,** the walnut tree; **el manzano,** the apple tree; **el naranjo,** the orange tree
There are some exceptions, as: **la encina,** the oak; **la higuera,** the fig tree.

(e) Oceans and seas: **el Atlántico, el Pacífico, el Mediterráneo, el Mar Caspio (Mar,** *Sea*)

(f) Rivers: **el Misisipí, el Amazonas** (*originally* **el Río de las Amazonas**)**, el Plata** (**el Río de la Plata**)

(g) Mountains and mountain chains: **el Aconcagua, los Alpes, el Himalaya,** the Himalayas

(5) Certain classes of things are feminine:

(a) The letters of the alphabet: **la e,** the *e;* **las eses,** the *s*'s

(b) Countries with names ending in unaccented –**a** (see 4c, above): **España,** Spain; **Inglaterra,** England; **Australia**

(c) Most names of towns and cities: **Madrid, Nueva York**

(d) Fruits (see 4d, above): **la manzana,** the apple; **la naranja,** the orange

(6) Nouns ending in –**l,** –**n** (except for the endings –**ción,** –**sión,** –**tión**), –**r** are masculine: **el sol,** the sun; **el corazón,** the heart; **el color,** the color

(7) Nouns ending in –**ción,** –**sión,** –**tión,** –**d,** –**umbre,** besides nearly all those in –**a,** are feminine: **la acción,** the action; **la visión,** the vision; **la cuestión,** the question; **la libertad,** liberty; **la virtud,** virtue; **la lumbre,** the firelight; **la muchedumbre,** the crowd

You need not memorize all these rules at present, but you should refer to them now and then and note exceptions to them.

NOUNS OF NATIONALITY. These nouns have distinctive endings to show gender and number; thus:

el inglés, the Englishman; **la inglesa,** the Englishwoman; **los ingleses,** the English, Englishmen; **las inglesas,** Englishwomen

el alemán, the German; **la alemana,** the German woman; **los alemanes,** the Germans; **las alemanas,** German women

el español, the Spaniard; **la española,** the Spanish woman; **los españoles,** the Spanish, *or* Spaniards; **las españolas,** Spanish women

el norteamericano, the North American; **la norteamericana,** the North American woman; *etc.*

El inglés, el alemán, el español also mean the languages English, German, Spanish.

§ 2. *Practicing Pronunciation — Double Letters — Some Exceptions to Rules regarding Diphthongs — Punctuation — Capital Letters — Syllables — Vocabulary*

PRACTICING PRONUNCIATION. You have probably realized by now that as regards pronunciation and vocabulary, Spanish is not very difficult. You will find most things straightforward and even easy in comparison with other European languages. But there is much to be learned, and it cannot be learned without effort. To learn Spanish requires concentration and practice and constant review.

For the present, make haste slowly. Memorize as much of the vocabulary as you can, and practice the pronunciation. Say the words aloud, at the same time thinking of their meaning. Go over them again and again.

IF YOU FIND A SECTION DIFFICULT, TAKE IT SLOWLY AND LEARN AS MUCH AS POSSIBLE. THEN GO ON TO THE NEXT SECTION, AND REVIEW DIFFICULT PARTS LATER.

DOUBLE LETTERS. You have already learned the pronunciation of **ll** and **rr.** The only other consonants that are doubled in Spanish are **c** and **n,** as in **acción, occidente, innumerable.** When two **c**'s come together, the first has the sound of *k* and the second **c** is *th* (Cast.) or *s* (SA). Thus:

$$\text{acción — Cast.: } ak\text{-}thion$$
$$\text{SA: } ak\text{-}sion$$

Note: The Spanish endings –ción, –sión, –tión do not have the *sh* sound that we use in *action, mission.*

Only the strong vowels **a, e, o** are doubled, and when this happens they are pronounced separately. Thus: **contraataque** (*counterattack*), **creencia** (*belief*). **cooperativo.**

SOME EXCEPTIONS TO RULES REGARDING DIPHTHONGS. Sometimes two vowels that usually form a diphthong have to be pronounced separately because one vowel is part of a prefix or suffix. In **coincidencia,** for example, we have the prefix **co–** followed by the prefix **in–,** so that it would be wrong to pronounce **coin–** as one syllable (compare English *coincidence*). Likewise, in **increíble** (*incredible*) there is the suffix **–ible,** which must be pronounced separately, and **ei** here is not a diphthong.

Often, as in **increíble,** a written accent shows that two letters which usually form a diphthong are pronounced separately: **baúl** (*trunk*), **grúa** (*derrick*), **tío** (uncle). This frequently happens in verb forms: **caído, reír, ríe, salíamos.**

The preceding exceptions to the rules given in Lesson I will not cause you any difficulty.

PUNCTUATION. Spanish punctuation is the same as that of English with the following exceptions: Inverted question marks and exclamation marks are placed *before* questions and exclamations, in addition to the regular marks at the end of the sentence. The nature of such sentences is thus indicated in advance:

> ¿ **Cómo está su padre?**   How is your father?
> ¡ **Qué vergüenza!**   What a shame!

You will sooner or later notice that occasionally an inverted question mark is used, not at the beginning of a sentence, but before a final interrogatory phrase or clause, as in:

> **Es su padre ¿ no es verdad?**   It's your father, isn't it?

CAPITAL LETTERS. The use of capitals is generally the same in Spanish as in English. But:

(1) No Spanish adjective is ever capitalized:

> **la bandera inglesa,** the English flag
> **un país sudamericano,** a South American country
> **un país cristiano,** a Christian country

(2) As regards nouns of nationality, usage varies. In Spanish newspapers it is not unusual to capitalize them: **los Ingleses,** the English; **el Sudamericano,** the South American. But in Spanish America these nouns are usually not capitalized: **el cubano,** the Cuban.

(3) The months and the days of the week are not capitalized:

> **de enero,** of January   **en diciembre,** in December
> **el domingo,** Sunday   **los lunes,** Mondays

DIVISION OF SYLLABLES IN WRITING. In Spanish, hyphens are used only when a word is broken at the end of a line (note that there are no hyphenated words).

Break a word in two only at the end of a syllable. If possible, a syllable should end with a vowel: **a-me-ri-ca-no**. But a syllable may end in a consonant when there is a good reason for it: **sud-a-me-ri-ca-no** (**sud**– means *south*), **nor-te** (**rte** would be unpronounceable), **des-cu-brir** (*discover*) (**des**– is a prefix).

Never divide **ll** or **rr**: **ca-ba-llo, pe-rro**.

Never divide a word so as to leave a single letter at the end or the beginning of a line: *not* **o-cupar** (*occupy*), but **ocu-par**.

VOCABULARY. In the first two lessons you should achieve a fair mastery of the elements of pronunciation and should learn the words used as examples. Many of the words are common and will recur again and again; so there is no need to learn them all now. But they are all important for pronunciation practice. Make sure that your pronunciation of these words is correct by referring to the rules and examples given on pages 3–7.

Those new words which have been used since the last vocabulary list (pages 9–10) are given below, in the order in which they were used. Look over the list and when you have forgotten the meaning of the word look back to the text for it. A few words are omitted as unnecessary. First review the vocabulary of Lesson I.

el muchacho — una muchacha — los — las — lo — útil — mío — posible — un amigo — la amiga — la señora — el diente — la carne — la mano — un día — el martes — la ciudad — una flor — la voz — el rey — el jardín — los niños — al — del — el pan — el sol — la luna — la cabeza — el or la guía — el or la indígena — el or la artista — el or la socialista — el or la mártir — el or la tigre — el cura — un poeta — la poetisa — el capital — la capital — el frente — la frente — el domingo — el lunes — el enero — el abril — el diciembre — el Perú — el Canadá — el nogal — el manzano — el naranjo — la encina — una higuera — el Atlántico — el Pacífico — el Mediterráneo — el mar — el Misisipí — el Amazonas — los Alpes — el Himalaya — España — Inglaterra — Nueva York — una manzana — una naranja — la libertad — la virtud — la acción — la visión — la cuestión — la lumbre — la muchedumbre — el inglés — un alemán — el español — un norteamericano — el occidente — el contraataque — la creencia — cooperativo — una coincidencia — increíble — el baúl — la grúa — el tío — ¿ Cómo ? — su — ¡ Qué ! — no — la verdad — la bandera — el país — sudamericano — cristiano — cubano — descubrir — ocupar

§ 3. *Adjectives — Agreement of Adjectives and Nouns — Some Useful Adjectives*

ADJECTIVES. An adjective is a descriptive word. In "a good man" *good* is an adjective. In "The man was good but timid" *good* and *timid* are adjectives.

AGREEMENT OF ADJECTIVES AND NOUNS. In Spanish the adjective, like the article, must agree with the noun in gender and number. The adjective is usually placed after the noun. Thus:

> **el hombre rico,** the rich man
> **los hombres ricos,** (the) rich men
> **la tinta negra,** the black ink
> **las tintas negras,** (the) black inks

Note: In the examples above, *the* is placed in parentheses in the plural to indicate that, although in English we often omit the article in the plural, in Spanish the article is nearly always used; **los hombres ricos** — *the rich men* or *rich men.*

As with nouns, the masculine form of the adjective usually ends in −o and the feminine in −a; plurals in −os and −as.

Adjectives which do not end in −o in the masculine singular retain the same ending in the feminine singular. Thus:

> **un hombre cortés,** a polite man
> **una mujer cortés,** a polite woman

In the plural the adjective adds −es for both genders:

> **los hombres corteses,** the polite men
> **las mujeres corteses,** the polite women

However, adjectives of nationality which do not end in −o in the masculine singular add −a in the feminine; plurals end in −es, −as:

> **el caballero inglés,** the English gentleman
> **la dama inglesa,** the English lady
> **los reyes ingleses,** the English kings
> **las reinas inglesas,** the English queens

THE GENERAL RULES FOR ADJECTIVES ARE THE SAME AS FOR NOUNS.

SOME USEFUL ADJECTIVES. The adjectives on page 20 should be memorized in tens. This list and its continuation in § 5 are useful for reference.

abierto, open

agradecido, grateful

alegre, gay, merry

algun(o), some

alto, high, tall

amargo, bitter

ambos, both

amistoso, friendly

ancho, broad, wide

atrayente, attractive

azul, blue

bajo, low

barato, cheap

bello, beautiful

blanco, white

bobo, silly, stupid

bonito, pretty

buen(o), good

cada,* each

cálido, warm, hot

caliente, warm, hot

cansado, tired

cariñoso, affectionate

caro, dear, expensive

ciego, blind

completo, complete, full

corto, short

cuadrado, square

cuidadoso, careful

chico, little, small

deleitoso, delightful

derecho, straight, right (*not left*)

deseoso, desirous

desgraciado, unfortunate

dichoso, lucky, happy

digno, worthy

dulce, sweet

duro, hard

enfermo, ill, sick

enojado, annoyed, angry

escondido, hidden

especial, special

estrecho, narrow

exterior, outer, exterior

fácil, easy

feliz, happy

feo, ugly

fiel, faithful

flaco, weak, feeble

flojo, lax, lazy

frío, cold

fuerte, strong

gordo, fat

gracioso, pleasing, amusing

gran(de), great, large, big

grueso, thick, stout

hermoso, beautiful

hondo, deep

hueco, hollow

inferior, inferior, lower

§ 4. *Adjectives That Lose −O before a Noun — GRAN(DE) — SAN(TO) — Two or More Adjectives in Series — Vocabulary — Practice*

CERTAIN adjectives are usually, or always, placed before their nouns and in this position drop the ending −o (but not the feminine ending −a). Thus:

alguno, some	algún amigo, some friend	alguna amiga
bueno, good	un buen hombre, a good man	una buena mujer
malo, bad	un mal hombre, a bad man	una mala mujer
ninguno, no	ningún hombre, no man	ninguna mujer

    * Cada is indeclinable: **cada hombre, cada mujer;** there is no plural.

primero, first	el primer señor, the first gentle-man	la primera señora
tercero, third	el tercer día, the third day	la tercera semana, the third week
uno, one, a, an	un alemán, a German	una alemana

GRAN(DE). When the word **grande** indicates importance or greatness, it is placed before the noun and usually drops **–de**. (Sometimes **–de** is retained before a vowel or **h**.) When it indicates physical bigness, it is placed after the noun and retains the **–de**. Thus:

> un gran (*or* grande) hombre, a great man
> un hombre grande, a big, *or* large, man
> un gran (*or* grande) edificio, a great building
> un edificio grande, a big building
> una gran mujer, a great woman
> una mujer grande, a big woman

SAN(TO). Santo (*holy, saint*) usually becomes **San** when used as a title: **San Juan,** *St. John;* **San Pedro,** *St. Peter.* But before **Do-** or **To-,** Santo is used: **Santo Domingo, Santo Tomás.** St. James, by the way, is not **San Diego,** but **Santiago.**

Since the adjectives given above are very common words, they should be memorized now.

Two or More Adjectives in Series. When two or more adjectives relate to one noun, they should ordinarily be placed after the noun, and **y,** *and,* must be placed between them. Thus:

> un hombre pobre y triste, a poor, sad man

Vocabulary. You should now be able to tell the meaning of the words already met. But you cannot *do* very much with them until you learn some of the words that make other words work, such as verbs and pronouns. Here are a few of them:

Usted, *pl.* **Ustedes** (usually written **Ud., Uds.,** or **Vd., Vds.,** or **V., VV.**) is the polite *you,* used with everyone but relatives and close friends. **Usted** is an abbreviation of **Vuestra Merced,** *Your Honor.*

¿ **Cómo** . . . ? How . . . ?	¿ **Dónde** . . . ? Where . . . ?
está, is, (*after* **Ud.**) are	**están** (*pl.*), are

¿ **Cómo está Ud.?** How are you?

muy, very   **bien,** well, all right   **gracias,** thanks

Muy bien, gracias. Very well, thanks.

Buenos días. Good morning.   **Buenas noches.** Good night.
Buenas tardes. Good afternoon. Good evening.

yo, I   **mi,** my   **él,** he   **ella,** she
ellos (*masc.*), **ellas** (*fem.*), they
su, (*before pl. nouns*) **sus,** your

yo tengo, I have	¿ **tengo yo?** have I? do I have?
él tiene, he has	¿ **tiene él?** has he? does he have?
ella tiene, she has	¿ **tiene ella?** has she? does she have?
ellos (ellas) tienen, they have	¿ **tienen ellos (ellas)?** have they? do they have?

With these and the words you already know it is possible to make many simple sentences. For example:

¿ **Cómo está su madre? Mi madre está bien. ¿ Y Ud.? Muy bien, gracias. ¿ Dónde está el cajón? Está ahí. ¿ Tiene Ud. una casa? Yo tengo una casa. ¿ Dónde están sus zapatos? Los zapatos están en la casa. ¿ Dónde está la casa? La casa está en la calle de San Juan.**

These are given merely as examples. From now on, make up your own sentences, using all the words that have been given.

If you have trouble remembering a word, write it out and say it aloud several times.

LEARN AT LEAST TEN NEW WORDS EVERY DAY.

§ 5. *Comparison of Adjectives — More Useful Adjectives — Adjectives as Nouns*

COMPARISON OF ADJECTIVES. We speak of the "comparison of adjectives" when we refer to a change of form which implies superiority or inferiority. Thus, in English: large, larg*er*, larg*est*; beautiful, *more* beautiful, *most* beautiful. Learn:

más . . . que, more . . . than	**el (la) más,** the most
menos . . . que, less . . . than	**el (la) menos,** the least

EXAMPLES:

El muchacho es (*is*) **más grande que la muchacha.** The boy is bigger than the girl.

Juan es más grande que Pedro, pero Tomás es el más grande. John is bigger than Peter, but Thomas is the biggest.

María es la más alta de las muchachas. Mary is the tallest of the girls.

El señor N. es menos amistoso que la mujer. Mr. N. is less friendly than the woman.

La sra. (señora) Gómez es la menos amistosa de las mujeres. Mrs. Gómez is the least friendly of the women.

To express *equality:*

> **tan . . . como,** as . . . as
> **tanto(-a) . . . como,** as much . . . as
> **tantos(-as) . . . como,** as many . . . as

EXAMPLES:

El hombre es tan feliz como la mujer. The man is as happy as the woman.

Yo tengo tanto pan como Ud. I have as much bread as you (have).

Él tiene tanta tinta como ella. He has as much ink as she (has).

El señor Pardo tiene tantos caballos como el señor Blanco. Mr. Pardo has as many horses as Mr. Blanco (has).

La niña tiene tantas flores como su madre. The little girl has as many flowers as her mother (has).

When *numerals* come into an affirmative sentence, **de** is used for *than* instead of **que.** Thus:

Él tiene más de tres casas. He has more than three houses.

But in a negative sentence **que** is used:

Él no tiene más que tres casas. He does not have more (*or* has no more) than three houses.

As much as is, in Spanish, **tanto cuanto** in a sentence like the following, when no noun follows **tanto:**

Yo tengo tanto cuanto quiero. I have as much as I want.

MORE USEFUL ADJECTIVES:

interior, inner, interior
izquierdo, left (*not right*)
joven, young
lento, slow
libre, free
ligero, light (*not heavy*)
limpio, clean
lindo, pretty, nice
liso, smooth, even
listo, ready, clever, apt

loco, mad, crazy
llano, plain, flat
lleno, full
mal(o), bad, ill
malsano, unhealthy
manso, tame, gentle
medio, half
mejor, better
mismo, same
moreno, swarthy, dark, brown

mudo, mute, dumb
muerto, dead
negro, black
ningun(o), no
nuevo, new
ocioso, idle, lazy
orgulloso, proud
pardo, brown, grey, drab
peligroso, dangerous
peor, worse

pequeño, small, little
pesado, heavy, dull
pobre, poor
poco, little (*amount*), (*pl.*) few
presto, quick, ready
primer(o), first
pronto, prompt, quick
propio, own, proper
querido, dear, darling
rápido, rapid, fast
raro rare, strange

rico, rich
rojo, red
sabio, wise
sano, healthy
seco, dry
segundo, second
semejante, similar
sencillo, simple
siguiente, following
sordo, deaf

súbito, sudden
sucio, dirty
suelto, loose
tercer(o), third
todo, all, every
tonto, stupid, silly
triste, sad
vacío, empty
verdadero, true
verde, green
viejo, old

ADJECTIVES AS NOUNS. Many adjectives can be used as nouns indicating a person:

    el ciego, the blind man
    la enferma, the sick woman, *or* girl
    el feo, the ugly man, the ugly one
    los fieles, the faithful
    el gordo, the fat man
    la hermosa, the beautiful girl, *or* woman
    los jóvenes, the young men, the young people
    el tonto, the stupid fellow
    el loco, the madman, the crazy man
    los muertos, the dead
    los pobres, the poor
    una vieja, an old woman

PRACTICE. Review all the vocabulary of Lessons I and II. Make as many sentences as you can. Practice using adjectives as nouns.

LESSON III

§ 1. *The Superlative of Adjectives — Irregular Comparison*

THE SUPERLATIVE OF ADJECTIVES. In Lesson II, § 5, you learned how to form the superlative by using **el más,** *the most,* and **el menos,** *the least.* The usual word order is:

(1) article   (2) noun   (3) **más**   (4) adjective
                                menos

as: **el**   **hombre**   **más**   **rico**
       la   **mujer**   **menos**   **fea**

There is also a form — called the "absolute superlative" — which is the equivalent of our *most* or emphatic *very* in such a statement as "He is most generous" or "He is *very* generous." It is formed by adding –ísimo(–a, –os, –as) to the adjective; for example:

> **liberal,** liberal, generous
> **liberalísimo,** most, *or* very, liberal

Note the difference in usage between the –ísimo form and the regular superlative:

> **Es liberalísimo.** He is most, *or* very, liberal.
> **Es el más liberal (de todos).** He is the most liberal (of all).

When –ísimo is added to an adjective that ends in a vowel, the vowel is dropped, as:

importante — importantísimo   feo — feísimo   viejo — viejísimo

At present you would do well to avoid using the effective and beautiful ending –ísimo, which has many pitfalls and demands a fairly advanced sense of both grammar and style if it is to be used correctly. Among the difficulties are various orthographic changes, as in **rico — riquísimo.**

You can express the meaning of –ísimo by using **muy,** *very,* and stressing it for emphasis, as:

> **Es *muy* liberal.** He is *very* liberal.

IRREGULAR COMPARISON. The following adjectives have comparatives which are different words. Some of them you already know; learn the others, as they are all commonly used.

25

buen(o), good
mal(o), bad
mucho, much, (*pl.*) **many**
poco, little, (*pl.*) few
gran(de), great, big

pequeño, small, little

mejor, better; best
peor, worse; worst
más, more; most
menos, less, fewer; least, fewest
mayor (*or* **más grande**), greater, bigger; greatest, biggest
menor (*or* **más pequeño**), smaller; smallest

Also note:

exterior, outer, exterior
interior, inner, interior
superior, upper, superior
ulterior, farther, ulterior

extremo, furthest, last, extreme
íntimo, in(ner)most, intimate
supremo, highest, supreme
último, farthest, last, latest, final, ultimate

Practice using the above words with nouns and in sentences.

§ 2. *Visualization; Thinking in Spanish*

IT IS IMPORTANT at this stage to get into the habit of thinking of persons and things in Spanish instead of translating Spanish words into English words. For example, you have learned that the Spanish word **caballo** means *horse,* and you can translate **caballo** into *horse,* and *horse* into **caballo.** In this process there is no direct *thinking* in Spanish, but a process which, if persisted in, retards progress in the achievement of an essential: *thinking in Spanish.*

What you must do is to connect the Spanish word or phrase with the person or thing, quality, relation, or action. Thus, when you see or say or write **caballo,** think of the animal instead of the word. **Una casa blanca** should make you think of a white house, not of three English words.

Visualize everything as you learn Spanish words and read Spanish. If you follow this practice, when you see a house it will be a **casa** as well as a *house.* Constant practice in visualizing will speed up your progress and enable you to reach the goal of thinking in Spanish.

Look over the vocabulary lists of Lessons I and II, visualizing those things that can be visualized (of course you can't visualize an **y** or a **de**). Then practice visualizing with the following:

un zorro — los zapatos — un mexicano — un oso — una sala — un perro — un carro negro — la tierra — la ropa de Ud. — la calle — la caja — unos huevos — una página — vacas — la boca — los dedos — una ruina — el fuego — el agua caliente — las aguas — un

diablo rojo — la viuda — el viudo — un burro — el papel blanco — una casa pequeña — una cama grande — un boletín — el barítono — un cajón — la tribu — una muchacha linda — unos niños — el padre de Ud. — el sol — la luna — el pan duro — la cabeza — unas manos sucias — el nogal — el naranjo — las naranjas — la encina — unos manzanos — unas manzanas — la bandera norteamericana — la tinta azul — un caballero inglés — la reina inglesa — una española — un buen amigo de Ud. — un edificio grande — un hombre gordo — un ciego — una mujer pobre y triste — la tercera casa — el tercer hombre

Now say the following phrases without thinking of the English translation:

Buenos días, señor. ¿Cómo está Ud.?
Muy bien, amigo. ¿Y Ud.?
Bien, gracias. ¿Tiene Ud. un cigarrillo (*cigarette*)?
Tengo aquí (*here*) un cigarrillo. ¿Cómo está su madre?
Está muy bien, gracias.
¿Dónde está ella ahora (*now*)?
Está en Madrid.
¿Y su padre?
Él está aquí en la Habana.
¿Tienen Uds. amigos aquí?
Muchos.

§ 3. *Personal Pronouns*

IN THIS section a table of Spanish pronouns is presented. In order to understand how to use them, you must clearly understand the terms that head the columns.

A *subject pronoun* indicates who is acting or, if no action is involved, who is the subject of the verb, as: *I* am studying Spanish, *They* are Mexicans.

A *direct object pronoun* indicates the recipient of the action, as: He hit *me*, I know *him*, They saw *us*.

An *indirect object pronoun* indicates the person to whom or for whom something is done when another person or a thing is the direct object, as: Give *her* the book, Read *them* the letter. In English, *to* or *for* is often used before an indirect object, as: Give the book to *her*, Read the letter to *them*, Read it for *them*.

After a preposition: In English the same pronouns are used as objects of verbs or prepositions, but in Spanish the pronouns used

PERSONAL PRONOUNS

Subject	Direct Object of Verb	Indirect Object	After a Preposition	Reflexive, Object of Verb	Reflexive, After a Preposition

SINGULAR

Subject	Direct Object of Verb	Indirect Object	After a Preposition	Reflexive, Object of Verb	Reflexive, After a Preposition
yo, I	me, me	me, me[4]	mí,[6] me	me, myself	mí, myself
tú, thou[1]	te, thee	te, thee	tí[6] thee	te, thyself	tí, thyself
él, he[2]	le, lo,[3] him	le,[5] him	él, him	se { himself	sí[7] { himself
ella, she[2]	la, her	le,[5] her	ella, her	se { herself	sí[7] { herself
ello, it[2]	lo, it	————	ello, it	se { itself	sí[7] { itself
Ud., you[1]	le, lo, la, you	le,[5] you	Ud., you	se { yourself	sí[7] { yourself

PLURAL

Subject	Direct Object of Verb	Indirect Object	After a Preposition	Reflexive, Object of Verb	Reflexive, After a Preposition
nosotros, –as, we	nos, us	nos, us	nosotros, –as, us	nos, ourselves	nos, ourselves
vosotros, –as, you[1]	os, you	os, you	vosotros, –as, you	os, yourselves	os, yourselves
ellos, –as, they	los, las, them	les,[5] them	ellos, –as, them	se, themselves	sí,[7] themselves
Uds., you[1]	los, las, you	les,[5] you	Uds., you	se, yourselves	sí,[7] yourselves

NOTES ON TABLE OF PRONOUNS

1. **Tú** and **vosotros** and their derived forms may be ignored for the present, as they are used only among members of the family and intimate friends. In speaking to an acquaintance or friend, use **Ud.** — unless he starts to address you as **tú**. Note that **Ud.** and **Uds.** are placed with the third person pronouns; these pronouns always take verbs in the third person (as we would say, "Your Honor *is*").

2. Grammars never give *it* as a translation of **él** or **ella**, but since all Spanish nouns are either masculine or feminine, **él** or **ella** referring to a thing is translated *it*. **Ello**, *it*, is used to refer to a fact, idea, or situation expressed in a clause or sentence; it cannot refer to a word.

3. Whether **le** or **lo** should be used as direct object has long been a matter of controversy. **Le** is preferred by scholars, but **lo** is more used in popular speech.

4. When the pronoun is an indirect object, *to* or *for* is implied, as in "Bring me some water." But in Spanish if a preposition is used, a pronoun from the fourth column is required.

5. When **le** or **les** immediately precedes another pronoun, it becomes **se**. This will be discussed later.

6. But when the preposition **con**, *with*, is used, **conmigo** and **contigo** are used instead of **con mí** and **con tí**.

7. Likewise **consigo** is used instead of **con sí**.

after prepositions are different from those used as direct or indirect objects of verbs.

The *reflexive pronoun* is used when a person or a thing does something to itself, as: You cut *yourself*. She dressed *herself*. We pride *ourselves*.

The *reflexive pronoun after a preposition* has no special form in English, but it does in Spanish.

The list of pronouns is for facility in reference and need not be memorized in full at present. It is better to learn the pronouns piecemeal, by means of phrases and sentences. Here are the subject pronouns with forms of **tener**, to have:

yo tengo, I have   **nosotros, –as tenemos,** we have
él, ella tiene, he, she has   **ellos, –as tienen,** they have
Ud. tiene, you (*sg.*) have   **Uds. tienen,** you (*pl.*) have

Do not proceed further until you know these pronouns.

§ 4. *NO with a Verb — SER and* **ESTAR** *— Position of Pronouns — Vocabulary and Practice — The Orthographic Accent*

NO with a Verb. *Not* is **no,** which always comes before the verb. Thus:

yo no tengo, I have no, I do not have
él no tiene, he has no, he does not have
Ud. no tiene, you have no, you do not have

A question is asked by putting the subject pronoun after the verb. Thus:

¿ **Tengo yo?** Have I? Do I have?
¿ **No tengo yo?** Haven't I? Don't I have?
¿ **No tienen Uds.?** Haven't you? Don't you have?

SER and **ESTAR.** There are two verbs in Spanish for *to be:*

Ser makes statements about the *permanent* or *essential* nature of a person or thing.

Estar makes statements about the *temporary* state or condition of a person or thing. It is used for location, even if the location is permanent (**Roma está en Italia**).

SER	ESTAR
Yo soy un hombre. I am a man.	**Yo estoy en casa.** I am at home.
Él es un cubano. He is a Cuban.	**Él está aquí.** He is here.
Ella es una viuda. She is a widow.	**Ella está ahí.** She is there.
Ud. es un loco. You are a mad-man.	**Ud. está loco.** You are mad (*to do or say so*).
Nosotros somos jóvenes. We are young.	**Nosotros estamos ocupados.** We are busy.
Ellos son buenos. They are good (people).	**Ellos están flojos.** They are lazy (SA).
Uds. son muy felices. You are very happy (*in general*).	**Uds. están muy felices.** You are very happy (*now*).

Practice using **ser** and **estar** with various nouns and adjectives that you have learned until you are thoroughly familiar with the forms and usages given above.

POSITION OF PRONOUNS.   It is necessary for you to learn the following rules regarding the position of pronouns:

1. A direct object pronoun follows a subject pronoun and precedes the verb.

> ¿ **Tiene Ud. la tinta?   Yo la tengo.** Do you have the ink?
> I have it.
>
> **Yo no lo creo.**   I don't believe it.

2. An indirect object pronoun precedes a direct object pronoun.

> **Tengo muchos libros.   Mi hermano me los da.** I have
> many books.   My brother gives them to me.

3. When the indirect object pronoun **le** or **les** precedes a direct object pronoun, it becomes **se**.

> **Ella no vende flores a Juan.   Ella se las da.** She does not
> sell flowers to John.   She gives them to him.

Note: Because of the ambiguity of **se** in such sentences as that above, it is customary — unless the reference is obvious — to add **a él, a ella, a Ud., a ellos, a ellas,** or **a Uds.,** as:

> **Él se las vende a ella (a Ud.).** He sells them (*flowers*) to her (to you).

VOCABULARY AND PRACTICE.   In order to use the pronouns, nouns, and adjectives that you have learned, you must know more verbs. The following are a few (including two just used above).

yo hablo, I speak, talk

él (ella) habla, he (she) speaks
Ud. habla, you speak

yo doy, I give
yo creo, I believe
yo escribo, I write
yo vendo, I sell

él da, he gives, *etc.*
él cree, he believes
él escribe, he writes
él vende, he sells

Practice saying *and thinking* these sentences:

Él me habla. Ella me habla el español. Él tiene un libro. Él me lo da. Ella escribe una carta (*letter*)**. Ella me la escribe. Le escribo una carta a ella. Yo la doy a Ud. Él da agua al hombre. Él le da agua. Él se la da. Mi padre me da dinero** (*money*)**. Él me lo da. Él da dinero a mi hermano. Él le da dinero. Mi padre se lo da a él. Él vende libros. Él vende un libro a Ud. Él lo vende a Ud. Él se lo vende a Ud. Ud. se lo da a ella. Ella me habla mucho de Ud.**

Before proceeding further, review the whole lesson. Learn as many words as possible. Practice using them in sentences.

THE ORTHOGRAPHIC ACCENT. When the accent mark is used, not to indicate the stress on a syllable, but to distinguish one part of speech from another, it is called the *orthographic accent*. You have already noticed that **el** appears with and without accent. Here is a list of such pairs of words:

el, the — **él,** he
mi, my — **mí,** me, myself (*after preposition*)
tu, thy — **tú,** thou
si, if — **sí,** yes; himself, *etc.* (*after prep.*)

There are others, which you need not learn at present.

§ 5. *The Cardinal Numbers — –UNO, CIENTO, MIL, MILLÓN — Learning the Numbers*

THE CARDINAL NUMBERS. Some of the commonest and most useful words in any language are the numbers. Learn the following cardinal numbers thoroughly. First learn the numbers 1 to 15 ·

1 un(o), una	6 seis	11 once
2 dos	7 siete	12 doce
3 tres	8 ocho	13 trece
4 cuatro	9 nueve	14 catorce
5 cinco	10 diez	15 quince

In the following group, the forms **dieciséis, veintiun(o),** etc., are usually used, but the original forms **diez y seis, veinte y uno,** etc., are still occasionally used.

16 dieciséis	20 veinte	25 veinticinco
17 diecisiete	21 veintiun(o), –a	26 veintiséis
18 dieciocho	22 veintidós	27 veintisiete
19 diecinueve	23 veintitrés	28 veintiocho
	24 veinticuatro	29 veintinueve

Now, to continue:

30 treinta	100 cien(to)	1,000 mil
31 treinta y un(o)	101 ciento (y) un(o)	10,000 diez mil
32 treinta y dos	200 doscientos, –as	100,000 cien mil
40 cuarenta	300 trescientos, –as	1,000,000 un millón
50 cincuenta	400 cuatrocientos, –as	
60 sesenta	500 quinientos, –as	
70 setenta	600 seiscientos, –as	
80 ochenta	700 setecientos, –as	
90 noventa	800 ochocientos, –as	
	900 novecientos, –as	

COMPOUNDS OF –UN(O). In compounds of un(o) (21, 31, 101, etc.) the –o is dropped before a noun, whether masculine or feminine; thus:

veintiún mujeres (note accent on –ún), **treinta y un mujeres**
capítulo (*chapter*) **veintiuno, página veintiuna**

CIEN(TO). **Ciento** drops –to before a noun and before **mil**:

cien soldados, one, *or* a, hundred soldiers
cien mil soldados, a hundred thousand soldiers
cientos de soldados, hundreds of soldiers

MIL. *Note:* **dos mil,** two thousand; *but:* **miles de,** thousands of.

Mil must be used for numbers between 1000 and 10,000; there is no Spanish equivalent of our "fifteen hundred," "thirty-six hundred," etc. The date 1950 is **mil novecientos cincuenta.**

MILLÓN. This word is a noun and must be preceded by the article: **un millón de soldados**
　　　　　dos millones de soldados

LEARNING THE NUMBERS. In learning the numbers, try to think in Spanish. That is, **cinco** — 5 (*****); not **cinco** — five — 5.
Practice saying in Spanish quantities and dates that occur to you. Here are a few to start on:

25 — 33 — 47 — 51 — 69 — 74 — 86 — 92 — 111 — 248 — 321 —
519 — 694 — 701 — 815 — 923 — 1066 — 1111 — 1288 — 1340 —
1492 — 1564 — 1660 — 1776 — 1861 — 1917

LESSON IV

§ 1. *Ordinal Numbers — Differing Usages in Spanish — Measurement*

ORDINAL NUMBERS indicate position in a series. Only the following need to be learned at this stage:

primer(o), first	**sexto**, sixth
segundo, second	**séptimo**, seventh
tercer(o), third	**octavo**, eighth
cuarto, fourth	**noveno** *or* **nono**, ninth
quinto, fifth	**décimo**, tenth

The ordinals must be regarded as adjectives and must agree in gender and number with the noun that follows; thus:

el primer hombre	**la primera mujer**
los primeros hombres	**las primeras mujeres**

The ordinals are sometimes abbreviated, usually by the figure followed by a small superior letter **o** or **a**: **2° = segundo, 2ª = segunda.**

Primero and **tercero** drop the –o before a masculine singular noun, even if another adjective precedes the noun: **el primer día, el primer buen día.**

Though usually adjectives, the ordinal numbers may be used as nouns: **el primero de mis amigos,** *the first of my friends.*

DIFFERING USAGES IN SPANISH. Spanish ordinal numbers exist for all the cardinal numbers, but because most of them are long and awkward, the ones above ten are commonly replaced by cardinals, except in formal, elegant, or ironical style. Thus:

el siglo veinte, the twentieth century
la página diecinueve, the nineteenth page

Ordinal numbers are used for kings and popes up to ten:

Felipe II (segundo)	**Alfonso XIII (trece)**
Carlos V (quinto)	**Luis XVI (dieciséis)**

Pío IX (nono — here **noveno** is never used)

The days of the month are expressed by cardinal numbers except for the first. Thus:

el primero de julio, the first of July
el dos de julio, the second of July

33

In speaking, the phrase **el día** is often used before the cardinal number, to express the date: **el día dos de julio**

el día dos, on the second

MEASUREMENT. To express measurements in Spanish, use the words **alto,** *height,* **largo,** *length,* and **ancho,** *width, breadth,* as follows:

Tiene (...) de alto.   It is (...) high.   ("It has ... of height.")
Tiene (...) de largo.   It is (...) long.   ("It has ... of length.")
Tiene (...) de ancho.   It is (...) wide.   ("It has ... of width.")

Thus:

La casa tiene 40 pies de alto, 60 de largo y 30 de ancho.
The house is 40 feet high, 60 long, and 30 wide.

§ 2. *Practice with Numbers — Some Quantitative Expressions*

PRACTICE WITH NUMBERS. As regards numbers, the best way to learn to think in Spanish is to do little arithmetic problems in Spanish. Let us begin with the numbers 1 to 10. First, say them over until you can count to 10 rapidly:

1   2   3   4   5   6   7   8   9   10

The word **y,** *and* or *plus,* is used in addition. We say "two and two *is* four"; in Spanish the plural verb is used.

Looking at the numbers above, say:

> **Uno y uno son dos.**
> **Uno y dos son tres.**
> Continue, up to 10.

Menos, as you know, means *less.* Now start with:

> **Diez menos uno son nueve.**
> Continue, down to 1.

Now try multiplication. *Times* is **por.**

> **Dos por dos son cuatro.**
> **Dos por tres son seis.**

Can you learn the whole multiplication table in Spanish?

Now practice adding, subtracting, and multiplying with numbers up to 20. For example:

> **Diez y uno son once.**
> **Seis y nueve son quince.**
> **Veinte menos uno son diecinueve.**

Veinte menos trece son siete.

Dos por diez son veinte.

Tres por seis son dieciocho.

Doce por doce son ciento cuarenta y cuatro.

CONTINUE THIS PRACTICE WITH NUMBERS AT ODD MOMENTS. IT IS
VERY VALUABLE IN HELPING YOU TO APPROACH YOUR GOAL OF
THINKING IN SPANISH

SOME QUANTITATIVE EXPRESSIONS. Learn the following words
and phrases:

una vez, one time, once
dos veces, twice
tres veces, three times
doble, double
triple, triple
la mitad, (a) half (*n.*)
medio, half (*adj.*) (**medias** = stockings)
una hora y media, an hour and a half
un tercio, a, *or* one, third
un cuarto, one-fourth, a room
un par, a pair, couple
una decena, ten, half a score
una docena, a dozen
una veintena, a score
un centenar, una centena, a hundred
un millar, a thousand
más o menos, more or less
cosa de, about, approximately (**cosa** = thing)
o cosa así, or thereabouts (**así** = thus)
ocho días = una semana, a week
quince días, a fortnight

Note: A hundred soldiers, a thousand soldiers, if expressing precise figures, would
be cien soldados, mil soldados; but if considered as round numbers or as units
of 100 or 1000 would be **un centenar de soldados, un millar de soldados.**

The material given in this section is all that is likely to be required
at present for practicing numbers.

§ 3. *Possessive Pronouns — Clarifying Phrases after SU — Adjectives as Pronouns*

POSSESSIVE PRONOUNS. There are two classes of possessive pronouns:

	I			II		
	Before a Noun [1]			*After a Noun or in Place of a Noun* [1]		
Sing.		*Pl.*		*Sing.*	*Pl.*	
mi		mis	my	mío, –a	–os, –as	my, (of) mine
tu [2]		tus	thy	tuyo, –a	–os, –as	thy, (of) thine
su		sus	his, her, its, your	suyo, –a	–os, –as	his, her(s), its, your(s) [3]
nuestro, –a	–os, –as		our	nuestro, –a	–os, –as	our(s)
vuestro, –a	–os, –as		your	vuestro, –a	–os, –as	your(s)
su		sus	their, your	suyo, –a	–os, –as	their(s), your(s)

Possessive pronouns, like adjectives, must agree in gender and number with the nouns they refer to. The following examples will illustrate their use:

mi libro, my book	**mis libros,** my books
mi casa, my house	**mis casas,** my houses
nuestro libro, our book	**nuestros libros,** our books
nuestra casa, our house	**nuestras casas,** our houses
su casa, his, her, its, your house	**sus casas,** his, *etc.,* houses

querido amigo mío (*more affectionate than* **mi querido amigo**), my *dear* friend

el libro mío (*more emphatic than* **mi libro**), *my* book

El libro es mío. The book is mine.

Es mío (*referring to* **libro**). It is mine.

Es un libro mío. It is a book of mine.

la casa nuestra, *our* house

La casa es nuestra. The house is ours.

Es nuestra (*referring to* **casa**). It is ours.

Son amigos nuestros. They are friends of ours.

Este (*this*) **sombrero es suyo.** This hat is yours.

Ese (*that*) **sombrero es mío.** That hat is mine.

---

[1] Some textbooks call I "possessive adjectives" and II "possessive pronouns," but the Grammar of the Spanish Academy regards both I and II as possessive pronouns.

[2] Tu, tus. tuyo, and vuestro are given for the sake of completeness, but you have no use for them now.

[3] Suyo, nuestro, and vuestro may = *of his, of hers,* etc.

CLARIFYING PHRASES AFTER **SU**. Because of the ambiguity of **su(s)**, which may mean *his*, *her(s)*, *its*, *their(s)*, or *your(s)* (referring to **Ud.** or **Uds.**), the explanatory phrases **de él, de ella**, etc., are used whenever there could be any doubt about the reference. (Compare Lesson III, § 4, *Note*.) Thus:

su libro de él, his book
sus libros de ella, her books
su madre de Ud., your (*sing.*) mother
su casa de Uds., your (*pl.*) house
su casa de ellos, their house

ADJECTIVES AS PRONOUNS. The following adjectives, some of which you know, are sometimes used as pronouns:

un(o), a, one; *pl.* some
algun(o), some
varios, several, various
ambos, both
todo, all; (*neuter pron.*) everything; *pl.* all, every (*see below*)
mucho, much; *pl.* many
otro, other, another

demás (*invariable*), other, rest of; (*pron.*) rest, remainder, *pl.* others
mismo, same
tal, such
cada (*invariable*), each, every
poco, little; *pl.* few
único, only, unique

Learn all these words now, and observe how they are used.

¿Hay un hotel? Sí, hay uno. Is there a hotel? Yes, there is one.
Tienen unas (*or* algunas) flores. They have some flowers. **Tienen algunas.**
¿La misma mujer? The same woman? **La misma.**
Hay varios hoteles. There are several hotels. **Hay varios.**
tal hombre, such a man   No hay tal (cosa). There is no such thing.
ambas mujeres, both women   Habla a ambas. He speaks to both.
cada hombre, each, *or* every, man
Cada tiene su caballo. Each has his horse.
todo el pan, all the bread; todos los huevos, all the eggs; toda la noche, all night; todas las noches, every night
Tengo todo. I have everything.
Todos están aquí. All (*the men*) are here.
mucho ruido, much noise; muchas niñas, many little girls
Hay muchas. There are many (*little girls*).
poco dinero, little money; pocas ciudades, few cities
Hay muy pocas. There are very few (*cities*).
otro hombre, another man; el otro hombre, the other man
Hay otros. There are others (*men*).

la demás gente, the rest of the people, the other people; **lo demás, the** rest (of it); **los demás,** the rest of them
la única muchacha, the only girl
Es la única. She is the only one.   **Es única.** She is unique.

§ 4. *Vocabulary — Practice Phrases and Sentences*

VOCABULARY.   The practice material that follows contains these new words.   Learn them before working on the phrases and sentences.

allí (= ahí), there, over there
con, with (see note 6, page 28)
para, for (*indicating purpose, destination*)
sobre, upon
este, esta, this (*adj.*)
ese, esa, that (*adj.*)
cierto, certain (*note:* **cierto hombre,** a certain man — *not* **un c. h.**)
solo, alone, single
sólo, only (*adv.*)

algo, something
nada, nothing
la culpa, fault, blame
la luz, the light
la suerte, luck
el alumno, la alumna, pupil
entero, whole, entire
el gusto, pleasure
la mesa, the table
la verdad, truth
la semana, the week

PRACTICE PHRASES AND SENTENCES.   You should be able to understand the following phrases and sentences, which illustrate the ground recently covered.   If you have trouble with some of them, you need to do some reviewing.

con mucho gusto — una semana entera — varias cosas — mi padre sólo — cierta muchacha — el primer hotel — unas pocas páginas — el tercer día — dos kilómetros de largo — el veintidós de abril — cuatro veces — una docena más o menos — la mitad de las casas — el día siete de enero — cosa de cincuenta — quinientos o cosa así — Uds. todos — su manzana de ella — todas mis flores — muchas de nuestras amigas — unos alumnos — de ambos hermanos — los mismos perros

¿Está en Inglaterra su tío de Ud.?   Estoy aquí toda la semana.   Él está allí todo el día y todos los días.   ¿Tienen Uds. todas las cosas?   Sí, todas.   Todo está listo.   Mis libros están aquí.   ¿Dónde están los suyos?   Nuestra casa está en la ciudad.   ¿Dónde está la suya?   Es culpa mía.   Es la verdad, toda la verdad.   Son unos amigos nuestros.   Habla una amiga de Ud.   Ella tiene mucha suerte ¿no es verdad?   Mucha.   Hay poca luz aquí.   Ese señor tiene mucho dinero ¿verdad?   No, tiene muy poco.   Pepe está solo.   Ella está sola todas las tardes.   Hay un libro para cada dos alumnos.   Cada libro vale cinco pesetas.   Los demás no hablan

inglés. **Esa es otra mujer. Hay algo aquí. No hay nada aquí. Sí, hay alguna cosa sobre la mesa. Ambos están en la calle. El gusto es mío. Tienen ciertos libros importantes. La carta es para mí. Ella habla con sus amigos. ¿ Lo cree Ud.? Soy el único hermano de María. Pero es mi propio perro. No hay tal animal.**

§ 5. *Relative Pronouns — Interrogative Pronouns — Exclamations — Impersonal Expressions — Telling Age — Practice Sentences — Practice for This Lesson*

RELATIVE PRONOUNS. A relative pronoun is one that connects the noun or pronoun to which it refers with the part of the sentence that follows. Thus, in "the man *who* said so," "the woman *whose* hat was lost," "the man *whom* I saw," "the noun or pronoun to *which* it refers," "the door *that* I closed," *who, whose, whom, which, that* are relative pronouns.

The Spanish relative pronouns are:

QUE, that, who, whom, which
QUIEN, *pl.* **QUIENES,** who, whom
EL CUAL, LA CUAL, LO CUAL, LOS CUALES, LAS CUALES, who, which
CUYO, –A, –OS, –AS, whose, of which

Que is the most commonly used, all-purpose relative pronoun, applicable to subjects or objects, persons or things, in all genders and numbers (like English *that*). Referring to persons, it must come right after the noun to which it refers; referring to things, it may be preceded by a preposition. Thus:

el hombre que habla, the man who, *or* that, is speaking
los hombres que hablan, the men who, *or* that, are speaking
el hombre que ella mató, the man whom, *or* that, she killed
  (We can say "the man she killed"; in Spanish the relative may not be omitted.)
las mujeres que el mató, the women whom, *or* that, he killed
el libro que tiene el muchacho, the book which, *or* that, the boy has
los libros de que hablo, the books of which I am speaking, the books that I am talking about
la casa en que escribo, the house in which I am writing
las manzanas que el manzano da, the apples which, *or* that, the apple tree bears

Quien must be used: (1) after a form of the verb **ser** *; (2) when the relative pronoun is the object of a preposition; and (3) when the relative clause is not essential to the meaning of the sentence. For example:

(1) **Es él quien habla.** It is he who is speaking.
 Son ellos quienes hablan. It is they who are speaking.

(2) **ella a quien escribo la carta,** she to whom I am writing the letter
 ellos con quienes Ud. habla, they with whom you are speaking

(3) **Escribo a mi amigo Roberto, quien está ahora en Nueva York.** I am writing to my friend Robert, who is now in New York. (Compare: **Escribo a un amigo que está en Nueva York.**)

A good rule to follow is to use **que** when it would be proper in English to use *that* and to use **quien** when it would be necessary or preferable to use *who(m)*.

El cual (**la cual,** *etc.*) is used when the relative pronoun is at a distance from its antecedent or when for some reason there might be doubt as to the reference. Thus:

Tengo una amiga, la hermana de Ramón, la cual me da lecciones. I have a friend, Raymond's sister, who gives me lessons.

Lo cual is used to refer to a fact or idea, not to a single word:

Él tiene muchos caballos, lo cual me interesa. He has many horses, which interests me.

Cuyo, *whose, of which,* may refer to persons or things:

el muchacho cuyas hermanas están aquí, the boy whose sisters are here

una ciudad cuyo nombre es muy raro, a city whose name is very strange

Two relative pronouns include their antecedents: **quien,** he who, *pl.* **quienes,** *those who;* **cuanto, –a, –os, –as,** *as much as, as many as, all that.* Thus:

Quien tiene dinero tiene ventaja. He who (*or* The one who) has money has an advantage.

* Forms of **ser** (present tense) are: **soy,** I am; **es,** he, she, it is, you are; **somos,** we are; **son,** they, you are.

Quienes tienen dinero tienen ventaja. Those who (*or* The
ones who) have money have an advantage.

Escribe cuanto sabe. He writes as much as (*or* all that) he knows.

Venden cuantas flores tienen. They sell as many flowers as
(*or* all the flowers that) they have.

INTERROGATIVE PRONOUNS. The relative pronouns can be used
as interrogatives, and then they are written with an orthographic
accent. The interrogatives do not correspond exactly, in use, to
the relatives — for example, **que** may refer to persons, but **¿ qué ?**
may not. **¿ Cúyo ?** is rarely used, its place being taken by **¿ de
quién ?** So we have, as interrogatives:

¿ QUIÉN, –ES ? who? **¿ DE QUIÉN, –ES ?** whose? **¿ A QUIÉN,
–ES ?** (to) whom? *

¿ QUÉ ? what? (*also used as adj.*)

¿ CUÁL, –ES ? which? what? (*also used as adj.*)

¿ CUÁNTO, –A ? how much? **¿ CUÁNTOS, –AS ?** how many?
(*also used as adj.*)

Before a form of **ser, ¿ cuál ?** is the word for *what ?* — except when
a definition is wanted. (See examples below.)

Examples of interrogative pronouns in use:

¿ Quién habla ? Who is speaking?

¿ Quiénes están allí ? Who are there?

¿ De quién (*rarely* **¿ Cúyo**) **es este sombrero ?** Whose hat is this?

¿ A quién(es) habla Ud. ? To whom are you talking?

¿ Qué (*or* **¿ Qué cosa**) **tiene Ud. en la mano ?** What do you
have in your hand?

¿ Qué es este quijotismo ? What is this *quijotismo ?*

¿ Qué significa juguetería ? What does *juguetería* mean?

¿ Cuál es el libro que tiene Ud. ? What is the book you have?

¿ Cuáles son sus ideas sobre la cosa ? What are your ideas on
the matter?

¿ Cuál es el sombrero de Ud. ? Which is your hat?

¿ Cuál sombrero es suyo ? Which hat is yours?

¿ De cuál país es Ud. ? What country are you from?

EXCLAMATIONS. **¡ Qué !** and **¡ cuánto !** are much used in exclamations. Note the following examples.

* The Spanish equivalent of *whom ?* is **¿ a quién ?** (not just **¿ quién ?**). See
Lesson VIII, § 2.

¡ **Qué hombre !** What a man !
¡ **Qué pobres son !** How poor they are !
¡ **Qué bien habla inglés !** How well he speaks English !
¡ **Cuántas flores hay !** How many flowers there are !
¡ **Cuánto habla !** How much he talks !

¡ **Cuánto !** becomes ¡ **cuán !** (translated *how !* and = ¡ **qué !**) before (1) an adjective not accompanied by a noun, and (2) an adverb. Thus:

¡ **Cuán** (*or* ¡ **Qué**) **inteligente es !** How intelligent he is !
¡ **Cuán** (*or* ¡ **Qué**) **mal escribe !** How badly he writes !

Often **tan** (*so*) or **más** is placed between a noun and an adjective in an exclamation beginning with ¡ **Qué !** Thus:

¡ **Qué hombre inteligente !**
¡ **Qué hombre tan inteligente !** } What an intelligent man !
¡ **Qué hombre más inteligente !**

IMPERSONAL EXPRESSIONS. Impersonal expressions such as the following are very useful in conversation. They are much used and are easy to learn.

es preciso, it is necessary	**es lástima,** it's a pity
es mentira, it's a lie	**es vergüenza,** it's a shame
es verdad, it's true	**es seguro,** it's sure
es posible, it's possible	**es cierto,** it's certain
es probable, it's probable	**es bueno,** it's good
es imposible, it's impossible	**es malo,** it's bad
es improbable, it's improbable	**está bien,** (it's) all right
es algo, it's something	**no es nada,** it's nothing
es todo, that's all	

Some of these words can be used as exclamations, with or without ¡ **qué !** Thus: ¡ **Bueno !** ¡ **Qué bueno !** ¡ **Mentira !** ¡ **Imposible !** ¡ **Qué lástima !** ¡ **Qué vergüenza !**

TELLING AGE. *How old are you?* is, in Spanish: "How many years have you?": ¡ **Cuántos años tiene Ud. ?** The reply is "I have (twenty-five) years": **Tengo (veinticinco) años.** In speaking of age, **cumplir** (*to fulfill*) is used to mean *reach* a certain age (**el cumpleaños,** *birthday*):

Mañana cumpliré treinta años. Mañana será mi cumpleaños.

PRACTICE SENTENCES: ¿ **Cuántos años tiene Ud. ?** **Tengo treinta y un años.** ¿ **Cuántos años tiene su hermano ?** **Él tiene veinticinco** años. ¿Y su hermana? Ella tiene dieciocho. ¿Cuántos tiene su padre? Él tiene treinta años más que yo. En junio Ud. cumplirá (*will reach*) treinta y dos años. ¡A la edad (*age*) de cuarenta años hablaré (*I'll speak*) español! Elena es muy joven. Ana está muy joven esta noche. (*Anna looks*, or *seems, very young tonight.*) Sí, está alegre.

PRACTICE FOR THIS LESSON. As with every lesson, review and practice all the new words and all the rules until you feel that you know them well. Make up as many sentences of your own as you can. When in doubt, review.

Make sure that you have mastered everything in Lessons I–IV before going on to Lesson V.

LESSON V

§ 1. *Words Common to English and Spanish — Orthographic Differences*

Words Common to English and Spanish. Allowing for certain orthographic changes, there are several thousands of words that are the same or almost the same in English and Spanish. Here are a few examples:

Nouns	Adjectives	Verbs
el accidente	activo	aceptar
la acción	actual, present, actual	acomodar
la adición	afortunado, fortunate	acostumbrar, to accustom
el adorno, adornment	agradable	admirar
el agente	amable	adoptar
la ambición	anterior	declarar
la arena, sand, arena	antiguo	dedicar
la ausencia, absence	anual	depositar
el automóvil	ausente	determinar
el azúcar, sugar	automático	doblar, to double, fold

The list could be extended almost indefinitely, because most modern scientific and technical words, such as **radio, telegrama, psicología, atómico,** are derived from Latin or Greek roots and therefore resemble one another.

Orthographic Differences. Nevertheless, even when words are common to both languages, there are certain differences in spelling that run consistently through them:

(1) Spanish nouns and adjectives very often end in –o, –a, or –e: **acto, persona, mucho, –a, aire, parte.**

(2) English double letters usually become a single letter in Spanish: **colegio,** *college;* **acomodación,** *accommodation.*

(3) The English prefixes *com-* and *im-* become **con-** and **in-** when the stem of the word begins with **m: conmoción,** *commotion;* **inmersión,** *immersion.*

(4) English *qu* becomes Spanish **cu: adecuado, frecuente, cuestión;** or (less often) **c: calidad,** *quality;* **cantidad,** *quantity;* **único.**

(5) English *r* may become Spanish **l: azul** (*azure, blue*), **papel.** Note **Argelia,** *Algeria.*

(6) English initial *s–* followed by another consonant becomes **es–** in Spanish: **España, espiritual, estricto.**

44

(7) In words of Greek origin:

Eng. *y* becomes Sp. **i: dinamita, sistema.**
" *ch* " " **c: carácter, Cristo, crónico;** or **qu: químico, psiquiatría.**
" *ph* " " **f: físico, fotográfico, frase.**
" *pn* " " **n: neumático, neumonía.**
" *rh* " " **r: rapsodia, reumático, rima.**
" *th* " " **t: autor, norte, teatro.**
" *ps* may become Sp. **s: salmista;** but: **psicología.**
" *pt* " " " **t: tolemaico;** but: **ptomaína.**

PRACTICE. Turn to the list of nouns, adjectives, and verbs in the next section, go through them, see how many Spanish words you can recognize, and note the differences in spelling between them and their English equivalents.

§ 2. *Similar English and Spanish Word Endings — Some Nouns, Adjectives, and Verbs Identical or Similar in Both Languages*

SIMILAR ENGLISH AND SPANISH WORD ENDINGS. The similarity between many English words and their Spanish equivalents is due to their common origin in Latin or Greek. Compare the following equivalent English and Spanish word endings:

English	*Spanish*	*Spanish Examples*
Nouns		
–ade	–ada	brigada, limonada
–age	–aje	coraje, lenguaje
–ance, –ancy	–ancia	importancia, discrepancia
–ence, –ency	–encia	experiencia, tendencia
–er, –or, –tor	–ero, –or, –dor	banquero, actor, aviador, emperador, explorador
–ic(s)	–ica	lógica, música, política
–ine	–ina	disciplina, quinina
–ion	–ión	religión, unión
–ism	–ismo	comunismo, idealismo, patriotismo
–ist	–ista	dentista, egoísta, materialista
–ment	–m(i)ento	argumento, departamento, sentimiento
–sion	–sión	misión, visión
–tion	–ción	acción, nación, observación
	–tión	cuestión, digestión
–tude	–tud	altitud, multitud
–ty	–dad, –tad	barbaridad, crueldad, libertad

English	Spanish	Spanish Examples
Nouns		
–ure	–ura	agricultura, cultura, temperatura
–y	–ia, ía	ceremonia, gloria, energía, geografía
Adjectives		
–able	–able	amable, innumerable
–acious	–az	sagaz, tenaz
–al	–al	usual, visual
–an	–ano	americano, cristiano
–ant	–ante	abundante, ignorante
–ate	–ado	delicado, duplicado
–ent	–ente	competente, valiente
–ible	–ible	elegible, increíble
–ic(al)	–ico	económico, público
–ile	–il	frágil, senil
–ine	–ino	equino, felino
–ist(ic, –al)	–ista	egotista, socialista
–ite	–ido, –ito	definido, infinito
–ive	–ivo	activo, destructivo
–ose, –ous	–oso	verboso, luminoso
–ure	–uro	futuro, puro
Verbs		
–ate	–ar	acomodar, calcular
–e	–ar	curar, imaginar, usar
–fy	–ficar	deificar, fortificar
–ize	–izar	civilizar, realizar

WARNING. It is not safe to assume that in every instance it is possible to make a Spanish word from an English one. But you can generally assume that when one of the above endings is attached to a Spanish word, the English equivalent will have the ending listed above. The above is not a complete list of equivalent endings.

SOME NOUNS, ADJECTIVES, AND VERBS IDENTICAL OR SIMILAR IN BOTH LANGUAGES. You have already looked over this list, noting orthographic differences between the Spanish and English words. Now look over it again, noting equivalent word endings. The similarities are obvious; pay attention to the *differences*. Learn all these words.

Nouns	Adjectives	Verbs
la paciencia, patience	blanco, blank, white	Ending in –AR
la página, page	capaz, capable, –cious	honrar, to honor
el papel, paper	central, central	ignorar, to be ignorant
el paquete, package	cierto, certain, sure	of, not know

Nouns

el **paralelo**, parallel
el **parque**, park
el **pasaje**, passage, fare
el **paso**, pace, step
el **pastel**, pastry, pie
el **patrón**, patron, landlord, boss
el **perdón**, pardon
el **período**, period
la **persona**, person
el **piano**, piano
la **planta**, plant
la **pluma**, plume, feather, pen
la **población**, population, town
el **poema**, the poem
el **poeta**, the poet
la **policía**, the police; el p., the policeman
la **porción**, portion, share
el **portero**, porter, doorkeeper
la **posesión**, possession
la **posición**, position
la **preferencia**, preference
el **presidente**, president, chairman
el **principal**, principal, chief
el **problema**, problem
el **producto**, product
el **profesor**, professor, teacher
el **progreso**, progress
el **proyecto**, project
el **público**, public
la **punta**, point, (sharp) end
el **punto**, point, dot, period

Adjectives

circular, circular
civil, civil
claro, clear, light (in color)
comercial, commercial
cómico, comic(al)
completo, complete, full
complicado, complicated
común, common
conciso, concise
consciente, conscious
contento, content
continuo, continual, –ous
contrario, contrary, opposite
cruel, cruel
culpable, culpable, guilty
curioso, curious, strange
delgado, delicate, thin
delicado, delicate, fine
delicioso, delicious
desconsolado, disconsolate, sad
diario, daily
diferente, different
distinto, distinct, different
doble, double
doméstico, domestic
eléctrico, electric, –al
entero, entire, whole
especial, special
exacto, exact
excelente, excellent
extraño, strange, queer
extraordinario, extraordinary

Verbs

imaginar, to imagine
importar, to be important, matter
inclinar, to incline, lean
indicar, to indicate
informar, to inform
iniciar, to initiate, begin
inspirar, to inspire
interesar, to interest

Ending in –ER

aparecer, to appear
atender, to attend, pay attention
cometer, to commit, entrust
comprender, to comprehend, understand
conceder, to concede, grant
contener, to contain, hold
convencer, to cònvince
corresponder, to correspond

Ending in –IR

admitir, to admit, receive, permit
aplaudir, to applaud
asistir, to assist, be present
batir, to beat, defeat
concluir, to conclude, end
construir, to construct, build
contradecir, to contradict
convertir, to convert, reform

§ 3. *Days of the Week — The Months — The Seasons — Dates — Dating a Letter*

Days of the Week:

el domingo, Sunday	**el jueves,** Thursday
lunes, Monday	**viernes,** Friday
martes, Tuesday	**sábado,** Saturday
miércoles, Wednesday	

The Months:

el enero, January	**el mayo,** May	**el septiembre,*** September
febrero, February	**junio,** June	**octubre,** October
marzo, March	**julio,** July	**noviembre,** November
abril, April	**agosto,** August	**diciembre,** December

The Seasons:

la primavera, spring	**el otoño,** autumn, fall
el verano, summer	**el invierno,** winter

Dates. In Spanish the date is placed before the name of the month. **De** is used before and after the month. **El** may or may not be used with the name of a day. **El** may or may not be used with the name of a month in general statements; it is not used in dates. The first of the month is always **el primero,** abbreviated **1º.** Thus:

¿ Cuál es la fecha de hoy? *or:* **¿ A cuántos estamos hoy?** ("At how many are we today?") What is the date today?

Hoy es el primero de marzo. Today is the first of March.

Estamos a dos de abril. It is April second.

Estamos a veinticinco de noviembre. It is November 25th.

Hoy es (el) miércoles, quince de mayo de 1957 (mil novecientos cincuenta y siete). Today is Wednesday, May 15, 1957.

Hoy es (el) martes, treinta y uno de diciembre de 1957. Today is Tuesday, the thirty-first of December, 1957.

El febrero es muy caliente aquí. February is very hot here.

Dating a Letter:

Nueva York, 1º de agosto de 1957
Wáshington, 2 de septiembre de 1958
La Habana, 3 de octubre de 1959

* **Septiembre** is sometimes spelled without the **p.**

Practice. Memorize the names of the days, months, and seasons. Practice dates by asking ¿ **A cuántos estamos hoy?** and giving various answers.

It is advisable at this stage to review sections 1–3 of this lesson. Learn as many words as you can from the word lists.

§ 4. *The Time of Day*

This section dealing with **la hora**, *the hour, the time (of day)*, is very important, and it provides excellent practice with numbers. Such practice as this helps the learner to *think in Spanish* and to think quickly. First learn the following words and phrases and then practice the sentences; finally make up questions and answers of your own regarding the time of day.

el reloj, clock, watch

adelantado, fast ⎫
atrasado, slow ⎬ *of clock or watch*
parado, stopped ⎭

el segundo, second

el minuto, minute

la hora, hour, time *(of day)*

un cuarto de hora, a quarter of an hour

una media hora, a half-hour

tres cuartos de hora, three-quarters of an hour

una hora y media, an hour and a half

una hora y tres cuartos, an hour and three-quarters

el día, day; **de día**, by day

mañana, tomorrow; **la mañana,** morning; **de**, *or* **por, la m.**, in the morning; **m. por la m.**, tomorrow morning; **pasado m.,** day after tomorrow

mediodía, midday, noon

tarde, late; **la tarde**, afternoon, evening; **de**, *or* **por, la t.**, in the a. or e.

la noche, night; **de**, *or* **por, la n.,** at n., in the n.; **de n.**, by n.

medianoche, midnight

ayer, yesterday

anteayer, day before yesterday

hoy, today

temprano, early

dar, to give, strike *(the hour)*

Note: With **mañana, tarde,** and **noche, de** is used if the hour is mentioned; otherwise **por** is used; thus: **ayer a las siete de la mañana (tarde)**, *yesterday at seven in the morning (evening)*; **ayer por la mañana (tarde)**, *yesterday morning (evening)*.

Practice:

¿ **Qué hora es?** or ¿ **Qué horas son?** What time is it?
Es la una (**hora** *understood after* **una**). It is one o'clock.
Son las dos (**horas** *understood after* **dos**). It is two o'clock.
¿ **Son las tres?** Is it three o'clock?
No, son las tres y diez. No, it's ten after three.
Mi reloj va atrasado. My watch is slow.

Está parado. It's stopped.

Llegan (They arrive) **mañana por la mañana.**

¿ A qué hora?

A las nueve y media de la mañana.

Hágame el favor de decirme qué hora es. Please tell me what time it is.

Son las cinco menos quince minutos. It's fifteen minutes till five.

Son las seis menos un cuarto. It's a quarter of six.

¿ Cuándo llegan? When do they arrive?

El jueves por la tarde.

El viernes a las cinco y media de la tarde.

¿ Tiene Ud. la hora? Do you have the time?

Son las ocho menos uno. Van a dar las ocho.

§ 5. *Geographical Names — Some Peculiar Regional Names and Nicknames — Reading Practice*

GEOGRAPHICAL NAMES. You have already learned the Spanish names of some countries and a few nouns and adjectives of nationality (review this material on page 15).

Here is a list of geographical proper names and derived adjectives and nouns, including some you already know. Remember that such forms as **inglés** may be either adjective or noun, and that they have endings indicating gender and number (**inglés, –a, –es, –as**). Translations are given only where they may be needed.

Most geographical names are used without the article; with some, the article must be used (as **el Perú**); with others the article may or may not be used (**China** or **la China, África** or **el África**).

América del Norte, Norteamérica; norteamericano
América Central, Centroamérica; centroamericano
América del Sur, Sudamérica; sudamericano

Europa; europeo   **Asia; asiático**   **el África; africano**
el Atlántico   **el Pacífico**   **el Mediterráneo**

las Antillas, the West Indies
las Indias Orientales, the East Indies
las Naciones Unidas, the United Nations
los Estados Unidos (de América), the United States (of America); **estadounidense,** (*more common*) **norteamericano**
la Gran Bretaña, Great Britain
las Islas Británicas, the British Isles; **británico**
Inglaterra, England; **inglés**

Escocia, Scotland; **escocés**   **Irlanda; irlandés**
Australia; australiano   **el Canadá; canadiense**

Alemania, Germany; **alemán**

Austria; **austríaco**

Bélgica; **belga, bélgico**

Checoeslovaquia; **checoeslovaco**

Dinamarca; **danés**

España; **español**

Finlandia; **finlandés**

Francia; **francés**

Grecia; **greco**

Holanda; **holandés**

Hungría; **húngaro**

Italia; **italiano**

Noruega; **noruego**

los Países Bajos, the Netherlands

Polonia; **polaco**

Portugal; **portugués**

Rumania; **rumano**

Rusia; **ruso**; Unión Soviética (U.R.S.S.)

Suecia, Sweden; **sueco**

Suiza, Switzerland; **suizo**

Turquía; **turco**

Yugoeslavia; **yugoeslavo**

China; **chino**

Egipto; **egipcio, egipciano**

la India; **indio**

el Japón; **japonés**

Méjico; **mejicano** — (*Mex. sp.*) México; **mexicano**

Cuba; **cubano**

Haití; **haitiano**

República Dominicana; **dominicano**

Puerto Rico; **portorriqueño** (*sometimes* **puerto-**)

Costa Rica; **costarriqueño, costarricense**

Guatemala; **guatemalteco**

Honduras; **hondureño**

Nicaragua; **nicaragüeño, nicaragüense**

el Panamá; **panameño**

el Salvador; **salvadoreño**

la (República) Argentina; **argentino**

Bolivia; **boliviano**

el Brasil; **brasileño**

Colombia; **colombiano**

Chile; **chileno**

el Ecuador; **ecuatoriano**

el Paraguay; **paraguayo**

el Perú; **peruano**

el Uruguay; **uruguayo**

Venezuela; **venezolano**

la América Hispana, Spanish America; **hispanoamericano**

la América Latina; **latinoamericano**

árabe, Arab   **blanco,** white   **negro,** black, Negro

indio, Indian (*of America or Asia*)   **judío,** Jewish, Jew

SOME PECULIAR REGIONAL NAMES AND NICKNAMES. Spanish adjective-nouns referring to inhabitants of certain regions and cities sometimes vary surprisingly from what is expected. The foreigner is tempted to say or write "andaluciano," "cataloniano," and "galiciano" for *Andalusian, Catalonian,* or *Galician* — but the correct forms are **andaluz, catalán,** and **gallego.** The inhabitants of Madrid, Malaga, Sevilla, and Cadiz are **madrileños, malagueños, sevillanos,** and **gaditanos.** A native of Buenos Aires is a **porteño** (*of the port*).

You are familiar with the term **gringo,** applied in Mexico and elsewhere to Anglo-Saxons, or to foreigners in general, a term sometimes expressing contempt or hostility. North Americans are also referred to familiarly as **yanquis.** Spanish Americans also have some slang terms for themselves, as **cholos** (properly, Peruvian Indians or mestizos) for Peruvians and **ticos** for Costa Ricans.

Diminutive endings may indicate affection and may even soften a contemptuous term, as **cholito, gringuito.**

READING PRACTICE. Before you attempt to read the following sentences you should review everything you have studied so far. When you feel that you have a good general grasp of the material in Lessons I to V, read the following sentences aloud and try to understand them:

El general Wéllington estaba (was) **al lado** (side) **de los españoles en la Guerra** (War) **de Independencia. El general pensaba** (thought) **que los guerrilleros españoles eran** (were) **buenos soldados.**

En una aldea (village) **de La Mancha vivía** (lived) **el hidalgo** (nobleman) **Don Quijote. Hay muchas traducciones** (translations) **del libro de Cervantes, y muchas son malas. En inglés no hay una perfecta traducción del** *Quijote.*

La muchacha Anita es muy bonita y muy inteligente.

El arte es inmortal.

Nuestro programa hoy consiste en práctica, especialmente (especially) **de pronunciación.**

Quevedo es un autor satírico interesantísimo pero muy difícil.

El curso principia (begins) **hoy, 15 de enero de 1958. Principia a las diez de la mañana. Hay que** (It is necessary to, One must) **entrar en la escuela** (school) **a las diez menos cinco para** (in order to) **estar a tiempo** (on time). **A las diez y media hay una lección en inglés y a las once una lección de aritmética.**

En España e (y *becomes* e *before* i– *or* hi–) **Hispano-América tienen el sistema métrico.**

¿ A qué hora tendrá (will you have) **su lección de español?**

¿ Cuántos años tiene su hermana de Ud.? Tiene catorce años.

¿ De qué color es este papel? Este papel es blanco.

Todo el día ese hombre está en casa.

¿ De quién es la casa verde? Es la casa de mi tío.

¿ De quién es este sombrero? Es mío. Ese sombrero es suyo.

Él es buen amigo mío. Y su hermana es buena amiga mía.

El profesor explica (explains) la lección en la clase y los alumnos la estudian en casa.

En el año 750 los árabes estaban (were) en España.

¿ Cómo está Ud.? Muy bien, gracias ¿ y Ud.?

En el año 1492 Cristóbal Colón descubrió (discovered) **América.**

¿ Es su amigo Juan un hombre rico? Sí, es riquísimo.

¿ Es inglés el maestro (teacher)? No, es español de origen mexicano.

¿ Es fácil hablar castellano? Sí, señor, pero no es fácil hablarlo (to speak it) bien.

¿ Cuándo está su amigo en la ciudad? Está aquí todos los días.

En el Café Madrid la comida (food) es muy cara, porque (because) es un café de primera clase.

¿ Es cara la vida (life, living) en los Estados Unidos? Sí, señor, carísima.

Pronuncie Ud. los números siguientes (following): 7 — 91 — 615 — 1958 — 20,422 — 331,711 — 1,753,555 — 10,876,543 — 123,456,789.

5 y 7 son.... 16 y 8 son.... 13 y 14 son.... 44 y 55 son.... 9 menos 6 son.... 12 menos 4 son.... 29 menos 10 son.... 4 por 4 son.... 6 por 7 son.... 21 por 3 son.... 512 por 2 son....

When you understand all the sentences above, read them a number of times, first slowly, and then more rapidly, until you can read them fluently. At the same time try to think in Spanish, without translating the sentences into English as you read them.

FROM NOW ON LISTEN TO SPANISH RADIO PROGRAMS

You should now begin to listen regularly to radio programs in Spanish. Write to the stations that you can listen to on your radio and request a schedule of programs in Spanish.

At first you may not be able to understand much, but you will recognize a word now and then, and listening to Spanish accustoms your ear to the sounds of Spanish. As you learn more Spanish and continue to listen to Spanish on the radio, you will understand more and more.

LESSON VI

§ 1. *Demonstrative Adjectives and Pronouns*

THERE ARE IN SPANISH three demonstrative adjectives, with their corresponding pronouns. They refer to: (a) the person or thing near the speaker; (b) the person or thing near the person addressed; and (c) the person or thing remote from either.

The demonstrative adjectives are:

	Singular		Plural	
	Masc.	Fem.	Masc.	Fem.
(a) this	este	esta	these estos	estas
(b) that	ese	esa	those esos	esas
(c) that	aquel	aquella	those aquellos	aquellas

When these words are used to indicate an unexpressed noun, they become pronouns and take the orthographic accent. The neuter pronouns take no accent because there are no neuter adjectives. The demonstrative pronouns are:

	Singular			Plural	
	Masc.	Fem.	Neuter	Masc.	Fem.
(a)	éste	ésta	esto	éstos	éstas
(b)	ése	ésa	eso	ésos	ésas
(c)	aquél	aquélla	aquello	aquéllos	aquéllas

EXAMPLES:

As Adjectives

(a) Near the speaker:

En este jardín hay muchas flores. In this garden there are many flowers.

(b) Near the person addressed:

Esas flores son muy hermosas. Those flowers are very beautiful.

(c) Remote from both:

Pero aquellas flores son más hermosas. But those flowers are more beautiful.

54

As Pronouns

(a) **Éste es mi sombrero.** This (one) is my hat.

(b) **Ése es el suyo.** That one (*you have*) is yours.

(c) **De todas las flores, aquéllas son las más hermosas.** Of all the flowers, those (over there) are the most beautiful.

A neuter demonstrative pronoun never refers to a word, since all Spanish words have gender. The neuter pronouns refer to unidentified objects, ideas, situations, etc. Examples:

¿ Qué es esto (eso)? What is this (that)?

Eso (*or* Aquello) no importa. That does not matter.

PRACTICE. Learn the demonstrative adjectives and pronouns well. Practice the following sentences, and make up some more of your own.

¿ De quién es este libro? ¿ Cuál? Éste. Es mío.

Este sombrero que yo tengo no es el mío.

Estos libros son muy interesantes.

Esa opinión que tiene Ud. y la que (that which) **yo tengo son diferentes.**

Esta mañana yo pensaba en (I was thinking of) **aquellos días.**

¿ Quién es aquella niña? Es mi hermana.

Ésas son flores bellísimas.

Aquélla es una casa histórica.

Aquéllos son indios.

§ 2. *Reflexive Pronouns and Reflexive Verbs — MISMO*

REFLEXIVE PRONOUNS are used with reflexive verbs. A reflexive verb is one in which the action is both performed and suffered by the subject. In "I wash myself" *wash* is a reflexive verb, and *myself* is a reflexive pronoun.

In Spanish, reflexive verbs may be used to express the passive, as: **se dice que,** *it is said that* ("it says itself that"); **él se llama,** *his name is* ("he calls himself").

LAVAR, to wash; LAVARSE, to wash oneself

yo ME lavo, I wash myself

él (ella) SE lava, he (she) washes himself (herself)

Ud. SE lava, you wash yourself

nosotros(–as) NOS lavamos, we wash ourselves

ellos(–as) SE lavan, they wash themselves

Uds. SE lavan, you wash yourselves

ME, NOS, and **SE** are reflexive pronouns (see table on page 28).

PRACTICE:

Se sabe que es viuda. It is known that she is a widow.

Aquí se habla inglés. English is spoken here.

¿ Se permite fumar? Is it permitted to smoke? Is smoking allowed? May one smoke?

Yo me llamo Carlos Smith. My name is Charles Smith.

Se habla de ello en todas partes. It is being talked about everywhere.

¿ Se venden diarios aquí? Are newspapers sold here? Do you sell newspapers here?

Los indios se bañan en el río. The Indians bathe in the river.

See whether, with the words you know, you can make some sentences using reflexive verbs.

MISMO is an *intensive* adjective and pronoun, meaning *same, very,* or *-self.* For example:

el mismo hombre, the same man

las mismas mujeres, the same women

hoy mismo, this very day; **ayer mismo,** only, *or* just, yesterday

aquí mismo, right here; **ahora mismo** right now

la misma mañana, the same morning

yo mismo(–a), I myself

él mismo, he himself; **ella misma,** she herself

ellos(–as) mismos(–as), they themselves

Ud. mismo(–a), you yourself; **Uds. mismos(–as),** you yourselves

los perros mismos, the very dogs, even the dogs

Mismo, though often translated *-self,* is not a reflexive pronoun. Compare:

Yo mismo lo ví. I myself (*intensive*) saw it.

Yo me ví en el espejo. I saw myself (*reflexive*) in the mirror.

Él habla a sí mismo. (**Sí** is reflexive; **mismo,** intensive.) He talks to himself.

§ 3. *Conjunctions*

CONJUNCTIONS are connecting words which serve to connect two or more parts of a sentence.

The two commonest conjunctions are **Y,** *and,* and **O,** *or.* Both of them change their form before certain words.

E (not **y**) is used before words beginning with **i-** or **hi-**, but not **hie-**. Thus:

Isabel y María	**padre e hijo,** father and son
María e Isabel	**nieve y hielo,** snow and ice

U (not **o**) is used before words beginning with **o-** or **ho-**:

obscuro o claro, dark or light
claro u obscuro   **mujer u hombre**

NI, *nor*, must be used in negative statements where we use *or*. The double negative is used in Spanish. Thus:

No hablan a Juan ni a su hermana. They don't speak to John or his sister. *Or:* . . . nor to his sister.
Sin estudiar no es posible ni hablar ni entender el español. Without studying it is impossible tc speak or understand Spanish.

Ni — or, more emphatic, **ni siquiera** — means *not even:*

No tengo ni (siquiera) un centavo. I don't (even) have a cent.

PERO, *but*, is much commoner but less emphatic than **MAS**, *yet*.

Thus: **Yo hablo castellano, pero no lo hablo bien.**

      Él dice eso, mas yo no lo creo (believe).

In negative statements **SINO**, *but, only*, must be used:

No son cubanos sino dominicanos. They are not Cubans but Dominicans.
No venden sino compran. They are not selling but buying.
Yo no tengo sino dos hermanos. I have but, *or* only, two brothers.
Yo no soy médico sino abogado. I am not a doctor, but a lawyer.

MAS, *yet*, is not to be confused with **MÁS**, *more*.

Certain conjunctions, in Spanish as in English, are used in pairs:

ASÍ . . . COMO, TANTO . . . COMO, both . . . and
O . . . O, either . . . or
NI . . . NI, neither . . . nor, (*in negative statements*) either . . . or

EXAMPLES:

Así (*or* Tanto) el padre como el hijo hablan inglés. Botn
the father and the son speak English.

O el padre o el hijo habla inglés.

Ni el padre ni el hijo habla inglés.

No habla inglés ni el padre ni el hijo.

No hablan ni francés ni alemán. They do not speak either
French or German.

Nunca tengo ni cigarrillos ni fósforos. I never have either
cigarettes or matches.

There are many other conjunctions and conjunctive phrases.
In the following brief list, the more important ones are capitalized:

QUE, that	**PUES,** since	**SI,** if
AUNQUE } although	**PORQUE,** because	
bien que } although	**PARA QUE,** in order that	
a menos que, unless	**ASÍ QUE**	
EN CASO QUE, in case, in the event that	**DE MODO QUE** } so that	
	de manera que	
LUEGO QUE, as soon as	**MIENTRAS QUE,** while	
supuesto que, granting, *or* granted, that		
no sólo ... sino también, not only ... but also		

At this stage it is not feasible to give examples of these conjunctions
in sentences, as you do not know enough verb forms. The last
expression in the list can, however, be illustrated:

No sólo habla inglés sino también francés. He speaks not only
English, but also French.

§ 4. *Interjections and Exclamatory Phrases*

THERE are many interjections, or exclamatory words, in Spanish,
almost every Spanish-speaking country having a number of its own.
In Catholic countries much use is made of expressions which in
Protestant countries are regarded as profane, but in Spanish they
are not considered improper. Here are some of them, with their
approximate English equivalents:

¡ Dios ! Heavens !	**¡ Dios mío !** Good gracious !
¡ Por Dios ! For Heaven's sake !	
¡ Ay, Dios mío ! Oh Heavens above ! Oh dear !	
¡ Válgame Dios ! Bless my soul !	

¡Ojalá ...! Would to God ...! If only ...! (**Ojalá**, *a relic of the Moorish invasion, invokes Allah.*)

¡Jesús! } expressions of astonishment
¡Ave María!

Most of the exclamations in the following list are common to all Spanish-speaking countries:

¡**Ay**! *expresses grief or pain:* Oh!

¡**Ay de mí**! Poor me! Woe is me!

¡**Pobre de mí**! Poor me! ¡**Pobre de él**! Poor fellow! ¡**Pobre de Juan**! Poor John! *etc.*

¡**Caramba**! *expresses astonishment or annoyance:* Well! Gee whiz! Damn! *etc.*

¡**Vamos**! Come on! Let's go!

¡**Anda**! ¡**Vaya**! ¡**Vamos**! *express disbelief:* Don't tell me! Go on! Really! Oh yeah?

¡**De veras**! ¡**Verdad**! *express surprise or doubt:* Is that so! Really! You don't say!

¡**Hombre**! My dear fellow! *Usually thrown in:* ¡**Vaya, hombre**! = ¡**Vaya**!

¡**Diga**! Go on (*with the story*)! Tell me!

¡**Oiga**! Listen! Hey!

¡**Calle**! Be still! ¡**Calle la boca**! Shut up!

¡**Olé**! Well done! (*used at bullfights, sports, and to cheer flamenco dancers*)

¡**Bravo**! Bravo!

¡**Otra vez**! Again! Encore!

¡**Adelante**! Come in! Go ahead!

¡**Cuidado**! Be careful! Look out!

¡**Pare**! Stop! ¡**Alto**! Halt!

¡**Ja, ja**! Ha ha!

Some exclamations are the same in both languages: *Ah! Oh! Ha! Bah!* Exclamations are more common in Spanish than in English.

§ 5. *The Adverb — Making Adverbs from Adjectives with* —*MENTE* — *Position of the Adverb — Invariable Adverbs*

THE ADVERB is a word that qualifies a verb, an adjective, or another adverb.

MAKING ADVERBS FROM ADJECTIVES WITH –MENTE. Adverbs can be formed from adjectives by adding the ending –mente, which corresponds to the English ending –ly:

(1) to the feminine singular of adjectives that end in –o, as: raro, rare; raramente, rarely.

(2) to the singular of adjectives that have the same form in both masculine and feminine, as: fácil, easy; fácilmente, easily; actual, present; actualmente, at the present time.

Note: If the adjective bears a written accent, the accent is retained. In fácilmente, both fá– and –men– are stressed.

Practice making adverbs in this way from the adjectives on pages 20, 23, 24, and 47.

POSITION OF THE ADVERB. In Spanish the adverb is normally placed immediately after the verb. Thus:

Mi amigo habla mal el español. My friend speaks Spanish badly.

Pero habla bien el inglés. But he speaks English well.

REFERENCE LIST OF INVARIABLE ADVERBS. In addition to the many adverbs that are derived from adjectives by the addition of –mente, there are many that are not formed in this way. For example, in the list below, the words despacio, temprano, and mal are sometimes adjectives but are also adverbs. And many adverbs, such as ahora and aquí, have no corresponding adjectives.

You have already learned a number of the words in the following list. Of the ones you do not know, learn now the ones in large type. After learning them, try to make sentences with them.

These words are all used adverbially. **Abajo** means down or below only adverbially; it cannot be used as a preposition.

ABAJO, down, below	**A LA IZQUIERDA**, to the left	al por menor, retail
acá, hither, here		alrededor, around
acaso, perhaps, by chance	a la moda, in fashion, in style	**ALTO**, (a)loud, high
ADELANTE, forward, ahead	al fiado, on credit, on trust	**ALLÁ**, thither, there
AFUERA, outside, abroad	**ALGO**, somewhat	**ALLÍ**, ahí, there
AHORA, now	al momento, instantly, right away	a más tardar, at the latest
A LA DERECHA, to the right	al por mayor, whole-sale	a menudo, often
		ANOCHE, last night
		ANTEAYER, day before yesterday

ANTES, before
apenas, scarcely
aprisa, quickly
AQUÍ, here
ARRIBA, up, upstairs
ASÍ, thus, so
a tiempo, in, *or* on, time
ATRÁS, backwards
aun, even, still, yet
a veces, at times, sometimes
AYER, yesterday

BAJO, under(neath), low
BASTANTE, enough
BIEN, well

CASI, almost
CERCA, near
CLARO, clearly
COMO, as, like, how
con todo, notwithstanding, in spite of everything
CUANDO, when

de buena gana, willingly, gladly
de mala gana, unwillingly, grudgingly
DE DÍA, by day
DE NOCHE, by night
DEMÁS, besides, over (*above a certain quantity*)
DEMASIADO, too much
dentro, within, inside
de nuevo, again, anew
DESPACIO, slow(ly)

DESPUÉS, after-(wards)
detrás, behind
de vez en cuando, from time to time, now and then
DONDE, where

encima, above, over
ENFRENTE, opposite
EN NINGUNA PARTE, nowhere
en otra parte, elsewhere
en todas partes, everywhere
EN SEGUIDA, right away, immediately, at once
ENTONCES, then

fuera, out, outside

harto, fully, enough, sufficiently, plenty
HOY, today

jamás, never (stronger than **nunca**)

LEJOS, far
LUEGO, soon

MAL, badly
MAÑANA, tomorrow
mañana por la mañana, tomorrow morning
MÁS, more
más o menos, more or less
MENOS, less

MUCHO, much
MUY, very

NO, no, not
NUNCA, never

pasado mañana, day after tomorrow
paso a paso, step by step
POCO, little, not much
poco a poco, little by little, gradually
por aquí, hereabouts
por allá, thereabouts
por último, finally, at last
PUES, then (*not of time*)

quizá, quizás, perhaps, maybe

raras veces, rarely, seldom

SÍ, yes
SIEMPRE, always
sin duda, without doubt, doubtless
sin embargo, however, nevertheless
SÓLO, only

TAL VEZ, maybe, perhaps
TAMBIÉN, also
TAMPOCO, neither
TAN, so
TANTO, so much
TARDE, late
TEMPRANO, early
todavía, yet, still

YA, already, now

LESSON VII

§ 1. *Prepositions — Simple Prepositions — Some Prepositions Explained*

PREPOSITIONS. A preposition is a word placed before a noun to show the relation in which a person or thing stands to something else. Thus, in "I go *to* the house," "he came *from* the theater," *to* and *from* are prepositions.

SIMPLE PREPOSITIONS. Spanish prepositions are simple or compound. The simple prepositions are:

a, to, at	**hacia,** toward(s)
ante, before, in front of	**hasta,** until, up to, to, as far as
bajo, under, below	**para,** for
con, with	**por,** by, for
contra, against	**salvo,** except, save
de, of, from	**según,** according to
desde, from, since	**sin,** without
durante, during	**sobre,** on, upon, about
en, in, into, at	**tras,** after, behind
entre, between, among	

SOME PREPOSITIONS EXPLAINED. The prepositions represent one of the more difficult aspects of Spanish, and it may be a little comfort to you to know that good Spanish writers often differ in regard to the usage of prepositions.

It is not proposed here to enter into subtleties, but to state merely the straightforward usages about which there is no doubt. Only wide experience and reading can teach the prepositions thoroughly. It is absolutely necessary for you to learn the following:

A, *to, at:* its basic meaning is to indicate *direction toward* a thing, a place, or a time:

Voy a casa. I am going home.
Vamos al teatro. We are going to the theater.
a la derecha (izquierda), to the right (left)
de calle a calle, from street to street
de las tres a las cinco, from three to five o'clock

A is also used in a variety of other ways — to include *location* in place or time (*at, on, upon*); for the *manner* of doing something; for the *instrument* with which something is done; and for *price, rate,* or *resemblance.* After verbs of depriving, it corresponds to English *from.* Note the following example.

sentarse a la mesa, to sit down at, *or* to, the table

a bordo del vapor, on board the steamer

a las cuatro de la tarde, at four in the afternoon

a mi llegada (salida), on, *or* upon, my arrival (departure)

a pie, on foot   **a mano,** by hand

a sangre fría, in cold blood

a manos de, at the hands of

a la española, in the Spanish manner, *or* style

¿A cuánto se vende? What does it sell for? ("At how much does it sell itself?") **A cinco pesos el metro.** At five pesos a meter.

dos a dos, two by two; **poco a poco,** little by little

Quité al marinero el sombrero. I took the sailor's hat. ("I took away from the sailor the hat.")

A is the most difficult and confusing of the Spanish prepositions. It has other important uses which will be explained later.

CON, *with*, indicates *accompaniment, instrumentality,* and *addition.* It sometimes means *with* in the sense of *in spite of.* **Con + mí = conmigo; con + tí = contigo; con + sí = consigo.** Thus:

Estoy con mi hermano. I am with my brother. **Él está conmigo.** He is with me.

Lo hago con mis propias manos. I make it with my own hands.

con todo, in spite of everything

Es inteligente y cortés, pero con todo no lo quiero. He is intelligent and polite, but still I don't like him.

DE, *of, from:* the basic meaning is to indicate *direction away from* a thing, a place, or a time. It is also used in indicating *origin;* the *material* of which something is made; *ownership; relation of a part to the whole;* and the *use* for which something is intended. Thus:

Vengo del hotel. I come from the hotel.

de Nueva York a San Francisco, from N.Y. to S.F.

Soy de los Estados Unidos. I am from the United States.

de hoy a mañana, from today to tomorrow

De las seis a las once son cinco horas. From six o'clock to eleven is five hours.

Hablo de memoria. I speak from memory.

una silla de madera, a wooden chair

la casa de mi padre, my father's house

las obras de Cervantes, the works of Cervantes

la cabeza del perro, the dog's head

un perro de caza, a hunting dog

una máquina de escribir, a typewriter ("a machine of writing")

Note also:

> **el camino de Oaxaca,** the road to Oaxaca
> **el avión de Nueva York,** the New York plane

After a superlative, **de** is to be translated *in:*

el hombre más gordo del mundo, the fattest man in the world

DESDE, *from, since,* is used in speaking of a *point of departure,* in place or time. Thus:

desde Nueva York a San Francisco, from N.Y. to S.F.

desde aquel año, since that year

desde niño, since I was a little boy

EN, *in, on, at, into,* is used of *place, time,* and *manner.*

Cuando lo vi en Córdoba en el verano pasado, él hablaba en serio. When I saw him in Cordoba last summer, he spoke in earnest.

en casa, at home   **en la escuela,** at school

en la mesa, on the table

entrar en la casa, to go into the house

After **de, en** is translated *to,* as in:

de día en día, from day to day

de vez en cuando, from time to time

§ 2. *More Prepositions Explained — Compound Prepositions*

HACIA, *toward(s),* means *in the direction of,* as:

Andamos hacia el parque. We are walking, *or* going, toward the park.

Hacia el norte hay una tempestad. Toward, *or* In, the north there is a storm.

HASTA means *until, (up) to, as far as:*

hasta mañana, until tomorrow

Hasta la vista. I'll be seeing you. *Au revoir.* ("Until the sight.")

Hasta luego. See you soon. So long. ("Until soon.")

desde Buenos Aires hasta Mendoza, from Buenos Aires to, *or* as far as, Mendoza

PARA and **POR** are both usually translated *for*, but their meanings are quite distinct in Spanish. **Para** expresses *purpose* or *destination:*

La carta es para Ud. The letter is for you.

el avión para Caracas, the plane for Caracas

¿ Es éste el camino para (*or* de) Puebla? Is this the road to P.?

Before an infinitive, **para** means *in order to:*

Hay que trabajar para comer. One must work (in order) to eat.

Por has many meanings. With the general meaning of *for*, it indicates an *equivalent, length of time, motive or reason, for the sake of, to get:*

Me dió su libro por el mío. He gave me his book (in return) for mine.

Vendió el caballo por cien pesetas. He sold the horse for a hundred pesetas.

Estaré de viaje por un año. I shall be traveling for a year.

por ahora, for the present, for the time being

Lo hace por amor. He does it for love.

Lo dice por ignorancia. He says it because of ignorance.

¡ Por Dios ! For Heaven's sake !

por la libertad, for the sake of liberty

Voy por pan. I am going for bread.

Por, translated *by*, indicates *agent* or *means:*

Fué construido por los indios. It was constructed by the Indians.

Lo hago por fuerza. I do it by force.

por fuerza de, by dint of

por lo que el dice, according to, *or* to judge by, what he says

Por sometimes means *along* or *through* (a place):

pasar por la calle, to walk along the street

Entró por la ventana. He entered through, *or* by, the window.

El tren pasa por aquí a las ocho. The train passes through here at eight o'clock.

por aquí, hereabouts, around here

por allí, *or* **ahí,** thereabouts, around there

SEGÚN means *according to, depending on:*

según los diarios, according to the newspapers
según las circunstancias, according to, *or* depending on, the
circumstances
Según. That depends.

SOBRE means *upon, on, about:*

sobre la mesa, upon the table
Él escribe sobre el derecho. He writes on law.
Hablamos sobre las cosas del día. We talk about the affairs
of the day, *or* current affairs.
Tomo sobre mí mucho trabajo. I take much work upon myself.

COMPOUND PREPOSITIONS. Compound prepositions are those composed of two or more words. Here are some of them:

a causa de, on account of, be- cause of	**acerca de,** about, concerning
a fuerza de, by dint of	**tocante a,** concerning
a través de, across	**cerca de,** near, *or* close, to
antes de, before (*time*)	**después de,** after (*time*)
delante de, before (*place*)	**atrás de, detrás de,** behind,
conforme a, according to	after (*place*)
(con) respecto a, with respect	**contrario a,** contrary to
to, respecting	**debajo de,** under(neath), be- neath
en vez de, in place of, instead	**frente a,** in front of, opposite
of	**junto a,** next to, adjoining
lejos de, far (away) from	**por razón de,** by reason of

THE WHOLE OF THIS SECTION ON PREPOSITIONS IS OF GREAT IMPOR-
TANCE. IT WILL BE NECESSARY FOR YOU TO REVIEW IT SEVERAL
TIMES AS THE COURSE PROCEEDS.

§ 3. *Negative Words and Their Use*

SOME of the negative words in the following list you already know,
but you must know all of them:

no, no, not
ni, nor, (*after not*) or; **ni ... ni,** neither ... nor; **ni siquiera,**
not even
ningun(o), no, not one, not any, none
nadie, no one, nobody, not anyone, not anybody

nada, nothing, not anything, (*adv.*) not at all; **una nada, a** nothing, nonentity, nothingness

nunca, jamás (*more emphatic*), never, not ever; **nunca jamás,** never, *or* not ever, again

tampoco (= **tan poco,** as little), neither; **ni . . . tampoco,** nor . . . either

Of the negative words, **NO** is the commonest. You are already familiar with **no** as the answer to a question and in negative statements. Thus:

¿ **Tiene Ud. el libro?** Do you have the book? **No, señor, no lo tengo.** No, I don't have it.

You have learned that **no** always precedes the verb, and that it also precedes an object pronoun, or two object pronouns. Thus:

¿ **Le dió a Ud. el libro?** Did he give you the book? **No me lo dió.** He didn't give it to me.

It has been mentioned, and you have observed, that Spanish, unlike English, uses the double negative: **No dice nada.** He says nothing. He doesn't say anything. In fact, a Spanish sentence can correctly contain three or four negatives, as:

No hay nunca ninguna carta de nadie. There is never any letter from anybody.

But the double negative need not be used if **no** is not used and another negative word comes at or near the beginning of the sentence. Thus:

Nadie está en casa. No está nadie en casa. No one is at home.

Nada hay en la casa. No hay nada en la casa. There is nothing in the house.

Ninguno de ellos habla inglés. No habla inglés ninguno de ellos. None of them speaks English.

Él nunca tiene cigarrillos. Él no tiene cigarrillos nunca. He never has cigarettes.

NI has been presented and explained with other conjunctions. Review Lesson VI, § 3, "**NI**" and "**NI . . . NI.**"

NINGUN(O), *no, not one, not any, none,* is the negative of **algun(o),** *some.* It is used as an adjective or a pronoun. Thus:

ningún hombre, no man; **ninguna mujer,** no woman

ninguno de los hombres, none of the men; **ninguna de las mujeres,** none of the women

De estos indios, ninguno habla español. None of these Indians speak Spanish.

¿Tiene Ud. alguna amiga? Do you have any girl friend? **Ninguna.** Not one.

Quiero algunas flores, pero no veo ningunas. I want some flowers, but I don't see any.

NADIE and **NADA** offer no difficulties:

No hay nadie aquí. There is no one here.

Nadie dice nada. Nobody says anything.

No es nada. It's nothing.

No es nada difícil (**nada** *an adverb*). It's not at all difficult.

Él es una nada. He is a nobody. He's nobody at all.

No tengo nada más que lo necesario. I don't have any more than what is necessary.

No quiero nada más. I don't want any more, *or* anything else.

De nada is much used in reply to an expression of thanks, as:

Mil gracias. Thanks a lot. Thanks ever so much. **De nada.** Don't mention it. It's nothing. You're welcome.

NUNCA and **JAMÁS** both mean *never*, *not ever*, but **jamás** is the more emphatic. **Jamás** is never used after **no**; it always begins a sentence. In conversation you would do well to use **nunca** — it is never necessary to use **jamás.**

Él no dice nada nunca. (*More emphatic*) **Jamás dice nada.** He never says anything. **¿No?** No? **Jamás.** Never.

Nunca jamás means *never again:*

No lo hago nunca jamás. I won't ever do it again.

TAMPOCO is used as follows:

Mi amigo no baila, ni yo tampoco. My friend doesn't dance, nor I either, . . . and neither do I, . . . and I don't either.

¿Habla Marta el español? Does Martha speak Spanish? **No.** No. **¿Y Juana?** And Jane? **Tampoco.** No, she doesn't either.

In Spanish America, the phrase **no más** is often colloquially used for *a little, just*, as:

Vengo no más. I have just come.

¿Quiere Ud. café? Will you have some coffee? **Un poco, no más.** Just a little.

§ 4. *Infinitives in –AR, –ER, –IR — Object Pronouns Attached to Infinitives — Present Tense of* COMPRAR, VENDER, VIVIR — TENER *and* HABER — *Past Participles — Present Perfect Tense*

INFINITIVES IN **–AR, –ER, –IR.** The infinitives of Spanish verbs end in –ar, –er, and –ir. Typical verbs are **comprar**, *to buy*, **vender**, *to sell*, and **vivir**, *to live*.

OBJECT PRONOUNS ATTACHED TO INFINITIVES. When a Spanish personal pronoun is the object of an infinitive, it is attached to the infinitive, as shown below (note the addition of a written accent to some forms):

Quiero comprarlas. I want to buy them (*flowers*).
Él quiere vendérmelas. He wants to sell them to me.
Quiero comprárselas. I want to buy them for him, her, them, *or* you.
Quieren comprárnoslas. They want to buy them for us.
Ella va a dármelo. She is going to give it (*book*) to me.
Voy a dárselos. I am going to give them (*books*) to him, her, them, *or* you.

PRESENT TENSE OF **COMPRAR, VENDER, VIVIR.** You have been using several –ar and –er verbs in the present tense. Here are the forms of the three types of verbs. Note the similarities and differences of the endings:

COMPRAR, to buy	**VENDER,** to sell	**VIVIR,** to live
yo compro, I buy, I am buying, I do buy	**yo vendo,** I sell, I am selling, I do sell	**yo vivo,** I live, I am living, I do live
tú compras, you buy	**tú vendes,** you sell	**tú vives,** you live
él (ella) compra, he (she) buys	**él (ella) vende,** he (she) sells	**él (ella) vive,** he (she) lives
Ud. compra, you buy	**Ud. vende,** you sell	**Ud. vive,** you live
nosotros(–as) compramos, we buy	**nosotros(–as) vendemos,** we sell	**nosotros(–as) vivimos,** we live
vosotros(–as) compráis, you buy	**vosotros(–as) vendéis,** you sell	**vosotros(–as) vivís,** you live
ellos(–as) compran, they buy	**ellos(–as) venden,** they sell	**ellos(–as) viven,** they live
Uds. compran, you buy	**Uds. venden,** you sell	**Uds. viven,** you live

EXAMPLES:

Yo no compro más papel. I am not buying any more paper.
Él me compra un diario. He is buying me a (news)paper.
Ni compran ni venden libros. They don't buy or sell books.
Vendemos automóviles. We sell automobiles.
Vivimos en Chicago. We live in Chicago.
¿Dónde vive Ud.? Where do you live?
¿Viven Uds. en la ciudad? Do you live in the city?

TENER AND **HABER.** **Tener** means *to have, possess.* You are
familiar with the present tense of this verb. **Haber,** *to have,* is an
auxiliary verb; that is, it is used to form "compound tenses"
of other verbs. Learn the following forms of **haber** (except for the
intimate second person):

HABER, to have

yo he, I have	**nosotros(–as) hemos,** we have
tú has, you have	**vosotros(–as) habéis,** you have
él (ella) ha, he (she) has	**ellos(–as) han,** they have
Ud. ha, you have	**Uds. han,** you have

PAST PARTICIPLES of regular verbs end in **–ADO** (**–ar** verbs) or
–IDO (**–er** and **–ir** verbs):

COMPRADO, bought   **VENDIDO,** sold   **VIVIDO,** lived

Since participles are adjectives, these forms have the usual
adjective endings, which are used when the participle refers to a
noun. Thus:

flores compradas en Xochimilco, flowers bought in X.
libros vendidos en la librería, books sold in the bookstore
la vida vivida por los indios, the life lived by the Indians

THE PRESENT PERFECT TENSE is formed by using the present of
haber (shown above) and the past participle (ending invariably
in **–o**). The present perfect tense is used to speak of an action
begun in the past and continuing to the present. Learn the present
perfect of **comprar** (except for the intimate second person):

yo he comprado, I have bought	**nosotros(–as) hemos comprado,** we have bought
tú has comprado, you have bought	**vosotros(–as) habéis comprado,** you have bought
él (ella) ha comprado, he (she) has bought	**ellos(–as) han comprado,** they have bought
Ud. ha comprado, you have bought	**Uds. han comprado,** you have bought

Write out and then say aloud the present perfect forms of **hablar, dar, vender, tener,** and **vivir.**

Now read aloud the following sentences several times, thinking of the meaning as you read them:

He comprado un perro.
Ella no me ha comprado un diario.
Los Álvarez me han dado un libro.
Hemos vivido en Tejas diez años.
No hemos hablado con los indios.
La niña ha vendido todas sus flores.
¿ Ha vivido su hermano de Ud. en los Estados Unidos?
El reloj ha dado la una.
El viejo ha tenido una buena vida.
Pablo no ha hablado nunca de sus padres.
Uds. nos han hablado muchas veces de él.
¿ Han vendido Uds. su casa?

§ 5. *Essential Parts of* SER *and* ESTAR — *The Use of* SER *and* ESTAR — *Essential Parts of* HABER — *Some More Past Participles*

ESSENTIAL PARTS OF **SER** AND **ESTAR.** The following table gives the forms of **ser** and **estar** in the simple tenses (intimate second person omitted). The imperfect expresses *continued* past action. The past definite expresses a *single* past action.

Infinitives:

SER	**ESTAR**	to be

Present:

yo soy	yo estoy	I am
él (ella) es	él (ella) está	he (she) is
Ud. es	Ud. está	you are
nosotros(–as) somos	nosotros(–as) estamos	we are
ellos(–as) son	ellos(–as) están	they are
Uds. son	Uds. están	you are

Imperfect:

yo era	yo estaba	I was
él (ella) era	él (ella) estaba	he (she) was
Ud. era	Ud. estaba	you were
nosotros(–as) eramos	nosotros(–as) estábamos	we were
ellos(–as) eran	ellos(–as) estaban	they were
Uds. eran	Uds. estaban	you were

SER	ESTAR	to be

Past Definite:

yo fuí	yo estuve	I was
él (ella) fué	él (ella) estuvo	he (she) was
Ud. fué	Ud. estuvo	you were
nosotros(–as) fuimos	nosotros(–as) estuvimos	we were
ellos(–as) fueron	ellos(–as) estuvieron	they were
Uds. fueron	Uds. estuvieron	you were

Future:

yo seré	yo estaré	I shall be
él (ella) será	él (ella) estará	he (she) will be
Ud. será	Ud. estará	you will be
nosotros(–as) seremos	nosotros(–as) estaremos	we shall be
ellos(–as) serán	ellos(–as) estarán	they will be
Uds. serán	Uds. estarán	you will be

Present Participle:

siendo	estando	being

Past Participle:

sido	estado	been

THE USE OF **SER** AND **ESTAR.** A peculiarity of Spanish is that it has two verbs * for our one verb *to be* — **ser** and **estar** — and these two verbs cannot be used interchangeably. As a rule, **ser** expresses *permanency* and **estar** expresses *the temporary* and *location* (temporary or permanent); but there are exceptions and ambiguous cases. The following table explains the uses of these verbs:

SER	ESTAR
I. Expresses the essential or permanent:	I. Expresses the temporary or accidental:
El perro es un animal. El hombre es mortal. Tres y tres son seis. ¿ Qué es eso? Mi madre es vieja.	El perro está enfermo (*sick*). El hombre está cansado (*tired*).
II. Expresses: (a) name: **Es el señor Martínez.** (b) origin: **La carta es de Alemania.**	II. Expresses location (temporary or permanent): La carta está en mi cuarto. Están en Madrid. Madrid está en España.

* We might say there are three, counting the impersonal **hay,** *there is, there are*

SER	ESTAR

SER

(c) nationality, race, religion:
  **Es cubano. Es árabe.
  Es cristiano.**

(d) profession or calling: **Soy
  médico.**

(e) ownership: **El libro es
  mío.**

(f) relationship: **Es mi hermano.**

(g) the material of which something is made: **La mesa
  es de madera.**

III. Is the auxiliary verb used in the
  passive:

  **El español es hablado por
  algunos indios.**

IV. Is used to state the time of day:
  Son las dos.

V. Is used in various impersonal
  expressions:

  **Es verdad.
  Es necesario.
  Es lástima.**

But **ser** is used of some matters which
  are or may be temporary (in the
  long run):

**María es joven.
Es la señorita Carmen Núñez Soto.
Es amada.
La casa es blanca.
Mi salud** (*health*) **es buena.
Son ricos.
Soy optimista.
Somos amigos.
Es temprano.**

ESTAR

III. Is used with the present participle, to form continuous
  tenses:

  Siempre están hablando.

IV. Is used to express the date:
  Estamos a dos de enero.

V. Is used in various impersonal
  expressions:

  Está bien.

But **estar** is used (before past participles) of some matters which
  are or may be permanent:

El caballo está muerto (*dead*).
Ella está casada (*married*).

The following examples further illustrate the difference between
ser and **estar**:

El hielo es frío. Ice is cold (*expresses permanency*).

Soy alegre. I am happy, gay, *or*
  cheerful (*by nature or generally*).

El agua está fría. The water is
  cold (*now, but not always*).

Estoy alegre. I am happy, gay, *or*
  cheerful (*at this time*).

Ella es amable. She is amiable *or* friendly (*by disposition*).

Ella está amable. She is amiable *or* friendly (*at this time*).

Mi madre es buena. My mother is good.

Mi madre está buena. My mother is well.

Es borracho. He is a drunkard.

Está borracho. He is drunk.

Fulano es loco. Fulano is crazy (*permanently*).

Fulano está loco. Fulano is crazy (*to act, or talk, as he does*).

ESSENTIAL PARTS OF **HABER**:

Infin.: **HABER**   *Present Participle:* **habiendo**   *Past Part.:* **habido**

Present	*Imperfect*	*Past Definite*	*Future*
he, I have	**había,** I had	**hube,** I had	**habré,** I shall have
ha	**había**	**hubo**	**habrá**
hemos	**habíamos**	**hubimos**	**habremos**
han	**habían**	**hubieron**	**habrán**

With these forms, compound tenses can be made:

Present Perfect: **he hablado,** I have spoken
Past Perfect: **había vivido,** I had lived
hube comprado, I had bought
Future Perfect: **habré vendido,** I shall have sold

SOME MORE PAST PARTICIPLES: Some of the following past participles are irregular (those in the second column); the others are regular, though some have an accent on the **i** to show that **ai** and **ei** are not diphthongs:

venido, come	**abierto,** opened, open
caído, fallen	**cubierto,** covered
creído, believed	**escrito,** written
leído, read	

Practice using these and the other past participles given in § 4 with various forms of **haber,** to form compound tenses.

Review this rather long and difficult lesson carefully, and make up as many sentences as you can, using the words, forms, and rules of this lesson.

KNOW HOW THE GRAMMAR *WORKS*. YOU WILL SOON BE READING NATIVE SPANISH WRITINGS WHICH WILL DRIVE IT HOME.

LESSON VIII

§ 1. *The Importance of* –AR *Verbs* — *Endings of* –AR *Verbs in the Simple Tenses* — *Progressive Forms with* ESTAR — *Some Common* –AR *Verbs* — GUSTAR

THE IMPORTANCE OF –AR VERBS. The majority of Spanish verbs end in –ar, and all but a few –ar verbs are regular in their conjugation. Others that are sometimes called irregular have parts in which the changes are merely orthographic. All verbs recently added to the language end in –ar, like **telefonear,** *to telephone.* The great importance of the –ar verbs and the need to know their conjugation need no emphasis.

ENDINGS OF –AR VERBS IN THE SIMPLE TENSES. The stem of a Spanish verb is found by dropping the infinitive ending –ar, –er, or –ir. Thus, the stem of **comprar** is **compr–**. The endings of the present, imperfect, and past definite tenses are added to the stem of the verb. The endings of the future tense are added to the *infinitive.* Here are the endings of the four simple tenses of –ar verbs, with the full forms of **comprar**. (The intimate second person is omitted.)

Infinitive:	–ar	**COMPRAR**	to buy
Pres. Part.:	–ando	comprando	buying
Past Part.:	–ado	comprado	bought

PRESENT TENSE:

Sing.	1	–o	compro	I buy, am buying, do buy, *etc.*
	3	–a	compra	
Pl.	1	–amos	compramos	
	3	–an	compran	

IMPERFECT TENSE:

Sing.	1	–aba	compraba	I was buying, I bought (*habit-*
	3	–aba	compraba	*ually*),[1] *etc.*
Pl.	1	–ábamos	comprábamos	
	3	–aban	compraban	

PAST DEFINITE TENSE:

Sing.	1	–é	compré	I bought (*on one occasion*),[1] *etc.*
	3	–ó	compró	
Pl.	1	–amos [2]	compramos	
	3	–aron	compraron	

[1,2] See note on next page.

75

FUTURE TENSE (*Endings Added to Infinitive*):

Sing.	1	–é	compraré	I shall buy, *etc.*
	3	–á	comprará	
Pl.	1	–emos	compraremos	
	3	–án	comprarán	

Note 1: Compare:

> En México yo compraba muchas veces chayotes. In Mexico I often bought chayotes. (*Imperfect tense*)
> Compré mi cámara en México. I bought my camera in Mexico. (*Past definite tense*)

Note 2: There is no difference in form, in the first person plural, between the present and past definite tenses. The context indicates the tense.

PROGRESSIVE FORMS WITH **ESTAR**. As indicated above, **compro** may be translated *I buy, I am buying,* or *I do buy.* The second and third forms are called the *progressive* and the *emphatic* forms of the present tense. The term *continuous present* (for *am buying,* etc.) is also used.

Forms of **estar** with the present participle provide distinctive progressive forms of the present and other tenses. For example:

I am buying: **estoy comprando** (*or* **compro**)
I was buying: **yo estaba comprando** (*or* **yo compraba**)
we shall be buying: **estaremos comprando**
they have been buying: **han estado comprando**

To emphasize the continuation of the action, use the forms with **estar**.

SOME COMMON –**AR** VERBS. Learn the following common –**ar** verbs. It should be mentioned here that those ending in –**car** are subject to orthographic changes (**c** becomes **qu** before **é**, as **apliqué,** *I applied*); but this matter will be taken up in detail in Part II.

aceptar, to accept	**certificar,** to certify, register
acompañar, to accompany	**comunicar,** to communicate
admirar, to admire	**consultar,** to consult
adoptar, to adopt	**contestar,** to answer, reply
anunciar, to announce	**copiar,** to copy
aplicar, to apply	**desear,** to desire, wish
avisar, to advise, warn	**doblar,** to double, fold
celebrar, to celebrate	**durar,** to last, endure

As the –**ar** verbs are of such importance, it is advisable to take each of the verbs above and, using the table on pages 75–76, apply all the endings of the simple tenses to it. In this way you will become thoroughly familiar with the endings.

GUSTAR: An important **-ar** verb is **gustar,** which usually means *to be pleasing to,* but, as illustrated below, becomes *to like:*

me gusta, it is pleasing to me, I like it
le gusta, he, she, *or* it likes it, you like it
nos gusta, we like it
les gusta, they, *or* you, like it
Me gusta el vino, pero me gusta más la cerveza. I like wine, but I like beer better.
Nos gusta bailar. We like to dance. We like dancing
¿ Le gustó a Ud. la música? Did you like the music?

Gustar also means *to taste, try:*

¿ Quiere Ud. gustar esto? Do you want to taste, *or* try, this?

And **gustar de** means *to like, enjoy:*

Gustamos de hablar español. We like to talk Spanish.

§ 2. *The Personal A — Practice Reading: Extract from* **La Vejez,** *by V. Blasco Ibáñez — Literal and Free Translations*

THE PERSONAL **A.** When the direct object of a verb is a *person or persons,* an *animal considered as a person,* a *country,* or a *personalized thing,* the preposition **a** must precede the object. This is called the "personal **a.**" Thus:

Consulté a mi amigo Ramón. I consulted my friend Ramón.
Consulté a Ramón y a su padre. I consulted Ramón and his father. (*Note repetition of* **a** *before second object.*)
No conozco al señor Rodríguez. I don't know Sr. Rodríguez.
El niño ama a su perro y a su gato. The little boy loves his dog and his cat.
Amamos a Guatemala. We love Guatemala.
Amamos a la libertad. We love freedom.

But:

No comprendo esta carta. I don't understand this letter. (*The letter is not a person.*)
No tengo amigos aquí. I have no friends here. ("*No friends*" *are not persons.*)
Tengo dos tíos en California. I have two uncles in California. (*The uncles are not thought of here as individuals.*)
Quiero comprar un perro. I want to buy a dog. (*A particular dog is not referred to.*)

The use of the personal **a** requires a bit of judgment.

PRACTICE READING. Hitherto you have been advised to practice
Spanish by making your own sentences from the material given.
Now we shall begin another kind of practice: the reading of Spanish
literature, which is excellent practice once you have a sufficient
knowledge of Spanish vocabulary and grammar. Here is a simple
passage, from a famous Spanish writer, with a literal translation.
First, study the Spanish in connection with the translation until
you understand the Spanish. Then read it over several times,
trying to follow the thought without referring to the English translation.

There are, of course, some words you have not yet met, and there
are some unfamiliar idioms. The notes give added information
about some words and explain the idioms.

When you have succeeded in understanding the passage well
enough to read it fairly rapidly with good comprehension, you should
have a feeling of accomplishment, for you are reading a selection
from Spanish literature, not an exercise in simplified Spanish for
students

LA VEJEZ[1]

OLD AGE

Ocurre [2] con la vejez lo que [3] con la muerte. Sabemos [4] que ha de [5]
There occurs with old age the same as with death. We know that it has

llegar, pero la vemos [6] tan lejos — ¡tan lejos! — durante una gran
to   arrive,   but   we   see   it   so   far — so   far! — during   a   great

parte de nuestra vida, que sólo nos inspira la falsa emoción de una
part of our life, that it only inspires in us the false emotion of a

catástrofe ocurrida en un lugar lejano [7] del globo. Nos lamentamos,[8]
catastrophe (that has) occurred in a distant place of the globe. We mourn over ourselves,

pero nuestro egoísmo, al ver [9] no nos toca [10] de cerca [11] el peligro, hace
but our egoism, on seeing (that) the danger does not touch us closely, makes (it)

que [12] las palabras no tengan [13] eco en el pensamiento. También estamos
that   the   words   have   not   any   echo   in   the   thought.   Also   we   are

seguros de que [14] algún día ha de llegar el fin del mundo, la muerte
sure   that   some   day   has   to   arrive   the end of the world, the death

de nuestro planeta, pero esto es tan remoto que no turba [15] ni por un
of our planet, but this is so remote that it does not disturb even for an

instante la paz de nuestros días.
instant the peace of our days.

— From **"La Vejez,"** in *Luna Benamor*, by Vicente Blasco Ibáñez

[1] Compare **viejo**, *old*. [2] From **ocurrir**, *to occur, happen*. [3] **lo que**, *that which;* **ocurre** is understood after **lo que**. [4] From **saber**, *to know*. [5] **ha de**, *has to* (a rather uncommon idiom). [6] From **ver**, *to see*. [7] Compare **lejos** (*adv*.) and **lejano** (*adj*.), both meaning *far* (*away*), *distant*. [8] From **lamentar**, *to lament, bewail, mourn over* (with object); **lamentarse**, *to lament, mourn* (no object). **Nos lamentamos** could mean either "we mourn over ourselves" or just "we mourn." [9] **al ver**, (*up*)*on seeing;* **que**, *that*, is understood after **al ver** (omission of **que** is very rare). [10] From **tocar**, *to touch*. [11] **de cerca**, *close at hand, closely;* compare **cerca**, *close, near*. [12] **hace que**, makes that (**hacer**, *to make, do*). [13] **tengan**, a subjunctive form from **tener**. [14] **seguros de que**, *sure of* (*the fact*) *that*. [15] From **turbar**, *to disturb, trouble*.

PRACTICE AND REVIEW THE SELECTION JUST STUDIED AND ALL LATER PRACTICE READINGS UNTIL YOU CAN READ AND UNDERSTAND THEM AS WELL AS IF THEY WERE WRITTEN IN ENGLISH.

LITERAL AND FREE TRANSLATIONS. At this stage you need a literal interlinear translation, but it is apparent that the translation given above is not a good literary English rendering. Here is a smoother, free translation of the passage, for comparison:

There happens with old age the same sort of thing as with death. We know that it has to come, but we see it so far away — so distant — during a great part of our life that it only inspires in us the false emotion of a catastrophe that has occurred in a distant part of the globe. We lament, but our egoism, on seeing that the danger is not imminent, prevents the words from having an echo in our thought. We are likewise sure that some day the end of the world must come, the death of our planet, but this is so remote that it does not trouble for an instant the peace of our days.

§ 3. *Word Order in Spanish — Position of Pronouns — Position of Adjectives — Position of Adverbs — Position of Negative Words — Word Order in Direct Statements — Word Order in Questions — Variety of Word Order*

WORD ORDER IN SPANISH. The order of words in a Spanish sentence is similar to that in English, but there are some important differences — as regards pronouns, adjectives, adverbs, negative expressions, and verbs. The rules you have learned at various times will be restated, together with some new ones.

POSITION OF PRONOUNS. Whereas in English, object pronouns follow the verb, in Spanish they precede it — unless they are attached to the verb. In either case the indirect object pronoun precedes the direct object pronoun. Note the following examples.

Siempre tengo muchas flores. Mi vecina me las da. Le gusta dármelas.
I always have many flowers. My neighbor gives them to me. She likes
to give them to me.

POSITION OF ADJECTIVES. In English, adjectives rarely follow the
noun ("the house beautiful"), but in Spanish they normally do so:

el libro rojo, the red book
mi hermana casada, my married sister

In Spanish, as you have learned, some adjectives change their
meanings with their position before or after a noun:

el pobre hombre, the poor (*unfortunate*) man
el hombre pobre, the poor (*impoverished*) man
el gran hombre, the great man
el hombre grande, the big man

A Spanish adjective placed before a noun is less emphatic than
one placed after the noun; before a noun the adjective tends to
be taken for granted or to have little force. Thus:

Es un hotel bueno. It's a *good* hotel.
Es un buen hotel. It's a good hotel. (*It's all right.*)
Es una mujer hermosa. She is a beautiful woman.
Aquella hermosa mujer es chilena. That beautiful woman is a
   Chilean.
Es una mujer inconstante. She is a fickle woman.
La inconstante mujer muere a manos de su amante. The fickle
   woman dies at the hands of her lover.

Sometimes a noun is preceded by and followed by an adjective;
the one following the noun is more important:

la pobre mujer ciega, the poor blind woman
el pequeño libro azul, the little blue book
el viejo palacio presidencial, the old presidential palace

If there are two or more adjectives in a series, they must follow
the verb and must be separated by **y:**

Es una mujer hermosa y inteligente y buena. She is a beautiful, intelligent, and good woman.

Using the lists of adjectives on pages 20, 23, and 24, make up sentences or phrases using the adjectives before and after the nouns
and in series.

Position of Adverbs. In English the adverb may precede or follow the verb, but usually follows it. In Spanish, adverbs and adverbial phrases normally follow immediately after the verb, but they may precede the verb. Thus:

Hablamos muy mal el español. We speak Spanish very badly.

Bailan todas las noches en el Hotel Palacio. They dance at the Hotel Palacio every night.

No tengo nunca la hora correcta. Nunca tengo la hora correcta. I never have the correct time.

Él siempre habla en serio. He always talks seriously.

Raras veces habla así. He rarely talks in this way.

EXCEPTIONS: some adverbs expressing time:

Vamos al parque hoy. We are going to the park today.

Vamos a la playa mañana. We are going to the beach tomorrow.

Position of Negative Words. Whereas in English we place a *no* or *not* between the parts of a compound verb, in Spanish **no** must precede the entire verb:

No he comprado nada en el mercado. I have not bought anything at the market.

Other negative adverbs follow immediately after the verb if **no** has been used; otherwise they precede the verb:

No he leído nunca los diarios españoles. Nunca he leído.... I have never read Spanish newspapers.

Word Order in Direct Statements. The usual word order in a simple Spanish declarative sentence is:

1	2	3	4	5	6
Art.	Noun	Adj.	Verb	Adv.	Obj. (Noun)
La	mujer	feliz	ama	locamente	a su marido.

This simple sentence should be memorized as a key to word order for direct statements, which are much the commonest kind of statements in everyday life.

But occasionally, for variety, emphasis, or other stylistic reasons, the verb may precede its subject:

Ama locamente a su marido aquella mujer feliz. That happy woman madly loves her husband.

Tienen estos indios mayas algunas costumbres muy interesantes. These Mayan Indians have some very interesting customs.

WORD ORDER IN QUESTIONS. As you have learned, in Spanish interrogative sentences the verb must precede its subject:

¿ Tiene Ud. aspirina?   Do you have aspirin?

Though a pronoun, such as **Ud.** in the sentence above, may come between the verb and its object, a noun must follow the object:

¿ Habla inglés la señora?   Does your wife speak English?

Likewise, a predicate adjective must follow immediately after the verb **ser:**

¿ Es inglés el maestro?   Is the teacher English?

VARIETY OF WORD ORDER. In Spanish, as in English, it is possible to say the same thing in a variety of ways. The more complicated the sentence, the more possibilities for various arrangements of the component ideas. For example, if we start with the English sentence:

Winston Churchill, Prime Minister of England during the war of 1939–45, occupied the first place among the world's great leaders and statesmen.

A direct translation into Spanish would be:

Winston Churchill, el primer ministro de Inglaterra durante la guerra de 1939–45, ocupaba el primer puesto entre los grandes caudillos y estadistas del mundo.

The following is a version that could be paralleled in English:

El primer ministro de Inglaterra durante la guerra de 1939–45, Winston Churchill, ocupaba el primer puesto entre los grandes caudillos y estadistas del mundo.

The word order of the following two versions, however, is typically Spanish:

Ocupaba el primer ministro Winston Churchill de Inglaterra durante la guerra de 1939–45 el primer puesto entre los grandes caudillos y estadistas del mundo.

El primer puesto entre los grandes caudillos y estadistas del mundo ocupaba Winston Churchill, el primer ministro de Inglaterra durante la guerra de 1939–45.

PRACTICE. Make up at least ten sentences of some length — say a dozen words or more — following the various rules for word order.

§ 4. *Forms of Address — Family Names — Introductions and Polite Expressions*

FORMS OF ADDRESS:

Señor (abbreviated **Sr.)** means Mr., Sir, gentleman
Señora (" **Sra.)** " Mrs., Madam, ma'am, lady
Señorita (" **Srta.*)** " Miss, young lady

The original meaning of **señor** was *elder, lord,* or *master,* and it still retains this meaning: **los señores de,** the lords of; **el Señor,** the Lord.

The title **Señorito,** *Master, young gentleman,* is rarely used today except familiarly (by servants), humorously, or contemptuously, and so it is best to avoid it.

In addressing a person you call him **"Señor N.," "Señora N.,"** or **"Señorita N."** But in speaking of someone you use the article: **"el señor N.," "la señora N.," "la señorita N."** Sometimes **de** is used with **señora: "la señora de N."**

These titles are used more lavishly than their English equivalents; that is, Spanish-speaking people use **señor** more than we use *sir.* Say **"Sí, señor," "No, señorita,"** not just **"Sí"** or **"No."**

The title **caballero,** *gentleman, sir* (originally *horseman, knight*), is sometimes used as a substitute for **señor.** In Spain it is somewhat more formal than **señor,** but in Spanish America it is less formal.

The respectful titles **Don** and **Doña** are much used among acquaintances. These titles are used either with the full name or with the Christian name:

In direct address: **Don Andrés, Doña Catalina.**
Speaking of them: **Don Andrés** *or* **Don Andrés Blanco, Doña Catalina** *or* **Doña Catalina Jiménez.**

Don and **Doña** are sometimes used in writing full names, in addition to **Sr.** and **Sra.:**

Sr. D. Andrés Blanco López
Sra. Dña. (*or* **Da.) Catalina Jiménez García**

Spanish-speaking people are much more formal and ceremonious than Americans. It is better to be overpolite than underpolite. Do not call anyone **"Don"** until he has called you **"Don."** Do not call anyone by his first name (without **Don**) until he has called

---

* Also abbreviated **Sta.,** which usually stands for **Santa.**

you by your first name. Do not use **tú** with anyone until he has begun to **tutear** you.

A man speaking of his wife may say **mi señora, mi mujer,** or **mi esposa;** but when he refers to another man's wife he will say **su señora.** A husband is referred to as **mi marido, su marido.**

FAMILY NAMES: Spanish family names are confusing, at first, to English-speaking people. The reason is that it is customary for a child to use the mother's name after the father's name. Thus, in the name of the novelist Vicente Blasco Ibáñez, Vicente is the given, or Christian, name, Blasco is the name of the writer's father, and Ibáñez the name of his mother. But because of our ignorance of the system, the novelist has usually been referred to by Americans (incorrectly) as "Ibáñez." He might correctly be referred to as "Blasco" or as "Blasco Ibáñez," the latter being the customary form of reference.

The Spanish dictator, Francisco Franco Bahamonde, became universally known as "Franco." Whether a person becomes known by his two family names or by his father's name alone is determined by such considerations as the length of the two family names, whether they sound well together, whether the mother's name is a distinguished or an ordinary one, and whether the person would be confused with someone else if only the father's name were used.

Sometimes, in accordance with the older style, **y** is used between the two family names: Sr. Miguel Rodríguez y Larrieta = Sr. Miguel Rodríguez Larrieta.

A woman may place her husband's name last, preceded by **de:** Sra. Dolores Fernández de Zayas = Sra. Dolores Zayas Fernández.

This is how the system works. We start with a young man and a young woman:

Sr. Enrique Federico García Velásquez
Srta. Inés Delgado y González.

After their marriage the wife is:

Sra. Inés García Delgado *or* Sra. Inés Delgado de García.

They have two children, Joaquín and Josefa, whose full names are:

Joaquín García Delgado,
Josefa García Delgado.

The mother's name may be represented by an initial, as is customary in parts of Spanish America, as: Horacio Rojas L.

Introductions and Polite Expressions. When you are introduced to a Spanish-speaking person, your best and safest response
is the common:

> **Tengo mucho gusto en conocerle (–lo, –la).** (Often reduced
> to **Mucho gusto**, or to **Encantado**.) I am pleased to meet
> you.

To introduce yourself:

> **John Doe, a sus órdenes.**

To introduce someone else:

> **Quiero,** *or* **Permítame, presentarle(s) a mi(s) amigo(s)** . . . .
> May I present . . . ?

Other useful expressions (besides those you already know) are:

El gusto es mío. The pleasure is mine.
Espero que nos encontremos otra vez. *Or:* **Espero verle**
(**–lo, –la**) **otra vez.** I hope we'll meet again. I hope to
see you again.
Con mucho gusto. With pleasure. I'd be delighted.
Con permiso. Excuse me. (Used when leaving the room
temporarily, when passing in front of someone, when
requesting someone to make way for you, etc.)
Perdóneme. Perdón. Dispénseme. (Add **señor, –a, –ita**
to a stranger.) Pardon me. Excuse me.
Permítame disculparme. Allow me to apologize.
Lo siento mucho. I am very sorry.
De nada. No hay de que. It's nothing. Don't mention it.
No se disculpe. Don't apologize.

§ 5. *Words of Relationship — Occupations — Some Personal Titles —
A Glance Backwards and Forwards*

Words of Relationship. The following list includes some words
you already know and others you should learn:

familia, family
padre, father; **madre,** mother
suegro, father-in-law;
  -a, m.-in-law
abuelo, grandfather; **-a, –**mother
bisabuelo, great-grandfather;
  -a, –mother
pariente, –a, relative
hijo, son; **hija,** daughter
yerno, son-in-law; **nuera,**
  daughter-in-law
nieto, grandson; **-a, –**daughter
biz-, or **bisnieto,** great-grandson;
  -a, –daughter

hermano, brother; **–a**, sister

cuñado, brother-in-law; **–a**, sister-in-law

tío, uncle; **tía**, aunt

sobrino, nephew; **–a**, niece

primo, **–a**, cousin

adoptivo, **–a**, adopted

novio (**–a**), fiancé (**–e**), sweetheart, groom (bride)

marido, husband; **esposa**, **señora** (**mi señora**, **su señora**), wife

matrimonio, married couple, *also* matrimony

padrino, godfather; **madrina**, god-mother

viuda (**–o**), widow (**–er**)

Remember that the masculine plurals of most of these words may refer to two or more males or to male(s) and female(s); as **padres** means *fathers* or *parents*.

OCCUPATIONS:

abacero, (*Mex.*) **abarrotero**, grocer

abogado, lawyer

actor, actor; **actriz**, actress

agente, agent, salesman

ama de casa, housewife

arquitecto, architect

artista, artist

autor, **–a**, author

aviador, **–a**, aviator

bailarín, **–ina**, dancer

banquero, banker

barbero, **peluquero**, barber

boticario, **farmacéutico**, druggist

cajero, **–a**, cashier

camarero (**–a**), steward (**–ess**), (chambermaid); **camarero** (**–a**), **mozo** (**–a**), waiter (**–tress**)

campesino, **–a**, peasant

cantante, singer

capitalista, capitalist

carnicero, butcher

carpintero, carpenter

cartero, postman, mailman

catedrático, (univ.) professor

científico, **–a**, scientist

cirujano, surgeon

clérigo, clergyman, minister

cocinero, **–a**, cook

comerciante, merchant

criado, **–a**, servant

cura, **padre**, priest

dentista, dentist

dependiente, clerk

dramaturgo, playwright

editor, **–a**, publisher (editor: **redactor**, **–a**)

empleado, **–a**, employee

escritor, **–a**, writer

estenógrafo, **–a**, **taquígrafo**, **–a**, stenographer

estudiante, **–a**, student

fabricante, manufacturer

ganadero, stock farmer

hacendado, (CA) **finquero**, (SA) **estanciero**, (*Mex.*) **ranchero**, planter, rancher, plantation owner

hombre de negocios, businessman

impresor, printer

ingeniero, engineer

joyero, jeweler

juez, judge

labrador, **agricultor**, **granjero**, farmer

lavandero (**–a**), laundryman (laundress)

librero, bookseller

maestro, -a, profesor, -a, teacher
mecánico, mechanic
médico, physician, doctor
niñera, nursemaid
novelista, novelist
óptico, optician
papelero, stationer
peón, farm hand
pescador, fisherman
poeta, poet; poetisa, poetess
político, politician
sastre, tailor
soldado, soldier
trabajador, -a, worker
zapatero, shoemaker

marinero, sailor
mecanógrafo, -a, typist
músico, musician
notario, notary
obrero, -a, laborer
panadero, -a, baker
pastor (-a), shepherd (-ess)
periodista, journalist
pintor, -a, painter
policía, policeman
relojero, watchmaker
secretario, -a, secretary
tendero, -a, storekeeper
viajante comercial, traveling salesman

SOME PERSONAL TITLES:

presidente, -a, president; vice-p., vice-p.

ministro, -a, minister, secretary (*of dept. of govt.*); primer ministro, prime minister

senador, -a, senator

diputado, -a, deputy, representative

gobernador, -a, governor

alcalde, mayor; alcaldesa, mayoress

embajador (-a), ambassador (-dress)

cónsul, consul

dictador, dictator

caudillo, leader

(See also rey, etc., page 12.)

almirante, admiral

comandante, commander, major

general, general

mariscal, marshal

mayor, major

capitán, captain

teniente, lieutenant

coronel, colonel

sargento, sergeant

cabo, corporal

el papa, the pope (*cf.* el papá, the papa, la papa, the potato)

cardenal, cardinal

(arz)obispo, (arch)bishop

amo, -a, owner, proprietor, boss

ayudante, assistant

caballero, gentleman

dama, lady

director, -a, director

doctor, -a, doctor

gerente, manager

jefe, chief, boss

licenciado (lawyer's title)

oficial, officer, official

patrón (-ona), proprietor (-tress), boss

Keep in mind that la presidenta may mean *the* (woman) *president* or *the president's wife;* and likewise for other such feminine forms.

A GLANCE BACKWARDS AND FORWARDS

In the extract from Blasco Ibáñez's "La Vejez" you had a good way of testing how far Part I of the course has taken you. You have, in fact, learned rather more than the "First Principles" of the language, as well as a fair number of words and many useful phrases. With a bigger vocabulary and these first principles you could make sense of a newspaper or a simple work of literature. But to understand and read Spanish with any accuracy and ease, rather than by merely guessing at what you hear and read, you must know much more. You must know much more about that most important part of speech, the verb — the full conjugations of regular and irregular verbs — as well as some other grammar; and, of course, you must have a much bigger vocabulary.

Part II contains as much of the "Framework of the Language" as you are likely ever to require, and in it you will be introduced to a careful selection of useful words and phrases.

It may have struck some learners that the method of practice in Part I differs from the old, orthodox methods of practicing with set exercises. I do not recommend this method for all languages. In the case of Spanish, because of the straightforward nature of the language, it provides rewarding results, especially if the learner has a teacher or friend to help him and to correct errors. With a teacher the results are rapid and highly satisfactory, as has been proved by tests.

But whatever the results, it will always pay the self-taught to go back over Part I at least once before proceeding to Part II.

At the end of the book you will find a Basic Vocabulary of 1,470 common words. Be sure you know all these words.

PART II

FRAMEWORK OF THE LANGUAGE

Quien no se aventura,
No ha ventura.

Spanish Proverb

How to Study Part II

Continue as recommended for Part I. But now, with readings in Spanish literature and Situation Material for practice, the language begins to be much easier to assimilate. You may now try to read a newspaper in Spanish, and you should be able to get the gist of it.

For those who do not have a teacher, listening to radio broadcasts is of great importance, so that the ear may become accustomed to the sounds of Spanish. (See page 203.)

Do not make heavy going of the grammar. Learn first how it works. When the working is understood, go over it again a few times and leave it. Proceed, and review grammar later.

CONCENTRATE ON READING.

LESSON IX

§ 1. *Introducing Part II — Regular Verbs in −ER and −IR — Conjugation of Simple and Compound Tenses of* **COMPRAR, VENDER,** *and* **VIVIR**

INTRODUCING PART II. If you have a fair mastery of Part I, you will not find Part II difficult. You will certainly find it much more interesting as you go along, because of the Situation Material and the Continuous Reading. As your knowledge of vocabulary and grammar increases, you will find that the Continuous Reading becomes easier. Because the Continuous Reading is of such importance, careful attention must be paid to the method of using it. The interlinear translation provides most of the explanation required; notes will supply the remainder.

The best way to learn grammar is to concentrate on *how it works*. Much of the grammar that you need to know will be found "in action" in the Continuous Reading and Situation Material, and thus it can be absorbed almost without need of explanation. Once you know how the grammar *works*, you will find that it is easily assimilated.

You should learn the vocabulary as you go along, and review it constantly.

Do not allow yourself to become impatient! Easier said than done, perhaps. But remember that neither you nor anybody else ever learned his own mother tongue in a day. You cannot expect to learn a foreign language in a few weeks — though with effort you can learn a great deal in a few weeks. Spanish is an easier and more encouraging language for the beginner than almost any other.

TAKE THE NEXT FEW LESSONS — ESPECIALLY THE PARTS ABOUT THE VERBS — SLOWLY; REVIEW CONSTANTLY UNTIL YOU KNOW THE MATERIAL THOROUGHLY. THE VERB IS THE MOST IMPORTANT PART OF SPEECH AFTER THE NOUN, AND THE VERBS GIVEN HERE, REGULAR AND IRREGULAR, ARE IN CONSTANT USE.

ALL THAT IS GIVEN IS ESSENTIAL FRAMEWORK SIMPLIFIED FOR EASY LEARNING.

REGULAR VERBS IN **–ER** AND **–IR**. The regular verbs which end in –er and –ir are conjugated on the same general principles as those ending in –ar. But in the –er verbs e replaces the a of the ending in the present tense; in the –ir verbs e and i replace the a in that tense. In –er and –ir verbs –ía replaces the –aba of the imperfect. The same endings are added to the infinitives of –ar, –er, and –ir verbs to form the future. In the past definite, –er and –ir verbs have endings different from those of –ar verbs, as shown below.

There are fewer Spanish verbs in –er and –ir put together than in –ar, but, as many of them are common, they have to be known. The following are common –er and –ir verbs; some have irregularities which you will learn later.

aparecer, to appear	**aplaudir,** to applaud
aprender, to learn	**asistir,** to be present, to assist
desaparecer, to disappear	**consistir,** to consist
meter, to put	**cubrir,** to cover
ofender, to offend	**divertir,** to amuse
proceder, to proceed	**existir,** to exist

SIMPLE TENSES OF **COMPRAR, VENDER, VIVIR.** Here are the simple tenses of three regular verbs set out for comparison (note that the endings are italicized):

Infinitives:

comprar, to buy	**vend**er, to sell	**viv**ir, to live

Present Participles:

comprando, buying	**vend**iendo, selling	**viv**iendo, living

Past Participles:

comprado, bought	**vend**ido, sold	**viv**ido, lived

Present Tense:

compro, I buy	**vend**o	**viv**o
compra, he, she buys, you (**Ud.**) buy	**vend**e	**viv**e
compramos, we buy	**vend**emos	**viv**imos
compran, they, you (**Uds.**) buy	**vend**en	**viv**en

Imperfect Tense:

compraba	**vend**ía	**viv**ía
compraba	**vend**ía	**viv**ía
comprábamos	**vend**íamos	**viv**íamos
compraban	**vend**ían	**viv**ían

Past Definite Tense:

compré	vendí	viví
compró	vendió	vivió
compramos *	vendimos *	vivimos *
compraron	vendieron	vivieron

Future Tense:

compraré	venderé	viviré
comprará	venderá	vivirá
compraremos	venderemos	viviremos
comprarán	venderán	vivirán

COMPOUND TENSES OF **COMPRAR, VENDER, VIVIR.** As you have learned (Lesson VII, § 5), the compound tenses are made with forms of **haber** and the past participle. And the progressive forms are made with forms of **estar** and the present participle (Lesson VIII, § 1).

EXAMPLES:

Ahora estoy comprando víveres. I am now buying provisions (groceries).

Él estaba aprendiendo el inglés. He was learning English.

Estarán llegando mañana a estas horas. They will be arriving at this time tomorrow.

No hemos comprado nada aquí. We have not bought anything here.

Han vivido aquí dieciocho años. They have lived here eighteen years.

Cuando al fin el sol hubo aparecido, inmediatamente desapareció. When at last the sun had appeared, it immediately disappeared.

En dos días habré aprendido todo esto. I shall have learned all this in two days.

§ 2. *Prepositions A, DE, and PARA after Verbs — Verbs Not Followed by Prepositions — DEBER Followed by Infinitive — The Infinitive Used as Noun — Situation Material: Greetings*

THE ENGLISH *to* before an infinitive may be translated by **a, de,** or **para,** or may not be translated by a Spanish preposition — it all depends on what verb has been used.

---

* Note that as regards the first person plural, –ar and –ir verbs have the same endings in the present and past definite; but –er verbs have different endings in these two tenses.

Among the verbs that are followed by **a** plus an infinitive are:

aprender, to learn	**invitar,** to invite
empezar, to begin	**persuadir,** to persuade
enseñar, to teach	

EXAMPLES:

Él ha aprendido a hablar inglés. He has learned to speak English.

Hemos empezado a hablar castellano. We have begun to speak Spanish.

Ella me enseña a pronunciarlo bien. She teaches me to pronounce it well.

Nos han invitado a visitarlos. They have invited us to visit them.

Verbs of motion are followed by **a,** before an infinitive or a noun Some of the commonest verbs of motion are:

andar, to walk	**ir,** to go	**volver,** to return
correr, to run	**salir,** to go out, leave	**venir,** to come

Note. Some of these verbs are irregular. See pages 154, 166, 170, 171.

EXAMPLES:

Él estaba andando a su casa. He was walking to his house.

Los niños corrieron a verlos. The children ran to see them.

Voy a estudiar mucho. I am going to study hard.

Voy a casa. I am going home.

Volvieron a su país. They returned to their country.

La niña volvió a llorar. The little girl began to cry again ("returned to crying").

Vienen a verme. They are coming to see me.

Vienen a mi hotel. They are coming to my hotel.

To must sometimes be translated by **de:**

tratar de comer, to try to eat

No tengo tiempo de hacer eso. I haven't time to do that.

Tengo un gran deseo de ir a Guatemala. I have a great desire to go to Guatemala.

If *to* expresses purpose (meaning *in order to*), **para** is used:

Corrimos para llegar a tiempo. We ran to arrive on time.

Necesito un lápiz para escribir una nota I need a pencil to write a note.

As you read you will note what verbs are followed by certain prepositions. The foregoing discussion is a mere introduction to the subject.

VERBS NOT FOLLOWED BY PREPOSITIONS. A number of common verbs rarely take a preposition when followed by an infinitive. Here is a list of some of the commonest verbs of this type:

AGRADAR, to gratify
BASTAR, to suffice, be enough
DEJAR, to allow, let
DESEAR, to desire, wish, want
ESPERAR, to wait (for), expect, hope (for)
IMPORTAR, to matter
NECESITAR, to need
OÍR, to hear
PARECER, to seem

PENSAR, to think, intend
PERMITIR, to permit, let
PODER, to be able, can
PREFERIR, to prefer
PROMETER, to promise
SABER, to know, know how to
SENTIR, to feel, be sorry
TEMER, to fear
VER, to see

EXAMPLES:

Me agrada estar aquí. I am glad to be here.
Basta decir unas pocas palabras. It is sufficient to say a few words.
Uds. no me dejan hablar. You don't let me speak.
Deseo saber algo. I want to know something.
Espero verla mañana. I hope, or expect, to see her tomorrow.
No necesito leerlo todo. I don't need to read it all.
Ella parece estar triste. She seems to be sad.
Pensamos salir pronto. We intend to leave soon.
No podemos oír nada. We can't hear a thing.
¿Se permite fumar? Is smoking permitted?
¿Sabe Ud. nadar? Do you know how to swim?
Me siento decirlo. I am sorry to say it.

DEBER FOLLOWED BY INFINITIVE. The primary meaning of **deber** is *to owe*, which may be expanded into *to owe it to oneself* — that is, *must, have to, ought to.* For example:

Mi hermano debe mucho dinero. My brother owes much money.
Yo no debo nada a Ud. I don't owe you anything.
Él debe su puesto a un amigo en el gobierno. He owes his job to a friend in the government.

Ud. debe venir por la mañana. You must come in the morning.

No debemos hacer eso. We must not do that.

Deber expresses an obligation; if it is merely a matter of physical or practical necessity, **tener que** is used for *to have to*:

Tengo que ir a casa. I have to go home.

Debo ir a casa. I must go home (*obligation*).

Deber de, as well as **deber,** is used to express probability:

Debe de ser verdad. It must be true.

Deben de ser las diez. It must be ten o'clock.

No debe ser difícil. It should not be difficult.

THE INFINITIVE USED AS NOUN. We say in English "The eating was good" or "The fishing was poor"; *eating* and *fishing* are gerunds — that is, present participles used as nouns. We also use infinitives as nouns; we may say "Seeing is believing" or "To see is to believe." There is no such choice in Spanish; the only verbal noun is the infinitive: **El comer era bueno, El pescar era malo, El ver es creer.**

When the Spanish infinitive is used as a subject, the article must be used with it:

El aprender inglés es difícil. Learning English is difficult.

Some Spanish infinitives have been used as nouns so frequently that they have, in effect, become nouns and may be used in the plural:

el ser, the being	**los seres,** the beings
un decir, a saying	**unos decires,** some sayings
un deber, a duty	**los deberes,** the duties

el Cantar de los Cantares, the Song of Songs

SITUATION MATERIAL — GREETINGS. To learn words and grammar is not enough. The problem of most importance in speaking any language is to be able to deal with *situations* as they arise. Every language has its own ways, its own words and turns of phrase for this purpose. To provide what is necessary for everyday situations, from now on "Situation Material" will be given in each lesson. In this lesson we begin with greetings:

Buenos días. Good morning.

Buenas tardes. Good afternoon. Good evening.

Buenas noches. Good night.

Very cordial: **Muy buenos días,** *etc.*

¿ **Cómo está Ud., señor?** (*more polite*) **caballero?**

¿ Qué tal, amigo? How are you, friend?

Muy bien, gracias. ¿ Y Ud.?

¿ Cómo le va? (SA) How are you getting on? How are things with you?

Bien. ¿ Y a Ud.?

¿ Qué tal se ha pasado la noche? How have you spent the night? (*I.e.,* Did you sleep well?)

¿ Sigue bien su familia de Ud.? Is your family well? ("Continues well . . . ?")

Perfectamente, gracias.

Me alegro. I'm glad. That's good.

Lo celebro. I'm delighted.

Recuerdos a los amigos. Regards to our friends.

Mis afectos a los niños. My love to the children.

Hasta mañana. See you tomorrow.

Hasta luego. See you soon. So long.

Hasta la vista. I'll be seeing you.

Siga Ud. bien. Take care of yourself.

Adiós. Good-by. *A traditional farewell:* **Vaya Ud. con Dios.**

§ 3. *The Verbs* CONOCER, SABER, *and* PODER — *Practice with Situation Material — Situation Material: Air Travel*

CARE must be taken in using the verbs **conocer** and **saber** because our word *know* may require one or the other according to the meaning. Each verb has its limitations.

CONOCER means *to know* in the sense of *be acquainted with* or *recognize*. **Conocer** is always used when we speak of knowing persons or places. Thus:

¿ Conoce Ud. a mi amigo Carlos? Do you know my friend Charles?

Lo conocí ayer. I met (*became acquainted with*) him yesterday.

No conozco la letra de esta carta. I do not know (*recognize*) the handwriting of this letter.

¿ Conoce Ud. el camino para Oaxaca? Do you know the road to Oaxaca?

No conocemos a Venezuela. We don't know (*have not been to*) Venezuela.

SABER means *to know a fact* or *to know how to;* **saber de** means *to know of:*

No saben el español. They don't know Spanish.

No saben hablar español. They don't know how to speak Spanish.

Conozco a su amigo Carlos, pero no sé si él me conoce.
I know your friend Charles, but I don't know whether he
knows me.

No sé si es bueno o malo el camino para Oaxaca. I don't
know whether the road to Oaxaca is good or bad.

Sabemos muy poco del asunto. We know very little of the
affair.

PODER means *to be able to, can*. **Saber** means *to be able to* or
can only in the sense of *know how to*. Thus:

No puedo leer sin más luz. I can't read without more light.

Miguelito no sabe leer. Miguelito can't (*has not learned to*)
read.

¿ Sabe Raúl nadar ? Can Raúl swim? (*Does he know how
to swim?*)

Sí, como un pez, pero no puede hoy porque no está bueno.
Yes, like a fish, but he can't today because he is not well.

PRACTICE WITH SITUATION MATERIAL. The self-taught have to
rely upon themselves for all kinds of practice with Spanish. The
Situation Material is intended to fill out what has been learned by
dealing with everyday situations. *It is not intended to be learned
parrot-fashion.* First, the sentences must be understood. Then the
new words and phrases must be learned, and the grammar in action
must be studied until you have mastered it. You must go over the
material several times until you find yourself thinking in Spanish.

If you have a teacher, everything is easier, for he can explain
things that puzzle you and can provide much more material from
his own experience.

Whether you have a teacher or are your own teacher, you should
not be content with the sentences presented. You should imagine
yourself in the situation, think of the various things you might
want to say, and see whether you can say them in Spanish.

SITUATION MATERIAL — AIR TRAVEL:

el avión, (air)plane (**aeroplano** *is rarely used today*)
aeropuerto, airport
aeródromo, airdrome
aterrizar, to land; **el aterrizaje,** landing; **campo de a.,** landing field
despegar, to take off
el aire, air; **aéreo,** air (*adj.*); **bolsa de aire,** air pocket
volar, to fly; **vuelo,** flight; **vuelo directo,** direct flight

subir, to go up, climb, get on; **subida,** going up, ascent, climb

bajar, to go down, descend, get off; **bajada,** descent

el aviador   el piloto   el navegador

¿ A qué hora sale el avión para Nueva York? What time does the plane
leave for New York?

¿ Cuándo llega el avión de Miami? When does the Miami plane arrive?

¿ Le gusta volar? Do you like flying?

Me encanta. I love it. ("It fascinates me.")

No me gusta volar, especialmente cuando hace mal tiempo. I don't like
flying, especially when the weather is bad.

¿ Qué tipo de avión es? What kind of plane is it? **Es un avión de
reacción.** It is a jet plane.

¿ Tendremos de cambiar de avión? Will we have to change planes?

¿ Cuánto equipaje se permite? How much baggage is permitted (*free*)?

¿ Cuánto cuesta el exceso? How much does the excess cost?

¿ Qué es el mejor remedio contra el mal de aire? What is the best
remedy for air sickness?

¿ Dónde está el retrete (SA: **excusado)?** Where is the toilet?

¿ Dónde está el lavabo? Where is the washroom, *or* lavatory?

¿ Se sirve el desayuno (el almuerzo, la comida)? Is breakfast (lunch,
dinner) served?

No, pero hay bebidas y sandwiches. No, but there are drinks and sandwiches.

¿ A qué velocidad (altura, altitud) volamos? At what speed (height) are
we flying?

¿ Cuál es el mejor medio de ir del aeropuerto al hotel? What is the best
way to get from the airport to the hotel?

Por taxi es el más rápido, pero hay un autobús. By taxi is quickest, but
there is a bus.

§ 4. *The Imperative — Polite Requests — Spanish Equivalents of* Let —
VAMOS, ¡ VIVA! — HAY — *Situation Material: Baggage — Reading:
Alarcón, Historia de Mis Libros (1)*

THE IMPERATIVE. The imperative expresses a command (*Close
the door, Be quiet*). In Spanish it has two forms, singular and plural;
for example: **compra, comprad,** *buy;* **vende, vended,** *sell;* **vive,
vivid,** *live.* (A few verbs have irregular imperatives in the singular;
these will be given later.)

Spanish-speaking people use the imperative in speaking to
children, servants, and inferiors. But foreigners would be wise
not to use it at all, and it is given here only that you may recognize
it when you hear it or see it in print.

POLITE REQUESTS. To make a polite request in English, we use the imperative with *please*. To make a polite request in Spanish, it is necessary to use a substitute for the imperative: the present subjunctive. At this time it is necessary to learn only two forms of the present subjunctive, those to be used with **Ud.** and **Uds.** (expressed or understood). In the present subjunctive the third person endings, singular and plural, are:

> **–ar** verbs: **–e, –en**   **–er, –ir** verbs: **–a, –an**

Thus: **comprar: compre   compren**
      vender: venda   vendan
      vivir: viva   vivan

In polite requests object pronouns are attached to these forms, unless **no** precedes the verb:

> **Cómpreme un diario.** Buy me a newspaper.
> **Cómpremelo.** Buy it for me.
> **No me compre un diario.** Don't buy me a newspaper.
> **No me lo compre.** Don't buy it for me.

Por favor, *please*, may be added, to make the request more polite:

> **Cómpreme un diario, por favor.**

Use **por favor** only at the end, never at the beginning, of a sentence.

Other, rather formal, polite expressions are:

> **Tenga la bondad de** (**hacerlo**). Will you be so good as to (do it).
> **Hágame el favor de** (*or just* **Favor de**) (**hacerlo**). **Sírvase** (**hacerlo**). Will you please (do it).

SPANISH EQUIVALENTS OF "LET." It is often necessary to know how to say, in Spanish, "Let's" do this or that. No Spanish word is used for the *let* * in *let us*, but the verb must be in the subjunctive. The first person plural of the present subjunctive is:

> **–ar** verbs: **–emos** (**compremos**)
> **–er, –ir** verbs: **–amos** (**vendamos, vivamos**)

Thus:

> **Compremos un diario.** Let's buy a newspaper.
> **Hablemos español.** Let's speak Spanish.
> **Subamos al autobús.** Let's get on the bus.

---

* *Let* meaning *allow* is **dejar** or **permitir**, but here we are not considering the word in that sense.

Let with the third person is **que**, followed by the subjunctive. This usage is not of much practical importance, but it should be known. For example:

> **Que compre ella algunas frutas.** Let her buy some fruit.
> **Que vivan felices.** Let them (*May they*) live happily.

VAMOS, ¡VIVA! The *indicative* form **vamos** (literally, *we go*) is used in place of the subjunctive for *let's go*, as:

> **¡Vamos!** Let's go! Come on! Let's get out of here!
> **Vamos al parque.** Let's go to the park.

¡Vámonos! is also often used. **¡Vamos!** may be used to express incredulity (like **¡Anda! ¡Vaya!** — see page 59).

The expression **¡Viva!** is used for **¡Que viva!**

> **¡Viva Fulano!** Long live So-and-so! Hurrah for So-and-so!

HAY. You have already learned the expression **hay** (a modification of **ha**, from **haber**). This impersonal expression may be used in all tenses:

> **hay,** there is, are
> **había,** there was, were (*imperfect*)
> **hubo,** there was, were (*past definite*)
> **habrá,** there will be
> **ha habido,** there has been
> **había,** *or* **hubo, habido,** there had been
> **habrá habido,** there will have been

SITUATION MATERIAL — BAGGAGE:

el equipaje, baggage; **e. de mano,** hand baggage; **depósito de e.,** baggage room, checkroom; **el vagón,** *or* **furgón, de e.,** baggage car
consigna, contraseña, check (*for baggage*)
asegurar, to insure; **seguro de equipaje,** baggage insurance
el baúl, trunk
mozo, porter, "boy"
maleta, suitcase; **el maletín,** small suitcase, bag
saco, bag; **saco de mano,** handbag (*but,* lady's purse: **bolsa**)
cartera, briefcase
la llave, key; **cerrado con llave,** locked
máquina de escribir (portátil), (portable) typewriter

Mozo, lléveme el equipaje. Porter, take my baggage.
¿Dónde está el depósito de equipaje? Where is the baggage room?
Quiero dejar estas cosas aquí. I want to leave these things here.
Cuide Ud. estas cosas. Take care of, *or* Look after, these things.

¿ Han encontrado mi baúl?   Have they found my trunk?

Me han robado la máquina de escribir.   My typewriter has been stolen.

Yo mismo llevo la cartera.   I'll carry the briefcase myself.

Espéreme en el andén.   Wait for me on the platform.

He perdido mi contraseña.   I have lost my check.

¿ Hay exceso de equipaje?   Is there any excess baggage?

¿ Cuánto cuesta el exceso?   How much is (*costs*) the excess?

Quiero asegurar mis equipajes.   I want to insure my baggage.   (**Equipaje**
is sometimes used in the plural.)

CONTINUOUS READING.   Experience has shown that reading, and especially continuous reading of some work by a good writer, is one of the best forms of practice for learners of a foreign language. This kind of practice, if provided with assistance on the difficulties, is of paramount importance to those who have no teacher. The assistance given here, to begin with, is an interlinear literal translation.

You are advised to approach each unit of reading in this way:

First, read the Spanish aloud slowly, making the best you can of the meaning.

Then read over the Spanish more quickly at least twice.

Next read over the translation to get the general sense.

Then go over the piece word for word — Spanish and English — until you understand the sense of each phrase and sentence.

Finally, read the Spanish aloud, *thinking with the text*, until you feel that you can follow the author as well as if he wrote in your own language.

When you have done this, you should be at home with the new words, grammatical forms, and idioms. Not until you have confidence that you have reached this stage should you proceed.

When you come to a new instalment, go back over the preceding instalments so that you will not forget the words, etc., that you have learned.

Pedro Antonio de Alarcón's **El Sombrero de Tres Picos** (*The Three-cornered Hat*) is the first book chosen for continuous reading. Something far less difficult could have been chosen, but this work is given for several reasons. It is not too difficult; it is both interesting and amusing; and it is world-famous. Furthermore, it is written in a pure Castilian which authors in all Spanish-speaking countries would willingly emulate. Alarcón lived from 1833 to 1891. Before proceeding to the work itself, let us hear what he says about it in his literary autobiography.

HISTORIA DE MIS LIBROS   (1)
HISTORY OF MY BOOKS

El Sombrero de Tres Picos
The Three-cornered Hat

Un día del verano de 1874, en Madrid, me apremiaba la obligación
One day in the summer of 1874, in Madrid, there was pressing me the obligation
de enviar a la isla de Cuba algún cuentecillo [1] jocoso, para cierto se-
to send to the island of Cuba some little humorous tale, for a certain
manario festivo que allí se publicaba.   Recordé, no sé cómo, el picaresco
gay weekly which was published there.   I remembered, I don't know how, the picaresque
romance [2] de El Corregidor y la Molinera, que tantas veces había oído
romance of the Magistrate and the Miller's Wife, that so often I had heard
relatar,[3] cuando niño, y me dije [4]:
told when a child, and I said to myself:

—¿Por qué no he de escribir una historieta [5] fundada en tan pere-
"Why have I not to write a little story founded on so wonder-
grino argumento?
ful a theme?"

— Porque es muy difícil, dentro de las conveniencias sociales...
"Because it is very difficult within the social conventions,"
— respondió mi buena crianza.
replied my good upbringing.

— ¡Razón de más [6] para intentar escribirla de modo que nadie se
"The more reason for trying to write it so that nobody becomes
escandalice! — arguyó mi temeridad de artista viejo, recordando
scandalized!" argued my temerity of (the) old artist, remembering
haber hecho un milagro semejante con el cuento de La Comendadora.
having performed a similar miracle with the tale of The Mother Superior.

— Pues, probemos... — contestó mi pereza, para librarse de seguir
"Well then, let us try," replied my laziness, to free itself from going
buscando asunto. — ¡En medio de todo,[7] el semanario de que se trata [8]
on seeking (a) subject.   "After all, the weekly in question

---

[1] **cuentecillo,** diminutive of **cuento,** *story, tale.*

[2] **picaresco romance.**   Spanish literature is famous for its picaresque ro-
mances, or novels about rogues.

[3] **había oído relatar.**   Note the use of the infinitive (**relatar**) where we use
the past participle (*told*).

[4] **dije,** irregular past definite of **decir.**

[5] **historieta,** diminutive of **historia,** *story, history.*

[6] **Razón de más.   De más** means *additional, extra, the more.*

[7] **En medio de todo,** literally "in the midst of all."

[8] **de que se trata,** literally "of which it is treated."

tiene pocos lectores, y tal vez ninguno de ellos resida en el continente
has few readers, and perhaps none of them resides on the Euro-

europeo!
pean continent!"

— ¡ Manos a la obra! — concluyó la parte atrevida de mi ser moral
"Hands to the work!" concluded the daring part of my moral being.

Y veinticuatro horas después había escrito diez o doce cuartillas, que
And twenty-four hours afterwards I had written ten or twelve little sheets, which

contenían, muy en compendio, todo El Sombrero de Tres Picos, o sea [1]
contained, very compressed, all of The Three-cornered Hat, *or, that is,*

toda la historia de El Corregidor y la Molinera, tal y como [2] me pareció
all the story of The Magistrate and the Miller's Wife, *such as it seemed to me*

prudente arreglarla y componerla ad usum [3] del respetable público.
prudent to arrange it and compose it for the use of the respectable public.

Iba ya a meterla en un sobre para echarla al correo,[4] cuando me
I was now going to put it in an envelope to throw (drop) it in the mail when

dijo repentinamente la conciencia artística:
suddenly the artistic conscience said to me:

— ¡ Qué lástima! Aquí hay materia para escribir una historia diez
"What a pity! Here there is material for writing a story ten

veces más larga. . . .
times longer. . . ."

— ¡ Ya [5] lo creo! — respondió la pereza. Y de ese modo nos ahorra-
"I should just think so!" replied (my) laziness. "And in that way we

ríamos,[6] durante dos meses, la penosa tarea de buscar asuntos para el
should spare ourselves, for two months, the painful task of looking for subjects for the

semanario. . . .
weekly. . . ."

§ 5. *PARA and POR — Situation Material: Sea Travel —* Historia de Mis Libros (2)

PARA AND **POR.** These two prepositions are often found trouble-some by advanced students and even by Spaniards themselves. They have already been explained briefly (see page 65), but will now be treated somewhat more fully.

[1] **sea,** subjunctive of **ser; o sea** is literally "or may (let) it be."

[2] **tal y como,** an idiom, literally "such and as," which should logically be **tal como.**

[3] *ad usum:* Latin.

[4] **echarla al correo. Echar a** means *to throw into;* **correo** means *mail.*

[5] **Ya** means *already, yet,* or *now,* but sometimes, as here, merely adds emphasis.

[6] **ahorraríamos,** the conditional mood, which you have not yet learned.

The basic meanings of the two prepositions are:

> **PARA:** destination or purpose
> **POR:** agency or cause

but in many idioms the basic meaning does not appear.

Examples of **para,** translated *for*, *to*, or *toward*, indicating destination or purpose:

Este paquete es para Buenos Aires. This package is for Buenos Aires.

Esa carta es para mí. That letter is for me.

Mañana sale el vapor para Nueva York. Tomorrow the boat leaves for New York.

¿ Es éste el camino para Guadalajara? Is this the road for Guadalajara?

Andemos para el hotel. Let's walk toward the hotel.

Este traje es para el verano. This suit is for summer.

Mi hermano está estudiando para abogado. My brother is studying to be (*for*) a lawyer.

Quiero un cuarto para un matrimonio. I want a room for a married couple.

Necesito aceite para cocinar. I need oil for cooking.

Tengo que comprar papel para escribir. I have to buy writing paper.

El pan es para comer. Bread is for eating. Bread is to eat.

¿ Para qué sirve eso? What is that for? (*For what does that serve?*)

Estar para means *to be about to:*

Estamos para salir. We are about to go out. We are just going out.

Estoy para ir al cine. I am about to go to the movies.

Está para llover. It's about to rain.

Para con means *toward*, expressing attitude or behavior:

Están muy amistosos para con nosotros. They are very friendly toward us.

No muestran mucho respeto para con el presidente. They do not show much respect for the president.

Sienten odio para con ellos. They feel hatred toward them.

Examples of **por**, translated *by* or *for*, indicating agency or cause:

La película ha sido bien recibida por el público.   The film has been well received by the public.

La muchacha es matada por su amante.   The girl is killed by her lover.

No se puede hacer por fuerza.   It can't be done by force.

Consiguió su puesto por mérito.   He got his post by merit.

Por falta de un sombrero ella no vino.   For want of a hat she didn't come.   (**Vino** *is irregular past definite of* **venir.**)

¿Por qué lo hacen?   Why (*For what*) do they do that?   (*Note the fine distinction between* **¿Para qué?**   *What for? For what purpose? and* **¿Por qué?**   *Why?*)

Porque es costumbre.   Because it is the custom.   (*Note that* **porque,** *because, is one word.*)

por causa de miedo, because of fear;   **por miedo,** for fear

No quiero hablar de ello por ser extranjero.   I don't want to speak of it on account of being a foreigner.

Por eso no quiero hablar de ello.   For that reason, *or* Therefore, I do not wish to speak of it.

Por also means (of places) *through, by, along, about, around:*

El ladrón entró por la ventana.   The thief entered by the window.

El tren no pasa por esa población.   The train does not pass through that town.

¿Pasamos por el mercado?   Do we pass by the market?

Paseábamos por la Avenida Bolívar.   We were strolling along the Avenida Bolívar.

por aquí, around here, hereabouts;   **por allí,** around there, thereabouts

Por, translated *for,* may indicate the equivalent of something:

Él me dió su libro por el mío.   He gave me his book (in exchange) for mine.

Dan tres mangos por diez centavos.   They give three mangos for ten centavos.

Compré una manta guatemalteca muy hermosa por ocho quetzales.   I bought a very beautiful Guatemalan blanket for eight quetzals.

¿Tiene Ud. cambio por este billete?   Do you have change for this bill?

Por, translated *for, in, during, about,* also indicates duration:

Estaré de viaje por varios meses. I shall be traveling **for**
several months.

Han vivido aquí por muchos años. They have lived here
for many years.

Basta por ahora. That's enough for the present.

por la mañana, tarde, noche, in the morning, afternoon, night

Tal vez por Navidad (enero). Maybe about Christmas
(January).

Por also means *for the sake of;* and *for* in the sense of *to get:*

Él lo hace por Ud. He does it for your sake.

¡Por Dios! For God's sake! For Heaven's sake!

Voy por cigarrillos. I am going for cigarettes.

The explanations and examples given above do not account for
all uses of **para** and **por.** The use of these and other difficult
prepositions (**a, de**) in various idioms and after various verbs must
be learned gradually by reading and by frequent reference to a
good dictionary, one that is generous with examples of words in use.

SITUATION MATERIAL — SEA TRAVEL:

el vapor, steamship, steamer, boat; **v. de pasajeros,** passenger ship; **v. de
carga,** cargo ship, freighter; **v. correo,** mail boat

la nave, el buque, vessel, ship	**el bote,** (*little*) boat
petrolero, (oil) tanker	**carbonero,** coal ship
el camarote, cabin, stateroom	**cubierta,** deck
marinero, sailor **el capitán,** the captain	**mayordomo,** chief steward
comisario, (SA) **contador,** purser	**camarera,** stewardess
el (*sometimes* **la**) **mar,** the sea	**ola,** wave **viento,** wind
puerto, port	**parada,** stop
tierra, land	**desembarcar,** to land, disembark
embarcar, salir, to sail, leave	**carga,** cargo
cargar, to load	**descargar,** to unload
mareo, seasickness	**marearse,** to get seasick

el salvavidas, life preserver; **el bote s.,** the lifeboat

¿A qué hora sale el vapor? What time does the ship sail?

¿Cuánto cuesta el pasaje a Los Ángeles? How much is the fare to Los
Angeles?

¿Puedo reservar un camarote? May I reserve a stateroom?

¿Dónde está la oficina del comisario (SA, contador)? Where is the
purser's office?

¿Es Ud. buen marinero(–a)? Are you a good sailor?

Yo no soy buen marinero(-a); me mareo. I'm not a good sailor; I get seasick.

Pero ahora se puede comprar remedios contra el mareo. But now one can buy remedies against seasickness.

Estoy un poco mareado(-a) ahora. I am a little seasick now.

Detesto viajar por mar. I hate traveling by sea.

Y yo adoro, *or* **me encantan, los viajes por mar.** And I love sea trips.

¿ Qué es aquel vapor en el horizonte? What is that ship on the horizon?

¿ Se ve la costa, la tierra? Can one see the coast, land?

¿ Cuándo llegamos a La Guaira? When do we arrive at La Guaira?

Quisiera hablar con el mayordomo, la camarera. I should like to speak with the steward, stewardess.

Es la estación de huracanes. It is the season of hurricanes.

Tengo un gran deseo de tocar tierra. I have a great desire to touch land.

HISTORIA DE MIS LIBROS (2)

— ¡Pues, recomencemos!
"Then, let us begin again."

— ¡Oh... no!...¿ Quién inutiliza lo ya redactado,[1] y se pone
"Oh...no! ... Who does not use the already written, and sets himself

ahora a volver a empezar la ración de mañana?
now to begin again tomorrow's ration (installment)?"

Vacilé algún tiempo, y esta vez triunfó la actividad. Comencé,
I vacillated some time, and this time activity triumphed. I began,

pues, de nuevo la historia de *El Sombrero de Tres Picos.*
then, afresh the story of The Three-cornered Hat.

Al otro día, iba yo a meter en un sobre la primera décima parte del
The other day, I was going to put in an envelope the first tenth part of the

segundo relato, o sea del relato actual, que llegaba a la descripción
second account — or, that is, of the present account — which arrived at the description

del tío Lucas, cuando entró en mi despacho un buen amigo, versado
of Uncle Lucas, when entered into my office a good friend, versed

en letras; referíle[2] el asunto de mi nueva obra; le leí lo que llevaba
in letters; I mentioned to him the matter of my new work; I read to him what I had

escrito,[3] y ved aquí sus terminantes palabras:
written, and see here his emphatic words:

— No envíe usted al otro mundo esas cuartillas. Reténgalas en
"Don't you send to the other world those sheets. Keep them in

---

[1] **redactado. Redactar** means *to write (for publication).*

[2] **referíle.** In literary style pronouns are often attached to verb forms contrary to conversational and everyday writing practice.

[3] **llevaba escrito = había escrito; llevar** is occasionally used for **haber** in compound tenses.

Madrid, y continúe la obra con amor, hasta acabarla y perfeccionarla
Madrid, and continue the work with love, until you complete and perfect
cuanto pueda. De este modo se encontrará usted, dentro de pocas
it as much as you can. In this way you will find yourself, within a few
semanas, con un libro que podrá convenirle publicar en Madrid, en
weeks, with a book which it can suit you to publish in Madrid, in
tomo. ¡El asunto es de perlas [1]!
volume (form). The subject is just right!"

Seis días después volvió a visitarme [2] el amigo, y se halló con que
Six days afterwards the friend came back to visit me, and it was found that
El Sombrero de Tres Picos estaba terminado y hasta puesto en limpio,
The Three-cornered Hat *was finished and even put in clean (form),*
en la forma que hoy tiene. Al siguiente día empezó a imprimirse en
in the form that it has today. On the following day it began to be printed in
la *Revista Europea*, que publicaban en esta corte los señores Medina y
the European Review, *which published in this court [3] the Messrs. Medina*
Navarro; al cabo de un mes se reimprimía solemnemente en tomo
y Navarro; at the end of a month it was reprinted solemnly in (a) separate volume,
aparte, y ésta es la hora en que van hechas, sólo dentro de nuestra
and   this   is   the   hour   in   which   are   made,   only   within   our
península, ocho numerosas ediciones.
peninsula, eight numerous editions.

Tal es la historia de este dichoso librejo,[4] contra el cual no se han
Such is the story of this happy little book, against which my adversaries
alzado mis adversarios.[5] Por la inversa, todo el mundo lo ha tratado
have   not   risen.   On   the   contrary,   everybody   has   treated   it
con mimo, así en el campo de los innovadores o blasfemadores del arte,
with indulgence, as well in the camp of the innovators or blasphemers of art,
de la moral y del alma,[6] como en él de los ortodoxos y arcaístas
of morality, and of the soul, as in that of the orthodox and archaists (outmoded writers)
de todas especies.
of all kinds.

---

[1] de perlas, literally, *as pearls* — a common idiom.

[2] volvió a visitarme. Volver a is a common idiom meaning *to . . . again* (as volver a decir, *to say again*).

[3] *court.* Madrid was called la corte because the king lived there.

[4] librejo, a contemptuous diminutive of libro, used humorously. The usual diminutive would be librito.

[5] mis adversarios. Alarcón was not approved of by the conservative writers of his time.

[6] el campo de los innovadores, *etc.* Alarcón speaks of himself and his school in the terms used by his literary enemies.

LESSON X

§ 1. *How to Use the Table That Follows — Full Conjugation of* **COMPRAR, VENDER, VIVIR** *in Simple Tenses — Situation Material: The Customs; At the Railway Station —* **El Sombrero de Tres Picos** (1)

How to Use the Table That Follows. The following table is intended primarily for reference. That is, it is not necessary for you to memorize now the new forms given, the conditional and subjunctive moods. (It is assumed that you are thoroughly familiar with all the other forms.) Some of the forms you will probably never use in conversation, but you will need to be able to recognize and understand them when you come across them in reading.

The endings are separated by hyphens from the stems, or infinitives, so that the table serves to give the endings of regular verbs and also the full forms of the model verbs. Furthermore, irregular verbs have the same *endings* as regular verbs in all but two or three forms.

The table may be used for the learning, or review, of the endings of any of the simple tenses, in any mood, and it may be used to identify an unfamiliar verb form. For example, in the reading selections to follow, you will come upon the forms **conducía, obsequiaba, exclamaréis, frisaría, añadid, careciese** — all verbs unknown to you. But you can identify the endings and decide that **conduc-ía** is imperfect indicative of **conducer** or **-cir; obsequi-aba** is imperfect indicative of **obsequiar; exclamar-éis** is future indicative of **exclamar; frisar-ía** is the conditional of **frisar; añad-id** is plural imperative of **añadir;** and **carec-iese** is past subjunctive of **carecer** or **-cir.** With forms that indicate either an **-er** or an **-ir** verb, it is not possible to know which is the ending of the infinitive unless you consult a dictionary.

Note on the Past Subjunctive: There is now no distinction as regards tense between the **r** and the **s** forms of the past subjunctive. As a rule they are interchangeable. The **s** forms are somewhat more commonly used.

FULL CONJUGATION OF **COMPRAR, VENDER, VIVIR** IN SIMPLE TENSES

Infinitive:

compr-*ar*	**vend-***er*	**viv-***ir*	to buy, *etc.*

Present Participle:

compr-*ando*	**vend-***iendo*	**viv-***iendo*	buying, *etc.*

Past Participle:

| compr–ado * | vend–ido | viv–ido | bought, *etc.* |

Imperative:

| compr–a | vend–e | viv–e | buy, *etc.* |
| compr–ad | vend–ed | viv–id | |

INDICATIVE

Present:

compr–o	vend–o	viv–o	I buy, am buy-
compr–as	vend–es	viv–es	ing, do buy,
compr–a	vend–e	viv–e	*etc.*
compr–amos	vend–emos	viv–imos	
compr–áis	vend–éis	viv–ís	
compr–an	vend–en	viv–en	

Imperfect:

compr–aba	vend–ía	viv–ía	I was buying,
compr–abas	vend–ías	viv–ías	used to buy,
compr–aba	vend–ía	viv–ía	bought (*more*
compr–ábamos	vend–íamos	viv–íamos	*than once*), *etc.*
compr–abais	vend–íais	viv–íais	
compr–aban	vend–ían	viv–ían	

Past Definite:

compr–é	vend–í	viv–í	I bought (*on*
compr–aste	vend–iste	viv–iste	*that occasion*),
compr–ó	vend–ió	viv–ió	*etc.*
compr–amos	vend–imos	viv–imos	
compr–asteis	vend–isteis	viv–isteis	
compr–aron	vend–ieron	viv–ieron	

Future:

comprar–é	vender–é	vivir–é	I shall, *or* will,
comprar–ás	vender–ás	vivir–ás	buy, *etc.*
comprar–á	vender–á	vivir–á	
comprar–emos	vender–emos	vivir–emos	
comprar–éis	vender–éis	vivir–éis	
comprar–án	vender–án	vivir–án	

* When used as adjectives, past participles must agree in number and gender with nouns they refer to: **la casa comprada, las flores vendidas.**

CONDITIONAL

comprar-*ía*	vender-*ía*	vivir-*ía*	I should buy,
comprar-*ías*	vender-*ías*	vivir-*ías*	*etc.*
comprar-*ía*	vender-*ía*	vivir-*ía*	
comprar-*íamos*	vender-*íamos*	vivir-*íamos*	
comprar-*íais*	vender-*íais*	vivir-*íais*	
comprar-*ían*	vender-*ían*	vivir-*ían*	

SUBJUNCTIVE

Present:

compr-*e*	vend-*a*	viv-*a*	(that) I buy, *etc.*
compr-*es*	vend-*as*	viv-*as*	
compr-*e*	vend-*a*	viv-*a*	
compr-*emos*	vend-*amos*	viv-*amos*	
compr-*éis*	vend-*áis*	viv-*áis*	
compr-*en*	vend-*an*	viv-*an*	

Past (S Form):

compr-*ase*	vend-*iese*	viv-*iese*	(*that or if*) I
compr-*ases*	vend-*ieses*	viv-*ieses*	should, *or*
compr-*ase*	vend-*iese*	viv-*iese*	might, buy,
compr-*ásemos*	vend-*iésemos*	viv-*iésemos*	*etc.*
compr-*aseis*	vend-*ieseis*	viv-*ieseis*	
compr-*asen*	vend-*iesen*	viv-*iesen*	

Past (R Form):

compr-*ara*	vend-*iera*	viv-*iera*
compr-*aras*	vend-*ieras*	viv-*ieras*
compr-*ara*	vend-*iera*	viv-*iera*
compr-*áramos*	vend-*iéramos*	viv-*iéramos*
compr-*arais*	vend-*ierais*	viv-*ierais*
compr-*aran*	vend-*ieran*	viv-*ieran*

Future:

compr-*are*	vend-*iere*	viv-*iere*	(*that or if*) I
compr-*ares*	vend-*ieres*	viv-*ieres*	may, *or shall,*
compr-*are*	vend-*iere*	viv-*iere*	buy, *etc.*
compr-*áremos*	vend-*iéremos*	viv-*iéremos*	
compr-*areis*	vend-*iereis*	viv-*iereis*	
compr-*aren*	vend-*ieren*	viv-*ieren*	

SITUATION MATERIAL — THE CUSTOMS:

aduana, custom house, customs; **derechos de aduana,** customs duties
aduanero, customs officer, inspector
registrar, revisar, to inspect, examine, search (*baggage*) (**registrar** *also means* to register, *and* **revisar,** to review)

registro, revisión, inspección, inspection, examination, search
efectos personales, personal effects   **compras,** purchases
muestras comerciales, commercial samples
el pasaporte, passport   **documento**   **declarar,** to declare
certificado de vacunación, vaccination certificate

¿ Cuándo registran, *or* **revisan, el equipaje?** *Or:* **¿ Cuándo se registra ...?** When do they inspect the baggage? When is the baggage inspected?

Al llegar. When you arrive. (*On arriving.*)

Primero revisan los pasaportes, y en seguida los equipajes. First they look at the passports, and right after that the baggage.

¿ Dura mucho el trámite? Does the business last long?

No, se termina pronto. No, it's soon over.

Aquí tiene Ud. mi pasaporte, y otros documentos para el automóvil. Here is my passport, and the other documents for the car.

No soy comerciante; soy turista. I'm not a businessman; I'm a tourist.

Estoy en este país solamente para las vacaciones. I am in this country only for my vacation.

No quedo en España; estoy de tránsito. I'm not staying in Spain; I'm in transit.

¿ Tiene Ud. algo que declarar? Do you have anything to declare?

No, señor, todos son efectos personales, cosas usadas. No, it's all personal effects, used things.

¿ Cuáles artículos pagan derechos? What articles pay duty?

Aquí tiene Ud. una lista de mis compras. Here is a list of my purchases.

¿ Tengo que pagar derechos? Do I have to pay duty?

Todo es franco de derechos. Everything is duty free.

¿ Quiere Ud. abrir el baúl? Will you open the trunk?

¿ Puedo cerrarlo ahora? May I close it now?

Abra Ud. la maleta. Open the suitcase.

Momentito. Está cerrada con llave. Just a moment. It's locked.

¿ Está terminado? Is it finished?

Todavía no, señor. Not yet.

¿ Qué tiene Ud. en ese saco? What do you have in that bag?

Ropa sucia, no más. Just dirty clothes.

¿ Quiere Ud. ver esta cartera? Do you want to see this briefcase?

SITUATION MATERIAL — AT THE RAILWAY STATION:

el ferrocarril, railroad, railway; **la estación de ferrocarriles,** railway station   **el tren,** train   **horario,** timetable
el billete, (SA) **boleto,** ticket; **b. sencillo,** *or* **de ida,** one-way ticket; **b. de ida y vuelta,** round-trip ticket; **b. de primera, segunda, tercera clase,** first-, second-, third-class ticket; **despacho de billetes,** *or* **boletos,** ticket office   **taquilla,** ticket window

sala de espera, waiting room   el andén, platform
sala para caballeros (damas), men's (ladies') room
el pasaje, passage, fare   pasajero, –a, passenger
locomotora, locomotive, engine   ¡A bordo! All aboard!
el coche, coach, car; c. restaurant, (SA) c. comedor, dining car; c. dormitorio, sleeping car
el vagón, car; el furgón, (freight or baggage) car
atrasarse, to be late   estar a tiempo, to be on time
subir, to get on; bajar, to get off   parar (v.), parada (n.), stop
asiento, seat   (des)ocupado, (un)occupied   ventana, window
litera, cama, berth (alta, upper, baja, lower)
trasbordo, transfer, change; trasbordar, to transfer

Pienso en hacer el viaje de México a Guatemala por tren. I am thinking of making the trip from Mexico to Guatemala by train.

A la estación de ferrocarriles, por favor. To the railway station, please.

¿Cuánto cuesta un billete de segunda clase a Sevilla? What does a second-class ticket to Seville cost?

Quiero dos boletos de ida y vuelta a Guadalajara, primera clase. I want two round-trip tickets, first class, to Guadalajara.

¿Quiere Ud. darme un horario? Will you give me a timetable?

¿A qué hora sale el próximo tren para Puerto Barrios? When does the next train leave for Puerto Barrios?

¿A qué hora llegaremos a la capital? What time will we get to the capital?

¿Tenemos que cambiar de tren? Do we have to change trains? **¿Hay que trasbordar?** Is it necessary to change, *or* transfer?

¿Tengo que pagar exceso de equipaje? Do I have to pay excess baggage?

¿Se sirven comidas en el tren? Are meals served on the train?

¿Se vende agua embotellada en el tren? Is bottled water sold on the train?

¿Hay un buzón en la estación? Is there a mail box in the station?

¿Se puede comprar cigarrillos, puros, tabaco, fósforos, dulces, tarjetas postales, sellos (SA, estampillas) aquí? Can one buy cigarettes, cigars, tobacco, matches, candy, post cards, stamps here?

EL SOMBRERO DE TRES PICOS   (1)

En aquel tiempo, pues, había cerca de la ciudad de ... un famoso
At that time, then, there was near the city of ... a famous
molino harinero (que ya no existe), situado como a un cuarto de legua [1]
flour mill (which no longer exists), situated at about a quarter of (a) league
de la población, entre el pie de suave colina poblada de guindos y
from the town, between the foot of (a) gentle hill covered with mazzard and

---

[1] legua, *league*, about three miles.

cerezos y una fertilísima huerta ¹ que servía de margen (y algunas veces
cherry trees and a most fertile vegetable garden which served as margin (ana sometimes
de lecho) al titular intermitente y traicionero río.
as bed) to the so-called intermittent and treacherous river.

Por varias y diversas razones, hacía ya algún tiempo ² que aquel
For several and diverse reasons, it was already some time since that
molino era el predilecto punto de llegada y descanso de los paseantes
mill was the favorite point of arrival and rest of the most distinguished
más caracterizados de la mencionada ciudad.... Primeramente,
strollers   of   the   (above)mentioned   city. ...   Firstly,   there
conducía a él un camino carretero, menos intransitable que los restantes
led   to   it   a   road   for   vehicles,   less   impassable   than   the   others
de aquellos contornos. En segundo lugar, delante del molino había
of those parts.   In (the) second place, in front of the mill there was
una plazoletilla ³ empedrada, cubierta ⁴ por un parral enorme, debajo
a   paved   little   square,   covered   by   a   huge   vine-bower,   below
del cual se tomaba muy bien el fresco en el verano y el sol en el in-
which was very welcome the coolness in the summer and the sun in the
vierno, merced a la alternada ida y venida de los pámpanos.... En
winter, thanks to the alternate going and coming of the young branches. ...   In
tercer lugar, el molinero era un hombre muy respetuoso, muy discreto,
(the) third place, the miller was a very respectful man, very discreet,
muy fino, que tenía lo que se llama don de gentes,⁵ y que obsequiaba
very fine, who had what is called winning ways, and who entertained
a los señorones ⁶ que solían honrarlo con su tertulia vespertina, ofre-
the great gentlemen who used to honor him with their evening gathering, offering
ciéndoles ⁷ ... lo que daba el tiempo, ora habas verdes, ora cerezas y
them . . . what the season gave, now fresh lima beans, now cherries and
guindas, ora lechugas en rama y sin sazonar (que están muy buenas
mazzards, now lettuces in (the) leaf and without seasoning (which are very good
cuando se las acompaña de macarros de pan y aceite; macarros que se
when they are accompanied with rolls of bread and olive oil, rolls which their

---

¹ huerta, *vegetable garden;* a flower garden is **un jardín.**

² hacía ya algún tiempo. There is no Spanish adverb meaning *ago.* Such
an expression as *a year ago* is usually expressed by **hace un año,** "it makes a
year."

³ plazoletilla, a double diminutive: a **plazoleta** is a little **plaza,** and a
plazoletilla is a little **plazoleta.** So **plazoletilla** is a *tiny little plaza.*

⁴ cubierta, irregular past participle of **cubrir,** *to cover.*

⁵ don de gentes, literally "gift of peoples."

⁶ señorones. **Señorón** is an augmentative of **señor.**

⁷ ofreciéndoles. The present participle is another form to which object pronouns may be attached — in speech or writing.

encargaban de enviar por delante sus señorías), ora melones, ora uvas
lordships took on themselves to send ahead of time), now melons, now grapes
de aquella misma parra que les servía de dosel, ora rosetas de maíz,[1]
from that same bower which served them as canopy, now popped corn,
si era invierno, y castañas asadas, y almendras, y nueces, y de vez en
if it was winter, and roasted chestnuts, and almonds, and walnuts, and occasionally,
cuando,[2] en las tardes muy frías, un trago de vino de pulso [3] (dentre
on very cold evenings, a swallow of homemade wine (now inside
ya de la casa y al amor de la lumbre [4]), a lo que por pascuas se solía
the house and in the glow of the fire), to which on Church holidays
añadir algún pestiño, algún mantecado, algún rosco o alguna lonja
would be added some kind of fritter, kneaded biscuit, twisted roll, or slice
de jamón alpujarreño.
of ham of the Alpujarras.[5]

[continuará
[*To be continued*

§ 2. *An Introduction to the Subjunctive — Situation Material: Asking the Way; Taxis — El Sombrero de Tres Picos (2)*

AN INTRODUCTION TO THE SUBJUNCTIVE. In order to understand the subjunctive in Spanish, it is necessary to understand the subjunctive in English.

In both English and Spanish the indicative mood makes a direct statement of fact. The subjunctive mood is used for various other kinds of statements, expressing doubt, supposition, desire, and so on. Usually a verb in the subjunctive is dependent on a verb in the indicative; for example, in "I insist that he apologize," *insist* is a verb in the indicative, stating a fact, and *apologize* is a verb in the subjunctive, expressing a desire or demand.

In English the subjunctive is not used as much as formerly, and some uses of the subjunctive have practically disappeared from everyday speech. For example, *be* after *if* ("if it be true"), expressing

---

[1] **rosetas de maíz,** literally "rosettes of maize."

[2] **de vez en cuando,** *from time to time,* an illogical idiom. **De . . . en** is used with various nouns, as **de día en día,** *from day to day.*

[3] **de pulso. Pulso** is pulse, and by extension the wrist, the hand; and so **de pulso,** *by hand, homemade.*

[4] **al amor de la lumbre. Amor,** *love,* is used in this phrase for the warmth and light of the fire; **lumbre** is the hearth fire, the common word for *fire* being **fuego.**

[5] *Alpujarras,* a region in southeastern Spain.

improbability, is still used in formal speech and writing, but is not used in conversation.

One reason the subjunctive is not very noticeable in English is that, except for the verb *be*, it differs from the indicative only in the third person singular of the present tense. Thus, in the sentence "It is necessary that you work hard," *work* is really subjunctive but the form does not show it.

The subjunctive *were* in a "contrary-to-fact condition" (as in "if I were you") seems to be fighting to hold its own against *was*. People who are careful of their speech still use *were*, but some linguistic radicals advocate *was* in speech and writing.

Some uses of the subjunctive, however, seem to be here to stay. No one would think of saying "I insist that he *apologizes*" or "I wish that I *have* been there."

The subjunctive is much more frequent in Spanish, and, as you have seen, there are a great many distinctive subjunctive forms. If you are to read Spanish literature, you need to be able to recognize all these forms and understand their uses. In conversation, however, you will never need to use the future subjunctive. You will rarely need the past subjunctive, and when you do you can stick to the *s* forms and ignore the *r* forms. (Originally the *r* form was the imperfect and the *s* form the past definite, but the distinction has been forgotten.) The present subjunctive you will be using constantly, so that it is necessary for you to know it as well as you know the present indicative.

Here are some examples of the subjunctive in use. The first three are uses you have already learned. Do not try to learn any other uses of the subjunctive at this time. The subjunctive forms are in italics:

(Subjunctive as imperative)

Déme (**Ud.**) **el horario.** Give me the timetable. (Orthographic accent on **dé.**)

Compremos **una piña.** Let's buy a pineapple.

Que la **compre** **si quiere.** Let him buy it if he wishes.

(Subjunctive as dependent verb)

Quiero que él me **venda** **la máscara.** I want him to sell (*that he sell*) me the mask.

Quisiera **subir al tren.** I should like to get on the train. (**Quisiera** is irregular past subjunctive of **querer,** a very useful form to know, as it is more polite than **quiero,** *I want.*)

Es posible que no *puedan* **venir.** It is possible that they may not be able to come.

No sé cuando *vengan.* I don't know when they may come. (**Vengan** is irregular present subjunctive of **venir**.)

Si yo *hubiese sabido.* . . . If I had known. . . . (**Hubiese** is irregular past subjunctive of **haber**.)

This is enough of an introduction to the subjunctive for the present. In a later chapter there will be a fuller explanation.

SITUATION MATERIAL — ASKING THE WAY; TAXIS:

la dirección, direction, address · · · **la calle,** street · · · **avenida,** avenue
cuadra, manzana, block · · · **esquina,** corner · · · **centro,** center
derecho, *adj.* straight, right; *adv.,* straight ahead · · · **para allá,** in that direction

a la derecha (izquierda), to the right (left)
correcto, correct, right · · · **errado,** wrong
informar, to inform; **informes,** information
edificio, building · · · **palacio, apartamiento, departamento,** apartment
la catedral, cathedral · · · **iglesia,** church · · · **escuela,** school
museo, museum · · · **mercado,** market · · · (**oficina del**) **correo,** post office
monumento, monument · · · **ruina,** ruin · · · **el parque,** park
el autobús, ómnibus, (*Mex.*) **camión,** (*Guat.*) **camioneta,** (*Cuba, P.R.*)
   guagua, bus · · · **el tranvía,** streetcar
el taxi · · · **libre,** free (*sometimes a taxi is called* **un libre**)
el chófer, (SA) **cochero,** driver · · · **tarifa,** fare
costar, to cost · · · **cobrar,** to charge · · · **parar,** to stop
aprisa, fast · · · **despacio,** slow
el guía, the guide; **la guía,** the guidebook · · · **el mapa,** map
Dígame, por favor, . . . **Favor de decirme.** . . . **Tenga la bondad de decirme.** . . . Please tell me, . . .
No entiendo; hable Ud. más despacio, por favor. I don't understand; please speak more slowly.
Quiero informes, un guía, un mapa. I want information, a guide, a map.
¿ Dónde puedo comprar, conseguir, encontrar, ver . . . ? Where can I buy, get, find, see . . . ?
¿ Cómo voy al palacio municipal? How do I go to the city hall?
¿ Puedo ir a pie? Can I go on foot?
¿ Puede Ud. decirme cómo se va al Parque Chapultepec? Can you tell me how to go to the Parque Chapultepec?
¿ Puede Ud. dirigirme al Zócalo? Can you direct me to the Zócalo?
¡ Se puede ir a la playa Miramar por autobús? Can one go to Miramar Beach by bus?

Estoy buscando la Avenida 5 de Mayo, número 66. I am looking for number 66, 5 de Mayo Avenue.

¿ Va al centro? Do you go to the center (of town)?

¿ Pasa Ud. por el mercado? Do you go past the market?

¿ Para aquí el autobús Hospital? Does the Hospital bus stop here?

¿ Pasa por aquí el ómnibus Condado? Does the Condado bus pass by here?

¿ A qué distancia está el Parque Zoológico? How far is it to the Zoo?

¿ Dista mucho de aquí la Universidad? Is the University far from here?

¿ Estamos en el camino de Cuernavaca? Are we on the road to Cuernavaca?

¿ Voy para la calle Cervantes? Am I going toward Cervantes Street?

Quiero alquilar un carro. I want to rent a car.

¡ Taxi! Está Ud. libre? Taxi! Are you free?

¿ Cuánto cuesta a esta dirección? What is the fare to this address?

¿ Cuánto nos cobra Ud. por llevarnos a las pirámides? What will you charge to take us to the pyramids?

Lléveme al Hotel España. Take me to the Hotel España.

Vaya por el camino más corto. Go by the shortest route.

¿ Cuánto tiempo se tardará en ir y volver? How long will it take to go and return?

Un poco más despacio, por favor. A little slower, please.

¿ Adónde vamos ahora? Where are we going now?

Quiero bajar aquí. I want to get out here.

EL SOMBRERO DE TRES PICOS   (2)

— **¿ Tan rico era el molinero, o tan imprudentes sus tertulianos? —**
"So rich was the miller, or so indiscreet his social companions?"
exclamaréis interrumpiéndome.
you will exclaim, interrupting me.

Ni lo uno ni lo otro. El molinero sólo tenía un pasar, y aquellos
Neither the one nor the other. The miller only had an existence, and those
caballeros eran la delicadeza y el orgullo personificados. Pero en unos
gentlemen   were   delicacy   and   pride   personified.   But   in
tiempos en que se pagaban cincuenta y tantas contribuciones diferentes
times   in   which   were   paid   fifty   and   more   different   contributions
a la Iglesia y al Estado, poco arriesgaba un rústico de tan claras luces [1]
to   the Church and to   the State,   little risked a rustic of such intelligence
como aquél en tenerse ganada la voluntad de regidores, canónigos,
as   that one in having gained the   (good) will of aldermen,   :anons,

---

[1] **claras luces,** literally, "clear lights."

frailes, escribanos y demás personas de campanillas.[1] **Así es que no**
monks, clerks of the court, and other persons of circumstance. So it is that there never
faltaba quien dijese[2] **que el tío Lucas (tal era el nombre del molinero)**
lacked someone who would say that Uncle Lucas (such was the miller's name)
se ahorraba un dineral[3] **al año a fuerza de agasajar a todo el mundo.**[4]
was saving a large sum of money yearly by dint of being kind to everybody.

— « **Vuestra merced me va a dar una puertecilla**[5] **vieja de la casa**
"Your Honor is going to give me a little old door from the house
que ha derribado » — **decíale a uno. « Vuestra señoría** — **decíale a**
he has demolished," he would say to one. "Your Lordship," he would say to
otro — **va a mandar que me rebajen el subsidio, o la alcabala, o la con-**
another, "is going to order that they lower for me the subsidy, or the sales tax, or the con-
tribución de frutos civiles. » « Vuestra reverencia me va a dejar coger
tribution to civil benefits." "Your Reverence will allow me to pick
en la huerta del convento una poca hoja[6] **para mis gusanos de seda. »**
in   the   convent   garden   a   few   leaves   for   my   silkworms."
« Vuestra ilustrísima me va a dar permiso para traer una poca leña[7]
"Most Illustrious Sir will give me permission to bring a little wood
del monte X. » « Vuestra paternidad me va a poner dos letras[8] **para**
from hill X." "You, Holy Father, will write two letters (lines) so that
que me permitan cortar una poca madera[7] **en el pinar H. » « Es**
they   allow   me   to   cut   a   little   wood   in   pine   grove   H."   "It
menester que me haga usted una escriturilla[9] **que no me cueste**[10]
is   necessary   that   you   write   something   for   me   which   won't   cost   me
nada. » « Este año no puedo pagar el censo. » « Espero que el pleito
anything." "This year I can't pay the rent." "I hope that the lawsuit
se falle a mi favor. » « Hoy le he dado de bofetadas[11] **a uno, y creo**
will   be   in   my   favor."   "Today   I   gave   blows   to   one,   and   I   believe

---

[1] **de campanillas,** literally, "of little bells" (**campana,** *bell*).

[2] **dijese,** irregular past subjunctive of **decir.**

[3] **dineral,** from **dinero,** *money.* The ending –al indicates a collection or
accumulation.

[4] **todo el mundo,** literally, "all the world," a very common phrase meaning
everybody.

[5] **puertecilla,** a diminutive of **puerta,** *door, gate.*

[6] **una poca hoja,** a colloquial expression used for **unas pocas hojas;** *a little*
leaf would be **una pequeña hoja.**

[7] **leña . . . madera.** The former is firewood, the latter lumber.

[8] **dos letras. Dos** is sometimes used to mean *two or three, a few.* **Letra** is a
letter of the alphabet; a letter (note) is a **carta.**

[9] **escriturilla,** diminutive of **escritura,** a *writing.*

[10] **cueste,** subjunctive, from **costar.**

[11] **he dado de bofetadas. Dar de** is used in many ways to mean *to treat with,*
to deal, give.

que debe ir a la cárcel por haberme provocado.» «¿Tendría su
that he should go to jail for having provoked me." *"Would Your*

merced tal cosa de sobra?» «¿Le sirve a usted de algo tal otra?»
Honor have such a thing left over?" *"Is such another thing any use to you?"*

«¿Me puede prestar la mula?» «¿Tiene ocupado mañana el
"Can you lend me the mule?" *"Will the cart be in use tomorrow?"*

carro?»...

Y estas canciones se repetían a todas horas, obteniendo siempre por
And these songs were repeated at all hours, obtaining always for

contestación un generoso y desinteresado...[1] «Como se pide.»
answer a generous and disinterested... "Just as you ask."

Conque [2] ya veis que el tío Lucas no estaba en camino de arruinarse.
From which you already see that Uncle Lucas was not on the way to ruin himself.

§ 3. *The Conditional Mood — Omission of Subject Pronouns — TÚ and*
VOSOTROS *— Situation Material: Money and Exchange — El Sombrero de Tres Picos* (3)

THE CONDITIONAL MOOD. The forms of the conditional mood
are very easy to learn. The endings are the same as those of –er
and –ir verbs in the imperfect tense (–ía, etc.), but these endings
are added to the infinitive, not the stem. The conditional is in
this way associated with the future, and the few verbs that are
irregular in the future are also irregular in the conditional (as
haber: fut., **habré;** cond., **habría**).

The conditional will be explained fully in a later lesson. For the
present, just look over the following examples of various uses
of the conditional (verbs in the conditional are italicized). Note
that what we call the conditional mood is called **modo potencial**
in Spanish, indicating not the *real* but only the *possible*.

Yo pensaba que Ud. *estaría* en casa. I thought you *would be* at home.
Ella me preguntó si yo *asistiría* al concierto. She asked me if I *would
attend* the concert.
Sería difícil hacerlo. It *would be* difficult to do it.
Si yo hablase francés, *hablaría* con ella. If I spoke French, I *should
speak* with her.
Yo lo *compraría* si tuviese el dinero. I *should buy* it if I had the money.
(Tuviese is irregular past subjunctive of **tener**.)
Si yo hubiese sabido eso, no *habría venido*. If I had known that, I
should not *have come*.

[1] desinteresado.... Probably the significance of the three dots is to cast
doubt on desinteresado.
[2] Conque, literally "with which," means *so* or *and so.*

Note 1: In the Spanish sentences on page 121, note that the verb with which the verb in the conditional is associated is in a past tense.

Note 2: Do not confuse the *should* of conditional sentences with *should* expressing obligation, which requires **deber**.

Note 3: **Querría** (irregular conditional of **querer**), *I should like*, is rarely used, its place being taken by **quisiera** (past subjunctive), as in **Quisiera comer algo,** *I'd like to eat something.*

OMISSION OF SUBJECT PRONOUNS. You have probably noticed that at the beginning of this book a pronoun was used with every Spanish verb but that later, verbs were often used without pronouns. The reason is that it was desirable for you to learn the pronouns with the verb forms, but that in practice the pronouns are often omitted. The subject pronoun may be omitted:

(1) When the verb form clearly indicates the subject, as in **vivo,** *I live;* **vivimos,** *we live;* **compré,** *I bought;* **vendí,** *I sold;* **he vivido,** *I have lived.* But: **yo había vivido,** *I had lived,* for **él, ella,** or **Ud.** could also be the subject of **había vivido.**

(2) When the reference is perfectly clear, as in:

Escríbame una carta. Write me a letter.

Isabel no está; ha salido. Isabel (*or* Elizabeth) isn't in; she has gone out.

José Martí no era mexicano; era cubano. José Martí was not a Mexican; he was a Cuban.

Permítame presentar a los Smith. Son amigos míos de Tejas. Están en el Hotel Palacio. May I introduce the Smiths? They are friends of mine from Texas. They are in the Hotel Palacio.

¿Quién es el hombre de la barba? Who is the man with the beard? **Es alemán, antropólogo.** He is a German, an anthropologist.

But the pronoun, even when unnecessary, may be used for emphasis, as: **Él sale mañana; yo quedo.** *He is leaving tomorrow; I'm staying.* And **Ud.** is often used for politeness. **¿Quiere Ud. un cigarrillo?** is less informal than **¿Quiere un cigarrillo?**

TÚ AND **VOSOTROS.** You have been advised not to use the pronouns **tú** and **vosotros** (and derived forms) or the second person of Spanish verbs — that is, in addressing people, to stick to **Ud.** and **Uds.,** the possessive **su,** and the object pronouns **se** and **sí.** The advice still holds. But here is a somewhat fuller explanation of the use of second person pronouns:

Tú (*thou*) is used by Spanish-speaking people only: when speaking to intimate friends, young children, or animals; when addressing servants; by officers to men of lower rank; when addressing God, Christ, the Virgin, and saints; and in sacred or poetic language. In rhetorical speech and in poetry it is used in addressing personifications like "Freedom" or "Love." The foreigner should never use it unless with someone he knows intimately, who has first addressed him as **tú**.

Vosotros(–as) (*ye, you*, plural of **tú**) is used in addressing two or more persons who would be addressed individually as **tú**. In rhetorical or poetic speech or literature it is otherwise used. It should never be used by the foreigner.

Vos (*you*) is an archaic form; it takes the second person plural of verbs but has a singular meaning. One finds it in literature, and it may still be heard in some regions.

SITUATION MATERIAL — MONEY AND EXCHANGE:

dinero, money
moneda, coin, currency, money
el billete, bill (*money*)
divisas extranjeras, foreign money (*bills*)
sencillo, change (*small bills or coins*)
suelto, (loose) change
menudo, (small) change
oro, gold   **plata,** silver   **níquel,** nickel   **cobre,** copper
banco, bank
ventanilla, window (*of bank, etc.*)
libreta, bank book   **el interés,** interest   **saldo,** balance
cuenta, account, bill (*owed*); **cuenta de ahorros (cheques),** savings (checking) account   **el cheque,** check; **ch. de viajero,** traveler's check
talonario, checkbook
endosar, to endorse
cobrar, to cash
giro, money order
firmar, to sign; **firma,** signature
descuento, discount
depositar, to deposit
retirar, sacar, to withdraw
cambiar, to change, exchange; **cambio,** (ex)change; **letra de cambio,** bank draft; **tipo de cambio,** rate of exchange
cotizarse, to be quoted (*at a certain rate*)   **el timbre,** tax stamp
¿Dónde está el Banco Nacional? Where is the National Bank?
Quiero cambiar divisas extranjeras. I want to exchange some foreign money.
¿A cómo se cotiza el peso hoy? How is the peso quoted today?
¿Cuánto vale el dólar hoy? What is the dollar worth today?
Deseo dinero mexicano. I want Mexican money.
Quiero pesos por (en cambio de) estos cien dólares. I want pesos for (in exchange for) these hundred dollars.
Creo que Ud. se equivoca. I think you are mistaken.
Lo siento; soy yo quien me equivoco. I'm sorry; I'm the one who is mistaken.

Ud. me cobra demasiado. You're overcharging me.

Quiero hablar con el director. I want to speak to the manager. (*A manager of an institution is* **un director;** *of a business,* **un gerente.**)

Es menester que alguien me acompañe como intérprete. It is necessary for someone to accompany me as an interpreter. (*Simpler:* **Necesito un intérprete.**)

Quisiera cobrar este cheque. I'd like to cash this check.

Déme cinco billetes de a veinte. Give me five twenties.

¿ Quiere Ud. aceptar un cheque de viajero? Will you take a traveler's check ?

¿ Debo firmar ahora? Shall I sign now?

¿ Dónde quiere Ud. mi firma? Where do you want my signature ?

¿ Qué pongo aquí? What do I put here ?

¿ Por qué no es pagadero a la vista? Why isn't it payable on sight ?

No tengo suelto. ¿ Puede Ud. cambiar este billete? I don't have any change. Can you change this bill ?

Sírvase darme suelto por esta peseta. Please give me small change for this peseta.

Déme dos bolívares en plata. Give me two B's in silver.

For the monetary units of Spanish-speaking countries, see pages 263–264.

EL SOMBRERO DE TRES PICOS   (3)

La última y acaso la más poderosa razón que tenía el *señorío* [1] **de la**
The ultimate and perhaps the most powerful reason which the gentry *of the*
ciudad para frecuentar por las tardes el molino del tío Lucas era . . .
city had for frequenting in the evenings Uncle Lucas's mill, was . . .
que, así los clérigos como los seglares, empezando por el señor obispo
that the clergy as well as the laity, beginning with the lord bishop
y el señor corregidor, podían contemplar allí a sus anchas una de las
and the magistrate, could contemplate there at their ease one of the
obras más bellas, graciosas y admirables que hayan salido [2] jamás [3]
most beautiful, pleasing, and admirable works that have ever come
de las manos de Dios, llamado entonces el Ser Supremo por Jovellanos [4]
from the hands of God, then called the Supreme Being by Jovellanos
y toda la escuela afrancesada de nuestro país. . . .
and all the Frenchified school of our country. . . .

[1] **señorío.** The ending **–ío** indicates a group, as **mujerío,** *crowd of women.*
[2] **hayan salido,** present perfect subjunctive; the subjunctive prevents the statement from being taken as a direct statement of fact.
[3] **jamás:** usually means *never,* but sometimes *ever.*
[4] **Jovellanos,** a Spanish philosophical poet (1744–1811), who was influenced by French rationalism.

Esta obra . . . se denominaba *la señora Frasquita.*[1]
This work . . . was called Señora Frasquita.

Empiezo por responderos[2] **de que la señora Frasquita, legítima**
I begin by assuring you that Señora Frasquita, legitimate

esposa del tío Lucas, era una mujer de bien, y de que así lo sabían todos
wife of Uncle Lucas, was an honest woman, and that thus all the

los ilustres visitantes del molino. Digo más: ninguno de éstos daba
illustrious visitors to the mill knew her. I say further: none of these gave

muestras de considerarla con ojos de varón[3] **ni con trastienda**[4] **pe-**
signs of regarding her with (the) eyes of (a) man nor with sinful

caminosa. Admirábanla, sí, y requebrábanla en ocasiones (delante de
caution. They admired her, yes, and courted her on occasions (in front

su marido, por supuesto), lo mismo los frailes que los caballeros, los
of her husband, of course), the friars as well as the gentlemen, the

canónigos que los golillas,[5] **como un prodigio de belleza que honraba**
canons as well as the ruffed justices, as a prodigy of beauty who honored

a su Creador, y como una diablesa de travesura y coquetería, que ale-
her Creator, and as a she-devil of mischief and coquetry, who

graba inocentemente los espíritus más melancólicos. « Es un hermoso
innocently cheered the most melancholy spirits. "She's a handsome

animal, » solía[6] **decir el virtuosísimo prelado. « Es una estatua de la**
animal," the most virtuous prelate would say. "She's a statue of

antigüedad helénica, » observaba un abogado muy erudito, académico
Hellenic antiquity," would observe a very erudite lawyer, a corresponding

correspondiente de la Historia.[7] **« Es la propia estampa de Eva, »**
academician of History. "She's the very image of Eve,"

prorrumpía el Prior de los Franciscanos. « Es una real moza, » ex-
would break forth the Prior of the Franciscans. "She's a regal girl," ex-

clamaba el Coronel de milicias. « Es una sierpe, una sirena, un de-
claimed the colonel of militia. "She's a serpent, a siren, a de-

monio ! » añadía el corregidor. « Pero es una buena mujer, es un
mon!" the magistrate would add. "But she is a good woman, she's an

---

[1] **la señora Frasquita.** In the original the dialectal form **Señá** is used throughout. **Frasquita** is a nickname for **Francisca** (*Frances*). So Señá Frasquita would be something like a Southern "Miz Fanny."

[2] **responderos:** for the –os, refer to the table on page 28.

[3] **varón,** *man* with emphasis on masculinity, *male.*

[4] **trastienda,** an amusing word, formed from **tras**, *behind*, and **tienda**, *store;* something like *underhandedness.*

[5] **los golillas. Golilla** means *ruff;* some justices wore a ruffed collar; note **los**, not **las**, **golillas**, as referring to men.

[6] **solía,** from **soler**, *to be accustomed to.*

[7] **académico correspondiente de la Historia:** a corresponding member of la Academia de la Historia.

ángel, es una criatura,[1] **es una chiquilla** [2] **de cuatro años, »** acababan
angel, she's a child, she's a little one of four years," they would all end
por decir todos, al regresar del molino atiborrados de uvas o de nueces,
by saying, on returning from the mill stuffed with grapes or with nuts,
en busca de sus tétricos y metódicos hogares.[3]
in search of their gloomy and methodical hearths.

§ 4. *Orthographic Changes in Verbs — Situation Material: Hotel and*
Boarding House — **El Sombrero de Tres Picos** (4)

ORTHOGRAPHIC CHANGES IN VERBS. Many regular verbs may appear to you to be irregular because of certain changes that occur
in the spelling of some of the forms. These orthographic changes
are necessary in order that the sound of the stem may be preserved.
For example, in the verb **tocar,** *to touch,* the stem is **toc–** and the
c has the *k* sound. Now if the past definite ending –**é** is added to
toc– we have **tocé** — but this will not do because before **e** the **c** no
longer has the *k* sound. It is necessary, therefore, that this form
be spelled **toqué.** The same is true of the present subjunctive.
Here is the conjugation of the verb **tocar** in the two tenses in which
orthographic changes occur:

Past Def. Indicative: **toqué, tocaste, tocó; tocamos, tocasteis, tocaron**
Present Subjunctive: **toque, toques, toque; toquemos, toquéis,**
    toquen

The following is a list of various classes of verbs with orthographic
changes. With some verbs the change does not appear in the past
definite indicative but does appear in the present indicative. One
example (the first person singular, present subjunctive) is given for
one typical verb of each class.

(1) Verbs ending in –**car: c** becomes **qu** before **e** (**tocar: toque**).
(2) Verbs ending in –**gar: g** becomes **gu** before **e** (**pagar: pague**).
(3) Verbs ending in –**guar: gu** becomes **gü** before **e** (**averiguar:**
    averigüe).
(4) Verbs ending in –**cer** or –**cir** *preceded by a consonant* (see Note,
    page 127): **c** becomes **z** before **o** or **a** (**vencer: venza; espar-**
    cir: esparza).

---

[1] **criatura,** *creature,* often used, affectionately, of a child.
[2] **chiquilla,** diminutive of **chico, –a.** **Chico** is the equivalent of our *kid;*
chiquillos, *little kids.*
[3] **hogares. Hogar** means *hearth* and by extension *home.*

(5) Verbs ending in –ger or –gir: g becomes j before o or a (coger: coja; dirigir: dirija).

(6) Verbs ending in –guir: gu becomes g before o or a (distinguir: distinga).

(7) Verbs ending in –iar or –uar: i becomes í and u becomes ú when accented (variar: varíe; continuar: continúe).

To the above list of necessary orthographic changes, may be added classes 8, 9, and 10:

(8) Verbs ending in –zar: z becomes c before e, as it is not customary to use z before e or i (gozar: goce).

In the following classes of verbs orthographic changes occur in the present participle and in the past and future subjunctives (two forms given as examples for each verb):

(9) Verbs ending in –llir, –ñer, –ñir: i is dropped from the ending –ió and from endings beginning with ie, as the i is absorbed by the preceding ll or ñ sound (bullir: bullendo, bullera; tañer: tañendo, tañera; bruñir: bruñendo, bruñera).

(10) Verbs in –er or –ir whose stem ends in a vowel: the i of the ending –ió and of endings beginning with ie is changed to y, as unaccented i may not be used between two vowels (creer: creyendo, creyera; huir: huyendo, huyera).

Note: One class of irregular verbs should be mentioned here, for comparison with class 4, above:

Verbs ending in –cer or –cir *preceded by a vowel:* In most, but not all, of these verbs, c becomes zc before o or a (conocer: conozco; lucir: luzca; but mecer: mezo). Verbs of this class must be learned individually.

Study this list until you thoroughly understand the reasons for the orthographic changes. You need not memorize the rules or the verb forms; it is only necessary to understand Spanish orthography. As far as speaking is concerned, there is no problem except for verbs of the type mentioned in the *Note,* above. As you read, observe verb forms that illustrate these rules.

SITUATION MATERIAL — HOTEL AND BOARDING HOUSE:

el hotel, hotel; h. comercial, commercial h.; h. de turistas, tourist h.;
h. de lujo, luxury h.   posada, inn
la pensión, casa de huéspedes, boarding house

céntrico, central, centrally located   **cuarto, habitación,** room

baño, bath   **ducha,** shower (bath)   **agua caliente,** hot water

cama, bed; **c. de matrimonio,** double bed

un matrimonio, a married couple

mosquitero, mosquito netting   **la chinche,** bedbug

comidas, meals; (SA) **comida criolla,** native food

desayuno, breakfast   **piso (bajo),** (ground) floor

caro, expensive; **barato,** cheap   **grande,** large; **pequeño,** small

claro, light; **oscuro,** dark   **limpio,** clean; **sucio,** dirty

ventana, window   **vista (a),** view (of)

vestíbulo, lobby   **el comedor,** dining room

el bar, bar   **piscina,** swimming pool

el ascensor, elevator   **mozo,** "boy"

camarera, chambermaid   **propina,** tip

los muebles, furniture   **mesa,** table   **silla,** chair

cómoda, dresser, bureau   **ropero,** clothes closet, wardrobe

percha, perchero, coat hanger   **la luz,** light

bombilla (eléctrica), (electric) light bulb

cuenta, bill   **recibo,** receipt   **por adelantado,** in advance

al día, a la semana, by the day, per day, by the week, per week

el gerente, manager   **amo, –a,** proprietor, –tress

apartamiento, departamento, apartment   **amueblado,** furnished

alquilar, to rent   **cocina,** kitchen

Busco una pensión o un hotel pequeño. I am looking for a boarding house or a small hotel.

¿ Conoce Ud. un buen hotel comercial, céntrico? Do you know a good commercial hotel, centrally located?

Conozco dos o tres; tal vez el París sería mejor para Ud. I know two or three; maybe the Paris would be best for you.

El mejor hotel es el Nuevo Mundo, pero es muy caro. Es un hotel de lujo. The best hotel is the Nuevo Mundo, but it is very expensive. It's a luxury hotel.

Cobran veinticinco dólares al día, y más. They charge twenty-five dollars a day and up. **¡ Ay!** Ouch!

Quisiera un hotel de segunda clase, pero limpio y cómodo. I'd like a second-class hotel, but clean and comfortable.

Quiero un cuarto con baño. Estoy solo. I want a room with bath. I am alone.

Queremos un cuarto de matrimonio. We want a room with a double bed.

Es mucho. ¿ Tiene Ud. cuartos más baratos? That's high. Do you have cheaper rooms?

Sírvase enseñarme el cuarto. Please show me the room.

Quisiera una habitación con vista al mar. I'd like a room with a view of the sea.

No quiero pensión completa, sólo desayuno. I don't want full board,
just breakfast.

¿ Qué cuesta la habitación con el desayuno? What does the room with
breakfast cost?

Bueno. Tomo la habitación para una semana. Good. I'll take the
room for a week.

**¿ Quiere Ud. darme una bombilla más fuerte? No puedo leer con esta
luz.** Will you give me a stronger bulb? I can't read with this light.

La lámpara no funciona, y necesito un cenicero y dos o tres percheros.
The lamp doesn't work, and I need an ash tray and two or three hangers.

EL SOMBRERO DE TRES PICOS   (4)

La chiquilla de cuatro años, esto es, la señora Frasquita, frisaría en
The little girl of four years — that is, the Sra. Frasquita — would be going on

los treinta. Tenía más de dos varas de estatura, y era recia a proporción,
thirty. She was more than two varas [1] in stature, and was robust in proportion,

o quizás [2] más gruesa todavía de lo correspondiente a su arrogante talla.
or perhaps even stouter than corresponded to her proud height.

Parecía una Niobe [3] colosal, y eso que no había tenido hijos; parecía
She seemed a colossal Niobe (and that although she had not had children); she seemed

un Hércules . . . hembra; parecía una matrona romana de las que aun
a Hercules . . . a female one; she seemed a Roman matron of those of which there

hay ejemplares en el Trastévere.[4] Pero lo más notable en ella era la
are still examples in Trastevere.   But the most notable in her was the

movilidad, la ligereza, la animación, la gracia de su respetable mole.
mobility, the lightness, the animation, the grace of her respectable bulk.

Para ser una estatua, como pretendía el académico, le faltaba el reposo
To be a statue, as the academician claimed, she lacked monumental

monumental. Se cimbreaba como un junco, giraba como una veleta,
repose.   She swayed like a reed, revolved like a weathercock,

bailaba [5] como una peonza. Su rostro era más movible todavía, y, por
spun like a top.   Her face was still more mobile and, for

---

[1] **dos varas.** The vara, usually translated *yard*, is a measure of varying length,
normally about 32 inches. So Frasquita's "proud height" was five feet, four
inches.

[2] **quizás.** This word also appears as **quizá.**

[3] **Niobe.** According to a Greek legend, Niobe was overproud of her many
children. The jealous gods Apollo and Artemis killed all the children and turned
the grieving mother to stone. The comparison of the smiling and lively Frasquita, who had no children, to Niobe is most inappropriate.

[4] **Trastévere,** a section of Rome.

[5] **bailaba.** The usual meaning of **bailar** is *to dance.*

tanto, menos escultural. Avivábanlo donosamente hasta cinco hoyuelos[1]**:**
all that, less sculptural.   There enlivened it prettily as many as five dimples:

dos en una mejilla; otro en otra; otro, muy chico, cerca de la comisura
two on one cheek; another on (the) other; another, very small, near the left corner

izquierda de sus rientes labios, y el último, muy grande, en medio de
of her laughing lips; and the last, very big, in (the) middle of

su redonda barba.[2] **Añadid a esto los picarescos mohines, los graciosos**
her round chin.   Add to this the roguish gestures, the droll

guiños y las varias posturas de cabeza que amenizaban su conversación,
winks, and the various postures of (her) head which enlivened her conversation,

y formaréis idea de aquella cara llena de sal[3] **y de hermosura y radiante**
and you will form (an) idea of that face full of life and of beauty and always radiant

siempre de salud y alegría.
with health and gaiety.

Ni la señora Frasquita ni el tío Lucas eran andaluces: ella era
Neither the Sra. Frasquita nor Uncle Lucas were Andalusians[4]*: she was*

navarra y él murciano. Él había ido a la ciudad de ——, a la edad de
Navarrese[5] *and he Murcian.*[6] *He had gone to the city of ——, at the age of*

quince años, como medio paje, medio criado del obispo anterior al que
fifteen years, as half page, half servant of the bishop before the one who

entonces gobernaba aquella iglesia.   Educábalo su protector para
then   governed   that   church.   His   protector   educated   him   to   be   a

clérigo, y tal vez con esta mira y para que no careciese de *congrua,*
cleric, and perhaps with that view and so that he would not lack a competence,

dejóle en su testamento el molino. . . .
left him in his will the mill. . . .

§ 5. *Full Conjugation of* **ESTAR** *and* **HABER** — *Uses of the Present and Future Tenses — Idioms — Situation Material: Getting Up —* **El Sombrero de Tres Picos** (5)

FULL CONJUGATION OF **ESTAR.   Estar** is an irregular verb.   It is unlike all other Spanish verbs in having an irregular *accent* in the present tense, both indicative and subjunctive (i.e., **está** and **esté** instead of **esta** and **este**) — the reason being to prevent con-

---

[1] **hoyuelos,** diminutive of **hoyo,** *hole.*

[2] **barba,** *beard* or *chin.*

[3] **sal,** *salt,* often used figuratively (*wit, piquancy*).

[4] Andalusia (**Andalucía**) is the southernmost region of Spain, embracing the eight provinces of Huelva, Cádiz, Sevilla, Málaga, Almería, Granada, Jaén, and Córdoba.

[5] Navarre (**Navarra**) is a province bordering on France.

[6] Murcia is a province in southeast Spain.

fusion with the pronoun-adjectives **este** and **éste**. Like three other verbs (**ser, dar, ir**) the first person singular, present indicative, ends in **–oy** instead of **–o**. Like a number of other verbs, it is irregular in the past definite in both stem and endings.

The full conjugation of **estar** follows (the irregular forms are italicized):

Infinitive: **estar**
Present Participle: **estando**
Past Participle: **estado** *
Imperative: está, **estad**

INDICATIVE:

Present: estoy, estás, está; **estamos, estáis,** *están*
Imperfect: **estaba,** *etc. (regular)*
Past Definite: estuve, estuviste, estuvo; estuvimos, estuvisteis, estuvieron
Future: **estaré,** *etc. (regular)*

CONDITIONAL: **estaría,** *etc. (regular)*

SUBJUNCTIVE:

Present: esté, estés, esté; **estemos, estéis,** *estén*
Past: estuviese, etc.
    estuviera, etc.
Future: estuviere, etc.

Important Note: Now that you have begun to learn the irregular verbs, it is necessary to point out that *the past and future subjunctives are based upon the past definite indicative.* That is, the endings of these tenses in the subjunctive are always regular, but they are added to the stem of the past definite, which may be regular or irregular. Thus:

Past Definite Indicative:	**estuv–e**
Past Subjunctives:	**estuv–iese**
	estuv–iera
Future Subjunctive.	**estuv–iere**

Therefore, in learning an irregular verb you usually need to learn only two or three irregular forms. In the case of **estar,** these would be **estoy** (ending *and* accent irregular) and **estuve.** All the other irregular forms are derived "regularly" from these two. (If the first person singular of the past definite ends in **–e,** the third person ends in **–o;** you will soon learn this when you learn more verbs with irregular past definites.)

You have already learned to form progressive tense forms by using **estar** as an auxiliary verb. The following is the conjugation of the progressive forms of **comprar** in the simple tenses (forms that do not occur or are extremely rare are omitted).

* **Estado** as a noun means *state.*

Infinitive: **estar comprando**

INDICATIVE:

Present: **estoy comprando,** *etc.*
Imperfect: **estaba comprando,** *etc.*
Future: **estaré comprando,** *etc.*

CONDITIONAL: **estaría comprando,** *etc.*

SUBJUNCTIVE:

Present: **esté comprando,** *etc.*
Past: **estuviese,** *or* **–iera, comprando,** *etc.*

Examples of progressive forms in the conditional and subjunctive:

Ella estaría llegando ahora si hubiese salido ayer. She would be arriving now if she had started yesterday.

Espero que ella esté llegando mañana a estas horas. I hope that she will be arriving at this time tomorrow.

Esperaba que ella estuviese llegando hoy. I hoped that she would be arriving today.

FULL CONJUGATION OF **HABER.** **Haber** has more irregular than regular forms. Here is the full conjugation of the verb (irregular forms italicized):

Infinitive: **haber**
Present Participle: **habiendo**
Past Participle: **habido**
Imperative: hé, **habed**

INDICATIVE:

Present: he, has, ha; **hemos, habéis,** *han*
Imperfect: **había,** *etc. (regular)*
Past Definite: hube, hubiste, hubo; hubimos, hubisteis, hubieron
Future: habré, habrás, habrá; habremos, habréis, habrán

CONDITIONAL: *habría, etc.*

SUBJUNCTIVE:

Present: haya, hayas, haya; hayamos, hayáis, hayan *
Past: hubiese, etc.
     hubiera, etc.
Future: hubiere, etc.

* **Haya** is exceptional because the stem of the present subjunctive is a.most always the same as the stem of the first person singular, present indicative

To learn the conjugation of **haber,** you must learn all of the present indicative plus the forms **hube, habré,** and **haya.**

Here is the conjugation of **comprar** in the compound tenses, in which **haber** is the auxiliary verb:

Perfect Infinitive: **haber comprado,** to have bought
Perfect Participle: **habiendo comprado,** having bought

INDICATIVE:

Present Perfect: **he comprado,** I have bought, *etc.*
Past Perfect: **había,** *or* **hube,*** **comprado,** I had bought, *etc.*
Future Perfect: **habré comprado,** I shall have bought, *etc.*

CONDITIONAL:

Perfect: **habría comprado,** I should have bought, *etc.*

SUBJUNCTIVE:

Present Perfect: **haya comprado,** (*that*) I have bought, *etc.*
Past Perfect: **hubiese,** *or* **–iera, comprado,** (*that* or *if*) I had bought, *etc.*
Future Perfect: **hubiere comprado,** (*that*) I shall have bought, *etc.*

There are progressive forms of the compound tenses. For example:

> **he estado comprando,** I have been buying
> **había estado comprando,** I had been buying
> **habré estado comprando,** I shall have been buying

USES OF THE PRESENT AND FUTURE TENSES:

(1) *The Present Tense:* The present tense may be used, in Spanish as in English, to express past or future time. What we call the "historical present" is more common in Spanish than in English. For example, if a person is relating an incident (and the historical present is used only in narration), he might say:

> **Yo estoy en la casa cuando él viene a sorprenderme.** I am in the house when he comes to surprise me.

Using the present in place of the future is perhaps equally common in both languages, as shown in the following sentences.

---

* The form **hube** as an auxiliary verb is used only after conjunctions of time (such as **cuando,** *when,* **después que,** *after*) and then only if the action is performed but once.

El vapor sale a las 6 de la tarde. The boat sails at 6 P.M.

El viernes que viene hay una corrida de toros. Next
Friday there is a bullfight.

(2) *The Future Tense:* In English, because we can use either *shall*
or *will*, we can make a distinction between simple futurity and more
emphatic statements of intention, prohibition, or prophecy, but
it is all the same in Spanish:

Lo veré. I shall see him. I *will* see him.

Habrá paz. There will be peace. There *shall* be peace.

No matarás. Thou shalt not kill. You will not kill.

In Spanish the future may express speculation or incredulity,
as in:

¿ Quién será? Who can it be?

Serán las doce. It must be about twelve o'clock.

¡ Será posible que esté enamorada! Can it be possible that
she is in love!

IDIOMS. Idioms constitute the greatest difficulty in learning a foreign language (because no rules apply). The most absurd blunders
result if a person translates his own idioms word-for-word into
another language.

If you wished to say, in Spanish, *from time to time* and translated
word-by-word, you would get **de tiempo a tiempo.** But the actual
Spanish phrase is **de vez en cuando** ("from time [occasion] in
when") — a good example of how illogical idioms can get. There
is nothing to do but learn idioms the way you learn words and to
remember that if you guess at a phrase you will be wrong nine
times out of ten.

The same kind of problem is presented in choosing the right
synonym when several are possible. *Time* may be **tiempo, vez,** or
hora, and where one is required the other two will not do. We
take a walk, but the Spanish expression is "give" a walk: **dar un
paseo.** In our country a machine *runs*, but in a Spanish-speaking
country it "walks" (**andar**).

A North American went into a liquor store and bought a bottle
of wine. The clerk offered to have it delivered (since Spanish
gentlemen will not usually carry packages). The American replied,
"No, puedo tomarla." Which means, "No, I can drink it" — *to
take*, meaning *carry*, is **llevar**, and while **tomar** is the usual word
for *take*, when liquor is spoken of, **tomar** is usually used instead of
beber, *to drink*.

Here are a number of common idioms based on **tener,** *to have* (possess):

tener que, to have to (**Tengo que salir.** I have to leave.)

tener (treinta) años, to be (thirty) years old

tener razón, to be right; **no tener razón,** to be wrong (**Ud. no tiene razón.** You are wrong.)

tener miedo, to be afraid (*followed by* **de** *or* **a,** *of;* *if a person is feared,* **a** *is used:* **Tengo miedo a aquel hombre.** I'm afraid of that man.)

tener vergüenza (de), to be ashamed (of)

tener hambre, sed, sueño, to be hungry, thirsty, sleepy

tener calor, frío, to be hot, cold (*of feelings*) — *but:*

hacer calor, frío, to be hot, cold (*of weather*)

Tengo mucho calor. I'm very hot. **Hace más calor hoy.** It's hotter, *or* warmer, today. **La sopa está muy caliente.** The soup is very hot. **La sopa está fría.** The soup is cold. **Hace frío aquí.** It's cold here. **¿ Tiene Ud. frío?** Are you cold?

Also learn these idioms:

¿ Qué hay? ¿ Qué pasa? What's going on? What's the matter?

¿ Qué pasa con Ud.? ¿ Qué tiene Ud.? What's the matter with you?

querer decir, to mean (*intend*); **significar,** to mean, signify

¿ Qué significa muñeca? What does **muñeca** mean?

¿ Qué quiere Ud. decir? What do you mean?

<small>SITUATION MATERIAL — GETTING UP AND STARTING THE DAY:</small>

dormir, to sleep	**descansar,** to rest	**despertar,** to wake up
levantarse, to get up	**madrugar,** to get up early	
mañana, morning	**madrugada,** early morning	
vestirse, to dress	**salir,** to go out	

Buenos días, señor. ¿ Ha descansado bien? Good morning. Did you sleep well?

Perfectamente, gracias. He dormido muy bien. Fine, thanks. I slept very well.

Ud. ha madrugado. You got up early.

Es mi costumbre. Suelo acostarme temprano y levantarme temprano. It is my habit. I usually go to bed early and get up early.

¿ Por qué se ha levantado Ud. tan temprano? Why did you get up so early?

Porque quiero aprovechar la mañana. Because I want to take advantage of the morning.

No conozco esta ciudad, y después del desayuno quiero dar un paseo (ir de paseo). I don't know this city, and after breakfast I want to take a walk (go walking).

¡ Ojalá tuviera un guía que hablara inglés! If only I had a guide who spoke English!

¿No conoce Ud. alguien que hable inglés? Don't you know anybody who speaks English?

No importa. Hablo bastante bien el castellano para pedir la dirección. No matter. I speak Spanish well enough to ask the way.

Volveré a las once, más o menos. I'll be back about eleven.

¿Hay cartas para mí? Are there any letters for me?

Dígame ¿ sería posible alquilar un radio? Tell me, would it be possible to rent a radio?

Sí, señor. Si Ud. quiere yo me encargaré de eso. Yes. If you wish, I will see to that.

¿Cuánto costará? How much will (*or* might) it cost? **¿Cuánto costaría?** How much would it cost? **Preguntaré.** I'll ask.

EL SOMBRERO DE TRES PICOS   (5)

En Estella [1] conoció a la señora Frasquita, que entonces sólo se
In Estella he knew Sra. Frasquita, who then was called only

llamaba Frasquita; la enamoró [2]; se casó con ella, y se la llevó a Anda-
Frasquita; he wooed her, he married her, and took her to Andalusia

lucía en busca de aquel molino que había de verlos tan pacíficos y
in search of that mill which was to see them so peaceful and

dichosos durante el resto de su peregrinación por este valle de lá-
happy during the rest of their peregrination through this vale of tears

grimas y risas.
and laughter.

La señora Frasquita, pues, trasladada de Navarra a aquella soledad,
Sra. Frasquita, then, removed from Navarre to that solitude,

no había adquirido ningún hábito [3] andaluz, y se diferenciaba mucho
had not acquired any Andalusian habit, and differed greatly

de las mujeres campesinas [4] de los contornos. Vestía con más sencillez,
from the peasant women of the vicinity. She dressed with more simplicity,

desenfado y elegancia que ellas; lavaba más sus carnes, y permitía
naturalness, and elegance than they; she washed her flesh more, and allowed

---

[1] Estella, a town in Navarre.

[2] enamorar, *to woo, make love to;* enamorarse (de), *to fall in love (with).*

[3] hábito: could mean *habit* or *attire;* both meanings are implied.

[4] campesinas: campo, *country;* campesino, *of the country, rural, peasant.*

al sol y al aire acariciar sus arremangados [1] **brazos y su descubierta** [2]
the sun and the air to caress her exposed arms and her uncovered

garganta. Usaba hasta cierto punto, el traje de las señoras de aquella
throat. She used to a certain point the dress of the ladies of that

época, el traje de las mujeres de Goya, el traje de la reina María Luisa [3]:
epoch, the dress of the women of Goya, the dress of Queen María Luisa:

si no falda de medio paso, falda de un paso solo, sumamente corta, que
if not (a) skirt of half (a) pace, (a) skirt of only one pace, extremely short, which

dejaba ver sus menudos pies y el arranque [4] **de su soberana pierna:**
allowed to be seen her tiny feet and the sudden start of her sovereign leg;

llevaba el escote [5] **redondo y bajo, al estilo de Madrid, donde se de-**
she wore the round low-cut neck, in the style of Madrid, where she stayed

tuvo [6] **dos meses con su Lucas al trasladarse de Navarra a Andalucía;**
two months with her Lucas on moving from Navarre to Andalusia;

todo el pelo recogido en lo alto [7] **de la coronilla,** [8] **lo cual dejaba**
all her hair gathered up on the top of the crown, which allowed

campear la gallardía de su cabeza y de su cuello; sendas [9] **arracadas** [10]
to excel the grace of her head and of her neck; earrings with pendants

en las diminutas orejas, y muchas sortijas en los afilados dedos de sus
in her very small ears, and many rings on the slender fingers of her

duras pero limpias manos. Por último, la voz de la señora Frasquita
hard but clean hands. Lastly, Sra. Frasquita's voice

tenía todos los tonos del más extenso y melodioso instrumento, y su
had all the tones of the most spacious and melodious instrument, and her

carcajada era tan alegre y argentina que parecía un repique de Sábado
burst of laughter was so merry and silvery that it seemed a peal of bells of Holy

de Gloria.
Saturday. [11]

Retrataremos ahora al tío Lucas.
We shall now portray Uncle Lucas.

[1] **arremangados. Manga** means *sleeve;* **arremangar,** *to roll up the sleeves.*

[2] **descubierta,** irregular past participle of **descubrir,** *to uncover, discover.*

[3] **María Luisa.** The reference is to the notorious María Luisa who lived at the time of Goya; she was the consort of Charles IV.

[4] **arranque,** *(sudden) start,* usually used of motion. The meaning here is that Sra. Frasquita's skirt did not reach her ankles.

[5] **escote,** *neck* of a dress; **cuello** is the *neck* of the body.

[6] **se detuvo,** from **detenerse,** *to stop* or *stay.*

[7] **lo alto.** The neuter **lo** indicates that **alto** is not an adjective but a noun (*the high part*).

[8] **coronilla,** diminutive of **corona,** *crown;* **coronilla** is the crown of the head.

[9] **sendas.** This word may be translated by *each,* but it is always used in the plural, as: **en sendas orejas,** *on each ear.*

[10] **arracadas,** *pendants,* here translated *earrings with pendants.*

[11] *Holy Saturday,* the Saturday before Easter.

LESSON XI

§ 1. *Full Conjugation of SER — The Passive Voice — Conjugation of AMAR in the Passive — Substitutes for the Passive — Situation Material: The Bathroom — El Sombrero de Tres Picos (6)*

FULL CONJUGATION OF **SER**. **Ser** is irregular in most of its forms (it looks like a composite of three different verbs). Since **ser** is such a basic verb, it must be thoroughly learned. You are already familiar with the present indicative. The key forms you must now learn are **era, fuí** and **fué,** and **sea.** In the full conjugation that follows, irregular forms are italicized. (This practice will be followed hereafter in the presentation of irregular verbs.)

Infinitive: **ser**
Present Participle: **siendo**
Past Participle: **sido**
Imperative: **sé,** [1] **sed**

INDICATIVE:

Present: soy, *eres, es;* somos, sois, son
Imperfect: era, eras, era; éramos, erais, eran
Past Definite: fuí, fuiste, fué; fuimos, fuisteis, fueron [2]
Future: **seré,** *etc.*

CONDITIONAL: **sería,** *etc.*

SUBJUNCTIVE:

Present: sea, seas, sea; seamos, seáis, sean
Past: fuese, etc. [2]
    fuera, etc. [2]
Future: fuere, etc. [2]

THE PASSIVE VOICE. We have been ignoring the fact that verbs have *voice* as well as tense and mood. The subject of a verb in the passive voice is acted upon. Verbs that do not express action —

---

[1] **Sé** is also the first person singular, present indicative, of **saber** (**yo sé, I know**).

[2] It happens that **ir,** *to go,* has the same forms as **ser** in the past definite and subjunctive tenses based on it. So you must depend upon the context to indicate whether **fuí** (etc.) means *was* or *went.*

138

like *be*, *seem*, *exist* — have no passive. The distinction between
an active verb and a passive verb is simple and clear: *The dog
chases* (active) *the cat. The cat is chased* (passive) *by the dog.*

All the verb forms so far presented have been active (with the
exception of the past participle, which is passive), and "full conjugation" has meant full conjugation of the verb (simple tenses)
in the active voice. Fortunately, learning to use verbs in the
passive voice does not require learning any new forms. The passive
is formed by using **ser** as an auxiliary verb with the past participle.

Note: In the passive voice, the ending of the past participle is varied as if it
were just an adjective. This is not true of the past participle used in compound
tenses with **haber**. Compare:

Las mujeres han comprado flores. The women have bought flowers.
Las flores fueron compradas por las mujeres. The flowers were bought
by the women.
Las flores compradas por las mujeres son hermosas. The flowers bought
by the women are beautiful.

The last sentence shows the past participle used as an adjective.

After a passive verb, **por,** *by,* is usually used to indicate the agent
(as in the second sentence above). But if the action is mental, **de**
is usually used: **Fué respetado de todos.** *He was respected by all.*
We might say *respected of all.*

CONJUGATION OF **AMAR** IN THE PASSIVE. The following is the
conjugation of **amar** in the passive, in both simple and compound
tenses, in the first person singular only:

INFINITIVES:

Present: **ser amado**(–a), to be loved
Present Perfect: **haber sido amado**(–a), to have been loved

PARTICIPLES:

Present: **siendo amado**(–a), being loved
Past: **amado**(–a), loved
Present Perfect: **habiendo sido amado**(–a), having been loved

IMPERATIVE: **sé amado**(–a), be loved

INDICATIVE:

Present: **soy amado** (–a), I am loved, I am being loved
Imperfect: **era amado**(–a), I was loved

Past Definite: **fuí amado(–a),** I was loved *

Future: **seré amado(–a),** I shall, *or* will, be loved

Present Perfect: **he sido amado(–a),** I have been loved

Past Perfect: **había,** *or* **hube,*** **sido amado(–a),** I had been loved

Future Perfect: **habré sido amado(–a),** I shall have been loved

CONDITIONAL:

Simple: **sería amado(–a),** I should be loved

Perfect: **habría sido amado(–a),** I should have been loved

SUBJUNCTIVE:

Present: **(que) sea amado(–a),** (that) I be, *or* may be, loved

Past: **(que) fuese,** *or* **fuera, amado(–a),** (that) I were loved

Future: **(que) fuere amado(–a),** (that) I shall be loved

Present Perfect: **(que) haya sido amado(–a),** (that) I have been loved

Past Perfect: **(que) hubiese,** *or* **hubiera, sido amado(–a),** (that) I had been loved

Future Perfect: **(que) hubiere sido amado(–a),** (that) I shall have been loved

Examples of verbs in the passive:

El ser amado es lo que todo el mundo quiere. To be, *or* Being, loved is what everyone wants.

No quiero ser visto con él. I don't want to be seen with him.

Habiendo sido atacados por la noche, fueron destruídos.† Having been attacked by night, they were destroyed.

Las señoritas serán llamadas primero. The young ladies will be called first.

Los dos jóvenes han sido condenados a seis meses en la cárcel. The two young men have been sentenced to six months in jail.

¡Qué vergüenza que fuesen perseguidos por decir la verdad! What a shame that they were persecuted for telling the truth!

Espero que la carta sea (fuere) recibida. I hope that the letter is (will be) received.

Si él hubiese sido matado entonces, habría sido amado del pueblo. If he had been killed then, he would have been loved by the people.

---

* With **amar** there would hardly be any occasion to use the past definite, which should refer to a single action. **Fuí atacado(–a),** *I was attacked*, would be a better example. The same thing is true of the past perfect with **hube.**

† When the stem of a verb ends in a vowel, **–ido** becomes **–ído.**

Substitutes for the Passive. In Spanish there is, especially in conversation, a tendency to avoid cumbersome verb forms by using substitutes.

It has already been mentioned that a common substitute for the passive is the reflexive form of the verb, as in:

> **Aquí se habla inglés.** English is spoken ("speaks itself") here.
>
> **Se dice que toma mucho.** It is said ("It says itself") that he drinks heavily.

In the above, **es hablado** and **es dicho** would *never* be used.

Another way of avoiding the passive is as follows:

> **Me han robado.** I have been robbed. ("They have robbed me.")
>
> **Me robaron la cámara.** My camera was stolen.
>
> **Me han dicho que. . . .** I was told that. . . .
>
> **Dicen que toma mucho.**

In English we may say *I was given a letter.* In this sentence, *was given* is passive in form, but the meaning is *A letter was given to me.* In Spanish this would be **Me dieron una carta,** *They gave me a letter.*

We use progressive forms of the passive, as: *We are being bitten by mosquitoes.* In Spanish this would be put in the active: **Los mosquitos nos pican.**

As a rule the passive is not used in Spanish if it can be easily avoided.

Situation Material — The Bathroom:

baño, bath; **cuarto de baño,** bathroom	**tina (de baño),** (bath)tub
bañar(se), to bathe	**lavatorio,** lavatory
palangana, wash basin	**toalla,** towel **el jabón,** soap
agua caliente, hot water	**ducha,** shower

Quisiera tomar un baño. ¿ Se puede? I'd like to take a bath. May I?

Sí, señor. En el cuarto piso hay baño con agua caliente. Yes. On the fourth floor there's a bath with hot water.

¿ Puedo bañarme allí? Can I bathe there?

¿ Cómo no? Suba Ud. El baño está al fondo del corredor. Sure. Just go up. The bathroom is at the end of the hall.

Mozo, el agua no está caliente. Porter, the water is not hot.

Espere un momento, señor. Yo sé lo que es. Wait a moment. I know what's the matter.

Ahora, señor, el baño está dispuesto. Now, sir, the bath is ready.

¡ Qué lástima que esta pensión no tiene baño ! What a pity this boarding house has no bath !

Es así en las pequeñas pensiones y en las posadas. No hay baños. It's
that way in the small boarding houses and inns. There are no baths.

Entonces ¿ qué se hace? Then what does one do?

Hay que lavarse en la habitación. You have to wash in your room.

Generalmente llevan agua caliente a la habitación. Generally they take
hot water to your room.

Pues, es mejor que nada. Well, it's better than nothing.

No se baña tanto aquí como en los Estados Unidos y Inglaterra. People
don't bathe as much here as in the United States and England.

Creo que no. I think not.

EL SOMBRERO DE TRES PICOS   (6)

El tío Lucas era más feo que Picio.[1] Lo había sido toda su vida, y
Uncle Lucas was uglier than Picio.   He had been so all his life, and
ya tenía cerca de cuarenta años. Sin embargo, pocos hombres tan sim-
now he was almost forty years old.   Nevertheless, few men so charming
páticos [2] y agradables habrá echado [3] Dios al mundo. Prendado de su
and   agreeable   can   God   have   given   to   the   world.   Taken   with his
viveza, de su ingenio y de su gracia, el difunto obispo se lo pidió a sus
vivacity, with his cleverness, and with his wit, the deceased bishop asked his parents
padres,[4] que eran pastores, no de almas, sino de verdaderas ovejas.
for   him,   who   were   shepherds,   not   of   souls,   but   of   true   sheep.
Muerto su Ilustrísima, y dejado que hubo [5] el mozo el seminario por
On the death of His Most Illustrious, and (when) the boy had left the seminary for
el cuartel, distinguiólo entre todo su ejército el general Caro, y lo hizo
the barracks, General Caro esteemed him among the whole of his army and made
su ordenanza más íntimo, su verdadero criado de campaña. Cumplido,
him   his   most   intimate   orderly,   his   real   campaign   servant.   Fulfilled,
en fin, el empeño militar,[6] fuéle tan fácil al tío Lucas rendir el corazón
at   last,   the   military   contract,   it   was   as   easy   for   Uncle   Lucas   to   over-

[1] **más feo que Picio,** a figurative and familiar expression meaning *uglier than
sin.* Nobody knows who Picio was.

[2] **simpáticos. Simpático,** literally "sympathetic," is usually translated *charming,* but there is no exact translation — it is something between *likable* and
lovable.

[3] **habrá echado,** future perfect of **echar,** *to throw,* which has been called a
general-purpose verb. The tense expresses speculation (see p. 134)

[4] **se lo pidió a sus padres. Se** means *for himself* (the bishop); **pedir** means
to ask for: we ask for something *from* or *of* a person, but in Spanish the preposition a is used.

[5] **y dejado que hubo.... Que** sometimes means *as;* the verb is **hubo
dejado,** *had left* — the two parts of the verb are not only separated by another
word but are put in reverse order — an unusual literary device.

[6] **Cumplido... el empeño militar.** If you have studied Latin, you will
recognize here the Spanish equivalent of the "ablative absolute" (*the military
contract having been fulfilled*)

de la señora Frasquita, como fácil le había sido captarse el aprecio del
throw Sra. Frasquita's heart, as it had been easy for him to capture the esteem of the
general y del prelado. La navarra, que tenía a la sazón veinte abriles,[1]
general and of the prelate. The Navarrese, who at the time was twenty,
y era el ojo derecho de todos los mozos de Estella, algunos de ellos
and was the right eye of all the youths of Estella, some of them
bastante ricos, no pudo resistir a los continuos donaires, a las chistosas
rich enough, could not resist the continuous witticisms, the amusing
ocurrencias,[2] a los ojillos [3] de enamorado mono y a la bufona y constante
remarks, the (dear) little eyes of enamored monkey, and the comical and constant
sonrisa, llena de malicia, pero también de dulzura, de aquel murciano
smile full of wickedness, but also of sweetness, of that Murcian,
tan atrevido, tan locuaz, tan avisado, tan dispuesto, tan valiente y
so daring, so loquacious, so well-informed, so ready, so valiant, and
tan gracioso, que acabó por trastornar el juicio, no sólo a la codiciada
so nice, that he ended by overturning the judgment, not only of the coveted
beldad, sino también a su padre y a su madre.
beauty, but also of her father and mother.

§ 2. *Reflexive Verbs — Situation Material: Going to Bed — El Sombrero de Tres Picos* (7)

REFLEXIVE VERBS. In §1 of this lesson you have learned how the
reflexive form of the verb is used as a substitute for the passive.
Now we shall go into the subject of reflexive verbs more thoroughly.

There is no occasion to speak of "reflexive verbs" in English.
An English "reflexive verb" would be just a verb with a reflexive
pronoun as object, as "I *cut myself*." The problem for the student
of Spanish is that there are some Spanish verbs which, always or
sometimes, take a reflexive pronoun as object although the English
equivalent is a verb or verb phrase without any object pronoun.
This can be made clear by examples:

atreverse (a), *to dare (to)* — atreverse is a reflexive verb, but *to dare*
    is just an ordinary verb, which is not followed by a reflexive
    pronoun.

irse, *to go away* — irse is the reflexive form of ir, *to go,* but *to go away*
    is just an ordinary verb phrase.

[1] veinte abriles, *twenty Aprils.* This expression is often used in giving the
age of young women. Tiene dieciséis abriles. *She is sweet sixteen.*

[2] ocurrencia, literally "happening," but often used, as here, to mean "bright
idea" or "clever remark."

[3] ojillos. Ojillo is the diminutive of ojo, *eye.* Diminutives usually express
affection; hence "the (dear) little eyes."

Atreverse is one of the few Spanish verbs that exist only in the reflexive form. Usually a verb may be reflexive or not reflexive — but with different meanings. Thus: **ir,** *to go;* **irse,** *to go away;* **ver,** *to see;* **verse,** *to be seen, to show, to be obvious;* **levantar,** *to raise, get . . . up;* **levantarse,** *to rise, get up.*

There may even be three forms of the verb — active, neutral, and reflexive. **Dar,** for example, has certain meanings as an active verb, other meanings as a neutral verb (with no object), and still other meanings as a reflexive verb. The Appleton-Century dictionary gives "**dar,** *va.* . . . **dar,** *vn.* . . . **dar,** *vr.* (**darse**) . . ."

There are no special forms for a reflexive verb; it is just a matter of using the verb with a reflexive pronoun as object. Thus:

(yo) me baño, I bathe	**(yo) me levanté,** I got up
él se baña, he bathes	**él se levantó,** he got up
nos bañamos, we bathe	**nos levantamos,** we got up
ellos se bañan, they bathe	**ellos se levantaron,** they got up

Study the following verbs with their meanings as nonreflexive and as reflexive verbs:

acostar, to put to bed; **acostarse,** to go to bed (*put oneself to bed*)

alegrar, to gladden; **alegrarse,** to be glad, rejoice (**de,** *of, at*)

acordar, (*va.*) to remind, (*vn.*) to agree; **acordarse,** to come to an agreement; **acordarse de,** to remember

dormir, to sleep; **dormirse,** to go to sleep, fall asleep

engañar, to deceive; **engañarse,** to deceive oneself, to make a mistake

equivocar, to mistake; **equivocarse,** to be mistaken

hacer, to make, to do; **hacerse,** to become

morir, to die; **morirse,** to be dying, to die

reír, to laugh; **reírse de,** to laugh at

olvidar *or* **olvidarse de,** to forget

sentar, to seat; **sentarse,** to sit down, be seated, take a seat

Now study the following sentences until you understand the grammatical construction and have the feeling of the Spanish reflexive verb:

No se sabe la fecha. The date is not known.

¿ **Qué se debe hacer ?** What ought to be done?

¿ **Se permite entrar ?** May one enter?

¿ **Cómo se llama Ud. ?** What is your name? ("How do you call yourself?")

Me acosté temprano anoche.   I went to bed early last night.

Me alegro mucho de eso.   I am very glad of that.

No puedo acordarme de la dirección.   I can't remember the address.

¿ Se acuerda Ud. de mí?   Do you remember me?

La gente se baña en el río.   The people bathe in the river.

El pobre no puede levantarse, y yo no puedo levantarlo.   The poor fellow can't get up, and I can't get him up.

Ud. se engaña.   You are making a mistake.

Mi hijo quiere hacerse médico.   My son wants to be a physician.

El perro se muere de hambre.   The dog is dying of hunger.

Se rieron de mí.   They laughed at me.

No voy a olvidarme de eso.   I am not going to forget that.

Siéntase Ud.   Won't you sit down?

Se acordaron pronto.   They soon came to an agreement.

¿ Cómo se atreve Ud. a decir eso?   How do you dare to say that?

No me atrevería a hacerlo.   I wouldn't dare to do it.

El dolor se ha ido.   The pain has gone (away).

Ya se ve que es verdad.   It is clear that it is true.

El remiendo no se vió.   The patch didn't show.

No me he sentado todo el día.   I have not sat down all day.

Some confusion may be caused by the fact that in English we may have a choice of whether or not to use the reflexive pronoun — *I wash* or *I wash myself*. There is no such choice in Spanish as a rule; it must be **me lavo.** (There are a few such choices in Spanish, as between **morir** and **morirse.**)

Another possible source of confusion derives from the fact that the pronouns *myself, yourself*, etc., may be either reflexive or intensive. For example:

Intensive: **Yo mismo lo vi.**   I myself saw it.
Reflexive: **Yo me vi en el espejo.**   I saw myself in the mirror.

This is a good place to mention a certain peculiarity of Spanish. When the object of a verb is a part of the body or an article of clothing, the idiom is as follows:

Me lavo la cara.   I wash my face.   ("I wash for myself the face.")

Se lavan la cara.   They wash their faces.   ("They wash for themselves the face.")

Me lavé la camisa.   I washed my shirt.

Situation Material — Going to Bed:

cansar, to tire; **cansarse,** to get tired; **estar cansado,** to be tired
acostarse, to go to bed; **estar acostado,** to be in bed
sábana, sheet   **manta, frazada,** blanket
dormido, asleep (*for* **dormir, -se,** *see page 144*)   **soñoliento,** sleepy
tener sueño, to be sleepy; **dar sueño,** to make sleepy
soñar (con), to dream (of)

Estoy muy cansado. Voy a acostarme. I am very tired. I'm going to bed.
¿ No tiene Ud. sueño? Aren't you sleepy?
Mire, Juan está dormido. Look. John's asleep.
Pues, buenas noches. Well, good night.
Duerma bien. Sleep well.
Que pase buena noche. Have a good night.
Mozo, despiérteme a las siete. Boy, wake me up at seven.
Póngame otra manta en la cama, por favor. Please put another blanket on my bed.
Sí, señor. ¿ Quiere Ud. desayuno? Yes sir. Would you like breakfast?
Sí, por favor. Y téngame preparado el baño. Yes, please. And have my bath ready.
¿ Y puede lustrarme los zapatos? And can you polish my shoes?
Tocaré la timbre. I'll ring the bell.
¿ Cómo puedo llamar a la camarera? How can I call the chambermaid?

Toque dos veces para el mozo y una vez para la camarera. Ring twice for the porter and once for the maid.
¿ A qué hora se puede bajar? When may one come down?
Cuando Ud. quiera. Whenever you like.
Mañana me voy. Téngame preparada la cuenta, por favor. I'm leaving tomorrow. Have my bill ready, please.
¿ A qué hora debo dejar la habitación? What time must I vacate my room?
A mediodía. Bajaremos su equipaje. At noon. We'll take your baggage down.
Aquí tiene Ud. la llave. Here's the key.

EL SOMBRERO DE TRES PICOS   (7)

Lucas era en aquel entonces,[1] **y seguía siendo en la fecha a que nos**
Lucas was at that time, and continued to be on the date to which we
referimos, de pequeña estatura (a lo menos con relación a su mujer),
refer, of small stature (at least in comparison with his wife),

[1] **en aquel entonces.** In this phrase, **entonces,** *then,* an adverb, is used as a noun !

un poco cargado de espaldas, muy moreno, barbilampiño, narigón,
a little heavy in the shoulders, very swarthy, beardless, big-nosed,

orejudo y picado de viruelas.[1] En cambio, su boca era regular y su
flap-eared, and pock-marked.   On the other hand, his mouth was regular and his

dentadura inmejorable. Dijérase que sólo la corteza de aquel hombre
set of teeth unsurpassable.   It might be said that only the outer husk of that man

era tosca y fea; que tan pronto como empezaba a penetrarse dentro de
was uncouth and ugly;   so that as soon as (one) began to penetrate inside of

él aparecían sus perfecciones, y que estas perfecciones principiaban
him,   his   perfections   appeared,   and   these   perfections   began   with

en los dientes.   Luego venía la voz, vibrante, elástica, atractiva;
his   teeth.   Soon   came   the   voice,   vibrant,   elastic,   attractive;

varonil y grave algunas veces, dulce y melosa cuando pedía algo, y
manly and grave sometimes, sweet and honeyed when he asked for something, and

siempre difícil de resistir. Llegaba después lo que aquella voz decía:
always difficult to resist.   Afterwards arrived what that voice was saying:

todo oportuno, discreto, ingenioso, persuasivo. . . . Y, por último, en
everything opportune,   discreet,   clever,   persuasive. . . .   And,   finally,   in

el alma del tío Lucas había valor, lealtad, honradez, sentido común,
the soul of Uncle Lucas there was valor, loyalty, honor, common sense,

deseo de saber y conocimientos instintivos o empíricos de muchas cosas,
desire to know and knowledge,   instinctive or empirical,   of many things,

profundo desdén a los necios, cualquiera [2] que fuese su categoría social,
profound contempt for fools,   whatever might be their social category,

y cierto espíritu de ironía, de burla y de sarcasmo, que le hacían pasar,
and (a) certain spirit of irony, of mockery, and of sarcasm, which made him pass,

a los ojos del académico, por un Don Francisco de Quevedo [3] en bruto.
in the eyes of the academician, for a Don Francisco de Quevedo in the rough.

Tal era por dentro y por fuera el tío Lucas.
Such was, inside and outside, Uncle Lucas.

§ 3. *Irregular Verbs — Classes of Irregularities — Compounds of Irregular
Verbs — Situation Material: At the Post Office — El Sombrero de Tres
Picos* (8)

IRREGULAR VERBS. Regular verbs are those in which there is
never a change in the stem of the verb and in which the endings are

---

[1] **picado de viruelas,** literally "bitten of smallpox."

[2] **cualquiera,** *whatever.* The plural is **cualesquiera.** It is followed by the
subjunctive.

[3] Don Francisco Gómez de Quevedo y Villegas (1580–1645) was one of the
great satirists and wits of the Golden Age (**Siglo de Oro**) of Spanish literature.

the usual ones — that is, those of the model verbs **comprar, vender,** and **vivir.** In irregular verbs the stem changes in certain forms, and there may also be some unusual endings.

As has been explained, orthographic changes do not constitute irregularity. They are merely changes in spelling that are necessary to maintain the regularity of the verb as regards sound. (See pages 126–127.)

The full list of Spanish irregular verbs is formidable (it runs into the hundreds), but such a list includes many rare or uncommon verbs. Such verbs, if met in reading, can be looked up in the dictionary.

In this book, which is not a complete textbook of Spanish, but an introduction to the language for beginners, only the common irregular verbs will be presented.

CLASSES OF IRREGULARITIES. Certain types of irregularities occur so frequently that we might almost speak of "regular irregularities." Among those that recur again and again are the following, which are listed here for reference and will be explained more fully in later sections:

I. CHANGES IN THE STEM:

(A) **E** to **IE:** The **e** of the stem of some –**ar** and –**er** verbs becomes **ie** *when accented* (**cerrar — cierro**).

(B) **O** to **UE:** The **o** of the stem of some –**ar** and –**er** verbs becomes **ue** *when accented* (**mover — muevo**).

(C) **E** to **IE** and **I:** The **e** of the stem of some –**ir** verbs becomes **ie** *when accented* and **i** *when unaccented and followed by certain endings* (**sentir — siento — sintió**).

(D) **O** to **UE** and **U:** The **o** of the stem of –**ir** verbs becomes **ue** *when accented* and **u** *when unaccented and followed by certain endings* (**dormir — duermo — durmió**).

(E) **E** to **I:** The **e** of the stem of some –**ir** verbs becomes **i** *when accented or followed by certain endings* (**pedir — pido — pidió**).

(F) **C** to **ZC:** In some verbs ending in –**cer** or –**cir**, the **c** becomes **zc** *before* **o** *or* **a** (**conocer — conozco; lucir — luzca**). (See page 127.)

(G) **U** to **UY:** In verbs ending in –**uir** (except for –**guir** and -**quir**, in which **u** is silent), **u** becomes **uy** *when accented or followed by certain endings* (**huir — huyo — huyó; argüir — arguyo — arguyó**).

(H) **G** added: A number of verbs add **g** to the stem *before the* *endings* **o** or **a.** The forms affected are the first person singular of the present indicative and all of the present subjunctive (**tener — tengo — tenga**).

(I) **E** lost in future tense: In some **–er** and **–ir** verbs the **e** of the infinitive is lost in the future and the conditional (which is derived from the future) (**haber — habré — habría**). The **e** may be replaced by **d** (**poner — pondré — pondría**).

A few other "regular irregularities" in the stem might be listed, but the number of verbs affected is too small to justify listing here.

Note: In some verbs, in addition to changes in the stem, orthographic changes occur; for example: **plegar — pliego — pliegue; torcer — tuerzo; regir — rijo; seguir — sigo.**

II. Irregular Endings:

(A) The past participle may end in **–to** (**escribir — escrito,** *not* **escribido**).

(B) The first person singular, present indicative, of the verbs **ser, estar, dar,** and **ir** ends in **–oy** (**soy, estoy, doy, voy**).

(C) Verbs with irregular stems in the past definite usually have the following endings: 1st pers. sing. **–e;** 3d pers. sing. **–o** (**poder — pude — pudo**).

Other irregular endings are too uncommon to be listed here.

Compounds of Irregular Verbs. A compound verb (a verb with a prefix) is conjugated like the basic verb. For example, **componer,** meaning *to put together, to compose, to repair, mend, "fix,"* is conjugated like **poner,** *to put:*

pongo	pondré	puse	puesto
compongo	compondré	compuse	compuesto

Situation Material — At the Post Office:

correo, mail; **echar al correo,** to mail; **casa,** *or* **oficina, de correos,** post office; **apartado (de correos),** (post office) box   **el buzón,** mailbox

lista de correos, general delivery

cartero, postman, mailman

sello, (SA) **estampilla,** stamp; **s. aéreo (ordinario), e. aérea (ordinaria),** airmail (regular) stamp

tarjeta (postal), (post)card

impresos, printed matter

asegurar, to insure

giro postal, postal money order

franqueo, postage

ventanilla, window

carta, letter

el paquete, package

certificar, to register

lacrar, to seal (*with wax*)

señas, (*written*) address

enviar, mandar, remitir, to send; **el remitente,** the sender
destinatario, addressee **la identificación**

¿ Hay correo para mí? Is there mail for me?

¿ Hay un buzón (cerca de) aquí? Is there a mailbox (near) here?

Dígame, por favor, cómo se va a la casa de correos. Please tell me how to get to the post office.

¿ Es aquél el edificio de correos? Is that the post office building?

¿ Qué es el franqueo para una tarjeta a los Estados Unidos, por correo aéreo? What is the postage for a postcard to the U. S., by air mail?

¿ Cuánto costará esta carta por correo aéreo? ¿ Y ordinario? What will this letter cost by air mail? And by regular mail?

Seis sellos aéreos de a veinticinco centavos, y diez ordinarios de a diez. Six twenty-five-centavo air-mail stamps and ten regular ten-centavo stamps.

¿ Cuánto tardará (en llegar) esta carta? How long will this letter take (to arrive)?

Favor de certificar esta carta. Please register this letter.

¿ Qué es la tarifa mínima de certificado? What is the minimum fee for registration?

Este paquete debe ser asegurado. This package is to be insured.

Este paquete tiene impresos, no más. This package contains printed matter — nothing else.

¿ Dónde está la ventanilla de poste restante? Where is the general delivery window?

Deseo un giro postal. I want a postal money order.

Quisiera alquilarme un apartado. I'd like to rent a box.

EL SOMBRERO DE TRES PICOS (8)

Amaba, pues, locamente la señora Frasquita al tío Lucas, y con-
Señora Frasquita, then, madly loved Uncle Lucas, and considered
siderábase la mujer más feliz del mundo al verse adorada por él. No
herself the happiest woman in the world to see herself adored by him. They
tenían hijos, según que ya sabemos, y habíase consagrado cada uno a
had no children, as we already know, and each one was consecrated to caring
cuidar y mimar al otro con esmero indecible, pero sin que aquella tierna
for and pampering the other with indescribable attention, but without that tender
solicitud ostentase el carácter sentimental y empalagoso, por lo zalamero,
solicitude showing the sentimental and cloying character, in the fawning,
de casi todos los matrimonios sin sucesión. Al contrario: tratábanse
of nearly all married couples without issue. On the contrary: they treated each

con una llaneza, una alegría, una broma y una confianza semejantes a
other with a frankness, a happiness, a jocularity, and a confidence similar to
las de aquellos niños, camaradas de juegos y diversiones, que se
those of those children, comrades in games and diversions, who love
quieren [1] con todo el alma sin decírselo jamás, ni darse a sí mismos
each other with all their soul(s), without ever saying so, or taking
cuenta de [2] lo que sienten.
account of what they feel.

¡Imposible que haya habido sobre la tierra molinero mejor peinado,
Impossible that there has (ever) been on the earth (a) miller better combed,
mejor vestido, más regalado en la mesa, rodeado de más comodidades
better clothed, more regaled at the table, surrounded by more comforts
en su casa, que el tío Lucas! ¡Imposible que ninguna molinera ni
in his home, than Uncle Lucas! Impossible that any miller's wife or
ninguna reina haya sido objeto de tantas atenciones, de tantos agasajos,
any queen should have been (the) object of so many attentions, so many kindnesses,
de tantas finezas como la señora Frasquita! ¡Imposible también que
so many courtesies as Sra. Frasquita! Impossible also that
ningún molino haya encerrado tantas cosas necesarias, útiles, agrada-
any mill should have held so many necessary, useful, agreeable,
bles, recreativas y hasta supérfluas, como el que va a servir de teatro
amusing, and even superfluous things, as that which is going to serve as theatre
a casi toda la presente historia!
(stage) for nearly all the present history!

Contribuía mucho a ello que la señora Frasquita, la pulcra, hacendosa,
It contributed much to it that Sra. Frasquita, the neat, hard-working,
fuerte y saludable navarra, sabía, quería, y podía guisar, coser, bordar,
strong, and healthy Navarrese, knew how to, loved to, and could prepare food, sew, em-
barrer, hacer dulces, lavar, planchar, blanquear la casa, fregar el cobre,
broider, sweep, make sweets, wash, iron, whitewash the house, burnish the copper,
amasar, tejer, hacer media,[3] cantar, bailar, tocar la guitarra y los pa-
knead, weave, make stockings, sing, dance, play the guitar and castanets,
lillos, jugar a la brisca y al tute, y otras muchísimas cosas cuya relación
play brisca and tute,[4] and very many other things the account of
fuera interminable.
which would be interminable.

[1] **se quieren.** You are familiar with **querer** as meaning *to wish, want;* it
also means *to love.*

[2] **darse cuenta de,** a common idiom: *to take account of, be aware of, notice.*

[3] **hacer media.** Except in this idiom, **media** is used in the plural: **medias,**
stockings.

[4] **brisca, tute:** card games.

§ 4. *Irregular Verbs with Change of* **E** *to* **IE** — *Change of* **O** *to* **UE** — *ANDAR, DAR, ESTAR, JUGAR* — *Situation Material: Drinking* — *El Sombrero de Tres Picos* (9)

IRREGULAR VERBS WITH CHANGE OF **E** TO **IE**. In a considerable number of –ar and –er verbs the **e** of the stem changes to **ie** *when it is accented*. Here is a synopsis of a typical verb with change of **e** to **ie**:

CERRAR, to shut, close   cerrando   cerrado

Imperative: **cierra, cerrad**

INDICATIVE:

Present: **cierro, cierras, cierra; cerramos, cerráis, cierran**
Imperfect: **cerraba,** *etc.* (*regular*)
Past Definite: **cerré,** *etc.* (*regular*)
Future: **cerraré,** *etc.* (*regular*)

CONDITIONAL: **cerraría,** *etc.* (*regular*)

SUBJUNCTIVE:

Present: **cierre, cierres, cierre; cerremos, cerréis, cierren**
Past: **cerrase,** *etc.;* **cerrara,** *etc.* (*regular*)
Future: **cerrare,** *etc.* (*regular*)

You see that the irregularity occurs only in the present tense, indicative and subjunctive, and in the singular of the imperative.

Some of the other verbs with change of **e** to **ie** are:

calentar, to warm, heat
COMENZAR, EMPEZAR, to begin, start (**a,** to)
confesar, to confess
despertar(se), to wake (up), (a)waken
gobernar, to govern
helar, to freeze
manifestar, to manifest, show, declare

negar, to deny; **–se a,** to refuse to
nevar, to snow
PENSAR, to intend, think (**de, en,** of)
plegar, to fold, bend
QUEBRAR, to break
recomendar, to recommend
SENTAR, to seat; **–SE,** to sit (down)

ascender, to ascend, rise, go up
atender, to attend, pay attention (**a,** to)
contender, to contend, struggle
defender, to defend

descender, to descend, go down
entender, to understand *
perder, to lose, miss (*not see*)
tender(se), extender(se), to extend, stretch (out)

* **Entender** is the common word for *understand:* **No entiendo a Ud.** I don't understand you. ¿ **Me entiende Ud.?** Do you understand me? But: **No comprendo sus ideas.** I don't understand his ideas.

There are orthographic changes (before **e**) in some of these verbs. Note the following present subjunctive forms: **comience, empiece, niegue, pliegue.**

The change of stem vowel is seen in nouns and adjectives derived from some of these verbs, as: **caliente**, *warm, hot;* **comienzo**, *beginning;* **gobierno**, *government;* **manifiesto**, *manifesto;* **nieve**, *snow;* **pliegue**, *fold;* **quiebra**, *break, crack;* **siento**, *seat;* **contienda**, *contest, struggle;* **tienda**, *tent, shop, store.* All these words could also be verb forms. The context indicates whether such a form is a verb or not.

CHANGE OF **O** TO **UE**. In many −**ar** and −**er** verbs the **o** of the stem changes to **ue** *when accented.* Here are the forms of an −**ar** and an −**er** verb, showing the irregularity:

COSTAR, to cost
Imperative: **cuesta, costad**
Pres. Indic.: **cuesto, cuestas, cuesta; costamos, costáis, cuestan**
Pres. Subj.: **cueste, cuestes, cueste; costemos, costéis, cuesten**
(All other forms regular)

MOVER, to move (*something*); **MOVERSE,** to move (*oneself*)
Imperative: **mueve, moved**
Pres. Indic.: **muevo, mueves, mueve; movemos, movéis, mueven**
Pres. Subj.: **mueva, muevas, mueva; movamos, mováis, muevan**
(All other forms regular)

Other verbs with change of **o** to **ue:**

ACORDAR, to remind; −**SE,** to agree; −**SE DE,** to remember
ACOSTAR, to put to bed; −**SE,** to go to bed, lie down
ALMORZAR, to (eat) lunch
COCER, to boil, to cook
colgar, to hang
concordar, to agree
consolar, to console, comfort
CONTAR, to count, to relate
DOLER, to ache, hurt
ENCONTRAR, to find, meet, come upon
forzar, to force
LLOVER, to rain

morder, to bite
oler, to smell (**a**, of, like); where **ue** is used, it becomes **hue,** since in Spanish a word never begins with **ue** (**huele,** smells)
PROBAR, to try, to prove
RECORDAR, to remind, to recall; −**SE DE,** to remember
resolver,* to resolve, to solve; −**se a,** to resolve to
ROGAR, to pray, beg
SOLER, to be accustomed *or* wont to (**suele llover,** it usually rains)
sonar, to sound
SOÑAR, to dream (**con,** of)

* **Resolver** has an irregular past participle: **resuelto.**

torcer, to twist, turn

tronar, to thunder

VOLAR, to fly

VOLVER,* to turn, to return, come *or* go back; V. A, to . . . again

Remember the orthographic changes. Note the following forms: (**-ar** verbs) **almuerce, cuelgue, fuerce, niegue;** (**-er** verbs) **cuezo, tuerzo, huelo.**

Related nouns include: **acuerdo,** *agreement,* accord (**de a.,** *agreed*); **almuerzo,** *lunch;* **consuelo,** *consolation;* **cuenta,** *account, bill;* **encuentro,** *encounter;* **fuerza,** *force;* **prueba,** *trial, proof;* **recuerdo,** *remembrance* (**recuerdos a,** *regards to*); **ruego,** *prayer, plea;* **sueño,** *sleep, dream;* **trueno,** *thunder;* **vuelo,** *flight;* **duelo,** *sorrow, grief;* **vuelta,** *turn.* These could all be verb forms.

ANDAR, DAR, ESTAR, JUGAR: These are the only **-ar** verbs with irregularities that are not "regular." Only the irregular forms are given below:

ANDAR, to walk, go, ride (*in car*), (*of machine*) run

Past Definite: **anduve, anduviste, anduvo; -imos, -isteis, -ieron** (*as if* **-er** *or* **-ir** *verb*)

Derived Subjunctive Forms: **anduviese, anduviera, anduviere,** *etc.* (*the endings are those of* **-er** *and* **-ir** *verbs*)

DAR, to give (*has various meanings in many idioms*)

Present Indicative: **doy, das, da; damos, dais, dan**

Present subjunctive is regular, but **dé** has orthographic accent, to distinguish it from preposition **de.**

Past Definite: **di, diste, dió; dimos, disteis, dieron** (*as if* **-er** *or* **-ir** *verb*)

Derived Subjunctives: **diese, diera, diere,** *etc.* (*endings of* **-er** *and* **-ir** *verbs*)

ESTAR: see pages 130–132.

JUGAR, to play (*the only verb in which* **u** *changes to* **ue**)

Imperative: **juega, jugad**

Present Indicative: **juego, juegas, juega; jugamos, jugáis, juegan**

Present Subjunctive: **juegue, juegues, juegue; juguemos, juguéis, jueguen**

SITUATION MATERIAL — DRINKING:

tener sed, to be thirsty

beber, to drink (*but* **tomar,** to take, *is usually used*); **bebida,** drink

* **Volver** has an irregular past participle: **vuelto.**

trago, copita, drink, "shot"; **traguito,** little drink

Of a drink: **caliente,** hot; **fría,** cold; **helada,** iced; **(no) alcohólica,** (non)alcoholic

vaso, glass   **copa,** (wine)glass   **taza,** cup

botella, bottle; **botellón,** large bottle; **embotellado,** bottled

agua, water; **agua mineral,** mineral water

la leche, milk (**pasteurizada,** pasteurized)   **la té,** tea

el café, coffee, café; **café con leche,** coffee with milk (*hot milk and coffee essence,* **esencia**); **café americano,** American-style coffee; **café negro,** black coffee; **cafecito,** demitasse

el chocolate, chocolate (**merengado,** whipped)

gaseosa, soft drink (*carbonated*)   **limonada,** lemonade

jugo (*Sp.* **zumo**) **de naranja, toronja, piña,** orange, grapefruit, pineapple juice

cerveza, beer (**clara,** light); **c. negra,** ale; **c. de presión,** draught beer

vino, wine (**blanco,** white; **tinto,** red)   **el jerez,** sherry

el whiskey   **el ron,** rum   **ginebra,** gin   **el licor,** liqueur

el aguardiente, brandy   **el coctel,** cocktail   **soda**

hielo, ice   **seco,** dry   **aperitivo,** apéritif

Tengo mucha sed. Quisiera un vaso de agua. I'm very thirsty. I'd like a glass of water.

El agua es para bañarse. Es mejor no tomar el agua aquí a menos que tenga Ud. pastillas para purificarla. Water is for bathing. You'd better not drink the water here unless you have tablets to purify it.

Pero hay agua embotellada, leche pasteurizada, Coca Cola y otras gaseosas. But there is bottled water, pasteurized milk, Coca Cola, and other soft drinks.

Voy a probar la cerveza del país. ¿Qué es la mejor marca? I'm going to try the domestic beer. What is the best brand?

Traíganos un botellón de Carta Blanca. Y para mí, una cajetilla de Elegantes. Bring us a large bottle of Carta Blanca. And for me a pack of Elegantes.

¡Qué bueno que este bar es airecondicionado; hace mucho calor afuera! I'm glad this bar is air-conditioned; it's very hot outside.

Tienen una lista muy larga de bebidas. Me parece que tienen todos los cocteles que tenemos en Nueva York. They have a very long list of drinks. It looks to me as if they have all the cocktails we have in New York.

Sí, los bares son internacionales. Yes, bars are international.

¿Tomamos una copita? Shall we have a little drink?

¿Quiere Ud. un trago? Would you like a drink?

Cuidado con los tragos en esta altitud, porque un trago va por dos. Be careful with your drinks in this altitude, because one drink has the effect of two drinks.

**Gracias, que no quiero emborracharme. . . . Me siento un poco (a)chis-
pado ahora.** Thanks, because I don't want to get drunk. I feel a little
tipsy now.

Aquel tipo ha tomado demasiado. Está bien borracho. That guy has
had too much. He's good and drunk.

**Con permiso de Ud., quiero escribir una tarjeta. A ver si puedo escri-
bir.** If you'll excuse me, I want to write a post card. Let's see if I can
write.

EL SOMBRERO DE TRES PICOS (9)

Y contribuía no menos al mismo resultado el que el tío Lucas sabía,
And it contributed no less to the same result that Uncle Lucas knew how to,
quería y podía dirigir la molienda, cultivar el campo, cazar, pescar,
liked to, and was able to manage the milling, cultivate the field, hunt, fish,
trabajar de carpintero, de herrero, de albañil, ayudar a su mujer en
work as carpenter, as blacksmith, as mason, help his wife in
todos los quehaceres [1] de la casa, leer, escribir, contar, etc., etc.
all the chores of the house, read, write, count, etc., etc.

Y esto sin hacer mención de los ramos de lujo, o sea de sus habilidades
And (all) this without making mention of the finer branches, that is, of his ex-
extraordinarias. . . .
traordinary accomplishments. . . .

Por ejemplo: el tío Lucas adoraba las flores (lo mismo que su mujer),
For example: Uncle Lucas adored flowers (the same as his wife)
y era floricultor tan consumado, que había conseguido producir ejem-
and was so consummate a floriculturist that he had succeeded in producing new
plares [2] nuevos, por medio de laboriosas combinaciones. Tenía algo
varieties by means of laborious combinations. He had something
de ingeniero natural, y lo había demostrado construyendo una presa,
of (the) natural engineer, and had demonstrated it (in) building a dam,
un sifón y un acueducto que triplicaron el agua del molino. Había
a siphon, and an aqueduct which tripled the water of the mill. He had
enseñado a bailar a un perro, domesticado una culebra, y hecho que
taught a dog to dance, domesticated a snake, and made
un loro diese la hora por medio de gritos, según las iba marcando un
a parrot give the hour by means of cries, as they were marked by a
reloj de sol [3] que el molinero había trazado en una pared; de cuyas
sundial which the miller had traced on a wall; from which

[1] **quehaceres,** plural of **quehacer** (**que,** what, **hacer,** to do).
[2] **ejemplares,** *varieties:* literally "examples."
[3] **según las iba marcando un reloj de sol:** literally, "as they (**horas**) went marking a sun-clock." The verb is active though it has to be passive in translation. Note **iba** used as an auxiliary verb; **ir** and **venir** are sometimes used
in this way.

resultas el loro daba ya la hora con toda precisión, hasta en los dias
results   the   parrot   gave   the   time   with   all   precision,   even   on   cloudy

nublados y durante la noche.
days and during the night.

Finalmente: en el molino había una huerta que producía toda clase
Finally: at the mill there was a garden which produced every class

de frutas y legumbres; un estanque encerrado en una especie de kiosco
of   fruits   and   vegetables;   a   closed-in   pool   in   a   kind   of   kiosk

de jazmines, donde se bañaban en verano el tío Lucas y la señora
of jasmins, where Uncle Lucas and Sra. Frasquita bathed in summer;

Frasquita; un jardín; una estufa o invernadero para las plantas exó-
a   flower   garden;   a   stove   or   hothouse   for   the   exotic   plants;

ticas; una fuente de agua potable; dos burras en que el matrimonio
a fountain of drinking water; two donkeys on which the married couple

iba a la ciudad o a los pueblos de las cercanías; gallinero, palomar,
went to the city or the towns of the neighborhood; chicken run, pigeon house,

pajarera, criadero de peces; [1] y muchas otras cosas. . . .
aviary, fish nursery; and many other things. . . .

---

§ 5. *Irregular Verbs with Change of* C *to* ZC — *Some Common Irregular*
-ER *Verbs* — *Situation Material:* Eating (1) — *El Sombrero de Tres*
Picos (10)

IRREGULAR VERBS WITH CHANGE OF C TO ZC. In most verbs that
end in −cer or −cir, *preceded by a vowel*, the c changes to zc before
o or a. (See page 127.) The change occurs only in the present
tense. Here is a synopsis of the conjugation of two typical verbs
of this class:

Infin.:	CONOCER, to know, be ac- quainted with	LUCIR, to shine
Parts.:	conociendo conocido *	luciendo lucido
Imper.:	conoce, conoced	luce, lucid

INDIC.:

Pres.:	conozco, conoces, *etc.*	*luzco,* luces, *etc.*
Imperf.:	conocía, *etc. (reg.)*	lucía, *etc. (reg.)*
Past Def.:	conocí, *etc. (reg.)*	lucí, *etc. (reg.)*
Fut.:	conoceré, *etc. (reg.)*	luciré, *etc. (reg.)*

[1] gallinero . . . criadero. The endings −ero and −era indicate a place; the
−ar of palomar means a collection, here of palomas.

* Conocido as noun means *acquaintance* (person)

COND.:   **conocería,** *etc.* (*reg.*)   **luciría,** *etc.* (*reg.*)

SUBJ.:

Pres.:   *conozca, etc.*   *luzca, etc.*
Past: **conociese, –iera,** *etc.* (*reg.*)   **luciese, –iera,** *etc.* (*reg.*)
Fut.:   **conociere,** *etc.* (*reg.*)   **luciere,** *etc.* (*reg.*)

Compounds: **desconocer,** *not to recognize, to disregard, disown, snub;*
         reconocer, *to recognize, to inspect, reconnoiter.*

Exceptions: **cocer,** *to cook:* **cuezo, cueza**
         escocer, *to smart:* **escuezo, escueza**
         mecer, *to stir, rock, swing:* **mezo, meza**
         Hacer, decir, yacer have other irregularities.

SOME COMMON IRREGULAR –ER VERBS. The following irregular –er verbs have their individual peculiarities. Only the irregular forms are given.

HABER: See pages 132–133.

CABER, to fit, *or* go, into (see examples, below)

INDICATIVE:

Present: **quepo, cabes,** *etc.*
Past Definite: **cupe, cupiste, cupo; cupimos, cupisteis, cupieron**
Future: **cabré,** *etc.*

CONDITIONAL: **cabría,** *etc.*

SUBJUNCTIVE:

Present: **quepa,** *etc.*
Past: **cupiese,** *etc.;* **cupiera,** *etc.*
Future: **cupiere,** *etc.*

Examples: **No cabemos en el carro.** There's no room for us in
         the car.
         Mis cosas no cabrán en la maleta. My things are
         not going to go into the suitcase.
         Tengo miedo de que las cosas no quepan. I am
         afraid the things won't go in.
         No cabe duda. There's no (room for) doubt.

HEREAFTER, SUBJUNCTIVE AND CONDITIONAL FORMS WILL NOT BE LISTED. THE PRESENT SUBJUNCTIVE IS BASED ON THE STEM OF THE FIRST PERSON SINGULAR, PRESENT INDICATIVE (quep–o: quep–a). THE PAST AND FUTURE SUBJUNCTIVES ARE BASED ON THE STEM OF

THE PAST DEFINITE (cup–e: cup–iese, cup–iera, cup–iere). THE
CONDITIONAL IS BASED ON THE STEM OF THE FUTURE (cabr–é:
cabr–ía).

CAER, to fall, befall
Participles: **cayendo, caído** (*orthographic changes; not irregular*)
Present Indicative: **caigo, caes,** *etc.*
The subjunctive forms **cayera,** *etc.,* are not irregular; **ca–iera**
  becomes **cayera** because unaccented **i** between vowels becomes **y**
  (see page 127).
Compounds: **decaer,** *to decay;* **recaer,** *to fall back, relapse.*

HACER, to do, make (has various meanings in many idioms)
Past Participle: **hecho** (also a noun meaning *deed, fact*)
Imperative: **haz, haced**
Present: **hago, haces,** *etc.*
Past Definite: **hice, hiciste, hizo; hicimos, hicisteis, hicieron**
Future: **haré,** *etc.*
Compounds: **deshacer,** *to undo, take apart, destroy;* **rehacer,** *to do*
  again, make over, remodel. **Satisfacer,** *to satisfy,* is conjugated
  like **hacer.**

PODER, to be able, can
Present Participle: **pudiendo**
Present: **puedo, puedes, puede; podemos, podéis, pueden.**
Past Definite: **pude,** *etc.*
Future: **podré,** *etc.*

PONER, to put, place
Past Participle: **puesto** (as noun, means *post, position*)
Imperative: **pon, poned**
Present: **pongo, pones,** *etc.*
Past Definite: **puse,** *etc.*
Future: **pondré,** *etc.*
Compounds: **componer,** *to put together, compose, repair, mend, "fix";*
  disponer, *to dispose, arrange;* **oponer,** *to oppose;* **posponer,** *to*
  postpone, put . . . after; **proponer,** *to propose;* **reponer,** *to replace,*
  restore (past def., **repuse,** *replied*); **suponer,** *to suppose;* and others.

QUERER, to wish, want, love
Past Participles: **querido** (which, as adj. or noun, means *dear,*
  beloved); **quisto** in **bien quisto,** *well liked, beloved;* **mal quisto,**
  disliked

Present: **quiero, –es, –e; queremos, queréis, quieren**
Past Definite: **quise,** *etc.*
Future: **querré,** *etc.*
Compounds: **bienquerer,** *to like well;* **malquerer,** *to dislike*
  (uncommon).

SABER, to know, know how to; **saber a,** to taste of
Present Indicative: **sé, sabes, sabe; sabemos, sabéis, saben**
Present Subjunctive: **sepa,** *etc.* (exceptional; not derived from **sé**)
Past Definite: **supe,** *etc.*
Future: **sabré,** *etc.*

TENER, to have, hold, possess
Imperative: **ten, tened**
Present: **tengo, tienes, tiene; tenemos, tenéis, tienen**
Past Definite: **tuve,** *etc.*
Future: **tendré,** *etc.*
Compounds: **abstenerse (de),** *to abstain (from);* **atenerse (a),**
  to hold (to), rely or *depend (on), abide (by);* **contener,** *to contain,*
  hold; **detener,** *to detain, stop, arrest;* **–se,** *to stop;* **entretener,** *to*
  entertain, amuse, put off; **obtener,** *to obtain, get;* **retener,** *to retain,*
  keep; **sostener,** *to sustain, maintain, support*

TRAER, to bring
Present: **traigo, traes,** *etc.*
Past Definite: **traje,** *etc.* (**traje** as noun: *suit, dress, costume*)
The participles, **trayendo** and **traído,** have orthographic changes,
  but are regular (compare **caer**).
Compounds: **atraer,** *to attract;* **contraer,** *to contract;* **–se,** *to*
  shrink; **distraer,** *to distract, bother, amuse;* **retraer,** *to bring back;*
  su(b)straer, *to subtract, deduct, withdraw;* and others.

VALER, to be worth
Present: **valgo, vales, vale,** *etc.* (a **vale** is an I O U)
Future: **valdré,** *etc.*
Compounds: **equivaler (a),** *to be equivalent (to);* **prevaler,** *to*
  prevail.

VER, to see, view; **VERSE,** to see oneself, find oneself, be obvious
Past Participle: **visto** (**vista,** noun: *sight, view*)
Present: **veo, ves, ve; vemos, veis, ven**
Imperfect: **veía,** *etc.*
Compounds: **prever,** *to foresee;* **rever,** *to review*

SITUATION MATERIAL — EATING (1). There follows a general vocabulary related to eating (and some sentences); then an outline of the Spanish menu. A long list of foods and dishes is presented in the next lesson.

el hambre,* hunger; **hambriento,** hungry; **tener hambre,** to be hungry
apetito, appetite   **alimentos,** food(s)
desayuno, breakfast; **desayunar,** to breakfast, have *or* eat breakfast
almuerzo, lunch; **almorzar,** to lunch, have *or* eat lunch
merienda, el piscolabis, lunch, "snack"; **merendar,** to lunch, have a
   "snack"
comida, dinner, meal, food; **comer,** to eat, dine, have *or* eat dinner; **el
   comedor,** dining room
cena, supper; **cenar,** to have *or* eat supper, sup
el restaurante, –ant, *or* **–án,** restaurant   **el café,** café, lunchroom
lista, menu   **mozo,** waiter; **moza,** waitress
servir, to serve; **servicio,** service   **servilleta,** napkin
mesa, table   **el mantel,** tablecloth
pedir, to order   **traer,** to bring
bastante, enough; **bastar,** to be enough; (**basta,** that's enough)
plato, dish, plate; **plato típico** *or* (SA) **criollo,** native dish
cuchillo, knife   **el tenedor,** fork
cuchara, spoon; **el cucharón,** soup *or* serving spoon; **cucharita,** teaspoon
azucarero, sugar bowl   **salero,** salt cellar
limpio, clean; **sucio,** dirty   **caliente,** hot; **frío,** cold
sabroso, delicious   **dulce,** sweet; **dulces,** candy
agrio, sour   **amargo,** bitter
picante, hot (*biting*)   **salado,** salty
tierno, tender   **verde,** green   **maduro,** ripe
pasado, spoiled   **podrido,** rotten   **duro,** hard, tough, stale
cuenta, bill   **pagar,** to pay (for)
propina, tip   **cajero(–a),** cashier
bodega, tienda de provisiones *or* **comestibles,** (*Mex.*) **el abarrote,** (*P.R.*)
   colmado, grocery (store)
panadería, bakery   **carnicería,** meat market
los víveres, groceries, provisions   **lata,** can; **en lata,** canned

¿Tiene Ud. hambre? Are you hungry?
Mucha. No he comido nada hoy sino un sandwich. ¿Y Ud.? Very.
   I haven't eaten anything but a sandwich today. How about you?
Yo también. ¿Dónde vamos a comer? Me too. Where shall we eat?
Pues, el Café Malagueño está cerca, a dos cuadras más o menos. Well,
   the Café Malagueño is near, about two blocks from here.
Es de los mejores, un poco caro; pero si Ud. quiere probar los platos

* **Hambre** is feminine, but **el,** you know, is used before a feminine noun beginning with accented **a–** or **ha** (as **el agua**).

españoles. . . . It's one of the best, a little expensive; but if you want to try Spanish dishes. . . .

La lista, por favor. The menu, please.

La paella es muy sabrosa. The *paella* is delicious.

¿Tal vez Ud. quiere probar los calamares? Maybe you want to **try** squids?

¿Qué quiere decir calamares? What does *calamares* mean?

¡Calamares en su propia tinta! Creo que no. Otra vez. Squids in their own ink! I think not. Another time.

Traíganos dos platos de paella. Bring us two dishes of *paella*.

Tengo miedo de comer las ensaladas. I am afraid to eat salads.

Las guías avisan a los turistas a no comer ensalada. The guidebooks advise tourists not to eat salad.

Ud. tiene razón. Pero aquí, pierda cuidado. Todo es higiénico, y no hay que temer las amebas. You're right. But here, don't worry. Everything is hygienic, and you don't have to fear amoebas.

Este tenedor está sucio; traígame otro tenedor, por favor. This fork is dirty; please bring me another fork.

Sí, señor; lo siento mucho. Yes sir; I'm very sorry.

¿Quiere un postre? Would you like a dessert?

¡Ay, no! No puedo más. Oh no! I'm stuffed.

Mozo, un flan y dos cafecitos. Waiter, one custard and two demitasses.

Yo pago la cuenta; Ud. puede pagar la próxima vez. I'll pay the bill; you can pay next time.

Gracias, don Pablo. Me he gustado mucho la comida. Thanks, don Pablo, I enjoyed my dinner very much.

THE SPANISH MENU. The Spanish menu does not correspond to the French, British, or American, either in the order of dishes or their nature. What follows is merely a sketch, and it is Spanish, not Spanish-American, although in the main the Spanish-American menu follows the Spanish, with innumerable local dishes added. The Spanish cuisine, according to the famous chef Nicolasa, goes in this order:

(1) **Caldos,** clear soups (broths), *or* **Sopas,** thick soups

(2) **Purés,** purees

(3) **Macarrones,** macaroni, *or* **Arroz,** rice (both in various forms)

(4) **Huevos,** eggs

(5) **Tortillas,** omelets

(6) **Fritos.** fried dishes

(7) **Pescados,** fish, including **Mariscos,** shellfish

(8) **Salsas,** sauces

(9) **Platos de carne,** meat dishes

(10) **Aves y Caza,** fowl and game

(11) **Cocidos o Potajes,** stews

(12) **Verduras,** vegetables

(13) **Asados de carne, ave y caza,** roasts of meat, fowl, and game

(14) **Fiambres,** cold meats   (16) **Helados,** ices

(15) **Compotas,** compotes, pre-   (17) **Repostería,** confectionery
serves

— and **Entremeses,** *hors d'œuvres,* called **Entradas** when they come
at the beginning.

Regarding the fifth item, the Mexican **tortilla** of cornmeal is
not an omelet, but in Mexico you can get an egg omelet by ordering
una tortilla de huevos.

Olives, radishes, and other small items (**entremeses**) accompany
the Spanish **almuerzo** and **comida** and **cena.** And sherry can be
drunk before, with, or after a meal: different kinds of sherry as an
appetizer, to accompany soup and at the end of a meal.

In addition to the above list, there is the regional cookery of
Spain, perhaps not so varied and not so interesting as French
regional cooking, but often very pleasing to strong palates. Garlic
and olive oil, two very healthful foods, enter into the preparation
of most things, if not substantially, then as a flavor or help.

Dishes alter from region to region, from one Spanish-speaking
country to another. Pages could be filled with lists of words and
explanations of dishes. Here only essentials are given. Each
traveler will make his own list, to his taste.

This is just an introduction to the Spanish menu. A vocabulary
of foods and dishes will be found in the next lesson.

EL SOMBRERO DE TRES PICOS   (10)

This is the last selection from **El Sombrero de Tres Picos** that will be
given. The story has not yet got started. This famous tale is interesting
and amusing. Perhaps you would like to complete it — if not in Spanish,
then in English. There are several English translations.

This time, as you see, the translation is not interlinear, but follows the
Spanish. Before reading the translation, see what you can make of the
Spanish text. If you find that you can understand most of it, write out as
full a literal translation as you can; then compare what you have written
with the printed translation. This procedure will serve as a sort of test;
it will give a good indication of how much you have learned so far.

Study your mistakes. Some will be due to carelessness. Some will be
due to unfamiliar or new words and idioms. Some mistakes in interpreting
the grammar may indicate that you need to review certain sections of the
book.

**Adorábanse, sí, locamente el molinero y la molinera, y aun se hubiera
creído que ella lo quería más a él que él a ella, no obstante ser él tan**

feo y ella tan hermosa. Dígolo porque la señora Frasquita solía tener celos [1] y pedirle cuentas al tío Lucas cuando éste tardaba mucho en regresar de la ciudad o de los pueblos adonde iba por grano, mientras que el tío Lucas veía hasta con gusto las atenciones de que era objeto la señora Frasquita por parte de los señores que frecuentaban el molino; se ufanaba y regocijaba de que a todos les agradase tanto como a él; y, aunque comprendía que en el fondo del corazón se la envidiaban algunos de ellos, la codiciaban como simples mortales y hubieran dado cualquier [2] cosa porque [3] fuese menos mujer de bien, la dejaba sola días enteros sin el menor cuidado, y nunca le preguntaba luego qué [4] había hecho ni quién [4] había estado allí durante su ausencia. . . .

No consistía aquello, sin embargo, en que el amor del tío Lucas fuese menos vivo que el de la señora Frasquita. Consistía en que él tenía más confianza en la virtud de ella que ella en la de él; consistía en que él la aventajaba en penetración, y sabía hasta qué punto era amado y cuánto se respetaba su mujer a sí misma; y consistía principalmente en que el tío Lucas era todo un hombre: un hombre como el de Shakespeare. . . .

Era, en fin, un Otelo de Murcia, con alpargatas [5] y montera.[6]

Pero ¿ a qué estas notas lúgubres en una tonadilla [7] tan alegre?

Vais a saberlo inmediatamente.

The miller and his wife indeed adored each other madly, and it might even have been believed that she loved him more than he (did) her, in spite of his being so ugly and she so beautiful. I say so because Sra. Frasquita was wont to be jealous and to ask for an accounting of Uncle Lucas when he was very late in returning from the city or from the towns where he went for grain, while Uncle Lucas viewed even with pleasure the attentions of which Sra. Frasquita was (the) object on the part of the gentlemen who frequented the mill; he was proud and rejoiced that she should please all as much as (she did) him; and, although he understood that in the bottom of (their) heart(s) some of them envied him her (and that) they coveted her as simple mortals and would have given anything that she might be a less honest woman, he left her alone whole days without the least worry and never asked her afterwards what she had done or who had been there during his absence. . . .

[1] **tener celos.** **Celo** means *zeal*, **celos** *jealousy;* **dar celos,** *to make jealous;* **tener celos,** *to be jealous.*

[2] **cualquier.** The word **cualquiera** drops the –a before a noun.

[3] **porque** usually means *because*, is used here for **que.**

[4] **qué, quién.** The orthographic accent on these words is used not only in a direct question but in an indirect or implied question.

[5] **alpargatas,** rope-soled sandals worn by Spanish peasants.

[6] **montera,** for **gorra montera,** *hunter's cap* (**montero,** *mountain (adj.),* *hunter;* from **monte,** *mountain, forest*).

[7] **tonadilla,** diminutive of **tonada,** *tune, song;* a **tonadilla** is also a musical interlude in the theater.

That did not mean, however, that Uncle Lucas's love was less lively than that of Sra. Frasquita. It meant that he had more confidence in her virtue than she in his; it meant that he had the advantage of her in penetration and knew to what point he was loved and how much his wife respected herself; and it meant, chiefly, that Uncle Lucas was a whole man: a man like that of Shakespeare. . . .

He was, in fine, an Othello of Murcia, with sandals and cloth cap.

But why these mournful notes in such a gay little tune?

You are going to know this immediately.

LESSON XII

§ 1. *Irregular –IR Verbs — Situation Material: Eating (2): Breakfast —* **Lazarillo de Tormes** *(1)*

IRREGULAR –**IR** VERBS. If you will glance back at the classification of irregularities on pages 148–149, you will see that all the irregularities listed except for I A and B may apply to –**ir** verbs.*

Let us consider first the types of changes that have already been discussed as occurring in –**ar** and –**er** verbs.

The change of **C** to **ZC** occurs in LUCIR (see page 148). It also occurs in **conducir**, which has an irregular past definite. The verb **ducir**, *to lead*, is obsolete, but the stem occurs in a number of compounds, all conjugated like **conducir**.

CONDUCIR, to conduct, lead
Present Indicative: **conduzco, conduces,** *etc.*
Past Definite: **conduje,** *etc.*
Related verbs: **deducir**, *to deduce, deduct;* **introducir**, *to introduce;* **producir**, *to produce;* **reducir**, *to reduce;* **reproducir**, *to reproduce;* **traducir**, *to translate;* and several others.

The addition of **G** to the stem in the present occurs in the following verbs:

ASIR, to seize, grasp
Present Indicative: **asgo, ases,** *etc.*
The past definite **así** may be confused with **así**, *thus.*

OÍR, to hear
Present Indicative: **oigo, oyes, oye; oímos, oís, oyen**
Note the orthographic changes: (1) **oyes** (for **oi–es**), etc.; (2) accented **í** in **oír, oído, oímos, oí.**
Oído as a noun means (inner) *ear, hearing.* ¡**Oiga**! *Listen! Hey there!* is much used.

SALIR, *to go out, set out, leave,* has the added **g** and also an irregular future:

Present Indicative: **salgo, sales,** *etc.*
Future Indicative: **saldré,** *etc.*

* Two not very common –**ir** verbs do belong in class I A: **concernir**, *to concern*, and **discernir**, *to discern.*

Now we must consider classes I C and D, with the changes
{ E to IE, I
{ O to UE, U   The change to **ie** or to **ue** occurs *when the stem is
accented*. The change to **i** or to **u** occurs *when the unaccented stem is
followed by a "strong" ending* — that is, before endings beginning with
a or **ie** and before the ending –**ió**. It may be easier for you just
to learn the forms affected in the model verbs **sentir** and **dormir.**

SENTIR, to feel, regret, be sorry

Participles: **sintiendo, sentido**
Imperative: **siente, sentid**

INDICATIVE:

Present: **siento, sientes, siente; sentimos, sentís, sienten**
Imperfect: **sentía,** *etc.* (*regular*)
Past Definite: **sentí, sentiste, sintió; sentimos, sentisteis, sintieron**
Future: **sentiré,** *etc.* (*regular*)

CONDITIONAL: **sentiría,** *etc.* (*regular*)

SUBJUNCTIVE:

Present: **sienta, sientas, sienta; sintamos, sintáis, sientan**
Past: **sintiese,** *etc.;* **sintiera,** *etc.*
Future: **sintiere,** *etc.*

In the present tense the forms of this verb may be confused with
those of **sentar;** thus, **sienta** may be from **sentar** (indicative)
or from **sentir** (subjunctive). There are also the nouns **siento,**
seat, and **sentido,** *sense, feeling, meaning.*

Compounds: **asentir,** *to assent* (**en,** *to*); **consentir,** *to allow, accept,
consent* (**en,** *to*); **disentir,** *to dissent, disagree;* **resentirse de** *or*
por, *to resent;* and others.

Conjugated like **sentir** are: **herir,** *to injure;* **hervir,** *to boil;* **mentir,**
to lie (tell a lie); **requerir,** *to require, summon;* and a number of
verbs ending in –**ferir** (as **preferir,** *to prefer*), –**gerir** (as **sugerir,**
to suggest), and –**vertir** (as **divertir,** *to divert, amuse*).

The change of **o** to **ue** and **u** parallels the change of **e** to **ie** and **i.**
That is, *when the stem is accented*, **o** becomes **ue.** The change
of **o** to **u** occurs *when the unaccented stem is followed by a "strong" ending* — that is, before endings beginning with **a** or **ie** and before the
ending –**ió.**

DORMIR, to sleep; –SE, to go to sleep

Participles: **durmiendo, dormido**
Imperative: **duerme, dormid**

INDICATIVE:

Present: **duermo, –es, –e; dormimos, dormís, duermen**
Imperfect: **dormía,** *etc. (regular)*
Past Definite: **dormí, dormiste, durmió; dormimos, dormisteis, durmieron**
Future: **dormiré,** *etc. (regular)*

CONDITIONAL: **dormiría,** *etc. (regular)*

SUBJUNCTIVE:

Present: **duerma, –as, –a; durmamos, durmáis, duerman**
Past: **durmiese,** *etc.;* **durmiera,** *etc.*
Future: **durmiere,** *etc.*

No other common verb is conjugated like **dormir** but **morir,** *to die.* **Morir** has the irregular past participle **muerto.** In compound tenses the verb may mean *murder* (**han muerto al hombre,** *they have murdered,* or *killed, the man,* but **han matado el perro,** *they have killed the dog*). **Estar muerto,** *to be dead.*

Another class of –ir verbs has the change of **E** to **I** *when the stem is accented or when a strong ending follows.* **Pedir** will serve as a model verb of this type.

PEDIR, to ask (for), order

Participles: **pidiendo, pedido** (as noun, means *order*)
Imperative: **pide, pedid**

INDICATIVE:

Present: **pido, pides, pide; pedimos, pedís, piden**
Imperfect: **pedía,** *etc. (regular)*
Past Definite: **pedí, pediste, pidió; pedimos, pedisteis, pidieron**
Future: **pediré,** *etc. (regular)*

CONDITIONAL: **pediría,** *etc. (regular)*

SUBJUNCTIVE:

Present: **pida,** *etc.*
Past: **pidiese,** *etc.;* **pidiera,** *etc.*
Future: **pidiere,** *etc.*

Compounds: **despedir,** *to dismiss,* *"fire";* **impedir,** *to impede, hamper, prevent;* and others.

Some common verbs conjugated like **pedir** are: **colegir,** *to collect, gather;* **corregir,** *to correct;* **elegir,** *to choose, elect;* **freír,** *to fry;* **gemir,** *to groan;* **medir,** *to measure;* **regir,** *to rule;* **reír,** *to laugh;* **sonreír,** *to smile;* **rendir,** *to render, subdue, overcome* [**rendir(se),** *to surrender, yield, give up*]; **reñir,** *to quarrel;* **seguir,** *to follow, go after;* **conseguir,** *to get;* **servir,** *to serve* *; **vestir,** *to dress, wear* (**vestirse,** *to dress oneself*).

Orthographic changes complicate the conjugation of some of these verbs. For example, from **regir: rijo,** *I rule;* from **reír: río,** *I laugh;* from **reñir: riñó,** *he quarreled*; from **seguir: sigo,** *I follow.*

In verbs that end in **–uir** *when the* **u** *is sounded* (i.e., excluding verbs ending in **–guir** or **–quir**) the stem is strengthened by the addition of **Y** *when the stem is accented or is followed by a strong vowel.* The verbs **argüir** and **huir** will serve as models:

ARGÜIR, to argue
Participles: **arguyendo, argüido**
Imperative: **arguye, argüid**

INDICATIVE:

Present: **arguyo, arguyes, arguye; argüimos, argüís, arguyen**
Imperfect: **argüía,** *etc.* (*regular*)
Past Definite: **argüí, argüiste, arguyó; argüimos, argüisteis, arguyeron**
Future: **argüiré,** *etc.* (*regular*)

CONDITIONAL: **argüiría,** *etc.* (*regular*)

SUBJUNCTIVE:

Present: **arguya,** *etc.*
Past: **arguyese,** *etc.;* **arguyera,** *etc.*
Future: **arguyere,** *etc.*

HUIR, to flee, run away
Participles: **huyendo, huido**
Imperative: **huye, huid**

* No **sirve,** *it's no good, it's no use;* **sírvase,** *please.*

INDICATIVE:

Present: **huyo, huyes, huye; huimos, huis, huyen**
Imperfect: **huía,** *etc. (regular)*
Past Definite: **huí, huiste, huyó; huimos, huisteis, huyeron**
Future: **huiré,** *etc. (regular)*

CONDITIONAL: **huiría,** *etc. (regular)*

SUBJUNCTIVE:

Present: **huya,** *etc.*
Past: **huyese,** *etc.;* **huyera,** *etc.*
Future: **huyere,** *etc.*

Conjugated like **huir** are: **atribuir,** *to attribute;* **concluir,** *to conclude;* **construir,** *to construct;* **contribuir,** *to contribute;* **destruir,** *to destroy;* **distribuir,** *to distribute;* **excluir,** *to exclude;* **fluir,** *to flow;* **influir,** *to influence;* **instruir,** *to instruct;* **obstruir,** *to obstruct;* and others.

The following verbs are irregular in various ways:

DECIR, to say, tell
Participles: **diciendo, dicho**
Imperative: **dí, decid**

INDICATIVE:

Present: **digo, dices, dice; decimos, decís, dicen**
Past Definite: **dije,** *etc.*
Future: **diré,** *etc.*
Compounds: **contradecir,** *to contradict;* **desdecir,** *to disagree, be unworthy of,* **–se,** *to retract;* **predecir,** *to predict;* and others. (Compounds have the singular imperative **–dice.**) **Bendecir,** *to bless,* and **maldecir,** *to curse,* have the future **–deciré,** etc. When used as adjectives, the forms **bendito,** *blessed,* and **maldito,** *(ac)cursed,* are used; otherwise the past participles are **bendecido, maldecido.**

IR, to go; **IRSE,** to go away
Participles: **yendo, ido**
Imperative: **ve, id** (**ve** *is also the imperative of* **ver**)

INDICATIVE:

Present: **voy, vas, va; vamos, vais, van** (*as if from* **–ar** *verb*)
Imperfect: **iba, ibas, iba; íbamos, ibais, iban**

Past Definite: **fuí, fuiste, fué; fuimos, fuisteis, fueron** (*same as for* **ser**)

Future: **iré**, *etc.* (*regular*)

SUBJUNCTIVE:

Present: **vaya, vayas, vaya; vayamos, vayáis, vayan**

VENIR, to come

Participles: **viniendo, venido**

Imperative: **ven, venid**

INDICATIVE:

Present: **vengo, vienes, viene; venimos, venís, vienen**

Past Definite: **vine,** *etc.*

Future: **vendré,** *etc.*

SITUATION MATERIAL — EATING (2): BREAKFAST: The typical **desayuno** of Spanish-speaking people is bread and chocolate, or coffee. The bread is often sweet rolls. But North American breakfasts are served wherever there are tourists in sufficient number. Here is a vocabulary of what North Americans eat for breakfast:

jugo (*Sp.* **zumo**) **de naranja** (**toronja, tomate**), orange (grapefruit, tomato) juice

el melón, melon   **papaya, lechosa,** (*Cuba*) **fruta bomba,** papaya

el pan, bread (**blanco,** white, **negro,** brown); **pan dulce,** sweet bread (rolls); **pan tostado,** toasted bread (**tostadas,** toast)

panecillo, roll   **mantequilla,** butter

jalea, jelly   **conserva,** preserves   **mermelada,** marmalade

huevos, eggs (**fritos,** fried, **revueltos,** scrambled, **pasados por agua,** soft-boiled)

                                                tocino, bacon

el jamón, ham   **lonja,** slice (*of meat*)

café, coffee (see page 155)   **el azúcar,** sugar

crema, cream (to order coffee with cream, order **café americano**)

Quisiera jugo de naranja, tostadas, huevos revueltos y café. I'd like orange juice, toast, scrambled eggs, and coffee.

Yo quiero pan dulce y chocolate. I want sweet rolls and chocolate.

¿ **Hay café americano? Entonces café con leche, la leche bien hervida.** Is there American-style coffee? Then coffee with milk, the milk well boiled.

¿ **Mozo, puede traerme un diario?** Waiter, can you bring me a paper?

¿ **Cuál quiere Ud.?** What one do you want? **Cualquiera. Es indiferente.** Any one. It doesn't matter.

¿ **A qué hora se puede almorzar?** At what hour may one have lunch?

CONTINUOUS READING. In this lesson you will read the beginning of the famous picaresque novel **La Vida de Lazarillo de Tormes,** published in Burgos in 1554. The identity of the author is unknown, though some scholars have attributed the book to Diego Hurtado de Mendoza. The novel is recognized as a work of genius and is written in a straightforward, pungent style that is not without occasional difficulties but is just as fresh as it ever was.

When we think of the difference between the English of Shakespeare and our present-day English, it is surprising to find that **Lazarillo de Tormes,** published ten years before Shakespeare and Cervantes were born, can be easily understood by anybody who has a good knowledge of modern Spanish. Castilian had reached maturity before the **Siglo de Oro,** the Golden Age of Spanish literature.

LAZARILLO DE TORMES   (1)

Cuenta Lázaro su vida y cuyo hijo fué.
Lázaro tells of his life and whose son he was.

Pues sepa V. M.[1] ante todas cosas que a mí llaman Lázaro de Tormes,
Then know, Your Honor, before all (other) things that they call me Lázaro de

hijo de Tomé González y de Antonia Pérez, naturales de Tejares, aldea
Tormes, son of Tomé (Tom) González and Antonia Pérez, natives of Tejares, (a) vil-

de Salamanca.[2] Mi nacimiento fué dentro del río Tormes, por lo cual
lage of Salamanca. My birth was within the River Tormes, for which

tomé el sobrenombre, y fué de esta manera. Mi padre, que Dios
I took the surname, and it was in this manner. My father, whom God

perdone, tenía cargo de proveer una molienda de una azeña, que está
pardon, had charge of providing meal from a water-mill, which is (on the)

ribera de aquel río, en la cual fué molinero más de quince años. Y
bank of that river, on which he was (a) miller more than fifteen years. And

estando mi madre una noche en la azeña, preñada de mí, tomóle el
my mother being one night in the water-mill, pregnant with me, was

parto[3] y parióme allí. De manera que con verdad me puedo decir
taken and bore me there. So that in truth I can say (myself)

nacido en el río.
born in the river.

---

[1] V. M., for **Vuestra Merced,** from which usted (**Vd., Ud.**) is derived.

[2] Salamanca. The reference here is to the province, not the city. The capital of a Spanish province usually has the same name as the province.

[3] **tomóle el parto,** literally "took her the birth."

Pues siendo yo niño de ocho años, achacaron a mi padre ciertas
Well, I being a child of eight years, they attributed to my father certain
sangrías malhechas en los costales de los que allí a moler venían, por
evil leakages in the sacks of those who came there for milling, for
lo cual fué preso [1] **y confesó y no negó y padeció persecución por jus-**
which he was seized and confessed and denied not and suffered prosecution by law.
ticia.   Espero en Dios que está en la gloria, pues el Evangelio los
I hope in God that he is in glory, for the Gospel calls (such
llama bienaventurados.   En este tiempo se hizo cierta armada contra
people) blessed.   At this time there was formed a certain armed force against
moros, entre los cuales [2] **fué mi padre, que a la sazón estaba desterrado**
(the) Moors, in which was my father, who at the time was deported
por el desastre ya dicho, con cargo de acemilero de un caballero que
for the disaster already mentioned, with (the) post of groom of a knight who
allá fué.   Y con su señor, como leal criado, feneció su vida.
was there.   And with his master, as (a) loyal servant, he ended his life.

§ 2. *Irregular Past Participles — Defective Verbs — Impersonal Verbs —
Situation Material: Eating (3): Lunch; Meats —* **Lazarillo de
Tormes** (2)

IRREGULAR PAST PARTICIPLES.   The following list contains some
irregular past participles that you have already met with plus a
few new ones:

	From:
ABIERTO, open(ed)	**abrir,** to open
CUBIERTO, covered	**cubrir,** to cover
DICHO, said, told	**decir,** to say, tell
ESCRITO, written	**escribir,** to write
HECHO, done, made	**hacer,** to do, make
IMPRESO, (im)printed	**imprimir,** to (im)print
MUERTO, dead, died, killed	**morir,** to die
(see page 168)	
PUESTO, put, placed	**poner,** to put, place
SUELTO, solved	**solver,** to solve
VISTO, seen	**ver,** to see, view
VUELTO, turned, returned	**volver,** to turn, return

[1] **preso,** irregular past participle of **prender,** *to seize.*
[2] **entre los cuales,** literally "among whom," referring to those taking part in
the expedition.

Compounds of these verbs have the same irregular past participle; for example: **descubrir,** *to uncover, discover;* **contradecir,** *to contradict;* **describir,** *to describe;* **rehacer,** *to do* or *make over;* **satisfacer,** *to satisfy* (**satisfecho,** *satisfied*); **suponer,** *to suppose;* **prever,** *to foresee;* **envolver,** *to involve, wrap up.* The verb **solver** is rarely used, its place being taken by **resolver,** *to solve, resolve;* **–se a,** *to resolve to.*

Related words: **cubierta,** *(n.) cover(ing), deck, cover charge;* **dicho,** *(adj.) said, (above-)mentioned, (n.) saying;* **escrito,** *(n.) a writing;* **hecho,** *(n.) deed, fact;* **impreso,** *(n.) pamphlet, (pl.) printed matter;* **muerto(-a),** *(n.) dead man (woman);* **puesto,** *(n.) post, position, job;* **puesto que,** *(conj.) since;* **vista,** *(n.) view;* **vuelta,** *(n.) turn, return.*

A number of verbs have two past participles, a regular one, which is, as a rule, only used in compound forms with **haber** or (passive) **ser,** and an irregular one used as an adjective. The following is not a complete list of such verbs:

Irreg. Past Part.	*Reg. P. P.*	*Infinitive*
ATENTO, attentive	**atendido**	**atender,** to attend, pay attention
BENDITO, blessed	**bendecido**	**bendecir,** to bless
CONCLUSO, concluded	**concluído**	**concluir,** to conclude
CONFUSO, confused	**confundido**	**confundir,** to confound, –fuse
DESIERTO, desert(ed)	**desertado**	**desertar,** to desert
DESPIERTO, awake	**despertado**	**despertar,** to (a)waken, wake up
DISTINTO, distinct	**distinguido**	**distinguir,** to distinguish
ELECTO, chosen, elected	**elegido**	**elegir,** to choose, elect
EXCLUSO, excluded	**excluído**	**excluir,** to exclude
FIJO, fixed	**fijado**	**fijar,** to fix, fasten
FRITO, fried	**freído**	**freír,** to fry
JUNTO, joined, together	**juntado**	**juntar,** to join
MALDITO, (ac)cursed	**maldecido**	**maldecir,** to curse
PRESO, seized, captive	**prendido**	**prender,** to seize, grasp
ROTO, broken, torn	**rompido**	**romper,** to break, tear
SUELTO, loose(ned)	**soltado**	**soltar,** to loose(n), let loose
TUERTO, *see below*	**torcido**	**torcer,** to twist

Note that **suelto** may be from **soltar** or **solver** (but the latter is rare). **Tuerto** as an adjective means *one-eyed* or *blind in one eye;* it also appears in a few idioms.

The following are related nouns: **desierto,** *desert, wilderness;* **junta,** *junta, council;* **preso,** *prisoner, convict;* **suelto,** *(small) change.*

Note: Some past participles (regular and irregular) have become true adjectives with *active* meanings. Note the following examples.

agradecido, grateful
atrevido, daring, bold
callado, silent
cansado, tiresome (*or* tired)
confiado, trusting, confident

descreído. unbelieving
desesperado, desperate
leído, well-read
osado, bold, daring
resuelto, determined

DEFECTIVE VERBS. A *defective verb* is one that is not used in all its forms.

Some verbs are restricted by their meanings. For example, **NACER,** *to be born,* would never be used in the imperative; there would be no occasion to use **nazco,** *I am born;* and there would be no need for the imperfect tense. **SOLER,** *to be accustomed, be wont, be in the habit of,* could not be used in the past definite, which refers to a single action; as a matter of fact, **soler** is used only in the present indicative (**suelo,** *etc.*) and the imperfect (**solía,** *etc.*).

Some verbs have become restricted in their use because other verbs have taken over some of their original uses or meanings. **Yacer,** *to lie,* is now used only in speaking of the dead, and so is restricted to the third person of the present and imperfect (**aquí yace,** *here lies*). [*To lie* (*down*) is **echarse** or **tenderse.**]

PLACER, *to please,* is now restricted to the third person singular. (The common word for *please, like* is **gustar: Me gustan los gatos,** *I like cats.*) **Placer** is highly irregular:

Present Indicative: **place** (**me place,** it pleases me)
Imperfect: **placía**
Past Definite: **plugo, plació**   *Future:* **placerá**
Present Subjunctive: **plegue** *or* **plazca**
Past Subjunctive: **pluguiera, –iese** (¡ **Pluguiera a Dios . . .** ! May it please God . . . ! Would to God . . . !)

Reponer in the sense of *reply* is used only in the past definite (**repuse,** *etc.*); **contestar** and **responder** both mean *reply.*

Ten **–ir** verbs (mostly uncommon) are now used only in thos forms with endings beginning with **i.** One of these verbs is **abolir,** *to abolish.* Thus, in the present indicative the forms in parentheses would not be used: (**abolo**), (**aboles**), (**abole**), **abolimos, abolís,** (**abolen**). The present subjunctive (**abola,** *etc.*) would not be used. But the imperfect, the past definite, the future, the conditional, and the past and future subjunctives could be used. **Suprimir,** *to suppress,* can be used in place of **abolir** in all forms. Another verb of the class of **abolir** is **garantir,** *to guarantee;* the forms not used can be replaced by forms of **garantizar.**

Other defective verbs are too uncommon to be worth listing in this book. If you come across them in reading, you can look them up in the dictionary.

IMPERSONAL VERBS. A number of verbs are used only impersonally. Although they have no real subject, in English we use *it* (without definite reference) as subject: **Llueve,** *It is raining.* Or a neuter pronoun may be the subject, in Spanish and English, referring to a fact or idea or situation, and not to any single word: **Eso me importa,** *That is important to me.* Impersonal verbs may all be used in the infinitive: **Va a llover,** *It is going to rain.*

Here are some common impersonal verbs:

acontecer (zc), to happen (**Acontece que** .. It happens that . . .)

atañer, concernir (ie), to concern. affect (**Eso no me atañe,** *or* **concierne.** That doesn't affect, *or* concern, me.)

BASTAR, to be enough *or* sufficient (**Basta.** That's enough.)

convenii (ie), to suit (**No me conviene.** It doesn't suit me. It is not convenient for me.)

IMPORTAR, to be important, to matter (**No importa mucho.** It's not very important. It doesn't matter much.)

PARECER (ZC), to seem (**Me parece que . . .** It seems to me that . . . **¿Qué le parece?** How does it seem, *or* look, to you? What do you think about it?)

precisar, to be necessary (**Precisa que . . .** It is necessary that . . .); *but* **ser preciso** *is more commonly used.*

ES DE (*followed by infinitive*), it is to be (**Es de esperar que . . .** It is to be hoped that . . .)

A number of impersonal expressions refer to the weather:

alborear, amanecer (zc),* to dawn (**Alborea,** *or* **Amanece.** Dawn is breaking.)

anochecer (zc), to get dark (**Anochece.** Night is falling.)

HELAR (IE), to freeze (**Hiela.** It's freezing.)

LLOVER (UE), to rain (**Llueve,** *or* **Está lloviendo, mucho.** It is raining hard.)

lloviznar, to drizzle (**Lloviznaba.** It was drizzling.)

NEVAR (IE), to snow (**Nieva.** It is snowing.)

RELAMPAGUEAR, to lighten (**Relampaguea.** It's lightening.) (**Relámpago** *is a* flash of lightning.)

TRONAR (UE), to thunder (**Truena.** It is thundering.)

---

* **Amanecer** is also used in this way: **Amanecí en París.** I arrived at Paris at dawn.

ventear, to blow (**Ventea.** The wind is blowing.) *But* **hacer** *or* **haber viento** *is more common* (**Hace mucho viento.** It is very windy.)

Some other impersonal expressions regarding weather are:

Hay sol (nubes). It is sunny (cloudy).
Hay viento (polvo, lodo). It is windy (dusty, muddy).
Hace calor (fresco, frío). It is hot (cool, cold).
Hace buen (mal) tiempo. The weather is good (bad).

SITUATION MATERIAL — EATING (3): LUNCH; MEATS. The Spanish **almuerzo** is a fairly heavy midday meal, which we might well call a *dinner.* In most Spanish-speaking countries the shops and offices are closed for two or three hours in the middle of the day while the employees — and bosses — eat the **almuerzo** and enjoy the **siesta.**

A North American light lunch, in which a sandwich is probably the main item, would hardly qualify as **almuerzo;** it would be more of a **merienda,** a "snack." If you eat your midday meal in a hotel, you will of course eat **almuerzo.**

Here is another list of foods, to be continued in the next section:

entradas, appetizers	**el entremés,** hors d'oeuvres
aceituna, olive **apio,** celery	**rábano,** radish
sopa soup	**caldo,** broth

la carne, meat, flesh; **carne de vaca,** beef; **c. de cerdo,** pork; **c. de cordero,** lamb; **c. de oveja,** mutton; **c. de ternera,** veal
el filete, steak, fillet **el bif–** *or* **bistek** *or* **–tec,** beefsteak **rosbif,** roast beef
asado, roast **el jamón,** ham
chuleta de cerdo (cordero), pork (lamb) chop **coteleta,** cutlet
bien cocido, well done; **poco cocido,** rare **grasa,** grease, fat
hígado, liver **salsa,** gravy
asar, to roast; **asar a la parrilla,** to broil, grill
cocer, to boil, cook; **cocer en horno,** to bake; **cocido español,** Spanish stew
guisar, to stew, cook **freír,** to fry
sausage: **salchicha,** (*pork*) **chorizo,** (*long*) **longaniza,** (salami) **salchichón**

Una mesa para dos, por favor. A table for two, please.
Tráiganos dos cervezas y la lista. Bring us two beers and the menu.
¿ **Qué es la sopa del día?** What is today's soup?
Quiero el biftek, bien hecho. I want the beefsteak, well done.
Para mí, la coteleta de ternera. For me, the veal cutlet.
He cambiado de mente — spaghetti con albóndigas. I have changed my mind — spaghetti with meat balls.
¿ **Tal vez tenemos un cocinero italiano?** Maybe we have an Italian chef?

LAZARILLO DE TORMES   (2)

Mi viuda madre, como sin marido y sin abrigo se viese,[1] determinó
My widow mother, as she saw herself without husband and shelter, determined
arrimarse a los buenos por ser uno de ellos y vínose a vivir a la ciudad
to draw near to good (people) to be one of them and came to the city to live
y alquiló una casilla y metióse a guisar de comer a ciertos estudiantes
and rented a small house and undertook to prepare food for certain students
y lavaba la ropa a ciertos mozos de caballos del Comendador [2] de la
and washed clothes for certain stable boys of the Comendador de la
Magdalena, de manera que fué frecuentando las caballerizas
Magdalena, so that she was frequenting the stables.

Ella y un hombre moreno, de aquellos que las bestias curaban,
She and a dark-skinned man, of those who cared for the beasts,
vinieron en conocimiento.   Éste algunas veces se venía a nuestra casa
became acquainted.   This (man) sometimes came to our house
y se iba a la mañana.   Otras veces de día llegaba a la puerta en achaque
and went away in the morning.   Other times by day he arrived at the door in (the) pre-
de comprar huevos y entrábase en casa.   Yo, al principio de su entrada,[3]
tense of buying eggs and entered into the house.   I, when he first came in,
pesábame con él [4] y habíale miedo,[5] viendo el color y mal gesto [6] que
disliked him and feared him, seeing the color and bad face he
tenía; mas, de que vi que con su venida mejoraba el comer, fuíle
had; but, as I saw that with his coming the food improved, I was
queriendo [7] bien, porque siempre traía pan, pedazos de carne y en
liking him well, because he always brought bread, bits of meat, and in
invierno leños, a que nos calentábamos.
winter (bits of) fuel with which we warmed ourselves.

De manera que, continuando la posada y conversación, mi madre
So (it was) that, the lodging and intercourse continuing, my mother
vino a darme un negrito muy bonito, el cual yo brincaba y ayudaba
came to give me a very pretty little black boy, whom I gamboled with and helped to
a calentar.
(keep) warm.

[1] **se viese.** In modern Spanish the indicative **se vió** would be used.

[2] **Comendador,** a rank (commander) in a Spanish order — in this case, of **la Magdalena.**

[3] **al principio de su entrada:** literally "at the beginning of his entrance."

[4] **pesábame con él. Pesar** means *to weigh;* **pesábame,** *it weighed upon me.*

[5] **habíale miedo,** "I had fear to him": **haber** was formerly used transitively, where **tener** is now used.

[6] **gesto,** not the usual word for *face* (**cara**); it means *facial expression* or *countenance.*

[7] **fuíle queriendo.   Ser** is now rarely used in the progressive forms of the verb.

Y acuérdome que, estando el negro de mi padrastro [1] trebejando con
And I remember that, my black stepfather being in play with

el mozuelo,[2] como el niño vió a mi madre y a mí blancos y a él no, huía
the little boy, as the child saw my mother and me white and him not, he fled

de él con miedo para mi madre y, señalando con el dedo, decía:
from him with fear to my mother and, pointing with his finger, said:

« ¡ Madre, coco [3] ! »
"Mother, bogy man ! "

Respondió él, riendo: « ¡ Hideputa [4] ! »
He replied, laughing: "Son of a gun ! "

Yo, aunque bien muchacho, noté aquella palabra [5] de mi hermanito
I, although a very young boy, noted that word of my little brother

y dije entre mí: « ¡ Cuántos debe de haber en el mundo, que huyen
and said to myself: "How many there must be in the world, who flee

de otros, porque no se ven a sí mismos ! »
fron others, because they do not see themselves!"

Quiso nuestra fortuna que la conversación del Zaide, que así se
Our fate willed that the intercourse of El Zaide,[6] for so he

llamaba, llegó a oídos del mayordomo y, hecha pesquisa, hallóse que
was called, reached the ears of the steward and, enquiry being made, it was found that

la mitad por medio de la cebada, que para las bestias le daban, hurtaba,
about the half of the barley that they gave him for the beasts, he stole,

y salvados, leña, almohazas, mandiles, y las mantas y sábanas de los
and bran, firewood, currycombs, leather aprons, and the blankets and cloths of the

caballos hacía perdidas, y, cuando otra cosa no tenía, las bestias des-
horses were missing, and, when there was nothing else, he unshod the animals,

herraba, y con todo esto acudía a [7] mi madre para criar a mi herma-
and with all this he came to my mother to bring up my little brother.

nico.   No nos maravillemos de un clérigo ni de un fraile, porque el
Let us not wonder at a priest or at a friar, because the

uno hurta de los pobres y el otro de casa para sus devotas y para ayuda
one steals from the poor and the other from (a) house for his devout women and for

de otro tanto,[8] cuando a un pobre esclavo el amor le animaba a esto.
other such aid, when love drove a poor slave to this.

[1] el negro de mi padrastro.   This construction is still much used; for example: el loco de mi hermano, *that crazy brother of mine.*

[2] mozuelo, diminutive of mozo.

[3] coco, usually *coconut.*

[4] Hideputa (= hijo de puta), a word not now used in polite society.

[5] aquella palabra: refers to coco.

[6] del Zaide.   The name indicates that the black man was Moorish.

[7] acudía a.   Acudir a usually means *to come to the aid (of).*

[8] para ayuda de otro tanto: literally "and for aid of other such."

§ 3. *How to Say SOME, ANY, NONE, Etc., in Spanish — IR and ANDAR — Situation Material: Eating (4): Dinner and Supper; Fowl; Seafood — Lazarillo de Tormes (3)*

How to Say SOME, ANY, NONE, Etc., in Spanish. No new Spanish words will be presented in this section, but there will be a general review of what are often called the "indefinite pronouns":

ALGUNO, *some, any.* This word can apply to persons or things and agrees with the noun it refers to or modifies. Before a masculine singular noun it drops the –o.

> **algún hombre,** some man; **alguna mujer,** some woman
> **algún día,** some day; **algunos días,** some days
> **¿Tiene Ud. algunas revistas mexicanas?** Do you have some, *or* any, Mexican magazines?

In the plural, **alguno** may be used as a pronoun:

> **¿Tiene Ud. algunos sobres? Sí, tengo algunos.** Do you have any envelopes? Yes, I have some.

Sometimes our *some* or *any* would not be expressed in Spanish:

> Do you have any money? **¿Tiene Ud. dinero?**
> Yes, I have some. **Sí, lo tengo.**
> Do you have any idea what happened? **¿Tiene Ud. una idea de lo que pasó?**
> Do you have any knowledge of Portuguese? **¿Sabe Ud. algo del portugués?**
> I have some work to do. **Tengo que trabajar un poco.**
> I still have some hope. **Todavía tengo esperanza.**
> He's some man! **¡Qué hombre! ¡Vaya un hombre!**

UNOS may be used in place of **algunos**:

> **¿Tiene Ud. unas estampillas?** Do you have any stamps?
> **Tengo unas de a diez centavos.** I have some ten-centavo ones.

The negative of **alguno** is **NINGUNO**, *no, not one, not any, none.* Like **alguno**, it drops –o before a masculine singular noun. **Ninguno** must be preceded by **no** unless it begins the sentence.

> **ningún hombre,** no man, not a man, not one man; **ninguna mujer**
> **ningunos hombres,** no men, not any men; **ningunas mujeres**
> **¿Tiene Ud. algunos cigarrillos? No, no tengo ningunos.** Do you have any cigarettes? No, I haven't any.

Ningunos de ellos son amigos míos. None of them are friends of mine.

No conozco a ningunos de ellos. I don't know any of them.

Unlike **alguno, ninguno** may be used as a pronoun in the singular:

Ninguno de mis amigos habla español. *Or:* **No habla español ninguno de mis amigos.** Not one of my friends speaks Spanish.

¿ Conoce Ud. a algunas de estas muchachas? No conozco a ninguna. Do you know any of these girls? I don't know any of them.

Not any would not always be expressed in Spanish:

Do you have any work to do? No, I haven't any. **¿ Tiene Ud. que trabajar? No.**

ALGUIEN, *somebody, anybody, someone, anyone,* is an invariable pronoun.

Alguien está a la puerta. Someone is at the door.

Busco a alguien que hable inglés. I am looking for someone who speaks English. (Note subjunctive **hable;** the subjunctive is used in a relative clause with an indefinite antecedent. Also note that although **alguien** is an indefinite pronoun, not referring to any certain person, it is preceded by the "personal a" when object of a verb.)

NADIE, *no one, nobody, not anyone, not anybody,* is the negative of **alguien.** It must be preceded by **no** unless it begins the sentence.

No hay nadie aquí. *Or* **Nadie está aquí.** There is no one here.

Nadie may be used as a noun: **Es un nadie.** He is a nobody.

ALGO, *something, anything,* and **NADA,** *nothing, not anything, not a thing,* are invariable. **Nada,** like **ninguno** and **nadie,** must be preceded by **no** unless it begins a sentence.

¿ Oye Ud. algo? Do you hear anything, *or* something?
No oigo nada. I don't hear anything.
¿ Hay algo de comer? Is there anything to eat?
Nada hay. *Or* **No hay nada.** There is nothing.
Aquí hay algo raro. There is something strange here.
No lo hago para nada. I wouldn't do it for anything.

Alguna cosa is sometimes used in place of **algo**, and **ninguna cosa** for **nada**:

> **Alguna cosa me preocupa.** Something worries me.
> **No falta ninguna cosa.** Nothing is lacking.

Algo and **nada** may be used as adverbs (**algo,** *somewhat, rather,* **nada,** *not at all*):

> **Volveré algo tarde.** I'll return rather late.
> **Esto es algo difícil.** This is somewhat difficult.
> **No es nada claro.** It is not at all clear.

Nada may be used as a noun: **Es una nada.** It's a mere nothing.
De nada (*Don't mention it*) is commonly said after one has been thanked.

When *there is* (*are*) precedes an indefinite pronoun, the Spanish equivalent is **hay** preceded by the article:

> **Necesito un lápiz rojo, si lo hay.** I need a red pencil, if there is one.
> **Yo buscaba una casa colorada, pero no la había.** I looked for a pink house, but there wasn't one.
> **Quiero comprar algunos dulces, si los hay.** I want to buy some candy, if there is any.
> **Tengo ganas de ver las orquídeas. Espero que las haya.** I am eager to see orchids. I hope there will be some.

IR AND **ANDAR: Ir** is the usual equivalent of *go.* It need not indicate actual motion. **Ir a** means *to go to* or *to be going to.* **Irse** means *to go away.*

> **Fuimos al cine.** We went to the movies.
> **La cosa no va bien.** The thing isn't going well.
> **¿Cómo le** (*or* **se**) **va?** How does it go? How are you doing?
> **Mañana me voy.** I'm leaving tomorrow.
> **Se me fueron los pies.** I slipped. (My feet went away from me.)
> **Voy a dar un paseo.** I am going to take a walk.
> **Ellos van en automóvil, pero yo prefiero ir a pie.** They are going to ride, but I prefer to walk.
> **¡Vamos!** Let's go. (Also expresses surprise, disbelief, disapproval.)

Andar means *to go* or *to walk.* It is used (as **ir** is not) of animals, vehicles, and machines. Note the following examples.

Andemos más rápidamente. Let's walk faster.

Andábamos más de cien kilómetros la hora. We were going
more than a hundred kilometers per hour.

Este caballo anda despacio. This horse goes slowly.

Mi reloj no anda bien. My watch doesn't run well.

Andan desnudos. They go naked.

SITUATION MATERIAL — EATING (4): DINNER AND SUPPER; FOWL;
SEAFOOD. A dinner at noon is **almuerzo**; evening dinner is the **comida.**
The **cena,** *supper,* may be (as with us) an evening family meal if lighter than
the noon meal, or a light meal in a restaurant after the theater or a social
evening.

It is not practicable or necessary to give you a complete vocabulary of
foods and dishes. There is no need for you to know the Spanish names for
foods unless you eat in Spanish or Spanish-American restaurants, and if you
do you will quickly acquire a food vocabulary. If you live in a city where
there is a Mexican or Spanish restaurant, or perhaps a number of them, you
will find bilingual menus, and you will find that the waiter can answer your
questions in English. The same is true of foreign hotels catering to tourists.

The following is a brief list of common dishes of fowl and seafood:

pollo, chicken; **arroz con pollo,** chicken and rice
Paella is chicken and rice with lobster or shrimp, olives, and other in-
gredients.   **pato,** duck
pavo, (*Mex.*) **guajalote,** (*Guat.*) **chompipe,** turkey
Mole de guajalote is perhaps the most typical Mexican dish. **Mole is a**
sweet-and-hot sauce.

el pez, fish (*in water*); **pescar,** to fish, catch (*fish*); **pescado,** fish (*to eat*)	
el filete, fillet, steak	**en escabeche,** pickled
mariscos, shellfish, seafood	**arenque,** herring
bacalao, cod	**escombro,** mackerel
lenguado, sole	**pargo,** red snapper
róbalo, bass	**pez espada,** swordfish
salmón, salmon	**atún,** tuna
calamares, squid(s)	**camarones,** shrimp(s)
cangrejos, crabs	**ostras,** oysters
langosta, lobster; **langostinos,** crawfish, rock lobsters	

¿ **A qué hora se sirve la comida?** What time is dinner served?

¿ **Dónde nos sentamos?** Where shall we sit?

Prefiero una mesa cerca de la ventana. I prefer a table near the window.

¿ **Qué hay de bueno hoy?** What's good today? **Me (Nos) recomienda**
algo especial? Do you recommend anything special?

Sírvanos lo antes posible, por favor. Tenemos prisa. Please serve us as
soon as possible. We are in a hurry.

No pidamos nada que requiera (necesita) mucho tiempo a guisar. Let's
not order anything that takes much time to prepare.

¿ Le gustó la comida? Did you like the dinner? Muchísimo.

Creo que la cuenta no es justa. I don't think the bill is correct. ¿ Qué
le parece? What do you think?

Es demasiado; creo que Ud. se ha equivocado. It's too much; I think
you have made a mistake.

Oh — se me olvidó de los puros. Oh, I forgot the cigars.

Pero hay un error en la adición. But there is an error in the addition.

LAZARILLO DE TORMES   (3)

Y probósele cuanto digo y aun más. Porque a mí con amenazas me
And all I say and even more was proved on him. Because they questioned me

preguntaban y como niño respondía y descubría cuanto sabía con
with threats and as (a) child I replied and disclosed all I knew with

miedo, hasta ciertas herraduras que por mandado de mi madre a un
fear, down to certain horseshoes that by order of my mother I sold to a

herrero vendí.
blacksmith.

Al triste de mi padrastro [1] azotaron y pringaron [2] y a mi madre
My unfortunate stepfather they flogged and lambasted and on my mother

pusieron pena por justicia, sobre el acostumbrado centenario, que en
inflicted penalty of law, of the usual hundred (lashes), that into

casa del sobredicho Comendador no entrase ni al lastimado Zaide en
(the) house of the aforementioned Comendador she should not enter nor receive in

la suya acogiese. [3]
hers the pitiable Zaide.

Por no echar la soga tras el caldero, [4] la triste se esforzó y cumplió
So as not to throw the ladle after the pot, the poor (woman) made an effort and ful-

la sentencia. Y por evitar peligro y quitarse de malas lenguas se fué
filled the sentence. And to avoid danger and free herself of evil tongues she went

a servir a los que al presente vivían en el mesón de la Solana. Y allí,
to serve those who at this time lived in the Solana inn. And there,

padeciendo mil importunidades, se acabó de [5] criar mi hermanico, hasta
suffering a thousand pesterings, she finally brought up my little brother, until

[1] **Al triste de mi padrastro.** The common meaning of **triste** is *sad*. As for
the construction, see note on **el negro de mi padrastro,** page 179.

[2] **pringaron,** *basted:* that is, tortured or beat up.

[3] **y a mi madre . . . acogiese.** The punishment was to be inflicted if the
woman disobeyed the orders of the court.

[4] **echar la soga tras el caldero,** literally "to throw the rope after the pot";
that is, to throw the minor thing away after the major is lost.

[5] **se acabó de. Acabarse de** means *to finish, to have finally*

que supo andar y a mí hasta ser buen mozuelo, que iba a los huéspedes
he could walk, and me until I was a fine little boy, who went for wine

por vino y candelas y por lo demás, que me mandaban.
and tapers for the guests, and for anything else they ordered.

En ese tiempo vino a posar al mesón un ciego, el cual, pareciéndole
At that time came to lodge at the inn a blind (man), who, it seeming to him

que yo sería para adestrarle,[1] me pidió a mi madre y ella me encomendó
that I would be (good) for leading him, asked my mother for me, and she entrusted

a él, diciendo como era hijo de un buen hombre, el cual por ensalzar
me to him, saying (that) as I was (the) son of a good man, who to exalt

la fe había muerto en la de los Gelves [2] y que ella confiaba en Dios
the faith had died in the (battle) of los Gelves, she trusted in God

no saldría peor hombre que mi padre y que le rogaba me tratase bien y
I would not turn out (a) worse man than my father, and she besought him to treat me well

mirase por mí, pues era huérfano.
and look after me, as I was (an) orphan.

Él respondió que así lo haría y que me recibía, no por mozo, sino
He replied that he would do so and that he received me, not as (a) servant, but

por hijo. Y así le comencé a servir y adestrar a mi nuevo y viejo amo.
as (a) son. And so I began to serve and to lead my new, and old, master.

Como estuvimos en Salamanca algunos días, pareciéndole a mi amo
As we were in Salamanca some days, it seeming to my master

que no era la ganancia a su contento, determinó irse de allí, y yo fuí a
that the gain was not to his liking, he determined to go away from there, and I went

ver a mi madre y ambos llorando, me dió su bendición y dijo:
to see my mother and, both weeping, she gave me her blessing and said:

§ 4. *Idioms with HACER, DAR, ECHAR, LLEVAR, PONER —* *Situation Material: Eating (5): Vegetables, Fruits — Lazarillo de Tormes (4)*

IDIOMS WITH SOME COMMON VERBS. A common verb is found in a variety of idioms in which its *translation* — but not its *meaning* — may vary widely from the basic one. For example, **hacer el mono** would be translated *to act the monkey*, but the basic meaning, *to make*, is there. If you know the component words it is rarely difficult to understand a Spanish idiom when you come upon it in reading. The difficulty is in saying idiomatically what you want to say.

---

[1] **adestrarle. Adestrar** means *to train* or *to guide*. Incidentally, because of the popularity of this novel, boys who led blind men came to be called **lazarillos**.

[2] **la de los Gelves. Batalla,** *battle*, is understood.

The only way to overcome this difficulty is to keep acquiring, by study and reading, more and more idioms. If you wish to make a serious attempt to master Spanish, you must have a good dictionary, which means a good-sized dictionary; such a dictionary will provide, when needed, several or many definitions of words, with explanation and illustration, and many idioms.

The following is a list of some of the idioms based upon certain common verbs:

HACER: The basic meaning is *to do* or *make*.
Expressions regarding the weather:

> **Hace buen (mal) tiempo.** The weather is good (bad). (**No pude asistir porque hizo mal tiempo.** I couldn't attend because the weather was bad.)
> **Hace buen día.** It's a nice day.
> **Hace calor (fresco, frío).** It is warm (cool, cold). (**Hace mucho calor.** It's hot. **Ayer hacía menos calor.** It wasn't so hot yesterday.)
> **Hace sol (viento).** It is sunny (windy). (**Hay** can be used instead of **hace.**)

Hacer with a period of time as object indicates a lapse of time; *ago* or (in negative statements) *since* is used in the translation:

> **Estuve aquí hace un año.** I was here a year ago.
> **¿ Cuánto tiempo hace que nos conocemos?** How long have we known each other?
> **Ayer hizo un año que me casé.** I got married a year ago yesterday.
> **Lo ví hace un año.** I saw him a year ago.
> **Hace un año que lo ví.** It has been a year since I saw him.
> **Hace un año que no lo veo.** I haven't seen him for a year.
> **Hacía un año que no lo veía.** I hadn't seen him for a year.

Hacer followed by an infinitive means *to cause to, order to, compel to:*

> **Yo lo hice ver a Ud.** I had him see you.
> **He hecho hacer un vestido.** I have had a dress made.
> **Yo lo hice pagarlo.** I made him pay for it.

Hacer de means *to act as:*

> **Ella hizo de maestra.** She acted as teacher. (*But:* **Ella hizo la maestra.** She played (*acted the role of*) the teacher.)

Hacer falta means *to be needed, be lacking:*

Eso me hace falta. I need that.

Me hace falta la práctica en hablar. I need practice in speaking.

¿ Qué hace falta? What is lacking, *or* missing?

Hacer por *or* **para** means *to make an effort to, try to, manage to:*

Haré por venir. I'll try to come.

Haga Ud. por escribirme una carta. Try to write me a letter.

The following idioms illustrate the variety of ways in which a verb may be used:

hacer agua, to leak (**El bote hace agua.** The boat is leaking.)

hacer las amistades, to make up (**Nos reñimos, pero después hicimos las amistades.** We quarreled, but afterwards we made up.)

hacer bancarrota, to go bankrupt (**La casa hizo b.** The firm went b.)

hacer la barba, to shave (*more common:* **afeitar, –se**)

hacer caso de, to pay attention to, take notice of (**No haga caso de ello.** Don't pay any attention to it.)

hacer la corte a, to pay court to, court, woo (**Él le hacía la corte a ella.** He was courting her.)

hacer daño a, to harm, disagree with, not be good for (**Los mariscos me hacen daño.** Seafood doesn't agree with me.)

hacer el favor de, to do the favor of (**Hágame el favor de traducírmelo.** Please do me the favor of translating it. Please translate it for me.)

hacer fiesta, to take a holiday

hacer fuego a, to fire on

hacer la guerra a, to make war on

hacer mal a, to wrong, injure (**Él no me hizo mal.** He did not wrong me.)

hacer pedazos, to break to pieces, shatter (**La taza se hizo pedazos,** *or* **añicos.** The cup broke to pieces, *or* shattered.)

hacer saber, to make known, let know, inform (**Quiero hacerlo saber que . . .** I want to let him know that . . . I want him to know that . . .)

hacer señas a, to make signs to, motion *or* signal to (**¿ Por qué me hacía señas?** Why were you motioning to me?)

hacer vela, to set sail

hacer la vista gorda, to wink at, overlook (**Lo sabían pero hacían la vista gorda.** They knew it, but they overlooked it, *or* closed their eyes to it, *or* pretended not to know it.)

tener que hacer con, *or* **ver con,** to have to do with (**¿ Qué tiene eso que hacer con ello?** What has that to do with it?)

Hacerse may mean *to become, grow:*

Él se hizo actor. He became an actor.

Se hace tarde. It is growing late.

DAR (basic meaning, *to give*) may be an active verb, a neutral verb, or a reflexive verb. Here are a few typical uses of **dar:**

dar una carcajada, to burst out laughing (*give a laugh*)

dar celos a, to make jealous (**Eso no me da celos.** That doesn't make me jealous.)

dar de comer, to feed

dar a conocer, to make known

dar a entender, to let it be known, suggest, hint

dar cuenta de, to take account of, take note of

dar ganas de, to make one want to (**La música me da ganas de bailar.** The music makes me want to dance. **No me da la gana.** I don't want to.)

dar guerra a, to make, *or* wage, war on

dar a luz, to bring forth, give birth

dar un paseo, to take a walk

dar que pensar, to give reason for thought (**Eso da que pensar.** That's something to think about.)

dar voces, to cry out, shout

La bala le dió en el brazo. The bullet hit him in the arm.

As a neutral verb, **dar** may mean *to give, yield, stretch,* etc.:

La puerta no da. The door won't give.

La ventana da a la calle. The window looks out on the street.

dar con, to run into, come upon, find (**Ayer di con él en el hotel.** Yesterday I ran into him in the hotel. **Dimos con una cabra.** We ran into a goat.)

dar contra, to hit against, run into

dar de, to fall on (**Dió de cabeza.** He fell on his head.)

dar en el clavo, to hit the mark, guess right

dar por, to consider as (**dar por supuesto,** to take for granted)

As a reflexive verb:

darse la mano, to shake hands (**Nos dimos la mano.** We
shook hands.) (*But:* I shook hands with him. **Le di la
mano.**)

darse prisa, to hurry up

ECHAR is a word of great range and can have all sorts of
meanings: *to throw, cast, hurl, fling, toss, put, throw off, throw out,*
"*kick out,*" *pour, produce, put forth, give off, give out, impute,* and so on.
For example:

echar en cara, to throw into one's face (**Me echó en cara
que . . .** He threw it into my face that . . .)

echar carnes, to get fat (*also* **engordar**)

echar al correo, to mail

echar a fondo, *or* **a pique,** to sink (*a ship*)

echar la llave a, to lock (*also* **cerrar con llave**)

echar de menos, to miss (**La echo de menos.** I miss her.)

echar de ver, to notice, observe (**Eché de ver que Ud
estaba cansado.** I noticed that you were tired.)

echar a perder, to spoil, ruin (**Lo echará a perder.** He will
spoil it.)

echar raíces, to take root

Echarse means *to throw oneself, lie down, stretch out:*

echarse a llorar, to burst out crying (**La niña se echó a
llorar.** The little girl started to cry.)

Me eché en la cama. I threw myself onto the bed.

LLEVAR means *to carry, take, lead, bear, wear, suffer,* etc. For
example:

Lléveme este paquete a esta dirección. Take this package
to this address for me.

Lléveme a Calle Independencia, número 436. Take me to
number 436 Independencia Street.

No llevo mucho dinero conmigo. I don't have much
money with me.

Nunca llevo sombrero. I never wear a hat.

Este arbol lleva mangos muy buenos. This tree bears very
good mangos.

Ha llevado un golpe serio. He has suffered a serious blow.

Llevar is sometimes used in place of **haber,** but the construction is different. Compare:

> **He escrito una carta.** I have written a letter.
>
> **Llevo escrita una carta.** I have a letter written. (Note that **escrita** modifies and agrees with **carta.**)

Llevar is sometimes used to express length of time, as follows:

> **¿ Cuánto tiempo lleva su hermano en la Argentina?** How long has your brother been in Argentina? (**lleva = ha estado**)
>
> **Llevo cuatro días en cama.** I have been in bed four days.

Some other idioms with **llevar:**

> **llevar a,** to be . . . older than (**Ella lleva tres años a el.** She is three years older than he.) (*But:* **Ella tiene más años que él.** She is older than he.)
>
> **llevar a cabo,** to carry out, accomplish, complete (**Han llevado a cabo todo el trabajo.** They have completed all the work.)
>
> **llevar libros,** to keep books (*ledgers*)
>
> **llevar la ventaja a,** to have the advantage of (**Ud. me lleva la ventaja en conocimiento del país.** You have the advantage of me in knowledge of the country.)

Llevarse means *to carry away* or *off, to get along:*

> **Los indios se llevaron todo.** The Indians carried off everything.
>
> **Me llevo mal con él.** I get along badly with him.
>
> **Nos llevamos bien.** We get along well.

PONER means *to put, place, lay, set, impose, bet, cause to be,* etc. Thus:

> **Ponga las maletas en el carro.** Put the bags in the car.
>
> **Han puesto las mesas.** They have set the tables.
>
> **Van a poner coto a eso.** They are going to put a stop to that.
>
> **La gallina pone huevos grandes.** The hen lays large eggs.
>
> **Tratan de poner paz a las dos facciones.** They are trying to impose peace on the two factions.
>
> **Pongo un peso a que no vengan.** I'll bet a peso they don't come.
>
> **Él me pone** (*or* **da**) **miedo.** He scares me.
>
> **Me pusieron de oro y azul.** They gave me a dressing down.

A few idioms with **poner:**

> **poner en claro,** to make clear
> **poner en duda,** to throw doubt on
> **poner fuego a,** to set fire to
> **poner por escrito,** to put in writing

Ponerse means *to put on, to become,* (of sun) *to set:*

> **Me puse el traje nuevo**   I put on my new suit.
> **Se puso la mano sobre el corazón.**   He put his hand over his heart.
> **Se puso colorada.**   She got red, *or* blushed.
> **El sol se pondrá pronto.**   The sun will set soon.

Also note:

> **ponerse a,** to set about, start to   (**Se puso a escribir la carta.** He set about writing the letter.)
> **ponerse de pie,** to stand up   (**Se pusieron de pie.** They stood up.)

SITUATION MATERIAL — EATING (5): VEGETABLES, FRUITS. If you travel to two or more Spanish-speaking countries, you will find that the names of some foods, especially vegetables and fruits, change from country to country. Pineapple may be **piña** throughout the Spanish-speaking world, but if you ask for **jugo de naranja** in Puerto Rico, the waiter may correct you: "**Jugo de china.**" (In Spain it would be **zumo de naranja.**) But the standard Spanish name for a food will no doubt be understood even if it is not popularly used.

You may find in the markets or on menus some foods that are unknown to you, such as **ujías,** land crabs, **chayotes** (a vegetable), or (fruits) **anonas, canepas, mangos, nísperas, zapotes.**

vegetables: (*botanical term*) **vegetales,** (*garden produce*) **hortalizas,** (*greens*) **verduras,** (*legumes*) **legumbres** (*the term is not restricted to legumes*)

beans: (*in general, also broad beans*) **habas,** (*kidney beans*) **habichuelas,** (*string beans*) **habichuelas, judías,** (*Mex.*) **ejotes,** (*black beans*) **frijoles; frijoles refritos,** bean cakes

col, repollo, berza, cabbage	**alcachofa,** artichoke
espinacas, spinach	**guisantes, chícharos,** peas
patatas, (SA) **papas,** potatoes; **puré de p.,** mashed p.	
nabos, turnips	**zanahorias,** carrots
remolachas, betarragas, (*Mex.*) **betabeles,** beets	
ensalada, salad; **e. de frutas,** fruit salad	
lechuga, lettuce	**aguacate,** avocado
tomate, (*Mex.*) **jitomate,** tomato	**pepino,** cucumber, pickle

papaya, lechosa, (*Cuba*) fruta bomba, papaya   melón

frutas, fruit(s) (fruto *is the* fruit *of labor or investment*)

banana, (SA) guineo, banana; plátano, plantain (*large banana for cooking*)

cerezas, cherries   ciruela, plum

durazno, melocotón, peach   fresas, strawberries

limón, lemon; limoncillo, lime   naranja, orange

manzana, apple (*also* block *of houses*)

pera, pear   piña, pineapple

toronja, grapefruit   uvas, grapes; pasas, raisins

LAZARILLO DE TORMES   (4)

« Hijo, ya sé que no te veré más. Procura de ser bueno, y Dios
"Son, I well know I shall see you no more. Try to be good, and God

te guíe. Criado te he y con buen amo te he puesto: válete por
guide you. I have brought you up and have placed you with (a) good master. Take

tí. »
care of yourself."

Y así me fui para mi amo, que esperándome estaba.
And so I went away to my master, who was awaiting me.

Salimos de Salamanca y, llegando a la puente, está a la entrada de
We left Salamanca and, arriving at the bridge, there is at its en-

ella un animal de piedra que casi tiene forma de toro, y el ciego man-
trance a stone animal which almost has (the) form of (a) bull, and the blind (man)

dóme que llegase [1] cerca del animal y, allí puesto, me dijo:
ordered me to go up close to the animal and, there placed, he said to me:

« Lázaro, llega [1] el oído a este toro y oirás gran ruido dentro de él. »
"Lázaro, put your ear to this bull and you'll hear (a) great noise inside it."

Yo simplemente llegué,[1] creyendo ser así. Y, como sintió que tenía
I simply did so, believing it to be so. And, as he felt that I had

la cabeza par de la piedra, afirmó recio la mano [2] y dióme una gran
my head by the stone, he hardened his hand and gave me a great

calabazada [3] en el diablo del toro, que más de tres días me duró el dolor
blow against the devil of the bull, so that the pain of the thrust lasted more than three

de la cornada [4] y díjome:
days, and he said to me:

[1] llegase, llega, llegué. Llegar means *to arrive, come, to reach* or *stretch out,
to bring near;* llegarse, *to approach, come near.*

[2] afirmó recio la mano. Afirmar means *to make firm, strengthen;* recio means
stout, strong; that is, he made a fist.

[3] calabazada. Calabaza is a *gourd* and slang for *head;* the ending –ada often
means a *blow.*

[4] cornada means, literally, *thrust with a horn* (cuerno), as a bull's horn.

« Necio, aprende: que el mozo del ciego un punto [1] ha de saber más
"Fool, learn: that the boy of the blind (man) has to know a bit more

que el diablo. »
than the devil."

Y rió mucho la burla.
And he laughed heartily at the joke.

Parecióme que en aquel instante desperté de la simpleza en que
It seemed to me that in that moment I awoke from the simplicity in which

como niño dormido estaba.   Dije entre mí:
as a child I was asleep.   I said within myself:

« Verdad dice éste, que me cumple avivar el ojo y avisar, pues
"This (man) says (the) truth, that it behooves me to keep a sharp eye and take heed,

solo soy, y pensar como me sepa valer. »
as I am alone, and to think how I may learn how to benefit myself."

Comenzamos nuestro camino y en muy pocos días me mostró jeri-
We set out on our road, and in (a) very few days he showed me rascality.

gonza.[2] Y, como me viese [3] de buen ingenio, holgábase mucho y decía:
And, as he saw me quite clever, he was very pleased and said:

« Yo oro ni plata no te lo puedo dar; mas avisos, para vivir, muchos
"I can give you neither gold nor silver; but advice, in order to live, I'll

te mostraré. »
show you plenty."

Y fué así, que, después de Dios, éste me dió la vida, y, siendo ciego,
And so it was, that, after God, this (man) gave me life, and, being blind,

me alumbró y adestró en la carrera de vivir.
he enlightened me and trained me in the way to live.

§ 5. *The Subjunctive: An Outline of Its Uses — Sequence of Tenses —
Situation Material: Eating (6):   Desserts;   Miscellaneous —* **Lazarillo
de Tormes** (5)

THE SUBJUNCTIVE: AN OUTLINE OF ITS USES.   Before going further
you would do well to review Lesson X, § 2, which explains the
subjunctive in a general way.   You presumably know by now the
subjunctive forms of verbs.   If you wish to test your knowledge of
the forms, write out the subjunctive, in all tenses, of **comprar,
vender,** and **vivir;** then compare what you have written with

---

[1] **punto,** literally "point."

[2] **jerigonza.**   The word now usually means *jargon, gibberish, slang,* or *clownish
antics.*

[3] **me viese.**   In modern Spanish the indicative **me vió** would be used.

the forms on page 112. You should know the rules for deriving the
subjunctive forms from the indicative — what are they? If in
doubt, turn to pages 100, 158–159.

What follows is an outline of the uses of the subjunctive, for
reference purposes. If you wish to learn to speak Spanish well, you
will need to learn how to use the subjunctive in all these ways. If
your ambition is more modest, you will still need to use the subjunctive in some of its uses, as in requests. And if you expect to
read Spanish, you will constantly come upon subjunctives, which
you will want to understand.

There are two general principles that apply to the subjunctive:
(A) The subjunctive does not make a direct statement of fact.
(B) The subjunctive follows and is dependent upon (*subjoined* to)
a verb in the indicative.

In apparent exceptions to the second rule, the indicative verb is
implied and, in the early days of the language, was no doubt
expressed. Thus we may say **Tráigame un vaso de agua** (*Bring
me a glass of water*). The original form of such a polite request
was no doubt **Quiero,** or **Ruego, que Ud. me traiga. . . .** This
was shortened to **Que me traiga . . .** (which may be used today).
Finally, by analogy with the imperative and the infinitive, the
pronouns came to be attached to the subjunctive: **Tráigame. . . .**
When you say, in English, "Bring me a glass of water," *bring* is
imperative, which you may soften by adding "please." But when
you say it in Spanish, it is "[I request that] you bring me a glass of
water."

Uses of the Subjunctive:

(1) In *polite requests* and *negative commands:*

> **Tenga cuidado.** Be careful.
> **Hablen Uds. español, por favor.** Speak Spanish, please.
> **Escríbame una carta.** Write me a letter.
> **No se mueva.** Do not move.

Que may be used before these expressions:

> **Que me escriba una carta.**

The Spanish imperative is never used in *negative commands.*
Compare:

> **¡ Siéntase !** Sit down ! (*command*)
> **Siéntese.** Sit down. (*request*)
> **No se siente.** Do not sit down. (*command or request*)

(2) *Imperative with* **que,** translated *let:* The **que** really means *that*, and in Spanish the construction is not really different from that of (1). But in both Spanish and English the expression is usually classified as an imperative. In the third person, singular and plural, it is used to express a commandment:

Que sea luz. Let there be light.
Que callen. Let them be silent.

In more commonplace statements, English *let* may mean *allow*, but the Spanish expression is the same:

Que lo lea. Let him read it (*I don't care*).

This is a shortened form of something like:

Permita que lo lea. Let him, *or* Allow him to, read it.

(3) *Exhortations* (*let us*):

Comamos algo. Let's eat something.

A much used exception is the indicative **vamos,** for **vayamos,** *let's go.*

(4) After verbs expressing a *command, request, permission,* etc.:

El capitán manda que ataquen. The captain orders them to attack.
Insistí en que me devuelvan el dinero. I insisted that they return the money.
Le ruego a Ud. que se vaya. I beg you to go (away).
No permiten que se hagan preguntas. They do not permit questions to be asked.

(5) After verbs expressing *desire, hope, fear,* etc.:

Deseo que sepan la verdad. I wish them to know the truth.
Espero que Ud. se divierta. I hope you are having a good time. *Or:* I hope you have a good time.
Temo que él se lo diga a ella. I am afraid that he will tell her.

The main verb may be implied:

Que pase buena noche. Good night. ([I hope] that you pass a good night.)
Que le vaya bien. Farewell. ([I hope] that it may go well for you.)
Que sean felices. May they be happy.

¡ **Viva la república !** Long live the republic !

¡ **Ojalá que él estuviera aquí !** Would that he were here !
(See 14.)

(6) To express *uncertainty* (in a dependent clause):

Es posible que no vengan. It is possible that they won't come.

Creo que él lo haya olvidado. I think he may have forgotten it.

Me extraño de que no hayan llamado. I am surprised that they have not called.

En caso de que lleguen, llámeme. In case they arrive, call me.

Note 1: In most clauses beginning with **si**, *if*, the indicative is used: **si vienen, llámeme.** But see (14).

Note 2: I wonder is expressed in Spanish by the future indicative:

¡ **Si vendrán ?** I wonder if they will come.

¡ **Qué pasará ?** I wonder what is happening? What can be happening?

Note 3: The present subjunctive is used after **cuando**, *when*, in speaking of the future, as:

Llámeme cuando lleguen los Gómez. Call me when the Gómez's come.

Juana será muy hermosa cuando sea grande. Juana will be very beautiful when she is grown up.

Vengan a visitarnos cuando estén en Nueva York. Come to see us when you are in New York.

(7) The subjunctive is often, though not always, used to express *negation in a dependent clause:*

Creo que él no la conozca. I don't think he knows her.

¡ **Qué lástima que él no esté aquí !** What a pity that he isn't here !

In everyday speech the indicative would probably be used: **conoce, está.**

(8) The subjunctive is used in *indirect statements or questions*, but may not be used in everyday speech:

Dicen que aquellos indios sean muy feroces. They say that those Indians are very fierce.

¿ **Cree Ud. que él se alegre mucho de eso?** Do you think that he is very happy about that?

In ordinary conversation the indicative would be used: **son, alegra.**

(9) *After a relative pronoun that does not refer to a definite person:*

Busco un amigo que hable español. I am looking for a friend who speaks Spanish. (But if the speaker is thinking of a certain friend: **Busco a un amigo, quien habla español.**)

Si Ud. quiere leer una novela española cuyo estilo sea bueno, le prestaré uno. If you want a Spanish novel whose style is good, I'll lend you one.

(10) *After words ending in –quiera* — **quienquiera** (pl. **quienesquiera**), **cualquier(a)** (pl. **cualesquiera**), **dondequiera, cuandoquiera, comoquiera:**

quienesquiera sean, whoever they may be, *or* are

cualquier cosa sea, whatever it may be, *or* is (But: **Cualquier libro servirá.** Any book will do. The subjunctive is not used unless *may* could be used in the translation.)

dondequiera esté, wherever it may be, *or* is

Cuandoquiera Ud. venga, será bienvenido. Whenever you come, you will be welcome.

Comoquiera se diga, es lo mismo. However you say it, it's the same thing.

However modifying an adjective is expressed as follows:

por difícil que sea, however difficult it may be

(11) *After certain conjunctions* if uncertainty is implied:

cuando, *when,* anticipating the future:

cuando vengan, when they come (*in the future*)
cuando vienen, when they come (*each time they come*)
cuando vinieron, *when they came*

aunque, *although:*

aunque sea difícil, although it may be, *or* is, difficult
aunque fué difícil, although it was difficult

en caso que, *in case:* see (6).
no obstante que, *notwithstanding that, in spite of the fact that*

Other conjunctions followed by the subjunctive when the future is anticipated or there is some uncertainty, are:

antes que, before	**aun cuando,** even if
después que, after	**para que,** in order that

hasta que, until	de manera que, de modo que, so
luego que, as soon as	that
mientras que, while	con tal que, siempre que, provided
siempre que, whenever	that

a menos que, a no ser que, excepto que, salvo que, unless

a pesar de que, in spite of the fact that

(12) *After many impersonal expressions:*

Importa que Ud. venga a tiempo. It is important that you come on time.

Basta que Ud. lo mencione. It is sufficient for you to mention it.

Es preciso que él se calle. It is necessary for him to keep quiet.

¡Imposible que sea verdad! Impossible that it should be true!

(13) *In certain expressions such as* **quisiera, pluguiera:**

Quisiera hablar con ella. I should like to speak with her.

¡Pluguiera a Dios que fuera así! Would to God it were so!

(14) *In wishes or suppositions contrary to fact,* the past subjunctive is used:

¡Ojalá que fuera así! Would that it were so!

Si yo fuera Ud., no haría nada. If I were you, I would do nothing.

Si él lo supiese, estaría muy alegre. If he knew it, he would be very happy.

Si él lo hubiese sabido, habría estado muy alegre. If he had known it, he would have been very happy.

Various kinds of conditional statements introduced by **si** will be discussed in Lesson XV.

SEQUENCE OF TENSES. The past subjunctive must be used if it is dependent on a verb in the imperfect or past definite. Thus:

Espero que Ud. venga. I hope you come.

Esperaba que Ud. viniese. I hoped you would come.

Le dice que espere. He tells him to wait.

Le dijo que esperase. He told him to wait.

This is not the whole story of sequence of tenses, but it is the chief thing to remember.

SITUATION MATERIAL — EATING (6): DESSERTS; MISCELLANEOUS

postre, dessert

pastel, pastry, pie

helado, mantecado, ice cream; **sorbete,** sherbet (*if* ice cream *is* **mantecado, helado** *is* ice, sherbet)

queso, cheese

azúcar, sugar

aceite, oil

pimienta, (*black*) pepper

nueces, walnuts, nuts

cacahuetes, (*Cuba*) **maní,** peanuts

flan, caramel custard

torta, cake

pudín, pudingo, pudding

galletas, crackers; **galleticas,** cookies

sal, salt   **ají,** garlic

vinagre, vinegar

mostaza, mustard

almendras, almonds

A ver si tienen pastel de manzana. Let's see if they have apple pie.

Creo que no. ¿ Ha probado Ud. cascos de guayaba con queso? I think not. Have you tried guava shells with cheese?

Me gusta helado de coco. I like coconut ice cream.

Hay varios sabores que no conozco. There are several flavors I don't know.

Yo siempre pido flan. I always order *flan*.

Tráiganos helado de coco, cascos de guayaba, y dos flanes. Bring us coconut ice cream, guava shells, and two *flans*.

Y un café con leche y tres cafecitos. And one *café con leche* and three demitasses.

Señorita ¿ puede traerme unos cerillos? Miss, can you bring me some (*wax*) matches?

Démonos prisa, para llegar al teatro. Let's hurry, to get to the theater. **Vamos.** Let's go.

¿ Cada cual paga su parte? Everyone pays his own bill?

LAZARILLO DE TORMES   (5)

Huelgo de contar a Vuestra Merced estas niñerías, para mostrar
I am pleased to tell Your Honor these childish things, to show

cuanta virtud sea saber los hombres subir siendo bajos y dejarse bajar
how much virtue it is for men to know how to rise, being low, and how great (a) vice to

siendo altos cuanto vicio.
let themselves fall, being high.

Pues tornando al bueno de mi ciego [1] **y contando sus cosas,** [2] **Ud. sepa**
Well, turning to my good blind (man) and counting his qualities, you may know

que, desde que Dios crió el mundo, ninguno formó más astuto ni sagaz.
that, since God created the world, he formed nobody more astute or sagacious.

[1] **al bueno de mi ciego,** literally "to the good (fellow) of my blind (man)."
[2] **cosas,** *things,* not used nowadays in the sense of qualities.

En su oficio era un águila. Ciento y tantas oraciones sabía de coro.[1]
In his business he was an eagle.   A hundred and more prayers he knew by heart.

Un tono bajo y muy sonable, que hacía resonar la iglesia donde rezaba,
A deep and very loud tone, which made the church resound where he prayed,

un rostro[2] **humilde y devoto, que con muy buen continente ponia,**
a humble and devout face, which with (a) very good mien he put on

cuando rezaba, sin hacer gestos[3] **ni visajes con boca ni ojos, como otros**
when he prayed, without making gestures or faces with mouth or eyes, as others

suelen hacer.
are wont to do.

   Allende de[4] **esto, tenía otras mil formas y maneras para sacar el**
   Besides this, he had a thousand other forms and ways of extracting

dinero.   Decía saber oraciones para muchos y diversos efectos: para
money.   He said he knew prayers for many and diverse effects: for

mujeres que no parían, para las que estaban de parto, para las que eran
women who did not give birth, for those who were expecting, for those who were badly

malcasadas, que sus maridos las quisiesen bien.   Echaba pronósticos a
married, that their husbands might love them well.   He made predictions for

las preñadas, si traía hijo o hija.
the pregnant, (telling) if they carried (a) son or (a) daughter.

   Pues en caso de medicina, decía que Galeno no supo la mitad que
   Then in matter of medicine, he said that Galen[5] *did not know the half (of) what*

él para muela,[6] **desmayos, males**[7] **de madre.   Finalmente, nadie le decía**
he (knew) for toothache, faintings, mothers' ills.   Finally, nobody told him

padecer alguna pasión, que luego no le decía:
of suffering any passion that immediately he did not say:

   « **Haced esto, haréis estotro,**[8] **coged tal yerba, tomad**[9] **tal raíz. »**
   "Do this, you'll do the other, gather such a herb, take such a root."

   Con éste andábase todo el mundo tras él, especialmente mujeres, que
   In this (way) everybody went after him, especially women, who

---

   [1] **de coro.**   Coro means *choir, chorus;* only in this idiom does it mean *memory*
or *heart.*   The word for *heart* is **corazón,** and it is never used in the sense of
memory.

   [2] **rostro,** *countenance, visage* (the common word for *face* is **cara**).

   [3] **gestos,** here *gestures;* you may recall the phrase **mal gesto,** in which **gesto**
meant *face.*

   [4] **Allende de.**   The literal translation would be *beyond* (*besides* is usually
además de).

   [5] *Galen,* the Greek "father of medicine."

   [6] **muela,** freely translated *toothache,* means *molar* or *grindstone.*

   [7] **males.**   You are familiar with **mal** as adjective; as noun it means *evil, ill.*

   [8] **estotro,** formed from **esto otro,** *this other* (thing).

   [9] **Haced, haréis, coged, tomad.**   These verbs are all plural.   In speaking
to a single person, the man would no doubt say **haz, harás, coge, toma.**

cuanto les decía creían. De éstas sacaba él grandes provechos con las
believed all that he told them.   From these he drew great benefits with the

artes que digo y ganaba más en un mes, que cien ciegos en un año.
arts I mention and earned more in one month than (a) hundred blind (men) in a year.

Mas también quiero que sepa Ud. que, con todo lo que adquiría y
But also I wish that you know that, with all that he acquired and

tenía, jamás tan avariento ni mezquino hombre no ví, tanto que me
had, I never saw so avaricious or stingy a man, so much that he

mataba a mí [1] de hambre y así no me demediaba de lo necesario. Digo
killed me with hunger and did not half support me with what was necessary. I tell

verdad: si con mi sutileza y buenas mañas no me supiera remediar,
(the) truth: if with my subtlety and good tricks I did not know how to remedy (this),

muchas veces me finara de hambre.
many times I should have perished with hunger.

[1] me mataba a mí. The a mí, not needed for clarity, is used for emphasis.

LISTENING TO RADIO

You should now be able to catch the gist of the Spanish that you hear on the radio. Persist with this practice and you will find it rewarding. There is much of interest to hear. Concentrate at first on the news bulletins (**noticias**). Later you may try to follow a play — the best listening practice, because you hear a variety of voices. The most difficult thing is to understand the words of songs, but you should be able to catch a word now and then in a song. PERSIST, PERSIST, PERSIST! If you continue to study and to listen to the radio, one day you will suddenly realize that you can understand most of what you hear.

LESSON XIII

§ 1. *Compound Nouns — Noun Phrases — Situation Material: At the Barber Shop and Hairdresser's — Carlos Octavio Bunge: El Gaucho*

COMPOUND NOUNS. In English a "compound noun" is a noun composed of two or more other words. An English compound noun may take the form of a single word, a hyphenated word, or two or three separate words (which have come to be thought of and used as a single word); for example, *doorbell, outlook, screwdriver, cross reference, to-do, son-in-law, grocery store, high school, life insurance, bird's-eye view, ice cream cone.*

With many English compounds there is a question of how to write them, and the authorities do not always agree. Fortunately for students of Spanish, the hyphen is not used in Spanish, and there does not seem to be any disagreement about whether to use one word or two.

There are innumerable Spanish compound nouns formed in various ways from various kinds of component words:

(1) *Noun plus adjective:*

aeropuerto, airport
agualluvia, rain water
el aguardiente (agua ardiente, *burning water*), brandy
buenaventura, fortune, good luck
el ferrocarril (ferro– *from* **hierro,** *iron (n.) or* **férreo,** *iron (adj.);* **carril,** *rail*), railway, railroad
hierbabuena (*good herb*), mint
librepensador, free thinker
nochebuena, Christmas Eve

(2) *Verb plus object:*

la guardarropa, wardrobe, clothes closet, check room
el limpiabotas, bootblack (*cleans-boots*)
el matafuego, fire extinguisher (*kills-fire*)
el matasiete, *or* **perdonavidas** (*pardons-lives*), bully, braggart
el mirasol, sunflower (*looks at sun*)
el mondadientes (mondar, *to clean, trim;* **diente,** *tooth*), toothpick
el pasaporte (–porte *related to* **portar,** *to carry*), passport

el **pasatiempo,** pastime

el **pisapapeles** (**pisar,** *step on*), paperweight

el **quitamanchas** (**quitar,** *to remove;* **mancha,** *spot*), spot remover, cleansing fluid

el *or* la **sábelotodo,** know-it-all

el **sacacorchos** (**sacar,** *to take out, extract;* **corcho,** *cork*), corkscrew

el **salvavidas,** life preserver

(3) *Preposition plus object:*

el **parabrisa** (**brisa,** *breeze*), windshield

el **paracaídas** (**caída,** *fall*), parachute; **paracaidista,** parachutist

el **paraguas,** umbrella

el **pararrayos** * (**rayo,** *ray, flash of lightning*), lightning rod

la **sinrazón,** injustice (*without reason,* or *right*)

el *or* la **sinvergüenza,** shameless person, scoundrel, (*f.*) hussy

(4) *Miscellaneous:*

la **bienvenida,** welcome

el **hazmerreír,*** laughing stock (*make me laugh*)

el **malhechor,** evildoer

el **puntapié** (*for* **punta de pie**), kick

el **pordiosero** (**por** + **Dios** + **-ero**), beggar

el **quehacer,** chore, task

NOUN PHRASES. Various kinds of noun phrases correspond to English noun phrases and compound nouns:

(1) *Noun plus one or more adjectives:*

el **gran escritor,** the great writer

la **tierra firme,** terra firma

la **bandera azul y amarilla y verde,** the blue, yellow, and green flag

los **hombres y las mujeres españoles,** Spanish men and women

el **viejo caballo blanco,** the old white horse

---

* When a word beginning with **r** forms the latter part of a compound, the **r** is doubled.

(2) *Noun plus noun (used as adjective):*

> **la lengua madre,** the mother tongue
> **la tierra virgen,** virgin soil
> **el canario hembra,** the female canary
> **el vapor correo,** the mail boat

(3) *Noun followed by prepositional phrase:*

> **los hijos de mi hermana,** my sister's children
> **las patas del gato,** the cat's paws
> **el exterior de la casa,** the outside of the house
> **un sombrero de paja,** a straw hat
> **anillos de oro,** gold rings
> **anteojos con aros de acero,** steel-rimmed glasses
> **una taza de té,** a cup of tea
> **un caballo de montar,** a riding horse
> **el hombre de la barba,** the man with the beard
> **el hombre de la calle,** the man in the street (*the common man*)
> **el camino de Sevilla,** the road to Seville
> **una máquina de escribir,** a typewriter
> **frutas en lata,** canned fruits
> **una taza para té,** a teacup
> **la mesa para escribir,** the writing table
> **el vestido negro de seda en el escaparate,** the black silk
> dress in the window
> **un camino sin fin,** an endless road

But there is no point in further examples. Perhaps the main thing to note is that an English compound noun is not necessarily a compound noun in Spanish: face towel, **toalla para la cara;** wineglass, **copa para vino,** *or just* **copa;** sugar bowl, **azucarero;** flower garden, **jardín;** oak tree, **roble;** pine grove, **pinar;** rainstorm, **aguacero;** washbowl, **palangana;** string beans, **judías.**

SITUATION MATERIAL — AT THE BARBER SHOP AND HAIRDRESSER'S:

peluquería (*from* **peluca,** *wig*), hairdresser's, barber shop; *also* **barbería** (*from* **barba,** *beard*), barber shop; **peluquero,** hairdresser, barber; *also* **barbero,** barber

pelo, hair, fur; **cabello,** hair (*of head*)   **el bigote,** mustache

cortar, to cut, trim; **un corte de pelo,** *or* **cabello,** a haircut

corto, short; **largo,** long; **medio largo,** medium

calvo, bald   **canas,** gray hair(s)

quemar las puntas, to singe

el champú, la fricción, shampoo; **dar ch.** *or* **fr.,** to shampoo

el peine, comb; **peinar,** to comb, dress, set (*hair*); **peinado,** hairdo, headdress

tijeras, scissors; **(tijeras) podaderas,** clippers

afeitar(se), to shave; *also* **afeitarse,** to groom oneself, primp

navaja, razor; **hoja de navaja,** razor blade

el salón de belleza, beauty parlor

ondular, to wave (*hair*); **ondulación permanente,** permanent wave

lavar, to wash   **teñir (i),** to dye

un masaje facial, a "facial"

el cutis, skin (*of face; of body:* **la piel**)

la tez, complexion

manicuro, manicure

uñas, nails; **uñas de los pies,** toenails

Deseo afeitarme. I'd like a shave.

Un corte de pelo (*or* cabello), por favor. A haircut, please.

Déjemelo en la misma forma. Leave it in the same style.

Córteme un poco la coronilla. Take a little off the top.

Límpieme la nuca y las patillas, no más. Just trim the back and sides.

Póngame loción en la cabeza. Put some hair tonic on my head.

Quisiera pedir hora para un champú. I'd like an appointment for a shampoo.

Se ha pedido hora para mí, para las dos y media. An appointment was made for me at two-thirty.

Hágame una fricción, una ondulación permanente, y peinarme. I'd like a shampoo, a permanent wave, and my hair set.

Péineme tal como estaba antes. Dress my hair as it was before.

Quisiera lavar la cabeza con alheña. I want a henna wash.

Quisiera oxigenar (teñir) el pelo. I want my hair bleached (dyed).

No quiero nada más. I don't want anything else.

¿ Cuánto debo? How much do I owe?

READING. From now on, you will not be given an interlinear translation of a selection in Spanish. You are to make what you can of each selection, consulting the notes, but not the translation. Only when you have done your best to understand the passage should you consult the translation; then study the passage, noting the meanings of unfamiliar words and difficult constructions. The translations are more literal than literary.

The Spanish of the following selection, from an Argentine writer, differs not at all from the Castilian of a good Spanish writer — except for a few local words. This holds true for all Spanish-American writing.

Argentine Writer   *Carlos Octavio Bunge* (1875–1918)

El Gaucho

El gaucho se formó en la planicie y bajo un clima templado. Fué el hijo de la pampa, aquel desierto siempre verde bajo un cielo siempre límpido, antes de que la moderna cultura la poblase de industrias y de ciudades. Entrecortaban la desolación del paisaje algún ombú[1] solitario, tal cual bosquecillo de talas,[1] y si acaso el rumor de los arroyos o el espejo de las lagunas, donde miríadas de aves reflejaban de púrpura y de nácar. A lo lejos sorprendía la vista fatigada por la sensación de la inmensidad, el grupo multicolor de caballos cimarrones. Salpicaban el mar de la llanura, como islotes, acá y allá, en grandes manchas calizas, montones de osamentas de vacas silvestres. Cuando por su copiosidad parecían cubrir la haz de la tierra, habían sido sacrificadas por tropas de gauchos, para vender los cueros y la grasa. La carne se abandonaba a los caranchos[1] y chimangos[1] que posados señorilmente sobre aquellos restos, se dirían mitos de una religión exterminadora. Tras la línea del horizonte estaban los indios, siempre en acecho. Al sonar la hora del malón brotaban entre el silencio y la sombra, alanceaban a los hombres y a los niños, arrebataban a las mujeres, dispersaban el ganado y huían mezclando en el viento sus ensangrentadas melenas con las crines de sus potros.

TRANSLATION:

The Gaucho [2]

The gaucho was formed on the plain and under a temperate climate. He was the son of the pampa, that ever green desert under an ever limpid sky, before modern culture settled it with industries and towns. The desolation of the landscape was partly cut by some solitary ombú, *here and there a coppice of* talas, *and perhaps the murmur of the streams or the mirror of the lakes, where myriads of birds gave reflections of purple and mother-of-pearl. In the distance the multicolored group of wild horses surprised the vision tired by the feeling of immensity. There sprinkled the sea of the plain, like islets here and there, in great limestone patches, heaps of bones of wild cattle. When by their abundance they seemed to cover the face of the earth, they had been sacrificed by troops of gauchos, to sell the horns and the fat. The flesh was abandoned to the* caranchos *and* chimangos, *which, posed in a lordly manner on those remains, one would say were myths of an exterminating religion. Beyond the line of the horizon were the Indians, always in ambush. When the hour of sudden attack struck, they rushed out amid silence and shade, speared the men and the children, carried off the women, dispersed the cattle, and fled, mixing in the wind their blood-stained locks with the manes of their ponies.*

[1] In the words *ombú, talas, caranchos,* and *chimangos*, the student has examples of a difficulty he will meet in most Spanish-American writings: local words to describe local flora and fauna. The *ombú* and the *tala* are Argentine trees. *Caranchos* and *chimangos* are local birds of prey.

[2] *Gaucho*, the Argentine cowboy.

§ 2. *Compound Adjectives — Adjectival Phrases — Situation Material:
At the Bullfight — Bartolomé Mitre:* **Bolívar y San Martín**

COMPOUND ADJECTIVES:

(1) Most Spanish compound adjectives have to do with physical characteristics and are composed of *noun plus adjective* (the ending of the noun is changed to **i**):

aliquebrado (**ala,** *wing;* **quebrado,** *broken*), broken-winged, disheartened
barbiblanco, white-bearded
barbicano (**cana,** *gray hair*), gray-bearded
barbinegro, black-bearded
boquiabierto (**boca,** *mouth*), open-mouthed
cariancho (**cara,** *face;* **ancho,** *wide*), broad-faced
caribobo (**bobo,** *stupid*), stupid-faced
carigordo (**gordo,** *fat*), fat-faced
manilargo, long-handed
ojialegre, bright-eyed
ojiazul, blue-eyed
peliblanco, pelicano, pelilargo, pelinegro, pelirrojo, white-haired, *etc.*
perniabierto (**pierna,** *leg*) bowlegged
pernituerto (**tuerto,** *twisted*), crooked-legged
airecondicionado, air-conditioned

(2) Other compound adjectives are composed of *adverb plus adjective:*

bienamado, (well-)beloved
bienaventurado (**ventura,** *fortune*), fortunate
bienintencionado, well-meaning
bienvenido, welcome
malacostumbrado, badly behaved *or* brought up, spoiled
malcriado (**criar,** *to bring up*), badly brought up, spoiled
malhablado, foul-mouthed
malhecho, ill-formed, misshapen
malhumorado, ill-humored, bad-tempered
malsonante, evil-sounding
todopoderoso, all-powerful

ADJECTIVAL PHRASES. Some English compound adjectives are translated into Spanish by adjectival phrases, others by single words (not compounds). The following are typical translations of English compound adjectives:

> two-headed, **de dos cabezas**
> two-and-a-half-hour, **de dos horas y media**
> three-volume, **de tres tomos**
> four-motored, **de cuatro motores**
> five-pointed, **de cinco puntas**
> six-story, **de seis pisos**
> seven-year-old, **de siete años**

> black-shirted, **de camisa negra**
> broad-brimmed, **de ala ancha**
> English-speaking, **de habla inglesa**
> first-class, **de primera clase**
> fun-loving, **ávido de diversión,** *(gay)* **alegre**
> good-hearted, **de buena corazón**
> half-dead, **medio muerto**
> horse-faced, **de cara acaballada**
> scatterbrained, **ligero de cascos**
> star-spangled, **sembrada de estrellas**

Note: In an adjective phrase, *with* after a past participle is translated **de** (as in **sembrada de** above, literally "sowed with"):

> covered with snow, **cubierto de nieve**
> adorned with flowers, **adornado de flores**

> rubber-soled, **con suelas de goma**
> silver-rimmed, **con aros de plata**
> wooden-wheeled, **con ruedas de madera**

Note: As illustrated in the three examples just above, **con . . . de** is used to avoid repetition of **de**.

Adjectives ending in *-colored* are translated in various ways:

> flame-colored, **color de fuego**
> mouse-colored, **color de ratón**
> chestnut-colored, **color castaño**
> olive-colored, **aceitunado**
> orange-colored, **anaranjado**

Often, an English compound adjective must be translated by a single Spanish word:

> one-armed, **manco**
> one-eyed, **tuerto, monóculo**

one-sided (*unfair*), **desigual, parcial**
eight-sided, **octágono, octagonal**
barefooted, **descalzo**
cross-eyed, **bisojo**
half-hearted, **indiferente**
half-witted, **imbécil**
happy-go-lucky, **despreocupado**
oil-bearing, **petrolífero**
so-called, **llamado**
up-to-date, **moderno**

Note: As some of the above examples suggest, when you are searching for the Spanish equivalent of an English expression, it often helps to think of synonyms of the English word or phrase, as *modern* for *up-to-date.*

SITUATION MATERIAL—AT THE BULLFIGHT. Most North Americans loathe bullfights, but if they visit a country where bullfights are held they usually see one out of curiosity, and are as uncomprehending as an Englishman seeing his first baseball game. If you are interested in bullfighting, which is, whether we like it or not, a part of Spanish culture, you will find a glossary of terms, with explanations — and also a gripping story — in Hemingway's *Death in the Afternoon.* Blasco Ibáñez's **Sangre y Arena,** *Blood and Sand,* is probably the best Spanish novel on the subject.

toro, bull; **corrida de toros,** bullfight; **plaza de toros,** bullring
tauromaquia, bullfighting; the art, *or* technique, of bullfighting; **tauro-máquico,** bullfighting (*adj.*)
arena, sand, arena   **asiento,** seat
sol, sun, the sunny side   **sombra,** shade, the shady side
barrera, *section where people sit on benches* (*usually of stone*)
almohadilla, cushion (*rented to sit on, in the barrera*)
tendido, *section above the barrera, with seats*
torero, bullfighter   **matador,** matador (*killer*)
cuadrilla, *the matador's "team" of seven*
picador (*from* **picar,** to sting, bite), picador, *who incites the bull on horseback* (*In these more humane days the horse is protected by padding from the horns of the bull, and the* **picador's** *lance is padded.*)
banderillero, *one who thrusts the* **banderilla** (*flagged barb*) *into the bull's shoulders*
muleta, *small red flag used by matador*   **capa,** cape
la espada, the sword; **el espada,** the matador
el presidente (**en su palco**), the president (*of the bullfight*) (*in his box*)

Yo quisiera ver una corrida de toros. ¿ Cuándo habrá una? I'd like to see a bullfight. When is there one?

No me gusta la sangre, pero es una cosa de ver. I don't like blood, but it is something to see.

¿ Puede Ud. conseguirme dos billetes para la corrida de miércoles? Can you get me two tickets for Wednesday's bullfight?

¿ Sol o sombra? Sunny or shady side?

Sombra, si es posible. The shady side, if possible.

Dos de sombra. Two on the shady side.

La muchedumbre me interesa más que los toros. The crowd interests me more than the bullfight.

Naturalmente no comprendo las finezas. Naturally I don't understand the fine points.

Argentine Writer   *Bartolomé Mitre* (1821–1906)

Bolívar y San Martín [1]

Bolívar era el genio de la ambición delirante, con el temple férreo de los varones fuertes, con el corazón lleno de [2] pasiones sin freno, con la cabeza poblada de [2] flotantes sueños políticos, sediento de [2] gloria, de poder, de resplandor, de estrépito, que acaudillando heroicamente una gran causa, todo lo refería a su personalidad invasora y absorbente. El [3] mismo se ha retratado así prorrumpiendo en uno de sus teatrales simulacros de renuncia del mando supremo: — « Salvadme de mí mismo, porque la espada que libertó a Colombia no es la balanza de Astrea.[4] »

San Martín era el vaso opaco de la Escritura,[5] que escondía la luz en el interior del alma: el héroe impersonal que tenía la ambición honrada del bien común, por todos los medios, por todos los caminos y con todos los hombres de buena voluntad, según él mismo se ha definido en la intimidad con estas sencillas palabras: — « Un americano, republicano por principios, que sacrifica sus mismas inclinaciones por el bien de su suelo. »

Por eso los dos murieron en el ostracismo. El uno en su edad viril, precipitado de lo alto, con las entrañas devoradas por el buitre de su inextinguible ambición personal, llorando hasta sus últimos momentos el poder

[1] Simón Bolívar, called El Libertador, is not only the national hero of Venezuela, where he was born in 1783 (d. 1830), but the great Spanish-American hero. Bolívar led the military forces that brought about the independence of Colombia, Venezuela, Ecuador, Bolivia, and Peru.

The Argentine José de San Martín (1778–1850) commanded the revolutionary armies that freed Argentina and Chile. Unable to come to an agreement with Bolívar at a meeting in Guayaquil, Ecuador, he abandoned his military career. San Martín is the national hero of Argentina.

[2] **lleno de, poblada de, sediento de:** examples of **de** translated *with*, as mentioned in this section.

[3] **El,** *he.* Here, and hereafter in the readings, the accent mark is not placed on capital letters. As a rule, an accent is placed on a capital only in elementary books and dictionaries.

[4] **Astrea,** goddess of justice.

[5] **el vaso opaco de la Escritura.** The reference is to the passage translated in the King James version as "Hide not thy light under a bushel."

perdido. El otro descendió sereno y resignado la pendiente del valle de la vida, con la estoica satisfacción del deber cumplido, guardando en su ancianidad el secreto roedor de sus tristezas, como en los heroicos días de su épica carrera había guardado el sigilo pavoroso de sus grandes concepciones militares.

TRANSLATION:

BOLÍVAR AND SAN MARTÍN

Bolívar was the genius of delirious ambition, with the iron disposition of strong men, with (his) heart full of unbridled passions, with his head full of floating political dreams, thirsty for glory, power, splendor, clamor, who, heroically heading a great cause, related everything (in it) to his invading and absorbing personality. He himself has portrayed himself thus, bursting forth in one of his theatrical fancies of renouncing the supreme command: "Save me from myself, because the sword which liberated Colombia is not the balance of Astraea."

San Martín was the opaque receptacle of the Scripture, who hid his light in the interior of his soul: the impersonal hero who had the honest ambition for the common welfare, by every means, by every way, and with all men of good will, as he himself has defined (it) privately in these simple words: "An American, republican in principles, who sacrifices his own inclinations for the well-being of his soil (land)."

For that the two (men) died in ostracism. The one in his virile age, precipitated from the height, with (his) entrails devoured by the vulture of his inextinguishable personal ambition, mourning until his last moments the lost power. The other went down, serene and resigned, the slope of the valley of life, with the stoical satisfaction of duty fulfilled, guarding in his old age the gnawing secret of his griefs, as in the heroic days of his epic career he had guarded the awful secret of his great military conceptions.

§ 3. *Verbs Formed from Nouns and Adjectives — Situation Material: Photography — Jorge Isaacs:* La Caza del Tigre

VERBS FORMED FROM NOUNS AND ADJECTIVES. It has already been emphasized that most Spanish verbs end in –ar and that few –ar verbs are irregular. Furthermore: (a) All new verbs added to the language end in –ar. (b) Almost all verbs made from nouns end in –ar.

Some verbs are made from nouns by using the stem of the noun as the stem of the verb; for example:

barniz, varnish; **barnizar,** to varnish
clavo, nail; **clavar,** to nail
martillo, hammer; **martillar,** to hammer
patín, skate; **patinar,** to skate
sierra, saw; **serrar (ie),** to saw
techo, roof; **techar,** to roof

Many verbs are formed by adding a prefix to the noun stem plus the –ar ending.

The prefix a(d)– means *to* and indicates the *application or use* of the thing:

> **carro,** cart; **acarrear,** to cart, carry, transport
> **cepillo,** plane; **acepillar,** to plane
> **frente,** front; **afrentar,** to affront
> **tornillo,** screw; **atornillar,** to screw

The prefix en– (em– before b or p) means *in* or *on* and indicates *putting something into* or *onto something else:*

> **bala,** bale; **embalar,** to bale
> **bolsilla,** pocket; **embolsillar,** to pocket
> **botella,** bottle; **embotellar,** to bottle
> **cola,** glue; **encolar,** to glue (**cola** *also means* tail)
> **jabón,** soap; **enjabonar,** to soap
> **papel,** paper; **empapelar,** to wrap in paper
> **paquete,** package; **empaquetar,** to pack, package
> **tierra,** earth; **enterrar (ie),** to inter, bury

The prefix **des–** is negative, like English *dis–,* and indicates *taking something away from something else:*

> **cabeza,** head; **descabezar,** to behead
> **cola,** tail; **descolar,** to cut off, *or* dock, the tail of
> **corteza,** bark, shell, hull, rind; **descortezar,** to strip the bark from, shell, hull, remove the rind from
> **hoja,** leaf; **deshojar,** to strip the leaves from
> **pelleja** *or* –o, skin, hide; **despellejar,** to skin, flay
> **pluma,** feather; **desplumar,** to pluck (*a fowl*)

Some verbs are made by using the stem of the adjective as the em of the verb, as:

> **alegre,** gay, happy, merry; **alegrar,** to gladden, cheer
> **ciego,** blind; **cegar (ie),** to blind
> **limpio,** clean; **limpiar,** to clean
> **seco,** dry; **secar,** to dry
> **vacío,** empty; **vaciar,** to empty

Various verbs are formed from adjectives by means of prefixes or certain endings (–ear, –ecer, –ficar, –izar):

> **grande,** large, big; **agrandar,** to enlarge
> **hondo,** deep; **ahondar,** to deepen
> **llano,** flat; **allanar,** to flatten

duro, hard; **endurar,** to harden
gordo, fat; **engordar,** to fatten
sucio, dirty; **ensuciar,** to dirty

blanco, white; **blanquear,** to whiten, whitewash, bleach
borracho, drunk; **borrachear,** to get drunk (*often*)
hermoso, beautiful; **hermosear,** to beautify

o(b)scuro, dark; **o(b)scurecer,** to darken, obscure
pálido, pale; **palidecer,** to become, grow, *or* turn pale
robusto, robust; **robustecer,** to strengthen

pobre, poor; **empobrecer,** to make poor, impoverish
rico, rich; **enriquecer,** to enrich, make rich
triste, sad; **entristecer,** to make sad, sadden

fuerte, strong; **fortificar,** to fortify
pacífico, peaceful; **pacificar,** to pacify
pétreo, stony, rocky; **petrificar,** to petrify

civil, civil; **civilizar,** to civilize
moderno, modern; **modernizar,** to modernize
social, social; **socializar,** to socialize

SITUATION MATERIAL — PHOTOGRAPHY:

fotografía, photography; **una foto(grafía),** a photo(graph); **fotografiar,**
to photograph; **fotógrafo,** photographer; **fotográfico,** photographic;
tienda fotográfica, camera store
en colores, color (*adj.*)   **blanco y negro,** black-and-white
cinematográfico, motion-picture, movie (*adj.*)
cámara, camera (*usually called* **aparato,** apparatus)
miniatura, miniature   **réflex,** reflex
el lente, lens; **l. de retrato,** portrait lens
filtro (amarillo, rojo), (yellow, red) filter
película, film; **p. de colores (blanca y negra),** color (black-and-white)
film
rollo, roll   **bobina,** spool   **revelar,** to develop
copia, prueba, print (*n.*); **hacer pruebas** *or* **copias de,** to print (*films*);
tirar una prueba de, to make a print of
negativo, negative (*n.*)   **transparencia,** transparency
instantánea, snapshot; **sacar una i.,** to take a picture
retrato, portrait; **retratar,** to make a portrait of, take a picture of
ampliar, to enlarge; **ampliación,** enlargement
¿Dónde hay una buena tienda de artículos fotográficos? Where is
there a good camera supplies store?

Hay una en la Avenida República, a la Calle Séptima, a la esquina. El nombre del propietario es Hoffmann, y es muy digno de confianza. There is one on Avenida República, at Calle Séptima, on the corner. The name is Hoffmann, and he is very reliable.

Quiero dos rollos de películas [marco] 120. I want two rolls of film [brand name] 120.

También quiero dos rollos regulares (blanco y negro). Also I want two rolls of ordinary (black-and-white) film.

Aquí tiene mi aparato. Hágame el favor de ponerme la película. Here's my camera. Would you do me the favor of putting the film in?

Quiero éstas reveladas, nada más; no quiero copias. I just want these developed; I don't want copies.

¿ Cuándo estarán listas? When will they be ready?

Yo dije muy claro, revelar no más, que no quise copias. I said very clearly just to develop them, that I didn't want prints made.

Quiero una copia, de este tamaño, de éstas, y dos copias cada una de éstas — el mismo tamaño. I want one print, of this size, of these (films), and two prints apiece of these — the same size.

¿ Cuándo pasaré a buscarlas? When shall I call for them?

Quiero dos ampliaciones, ocho pulgadas * por cinco, brillantes (mates), de ésta. I want two enlargements, eight inches by five, glossy (mat) of this.

Hágame una docena de tarjetas postales con este negativo. Make me a dozen postal cards with this negative.

Cochero, pare un momento, que quiero sacar una instantánea. Driver, stop a moment; I want to take a picture.

Quisiera retratar a los hombres de las máscaras. ¿ Puede Ud. arreglarlo? I'd like to get a picture of the men in the masks. Can you arrange it?

Niño, ¿ puedo retratar a Ud. y a su hermanita? Little boy, may I take a picture of you and your little sister? **Le doy diez centavos.** I'll give you ten centavos.

Colombian Writer   *Jorge Isaacs* (1837–95)

La Caza del Tigre

No convenía dar tregua a la fiera, y se evitaba así riesgo mayor a Braulio.

Los perros volvieron al ataque simultáneamente. Otro de ellos quedó muerto sin dar un quejido.

El tigre lanzó un maullido horroroso.

Braulio apareció tras el grupo de robles, hacia nuestro lado, empuñando el asta de la lanza sin la hoja.

* A **pulgada,** *inch,* is a "flea jump" (from **pulga,** *flea*). The metric system is used in Spanish-speaking countries, but inches, feet, and miles are generally understood.

La fiera dió la misma vuelta en su busca; y él gritó:

— ¡Fuego! ¡Fuego!, volviendo a quedar de un brinco en el mismo punto donde había estado la lanza.

El tigre lo buscaba. Lucas había desaparecido. Tiburcio estaba de color de aceituna. Apuntó y sólo se quemó la ceba.

José disparó; el tigre rugió de nuevo tratando como de morderse el lomo, y de un salto volvió instantáneamente sobre Braulio. Este dando una nueva vuelta tras de los robles, lanzóse hacia nosotros a recoger la lanza que le arrojaba José.

Entonces la fiera nos dió frente. Sólo mi escopeta estaba disponible: disparé; el tigre se sentó sobre la cola, tambaleó y cayó.

Braulio miró atrás instintivamente para saber el efecto del último tiro. José, Tiburcio y yo nos hallábamos ya cerca de él, y todos a un tiempo dimos un grito de triunfo.

La fiera arrojaba sanguaza espumosa por la boca: tenía los ojos empañados e inmóviles, y en el último parasismo de muerte estiraba las piernas temblorosas y removía la hojarasca al enrollar y desenrollar la hermosa cola.

— ¡Valiente tiro!... ¡Qué tiro!...— exclamó Braulio poniéndole un pie al animal sobre el cogote. — ¡En la frente! ¡Ese sí que es pulso firme!

TRANSLATION:

THE TIGER * HUNT

It was not advisable to give (any) respite to the beast, and thus greater risk to Braulio was avoided.

The dogs returned to the attack simultaneously. Another of them lay dead without uttering a yelp.

The tiger let out a frightful roar.

Braulio appeared behind the group of oaks, to our side, holding the shaft of the lance without the blade.

The (savage) beast took the same turn seeking him; and he shouted:

"Fire! Fire!" returning with one leap to the same point where the lance had been.

The tiger was looking for him. Lucas had disappeared. Tiburcio was olive-colored (green). He aimed and the priming only burned out.

José fired. The tiger roared again, trying as if to bite its loin, and with one spring came instantaneously upon Braulio. The latter, taking a new turn behind the oaks, hurled himself towards us to recover the lance which José threw him.

Then the wild beast faced us. Only my shotgun was available: I fired; the tiger sat on its tail, tottered, and fell.

Braulio looked behind instinctively to know the effect of the last shot. José, Tiburcio, and I now found ourselves near him, and all (of us) gave at one time a shout of triumph.

* The American **tigre** is really a jaguar, not a tiger.

The beast was emitting bloody froth from its mouth: its eyes were blurred and immobile, and in the last paroxysms of death it stretched its trembling legs and removed the dead leaves in coiling and uncoiling its beautiful tail.

"A fine shot!   What a shot!" exclaimed Braulio, putting a foot on the back of the animal's neck.   "In the forehead!   That indeed is a steady hand."

§ 4. *Words for Males and Females — Situation Material: Doctor and Dentist — Ricardo Palma:* Carta

WORDS FOR MALES AND FEMALES.   As you know, a great many Spanish words end in –o and –a, and nearly all of them are masculine and feminine, respectively.

Some words have alternative endings, according to whether a male or female is meant, as:

> **amo,** master, proprietor, boss (*male*);   **ama,*** mistress, proprietress, landlady, lady of the house, boss (*female*)
>
> **mozo,** youth, lad, young fellow;   **moza,** lass, (young) girl
>
> **pasajero,** passenger;   **pasajera,** (female) passenger
>
> **maestro,** teacher;   **maestra,** teacher (*female*)
>
> **católico,** Catholic;   **católica,** Catholic (*female*), C. woman
>
> **italiano,** Italian;   **italiana,** Italian woman
>
> **vegetariano, –a,** vegetarian
>
> **médico,** doctor, physician;   **médica,** woman doctor (*also* doctor's wife *or* medicine [*the science*])
>
> **hijo,** son;   **hija,** daughter
>
> **muchacho,** boy;   **muchacha,** girl
>
> **niño,** little boy;   **niña,** little girl
>
> **tío,** uncle;   **tía,** aunt
>
> **sobrino,** nephew;   **sobrina,** niece
>
> **abuelo,** grandfather;   **abuela,** grandmother
>
> **nieto,** grandson;   **nieta,** granddaughter
>
> **cuñado,** brother-in-law;   **cuñada,** sister-in-law
>
> **perro,** dog;   **perra,** (female) dog, bitch
>
> **gato,** cat, tomcat;   **gata,** female cat
>
> **paloma,** pigeon, dove;   **palomo,** male, *or* cock, pigeon, *or* dove

Some words do not vary the ending to indicate gender, which is indicated by the article.   Thus:

> **el joven,** the young man;   **la joven,** the young woman
>
> **el tigre,** the tiger;   **la tigre,** the tigress

---

* Though **ama** is feminine, **el ama** must be used because **el** precedes any noun beginning with accented a– or ha–.

el *or* la **centinela,** the sentinel

el *or* la **cómplice,** the accomplice

el *or* la **compatriota,** the compatriot, fellow countryman

el *or* la **espía,** the spy

el *or* la **guía,** the guide

el *or* la **reo,** the criminal, culprit

el *or* la **testigo,** the witness

un *or* una **liberal,** a liberal

un *or* una **protestante,** a Protestant

To the same class belong all the numerous words ending in
–ista (Eng. *–ist*), such as **artista, comunista, idealista, lingüista,
pacifista, turista;** as: **Él es artista.** *He is an artist.* **Ella es artista.**
She is an artist.

Nouns referring to persons or animals, which end in **–e** usually
(but not always — e.g., **cómplice, tigre**) have a feminine form
ending in **–a.** Thus:

el gigante, the giant; **la giganta,** the giantess

el monje, the monk; **la monja,** the nun

el pariente, the relative; **la parienta,** the (female) relative

el elefante, the elephant; **la elefanta,** the female elephant

Most nouns referring to persons or animals, which end in a
consonant have a feminine form ending in **–a:**

el autor, the author; **la autora,** the authoress, (female) author

el escritor, the writer; **la escritora,** the (female *or* woman)
   writer

el pensador, la pensadora, the thinker

el dios, the god; **la diosa,** the goddess

el colegial, the college student; **la colegiala,** the college
   student (*female*), college girl

señor; señora   español; española

Some words add **–esa** or **–isa** (our *–ess*):

el abad, the abbot; **la abadesa,** the abbess

el alcalde, the mayor; **la alcaldesa,** the mayoress (*or* mayor's
   wife)

el barón, the baron; **la baronesa,** the baroness

el conde, the count; **la condesa,** the countess

el duque, the duke; **la duquesa,** the duchess

el poeta, the poet; **la poetisa,** the poetess

el sacerdote, the priest; **la sacerdotisa,** the priestess

A considerable number of words have feminine counterparts that do not conform to any of the preceding rules:

> **Don; Doña**   **actor; actriz**
> **héroe; heroína**   **emperador; emperatriz**
> **el rey,** the king; **la reina,** the queen
> **el príncipe,** the prince; **la princesa,** the princess
> **el gallo,** the cock, rooster; **la gallina,** the hen

Some pairs of words do not have the same stem (as in English):

> **hombre; mujer**   **padre; madre**
> **caballero; dama**   **caballo,** horse; **yegua,** mare
> **marido,** husband; **esposa,** wife (**esposo,** spouse, *is little used*)
> **varón,** male (*human being*), **macho,** male (*animal*); **hembra,** female
> **yerno,** son-in-law; **nuera,** daughter-in-law
> **toro,** bull; **vaca,** cow

As in English, if the sex is not specified or if the sexes are mixed, the masculine is used:

> **un pasajero,** a passenger (*male or female*); **los pasajeros,** the passengers
> **un hijo,** a son, a child; **los hijos,** the sons, the children

SITUATION MATERIAL — DOCTOR AND DENTIST:

el dolor, pain; **d. de cabeza,** headache; **d. de estómago,** stomach ache; **d. de oídos,** earache; **d. de garganta,** sore throat

doler(ue), to pain, hurt, ache (**Me duele. . . .** My . . . hurts; *as* **Me duelen los pies.** My feet hurt.)

enfermo, ill, sick; **enfermar,** to make ill, get sick; **la enfermedad,** illness, sickness; **enfermera, –o** nurse

el mal, evil, harm, illness; **mal de corazón (estómago),** heart (stomach) trouble; **(mal de) puna (SA),** altitude sickness

médico, medical, (*n.*) physician, doctor (*the* **médico** *is addressed as* **doctor**); **medicina,** medicine   **especialista**

el hospital   **clínica**

farmacia, botica, droguería, pharmacy, drugstore

el síntoma, symptom   **temperatura   pulso   náusea**
la fiebre, fever   **la tos,** cough; **toser,** to cough
el ataque, attack   **(es)calofríos,** chills (*hot-colds*)
diarrea, diarrhea   **vértigo,** dizziness, dizzy spell
la inflamación   **la infección**
un catarro, resfriado, resfrío, a cold; **resfriarse, constiparse,** to catch cold   **estreñimiento,** constipation

disentería (**amiboidea**), (*amoebic*) dysentery   **paludismo**, malaria

pulmonía, pneumonia (**pulmón**, lung)

la apendicitis, appendicitis

grave, serious, grave   **crónico**, chronic

débil, weak

vacunar, to vaccinate; **vacunación**, vaccination; **certificado**, certificate

píldora, pill

pastilla, tablet   **cápsula**, capsule   **aspirina**, aspirin

el dentista, the dentist   **el diente**, tooth

dolor de muelas, toothache (**muela**, molar)

la cavidad, cavity   **empastar**, to fill; **empastadura**, filling

el oculista, oculist

óptico, optician

ojo, eye   **pupila**, pupil (*of eye*)

el choque, collision, (*auto*) accident   **el accidente**, accident

caer(se), to fall; **caída**, fall

herir (ie), to injure (**injuriar**, *means* to insult); **herida**, injury

¿**Puede Ud. recomendarme un buen médico (hospital)?** Can you recommend a good doctor (hospital) to me?

¿**Sabe Ud. de un médico norteamericano?** Do you know of a North American doctor?

Hágame el favor de llamar al médico. Please call the doctor. (Do me the favor of calling a doctor.)

Sírvase indicarme una farmacia. Please direct me to a drugstore.

Me encuentro, *or* siento, malo. I feel bad.

Creo que estoy enfermo. I think I'm sick.

Tengo dolor de estómago y diarrea. I have a stomach ache and diarrhea.

Espero que no sea la disentería amiboidea. I hope it isn't amoebic dysentery.

Doctor, tengo dolor de cabeza y vértigos. Doctor, I have a headache and dizzy spells.

Tengo fiebre y escalofríos. I have fever and chills.

Me duele la garganta. My throat is sore.

Estoy (muy) constipado. Tengo un resfriado (fuerte). I have a (bad) cold.

Quiero un poco de aspirina. I want some aspirin.

Quiero unas pastillas a poner en el agua, para purificarla. I want some tablets to put in the water, to purify it.

Sírvase darme algo contra el estreñimiento. Please give me something for constipation.

Tengo mucho dolor. I am in much pain.

¡**Socorro!** Help!

Ha habido un choque, y dos personas están gravemente heridas. There has been an accident, and two people are seriously injured.

Peruvian Writer *Ricardo Palma* (1833–1919)

CARTA DEL SEGUNDO COMANDANTE DEL GERONA A SU AMIGO DEL IMPERIAL ALEJANDRO

Sama, 28 de diciembre de 1822.

Mi inolvidable camarada y pariente: Te escribo sobre un tambor en el momento de alistarse el batallón para emprender marcha a Tacna,[1] donde tengo por seguro que vamos a copar al gaucho Martínez antes de que se junte con las tropas de Alvarado, a quien después nos proponemos hacer bailar el zorongo.[2] El diablo se va a llevar de esta hecha[3] a los insurgentes. Ya es tiempo de que cargue Satanás con lo suyo y de que las charreteras de Coronel luzcan sobre los hombros de este invariable amigo.

Te doy las gracias por haberme proporcionado la amistad del capitán Uriondo. Es un muchacho que vale en oro lo que pesa, y en los pocos días que le hemos tenido en el Cuartel General ha sido la niña bonita[4] de la oficialidad. ¡ Y lo bien que canta el diantre[5] del mozo ! ¡ Y vaya si sabe hacer hablar las cuerdas de una guitarra !

Mañana saldrá, de regreso para el Cuzco, con comunicaciones del General para el Virrey.

Siento decirte que sus laureles como ganador de apuestas van marchitos. Sostuvo esta mañana que el aire de vacilación[6] que tengo al andar dependía, no del balazo que me plantaron en el Alto Perú, cuando lo de Cuaqui, sino de un lunar, grueso como un grano de arroz, que, según él afirmaba, como si me lo hubiera visto y palpado, debía yo tener en la parte baja de la pierna izquierda. Agregó, con un aplomo digno del físico de mi batallón, que ese lunar era cabeza de vena y que, andando los tiempos,[7] si no me lo hacía quemar con piedra infernal, me sobrevendrían ataques mortales al corazón. . . .

Dios te guarde de una bala traidora, y a mí . . . lo mismo.

Domingo Echizarraga.

TRANSLATION:

LETTER FROM THE SECOND COMMANDER OF GERONA TO HIS FRIEND OF THE IMPERIAL ALEJANDRO[8]

Sama, 28th December 1822

My unforgettable comrade and kinsman: I write to you on a drum at the moment the battalion gets ready to undertake (the) march to Tacna, where I take it for certain

[1] Tacna and Cuzco (mentioned below) are in Peru.

[2] zorongo, an Aragonese dance; hacer bailar el z. freely translated *to lead a nice dance.*

[3] hecha, the old form of fecha, *date.*

[4] la niña bonita, literally "the pretty little girl"; "the fair-haired boy."

[5] el diantre (euphemism for el diablo), *the deuce.*

[6] el aire de vacilación, literally "the air of hesitation" — that is, a limp.

[7] andando los tiempos, *as time goes on.* Commonly, andando el tiempo.

[8] refers to the second-in-command of the Army of Gerona and his friend of the Imperial (Spanish) Army in Peru.

that we're going to surprise the gaucho Martínez before he joins with the troops of Alvarado, whom afterwards we propose to lead a nice dance. The devil is going to carry off the insurgents from now onward. It's time already that Satan should carry away his own and that the epaulets of (a) colonel should shine on the shoulders of this invariable friend.

I give you thanks for having provided me with the friendship of Captain Uriondo. He's a boy worth his weight in gold, and in the few days we've had him in General Headquarters he has been the darling of the officers. And how well the devil of a boy sings! And does he know how to make the strings of a guitar speak!

Tomorrow he will set out on return to Cuzco, with communications from the General for the Viceroy.

I regret to tell you that his laurels as winner of wagers are becoming withered. He maintained this morning that the difficulty which I have in walking depended, not ʌ⸱ the bullet wound they planted on me in Upper Peru, on the occasion of Cuaqui, but on a mole as thick as a grain of rice which, as he affirmed, as if he had seen and touched it, I ought to have in the lower part of the left leg. He added, with an aplomb worthy of the physician of my battalion, that that mole was (the) head of (a) vein and that, as time goes on, if I did not have it burned (off) with infernal stone (caustic), mortai heart attacks would supervene on me. . . .

May God guard you from a traitorous bullet, and myself . . . the same.

Domingo Echizarraga.

§ 5. *MACHO* and *HEMBRA* — *Nouns with Two Genders and Two Meanings* — *Geographical Adjectives* — *Situation Material: Clothes; Laundry and Cleaning* — *Rubén Darío: Palimpsesto*

MACHO AND **HEMBRA.** The **macho** is the male of animals, and the term is sometimes applied to a man, as: **Es muy macho.** *He's a real he-man.* **Hembra** is applied to women or female animals. As explained in the preceding section, most of the names of the higher animals have different forms for males and females (**burro, burra; elefante, elefanta; toro, vaca**). But the case is different with the smaller or less common animals, and with birds, fish, and insects. With these **macho** and **hembra** are used to indicate sex, as:

> **la ardilla macho,** the male squirrel; **la a. hembra,** the female s.
> **el canario macho,** the male canary; **el c. hembra,** the female c.
> **el tiburón macho,** the male shark; **el t. hembra,** the female s.
> **el saltón,** *or* **saltamontes, macho** (**hembra**), the male (female) grasshopper

You note, of course, that the article does not change to indicate sex.

Nouns with Two Genders and Two Meanings. In the fol lowing pairs, most, but not all, of the masculine nouns seem to be derived from the feminine nouns:

> la ayuda, aid; el ayuda, aide, assistant
> la calavera, skull; el calavera, rake (*man*)
> la capital, capital (*city*); el capital, capital (*money*)
> la cólera, anger, wrath; el cólera, cholera
> la corte, court, courtship; el corte, cutting edge, cut
> la espada, sword; el espada, swordsman
> la frente, forehead; el frente, front
> la guardia, guard (*body of men, guarding*); el g., guard (*man*)
> la guía, guide(book); el *or* la guía, guide (*person*)
> la parte, part; el parte, message
> la pez, pitch; el pez, fish
> la policía, police; el policía, policeman
> la recluta, recruiting; el recluta, recruit
> la orden, order (*command, brotherhood*); el orden, order (*arrangement, system, classification*); *in ecclesiastical usage the gender is inconsistent, as* las sagradas órdenes, holy orders, el orden de predicadores, the order of preachers.

There are some pairs of words which end in –o and –a, with distinct meanings, as:

> fruta, (*edible*) fruit; fruto, fruit (*reward, profit*)
> grito, shout, cry; grita, shouting
> leña, (fire)wood, kindling; leño, stick of wood
> madera, wood, lumber; madero, board, beam (*also* el madera, Madeira wine)

A few words exist in two forms (–o, –a) without distinction of meaning. For example, saco, saca, *sack, bag;* bolsa, bolso, *purse;* cribo, criba, *sieve.* The others are uncommon or rare.

There are also a few words of ambiguous gender. Most of them have come to be used in only one gender today. One exception is mar, *sea.* It is generally el mar, but in poetry or literary usage it is often la mar.

Geographical Adjectives. These are formed from their nouns by the addition of various endings — –ano, –ense, –eño, –ero, –és, –ino, –no, –o, –teco — and irregularly. The following list illustrates the variety of endings.

−(a)no:

Australia: australiano
Bolivia: boliviano
Colombia: colombiano
Cuba: cubano
Italia: italiano
México: mexicano
Norte América: norteameri-
  cano
el Perú: peruano
Venezuela: venezolano
Jerez: jerezano
Puebla: poblano
Sevilla: sevillano
Vera Cruz: veracruzano

−ense:

el Canadá: canadiense
Costa Rica: costarriquense
Estados Unidos: estadounidense
Cuenca: conquense, cuencano
Montevideo: montevidense

−eño:

Brasil: brasileño
Honduras: hondureño
Nicaragua: nicaragüeño
el Panamá: panameño
El Salvador: salvadoreño
Caracas: caraqueño
Gibraltar: gibraltareño
Lima: limeño
Málaga: malagueño
Oaxaca: oaxaqueño
Quito: quiteño

−ero:

la Habana: habanero
Maracaibo: maracaibero

−és:

Escocia: escocés
Finlandia: finlandés
Francia: francés
Holanda: holandés
Irlanda: irlandés
el Japón; japonés
el Portugal: portugués
Cuernavaca: cuernavaqués

−ino:

Bilbao: bilbaíno
Granada: granadino
Salamanca: salamanquino

−o:

Bulgaria: búlgaro
Checoeslovaquia: −vaco
China: chino
Noruega: noruego
Prusia: pruso
Rumania: rumano
Rusia: ruso
Suecia (*Sweden*): sueco
Suiza (*Switz.*): suizo
Turquía: turco
Yugoeslavia: −vo
Argentina: argentino
el Paraguay: −guayo
el Uruguay: −guayo

−teco:

Guatemala: −malteco
Tlascala: tlascalteco

Some unusual geographical adjectives:

Asia: asiático
la Gran Bretaña: británico
Austria: austríaco
Dinamarca: danés
España: español
Hungría: húngaro
Polandia: polaco

Europa: europeo
Alemania: alemán
Bélgica: belga, bélgico
Gales (*Wales*): galés
Grecia: griego (*Greek*), greciano
  (*Grecian*)
Inglaterra: inglés

Chile: chileno
Santo Domingo: dominicano
Madrid: madrileño
Buenos Aires: porteño
Estremadura: estremeño
Salamanca: salmantino, salamanquino

Egipto: egipcio, –ciano
el Ecuador: ecuatoriano
Londres: londinense
Badajoz: pacense
Cádiz: gaditano
Mallorca: mallorquín

SITUATION MATERIAL — CLOTHES; LAUNDRY AND CLEANING.

ropa, clothes; **ropa interior,** underwear   **prenda,** garment

limpio, clean: **limpiar,** to clean; **l. a secas,** to dry clean

sucio, dirty   **lista,** list

lavar, to wash; **lavado,** washing (*dirty clothes*); **lavandero,** laundryman; **lavandera,** laundress; **lavandería,** laundry

planchar, to press   **chamuscar,** to scorch

remendar (ie), to mend   **zurcir,** to darn

quitar, to remove   **mancha,** spot

coser, to sew; **pegar,** to sew on   **descolorarse,** to fade

encogerse, to shrink   **el almidón,** starch; **–donar,** to st.

devolver, to return   **faltar,** to be missing

el sastre, tailor; **sastrería,** tailor shop

tintorería, dry cleaning shop; **tintorero,** cleaner (*man*)

vestir (i), to dress; **vestido,** dress; **v. de gala,** evening dress

el traje, suit; **t. de etiqueta** *or* **ceremonia,** dress suit; **t. de baño,** bathing suit

el smoking, tuxedo   **saco,** (*man's*) coat   **chaqueta,** jacket

caer, *or* **sentar (ie), bien (mal),** to fit well (badly)

los pantalones, trousers   **falda,** skirt

camisa, shirt, chemise, slip; **c. de noche,** nightgown; **c. de caballero,** man's shirt; **camiseta,** undershirt

blusa, blouse   **cuello,** collar   **puños,** cuffs

los calzones, breeches, panties; **calzoncillos,** shorts (*underwear*)

los calcetines, socks   **medias,** stockings

los pijamas   **el ropón,** robe   **el sweater**

faja, girdle   **corpiño,** brassière   **corbata,** (neck)tie

el cinturón, belt   **sombrero,** hat

pañuelo, handkerchief   **los guantes,** gloves

sobretodo, abrigo, overcoat   **el impermeable,** raincoat

zapato, shoe; **calzado,** footwear; **zapatilla,** slipper; **cordones de z.,** shoelaces   **suela,** sole; **poner media suela a,** to halfsole

taco, heel; **el tacón,** (high) heel; **de goma** *or* **hule,** rubber (*adj.*)

sandalias, alpargatas, (*Mex.*) **huaraches,** sandals

¿ **Hay servicio de lavandería?** Is there laundry service?

Busco un lavandero (una lavandera, una lavandería). I am looking for a laundryman (a laundress, a laundry).

Aquí tiene Ud. el lavado y la lista.   Here is the laundry and the list.

¿ Cuándo devolverá la ropa?   When will you return the clothes?

¿ Puede Ud. darme una lista de precios?   Can you give me a price list?

Falta una camisa deportiva y dos pañuelos.   A sport shirt and two handkerchiefs are missing.

Que me lave a secas este traje.   Quiero este traje limpiado.   I want this suit cleaned.

Lo necesito tan pronto sea posible.   I want it as soon as possible.

Lo necesito para mañana a las seis.   I need it for six o'clock tomorrow.

Esta blusa no es mía.   This blouse isn't mine.

Aquí está una mancha a quitar si es posible.   Here is a spot to take out, if possible.

La manga de esta camisa está rasgada.   ¿ Puede Ud. remendarla?   The sleeve of this shirt is torn.   Can you mend it?

Y pégueme un botón aquí.   And put on a button here.

Este vestido no me cae bien; está apretado.   This dress doesn't fit me well; it's tight.

Las viejas visten de negro.   The old women wear black.

¿ Hay que vestir traje de ceremonia?   Is it necessary to wear a dress suit?

¿ Se puede alquilar un smoking?   Can one rent a tux?

Nicaraguan Writer   *Rubén Darío* (1867–1916)

PALIMPSESTO

Ciento veintinueve años habían pasado después de que Valeriano y Decio, crueles emperadores, mostraron la bárbara furia de sus persecuciones sacrificando a los hijos de Cristo; y sucedió que un día de claro azul, cerca de un arroyo, en la Tebaida, se encontraron frente a frente un sátiro y un centauro.

(La existencia de estos dos seres está comprobada con testimonios de santos y sabios.)

Ambos iban sedientos bajo el claro cielo, y apagaron su sed: el centauro, cogiendo el agua en el hueco de la mano; el sátiro, inclinándose sobre la linfa hasta sorberla.

Después hablaron de esta manera:

— No ha mucho * — dijo el primero —, viniendo por el lado del Norte, he visto a un ser divino, quizá Júpiter mismo bajo el disfraz de un bello anciano.

Sus ojos eran penetrantes y poderosos, su gran barba blanca le caía a la cintura; caminaba despaciosamente, apoyado en un tosco bordón. Al verme se dirigió hacia mí, hizo un signo extraño con la diestra y sentíle tan grande como si pudiera enviar a voluntad el rayo de Olimpo. No de otro modo quedé que si tuviera ante la mirada mía al padre de los dioses.

---

* **No ha mucho** = no hace mucho, *not long ago.*

Háblóme en una lengua extraña, que, no obstante, comprendí. Buscaba
una senda por mí ignorada, pero que sin saber cómo pude indicarle, obe-
deciendo a raro o desconocido poder.

Tal miedo sentí, que antes de que Júpiter siguiera su camino, corrí
locamente por la vasta llanura, vientre a tierra y cabellera al aire.

—¡ Ah ! — exclamó el sátiro —.   ¿ Tú ignoras acaso que una aurora
nueva abre ya las puertas del Oriente, y que los dioses todos han caído
delante de otro Dios más fuerte y más grande?   El anciano que tú has visto
no era Júpiter, no es ningún ser olímpico.   Es un enviado del Dios nuevo.

TRANSLATION:

PALIMPSEST

*One hundred and twenty-nine years had passed since Valerian and Decius, cruel
emperors, showed the barbarous fury of their persecutions (in) sacrificing the sons of
Christ; and it happened that on a clear blue day, near a brook, in the Thebaid, a
satyr and a centaur found themselves face to face.*

(The existence of these two beings is confirmed by testimonies of saints and sages.)

*Both were thirsty under the clear sky, and they quenched their thirst: the centaur
catching the water in the hollow of his hand; the satyr bending over the water till he
could suck it up.*

Afterwards they spoke in this manner:

*"Not long ago," said the first, "coming from northwards, I saw a divine being
perhaps Jupiter himself in the disguise of a handsome old man.*

*"His eyes were penetrating and powerful, his great white beard reached down to
his waist; he was walking slowly, leaning on a rough staff.   On seeing me he came
towards me, made a strange sign with his right hand and I felt him to be so tall (that)
he could at will send the lightning from Olympus. I remained in no other way than
if I had before my gaze the father of the gods.   He spoke to me in a strange tongue,
which, nonetheless. I understood. He was seeking a path by me unknown, but which,
without knowing how, I could indicate to him, obeying a rare or unknown power.*

*"Such fear I felt that, before Jupiter went on his way, I ran madly over the vast
plain, belly to earth and head in the air."*

*"Ah!" exclaimed the satyr.   "Perhaps you do not know that a new dawn already
opens the doors of the East and that the gods have all fallen before another God,
stronger and greater? The old man you have seen was not Jupiter, is no Olympic
being.   He is an envoy of the new God."*

LESSON XIV

§ 1. *Word-building by Derivatives — Augmentatives — Pejoratives —*
Situation Material: Motoring — Amado Nervo: **Las Nubes**

WORD-BUILDING BY DERIVATIVES. In English we make many new
words by adding certain suffixes to basic words; for example:
*buyer, youngster, Johnny, booklet, floweret, rosette, lambkin, princeling,
birdie, foolish, childlike, troublesome, globule, poetaster.* The Spanish
language is far richer than English in such derivatives and in the
endings that make them. Especially numerous, interesting, and
effective are the augmentative and diminutive endings. Where
we must use adjectives such as "little," "very small," "dear little,"
"tiny little," "big," "very big," "great big," "tremendous,"
Spanish expresses these ideas and attitudes by diminutive and
augmentative suffixes.

Before you can use these suffixes correctly and confidently you
must hear and read a great deal of Spanish. Matters of taste are
involved. Also, certain endings may be popularly used in one
country and not much used in another. Thus it is said that the
Costa Ricans are called by their neighbors **"ticos"** because of
their fondness for the diminutive ending **–ico.** Children in one
country may call "Daddy" **papacito,** while in another country
they say **papaíto.**

In this lesson the common suffixes used to form derivatives will
be presented. The following general principles apply in the
formation of new words by the addition of suffixes:

(1) A final unaccented vowel of the basic word is dropped before
   a suffix beginning with a vowel; as: **libro** *(book)* + **–ito**
   = **librito** *(little book);* **cuchara** *(spoon)* + **–ón** = **cucharón**
   (soup spoon, ladle); **plaza** + **–uela** = **plazuela** *(little plaza).*

(2) A basic word ending in a consonant or an accented vowel
   retains its full form when a suffix is added: **señor** + **–ito**
   = **señorito** *(young gentleman);* **pan** + **ecillo** = **panecillo** *(roll);*
   jardín + **–cito** = **jardincito** *(little flower garden);* **mamá** + **–cita**
   = **mamacita.**

(3) Orthographic changes take place according to the rules you
   are familiar with, as: **pedazo** *(piece)* + **–ito** = **pedacito** *(little*

229

piece); **chico** (*little,* "*kid*") + –**illo** = **chiquillo** (*very little, little kid*); **lengua** (*tongue*) + –**ecita** = **lengüecita** (*little tongue*).

(4) An accented **ie** or **ue** in the basic word may become **e** or **o** when the accent shifts to the ending (as in numerous irregular verbs), but this does not take place consistently, so no rule can be applied: **bueno** + –**achón** = **bonachón** (*good-natured* or *good-hearted fellow*); **viejo** (*old man*) + –**ete** = **vejete** (*silly old man*), but **viejo** + –**ito** = **viejito** (*little old man*); **puerta** (*door*) + –**ezuela** = **portezuela** (*little door*), but **puerta** + –**ecita** = **puertecita**.

(5) Masculine derivatives ending in –**o** or –**e** may have a feminine form ending in –**a,** as: **chiquillo, –a** (diminutive of **chico**); **feote, feota** augmentative of **feo,** *ugly*).

(6) Masculine derivatives ending in a consonant may have a feminine form ending in –**a,** as: **solterón** (*old* or *confirmed bachelor*), **solterona** (*old maid, spinster*), augmentatives of **soltero, –a** (*bachelor, b. girl*).

AUGMENTATIVES. The endings –**ón,** –**azo,** and –**ote** add to the original meaning — as regards *size, degree,* or *quality* — and –**ote** may also be depreciatory.

The endings –**ÓN,** –**ONA** usually merely indicate bigness, as:

> **hombrón,** big man; **mujerona,** big woman
> **sillón,** easy chair, armchair, big chair (**silla,** chair)
> **borrachón,** sot (**borracho,** drunkard)
> **casón** *or* **casona,*** big house, mansion

Also see examples in (1), (4), (6), above.

Exceptions: In a few words, alas, –**ón** acts as a diminutive; for example:

> **cordón,** cord, twine, strand [**cuerda,** rope, (*heavy*) cord]
> **plumón,** down (**pluma,** feather)
> **ratón,** mouse (**rata,** rat)

The endings –**AZO,** –**AZA** are more emphatic than –**ón,** –**ona:**

> **hombrazo,** tremendous, *or* huge, man   **librazo,** great big book
> **perrazo, –a,** great big dog, huge dog
> **longazo,** very *or* "awfully" long (**luengo,** long) (*Note:* augmentative and diminutive endings may be added to adjectives.)

---

* As a rule, the ending –**ona** is used only in referring to females; so **casona** is exceptional.

If **–azo** is added to **–ón**, we get the ultimate in bigness or degree: an **hombronazo** would be a "man mountain"; a **borrachonazo** would be perpetually drunk.

Note: The endings **–ón** and **–azo** have other meanings, to be explained in sections 3 and 4.

The endings **–OTE, –OTA** are augmentatives which are also usually pejorative (depreciatory). Thus:

> **feote, –a,** extremely, *or* frightfully, ugly (**feo,** ugly)
> **palabrota,** big word, bad word, offensive word (**palabra,** word)
> **francote,** very frank, ingenuous, naïve (**franco,** frank)
> **librote,** big, heavy old book

Just as with **–ón, –ote** is diminutive in a few words:

> **camarote,** stateroom (**camara,** chamber)
> **islote,** islet (**isla,** island)

PEJORATIVES. The following endings (sometimes considered augmentatives) express contempt: **–AJO, –ACHO(–A), –UCHO(–A), –UCO(–A).** Thus:

> **un espantajo,** a scarecrow, "a fright" [**espanto,** fright, (SA) spook]
> **Latinajo,** dog-Latin
> **terminajo, terminacho,** vulgar expression (**término,** term)
> **ricacho,** "filthy rich"
> **vinacho,** poor wine
> **casucha, casuca,** hovel, shanty, shack

There are a few other uncommon augmentatives and pejorative endings. A few examples:

> **libraco,** bad, *or* poor, book (**libro,** book)
> **ventarrón,** violent wind (**viento,** wind)
> **narigón,** big nose, big-nosed (**nariz,** nose)
> **ventorro,** vile inn (**venta,** inn)
> **vivaracho,** frisky, spry (**vivo,** lively)
> **gentuza,** riffraff, rabble (**gente,** people)

SITUATION MATERIAL — MOTORING:

el **automóvil,** automobile; **auto,** auto   **carro, el coche,** car
manejar, conducir, to drive (*car*); **conductor, –a,** driver   **motorista**
el **chófer, cochero,** chauffeur   el **carnet,** (driver's) license
matrícula, license plate   el **garage** *or* **–je,** garage

estacionarse, parcar, to park; **estacionamiento,** parking; **un parque de automóviles,** a car park, parking lot

camino, road	**carretera,** highway	**calzado,** paved
(in)transitable, (im)passable	**gasolina**	**el aceite,** oil
el motor, engine	**llanta, neumático,** tire (**llanta** *may mean* rim)	
cubierta, hood, (tire) cover	**cámara,** (inner) tube	
la presión (de aire), (air) pressure	**un revent(az)ón,** a blowout	
reparar, to repair; **reparaciones,** repairs	**ajustar,** to adjust, fix	
freno, brake	**válvula,** valve	**faro,** headlight	**el parabrisas,** windshield

Road Signs

¡Pare! Stop!   **¡Prohibido Parar!** Do Not Stop!

¡Continúese! Keep Going!   **Sentido Unico** One Way

No Se Estacione, Estacionamiento Prohibido, Prohibido Parcar Do Not Park, No Parking

Prohibido el Paso No Thoroughfare   **Carretera Importante** Main Highway

Camino Interceptado Closed Road   **Desvío** Detour

Trabajos (Works) Road under Repair   **Fin de Ruta** End of Road, Dead End

A la Izquierda (Derecha) Turn Left (Right)   **Derecho** Straight Ahead

Velocidad Máxima Speed Limit   **Peligro(so)** Danger(ous)

¡Despacio! Slow!   **Toque Su Bocina** Sound Your Horn *

Curva Curve   **Cruce** Crossing   **Peatones** Pedestrians

Muy Poblado Thickly Populated   **Escuela** School

Declive Descent, Downgrade   **Resbaladizo** Slippery

Paso a Nivel Railway Crossing   **Camino Bacheado** Bad (bumpy) Road

Puente Angosto Narrow Bridge   **Puente Levadizo** Drawbridge

Altura Máxima Maximum Height   **Ancho Máximo** Maximum Width

Peso Máximo Maximum Weight   **Trasbordador** Ferry

Quiero diez litros de gasolina. I want ten liters of gasoline.

¿Necesito aceite? Do I need oil?

¿Cómo está la presión en las llantas? How is the pressure in the tires?

Favor de limpiarme el parabrisas. Please clean the windshield.

Se necesita agua. It needs water.

¿Cuánto cuesta el garage para una noche? How much does garage room cost for one night?

Quiero que me lave el carro. Quiero el carro lavado. I want the car washed.

Los frenos no funcionan bien. The brakes don't work well.

Creo que hay una válvula que se debe ajustar. I think there is a valve that needs seeing to.

---

* In some cities it is prohibited to sound your horn.

Hay que cambiar la llanta, *or* **el neumático.**   The tire must be changed.

¿ Cuándo estará listo?   When will it be ready?

Lo necesito mañana por la mañana.   I need it tomorrow morning.

¿ Cuánto me cobrará por las reparaciones?   What will you charge me for
the repairs?

¿ Cómo es el camino de aquí a Quezaltenango?   How is the road from
here to Quezaltenango?   **¿ Está en buena condición?**   Is it in good
condition?

Aquí tiene Ud. mi carnet.   Here is my license.

Mi velocímetro indicó cuarenta millas por hora.   My speedometer
showed forty miles an hour.

Mexican Writer   *Amado Nervo* (1870–1919)

Las Nubes

Un día llegará para la tierra, dentro de muchos años, dentro de muchos
siglos, en que [1] ya no habrá nubes.

Esas apariciones blancas o grises, inconsistentes y fantasmagóricas, que
se sonrosan con el alba y se doran a fuego con el crepúsculo, no más, in-
cansables peregrinos, bogarán [2] por los aires.

Los grandes océanos palpitantes, que hoy ciñen y arrullan o azotan a los
continentes, se habrán reducido a mezquinos mediterráneos, y en sus cuencas
enormes, que semejarán espantosas cicatrices, morará el hombre entre
hídridas faunas y floras.

Debido a incesantes filtraciones, el agua en las honduras de la tierra,
amalgamada con otras substancias, tendrá otras propiedades y se llamará
de otro modo.

El sol, padre de la vida, llegado a un ciclo más avanzado de su evolución,
alumbrará y calentará menos.   Su luz, que en épocas prehistóricas pasó del
blanco al amarillo, habrá pasado ya del amarillo al rojo, como Antarés y
Aldebarán.

Por efecto del menor calor y del menor caudal de las aguas, la evapora-
ción habrá de ser muy menos considerable que ahora, y una gran sequedad
reinará en la atmósfera.

¡ Ni nubes, ni lluvia !

El cielo, de un incontaminado azul, se combará serenamente sobre la
tierra.

Por las mañanas, un leve tinte rojo, en el orto, anunciará la aurora; por
las tardes, un descrecimiento brusco de la luz presidirá a las tinieblas.

No más volcanes ignívomos, no más prodigiosas cordilleras de oro, no
más inmensos abanicos de fuego con varillajes nacarados,[3] no más piélagos

---

[1] **que** refers to **día.**

[2] **bogarán.**   The usual meaning of **bogar** is *to row.*

[3] **nacarados,** from **nacar,** *mother-of-pearl.*

de llamas, no más entonaciones malva, lila y heliotropo, entre los cuales
bulle [1] la estrella de la tarde.

Los poetas experimentarán una suprema tristeza; pero ya no existirán
los poetas. El último se habrá extinguido hará muchos siglos.

TRANSLATION:

THE CLOUDS

*A day will arrive for the earth, within many years, many centuries, in which there
will no longer be (any) clouds.*

*Those white or gray apparitions, inconsistent and phantasmagorical, which blush
with the dawn and become gilt with twilight, indefatigable pilgrims, will no longer
sail through the air.*

*The great palpitating oceans, which today gird and court or lash the continents,
will have become reduced to minute Mediterraneans, and in their enormous basins,
which will resemble frightful scars, man will dwell among (the) hydrid floras and
faunas.*

*Owing to incessant infiltrations, the water in the depths of the earth, amalgamated
with other substances, will have other properties and will be called otherwise.*

*The sun, father of life, (having) reached a more advanced cycle of his evolution,
will give less light and heat. His light, which in prehistoric epochs passed from white
to yellow, will by now have passed from yellow to red, like Antares and Aldebaran.*

*Through (the) effect of less heat and the lesser volume of the waters, the evaporation
will have to be much less considerable than now, and a great dryness will reign in
the atmosphere.*

Neither clouds nor rain!

The sky, of an uncontaminated blue, will curve serenely on (around) the earth.

*In the mornings, a light red tint in the rising sun will announce the dawn; in the
evenings a brusque decrease of light will preside over darkness.*

*No more volcanoes vomiting fire, no more prodigious golden mountain ranges, no
more immense fans of fire with nacred ribs, no more seas of flames, no more mallow,
lilac, and heliotrope tones among which the evening star dances.*

*The poets will experience a supreme sadness; but (by then) the poets will no longer
exist. The last one will have been extinguished many centuries before.*

§ 2. *Diminutives — Situation Material: Theater and Cinema — Juan Montalvo: Elogio de la Pobreza*

DIMINUTIVES. Spanish is extraordinarily rich in diminutives.
They are used to indicate smallness of size, degree, or value and
also to express affection for persons or liking for things and sometimes to express contempt.

The following is a list of the diminutive endings. Those in
capitals are the most common.

[1] **bulle.** The usual meaning of **bullir** is *to bubble.*

–ITO	**–CITO**	**–ecito**	**–ececito**
–ILLO	**–CILLO**	**–ecillo**	**–ececillo**
–ico	–cico	–ecico	–ececico
–UELO	**–zuelo**	**–ezuelo**	**–ececuelo**
–ete	–cete	–ecete	
–ejo			
–in, –ino, –iño			

The diminutive endings **–ITO** and **–CITO** are the commonest ones. Usually they express affection, sentiment, or liking, and rarely indicate mere smallness. They may sometimes have a flavor of irony, as when applied to the names of famous persons not universally respected.

Words ending in –**ito** are the basis of Spanish "baby talk" (**gatito,** *kitty,* **caballito,** *horsey*). A child may say, "**Déme mi pañuelito, mamacita.**" And the mother may say to the child, "**¿ Te has levado la carita y las manitos ?**"

A fruit-seller may say, "**¿ Quiere Ud. naranjitas, señor ?**" The oranges may or may not be small; the diminutive is used to make them seem desirable.

Personal names have their diminutives: **Miguelito,** *Mike;* **Juanito,** *Johnny;* **Anita,** *Annie.* Even nicknames have diminutives: **Pepe** (*Joe*), **Pepito.**

The ending –**ito**(–**a**) is sometimes added to adverbs: **ahora,** *now,* **ahorita,** *right now;* **pronto,** *soon,* **prontito,** *very soon;* **¡ Adiós !** *Good-by!* **¡ Adiosito !** *Bye-bye!*

If the basic word ends in –**s,** the **s** is retained after –**ito**: **Carlos,** *Charles,* **Carlitos,** *Charley;* **Dolores, Dolorcitas; lejos,** *far,* **lejitos,** *rather far* (but **Adiosito,** not –**tos**).

The endings –**ito,** –**cito,** etc., sometimes merely indicate smallness, as: **casita,** *little house, cottage;* **chiquito; momentito,** *just a moment;* **poquito,** *just a little.*

Sometimes these endings have an intensifying effect: **ahorita,** *right now;* **cerquita,** *very near;* **mismito,** *very same.*

The endings –**ILLO,** –**CILLO,** etc., merely indicate smallness without emotional connotations: **cigarro,** *cigar,* **cigarrillo,** *cigarette;* **chico,** *kid,* **chiquillo,** *little kid;* **guerra,** *war,* **guerrilla,** *guerrilla warfare;* **palo,** *stick, pole;* **palillo,** *little stick, rolling pin, toothpick, drumstick,* (pl.) *castanets;* **pícaro,** *rascal,* **picarillo,** *little rascal;* **ventana,** *window,* **ventanilla,** (*little*) *window* (as of a bank teller or ticket seller); **viaje,** *journey,* **viajecillo,** *little trip.*

The endings –ico, –cico, etc., may be used locally in place of –ito, –cito, or they may be used sarcastically, as **angelico**, *little angel*.

The endings **–UELO, –ZUELO**, etc., indicate smallness of size or importance, and usually express contempt: **castaña**, *chestnut*, **castañuelas**, *castanets;* **pintorzuelo**, *dauber* (painter without talent), **plazuela**, *little plaza;* **portezuela**, *door* (of automobile, carriage).

The ending –ete generally indicates smallness and sometimes contempt: **burla**, *trick*, **burleta**, *little trick*, *dirty trick;* **historia**, *story*, **historieta**, *little story*, *short story;* **juguete**, *toy*, *plaything* (from **jugar**, *to play*).

The ending –ejo indicates smallness and worthlessness: **papelejo**, *scrap of paper*. An **animalejo** is a little animal of no value for which one feels little or no liking. (An **animalito** is an animal, probably small, of which one is fond.)

The uncommon endings –in, –ino, –iño indicate smallness: **chiquitín**, *baby boy*, **chiquitina**, *baby girl;* **langosta**, *lobster*, **langostino**, *crayfish;* **cuerpo**, *body*, **corpiño**, *bodice*.

Two or more diminutive endings may be added to a word: **chiquitillo**, *tiny*, *little one;* **poquitito**, *a tiny little bit*.

Finally, both a diminutive and an augmentative ending may be used at the same time; as: **grandillón**, *overgrown* (of a child) — grande + –illo + –ón; **picaroncillo**, *little big-rascal;* **callejón**, *alley*, *lane* — calle + –ejo + –ón. But such forms are rather rare curiosities.

Situation Material — Theater and Cinema:

teatro, theater; **t. de variedades**, vaudeville theater

el drama, drama, play; **dramático**, dramatic; **dramatista**, dramatist, playwright   **tragedia**, tragedy; **trágico**, tragic

comedia, comedy; **cómico**, comic(al), comedian

zarzuela, musical play   **el sainete**, farce

acto, act; **entreacto**, interlude, intermission

escena, scene (*part of act*); **escena, escenario**, scenery, set, stage; **poner a escena, representar**, to stage, perform, present (*a play*)

estreno, opening (performance); **estrenar**, to open, be performed for the first time   **la función**, show

actor, actriz, actor, actress   **reparto**, cast

héroe, heroína, hero, –ine   **el galán**, leading man

interpretar, hacer, to act, play (*a role*)

el cinema, cinema, motion pictures; **el cine**, movies; **cinematográfico**, motion-picture (*adj.*); **del cine**, movie (*adj.*); **el** *or* **la artista del cine**, movie actor (actress)   **pantalla**, screen película, cinta, el film, film, movie

música, music; músico, musician   tocar, to play (*instrument*)

orquesta   el director   el programa   concierto   ópera

piano; pianista   violín; violinista   guitarra; guitarrista

cantar, to sing; el cantar, singing, song; la canción, song; el *or* la
    cantante, la cantatriz, singer

bailar, danzar, to dance; el baile, dance; la danza, the (*artistic or re-*
    ligious) dance; bailador, –a, dancer; bailarín, –ina, (*professional*)
    dancer; danzante, (*artistic or religious*) dancer

taquilla, box office, ticket window	el billete, (SA) boleto, ticket
asiento, localidad, seat	reservar, to reserve
la admisión, entrada, admission	entrada, entrance; salida, exit
luneta, orchestra seat	butaca, orch. seat (*soft chair*)
anfiteatro, balcony	paraíso, galería, gallery
palco, box	fila, row
gemelos, opera glasses ("*twins*")	espectáculo, spectacle
éxito, success, hit; exitazo, big hit	

¿Qué vamos a hacer esta noche? What are we going to do tonight?

Quisiera oír cantar y ver bailar cosas típicas de este país. I'd like to
    hear some singing and see some dancing typical of this country.

Pues, no hay nada al momento. Pero estrena esta noche en el Teatro
    Nacional una comedia que era un exitazo en España. Well, there's
    nothing at the moment. But there's a comedy opening tonight at the
    Teatro Nacional which was a big hit in Spain.

Probablemente yo no podría entender mucho de ella. Probably I
    wouldn't understand much of it.

A ver si podemos conseguir localidades. Let's see if we can get seats.

Puedo telefonear. ¿Qué le parece? I can phone. What do you say?

Tienen unas pocas butacas. They have a few orchestra seats.

Apárteme dos butacas, por favor. Hold two seats for me, please.

¿A qué hora comienza? When does it begin?

Tal vez le interesa el teatro popular. El cómico Chamacote es muy
    divertido. Maybe you'd be interested in the popular theater. The
    comedian Chamacote is very amusing.

¿Qué hay en el cine? What is there in the way of a movie?

Películas de todas clases. Hay una cinta sueca que los críticos dicen es
    muy fina. Pictures of all kinds. There's a Swedish film that the critics
    say is very fine.

¿Ha visto Ud. las danzas indígenas en el Palacio de Bellas Artes? Have
    you seen the native (Indian) dances at the Palacio de Bellas Artes?

¿Qué le parece la música? What do you think of the music?

Muy interesante, y bien ejecutada. Very interesting, and well played.

¿Quién es el compositor de la última pieza? Who is the composer of
    the last piece?

Es un joven mexicano, indio, un verdadero genio. He is a young Mexican, an Indian, a real genius.

Ecuadorian Writer   *Juan Montalvo* (1833–89)

ELOGIO DE LA POBREZA

. . . Pero no hay manjar como la buena disposición, y el hambre adereza maravillosamente hasta las cosas humildes; ella es la mejor cocinera del mundo; todo lo da lampreado y a poquísima costa. Dichosos los pobres, si tienen que comer, porque comen con hambre. La salud y el trabajo tienden la mesa, bien como la conciencia limpia y la tranquilidad hacen la cama: el hombre de bien, trabajador,[1] se sienta a la una, se acuesta en la otra, y come y duerme de manera de causar envidia a los potentados. La pobreza tiene privilegios que la riqueza comprara a toda costa si los pudiera comprar, mientras que la riqueza padece incomodidades contra las cuales nada pueden [2] onzas de oro. ¿ Cuánto no daría un magnate por un buen estómago? El pobre nunca lo tiene malo, porque la escasez y moderación le sirven de tónico, y el pan que Dios le da es sencillo, fácil de digerir, como el maná del desierto. El rico cierne la tierra, se va al fondo del mar, rompe los aires en demanda de comestibles raros y valiosos con que se emponzoña lentamente para morir en un martirio, quejándose de Dios; el pobre tiene a la mano el sustento, con las suyas lo ha sembrado enfrente de su choza, y una mata le sobra para un día. El faisán, la perdiz son necesidades para el opulento, hijo de la gula; al pobre, como al filósofo, no le atormentan deseos de cosas exquisitas.

TRANSLATION:

EULOGY OF POVERTY

. . . *But there is no sustenance like a good state of health, and hunger seasons marvelously even humble things; it is the best cook in the world; it gives everything good flavor and at very little cost. Happy (are) the poor if they have (the wherewithal) to eat, because they eat hungrily. Health and work lay the table, just as clear conscience and peace of mind make the bed: the honest man, hard-working, sits down at the one, lies down on the other, and eats and sleeps in a way to cause envy to potentates. Poverty has privileges which wealth would buy at any cost if it could buy them, while wealth suffers inconveniences against which ounces of gold can do nothing. How much would not a magnate give for a good stomach? The poor (man) never has anything wrong with it, because scarcity and moderation serve him as (a) tonic, and the bread God gives him is simple, easy to digest, like the manna of the desert. The rich (man) sifts the earth, goes down to the bottom of the ocean, tears the airs apart in demand of rare and esteemed viands with which he poisons himself slowly to die in martyrdom, grumbling at God; the poor (man) has his sustenance in his hand, with*

[1] **trabajador,** *hard-working;* as noun means *worker.*
[2] **nada pueden.** **No poder** often means *to be of no avail.*

*his own (hands) he has sown it in front of his cabin, and a plant is more than enough
for him for one day. The pheasant, the partridge are necessities for the opulent (man),
(the) son of gluttony; desires for exquisite things do not torment the poor (man), as
(they do not) the philosopher.*

§ 3. *Derivatives with Special Meanings — Nicknames — Situation
Material: Paying Accounts — José Martí: **Un Cuento de Elefantes***

DERIVATIVES WITH SPECIAL MEANINGS. One of the difficulties of
derivatives — especially augmentatives and diminutives — is that
they sometimes have a meaning quite different from that of the
basic word. In sections 1 and 2 you found, for example: **panecillo,**
roll; **ratón,** *mouse;* **camarote,** *stateroom;* **espantajo,** *scarecrow;*
cigarrillo, *cigarette;* **palillos** and **castañuelas,** *castanets;* **langostino,**
crayfish; **corpiño,** *bodice;* **callejón,** *alley.* You know that **leche**
means *milk* and that **–ón** is an augmentative ending, but try to
guess what a **lechón** is. (Answer at bottom of page.*)

You may recall the multiple meanings of **palillo** (see page 235).
Manza ʾlla (from **manzana,** *apple*) has the following meanings:
camomile, a certain kind of olive, a white Andalusian wine, an
ornamental knob, point of the chin, pad of animal's paw.

Take warning, then, that derivatives often have meanings that
you cannot guess by merely knowing the meaning of the basic
word and the significance of the ending.

Be careful, also, of words with endings that look like but are not
suffixes; for example, **abrazo,** *embrace;* **espejo,** *mirror;* **botica,**
drugstore; **pabellón,** *pavilion.*

NICKNAMES. Some Spanish nicknames are just diminutives, as
Juanito, *Johnny,* and **Evita,** from **Eva.** The ending **–ito, –a** is the
usual one used with personal names, but other endings are used.
José may be called **Joseíto** or **Josecito.** Various diminutives,
including some double ones, are used for **María: Marica, Mari-
quita, Mariquilla, Maruca, Marucha,** and **Maruja.** As has been
mentioned, if the name ends in **–s** the **–s** is retained after **–ito:
Carlos, Carlitos; Dolores, Dolorcitas.** You must remember, also,
the orthographic changes: **Diego, Dieguito; Francisca, Francis-
quita; Luz, Lucita; Antonio, Antoñito.**

There are some Spanish nicknames as different from the proper
names as *Peg* from *Margaret.* The following is a list of nicknames,
with the simple diminutives omitted.

---

* Spelled backwards: gipgnilkcus.

Antonio, –a: Toño, –a, Toñico, –a
Bartolomé: Bartolo, Bartolito
Catalina, Catarina (Catherine):   **Catana, Catuca, Catuja.**
   Catujita
Cayetano: **Tano, Tanito**
Cristóbal (Christopher): **Tobal, Tobalito**
Francisca (Frances): **Frasca, Frascuela, Frasquita, Paca, Paquita**
   Pacorra, Pancha, Panchita, Curra, Currita, Farruca
Francisco (Francis, Frank): **Frasco,** *etc.* (*as above*)
Gertrudis: **Tula, Tulita**
Gregorio: **Goyo, Goyito**
Isabel (Elizabeth, Isabel, –la): **Bela, Belica, Belisa, Belita**
Jesús (a common Christian name)· **Chucho, Chuchito**
José: **Pepe, Pepito, Pepillo, Chepe, Chepito**
Josefa, Josefina: **Pepa,** *etc.* (*as above*)
Manuel: **Manolo, Manolito**
María de la Concepción: **Concha, Conchita**
María de los Dolores: **Lola, Lolita**
María de Jesús: **Jesusa, Jesusita, Chucha, Chuchita**
María de la Luz: **Lucecita, Lucita**
Pedro: **Perico, Perucho**

SITUATION MATERIAL — PAYING ACCOUNTS:

Dígame, por favor, el total de mi cuenta. Please tell me the total amount
   of my bill.
Son seiscientos cincuenta y cinco pesos. Aquí esta la cuenta. It is six
   hundred and fifty-five pesos. Here is the account.
Bueno. Voy a repasarla. All right. I'll look over it.
Me parece que no está bien It seems to me it's not right.
Veo aquí unas partidas que no recuerdo. I see here some items I don't
   remember.
Pues, señor, hay sesenta y cinco pesos que son por extras. Well, there
   are sixty-five pesos for extras.
¡Ah ! Olvidaba las extras. Oh, I forgot the extras.
Permítame explicar. Este cargo de veinte pesos es por un almuerzo.
   Let me explain. This charge of twenty pesos is for a lunch.
Y quince pesos por el telegrama. And fifteen pesos for the telegram.
Entonces todo está correcto. Then everything is correct.
Ahí van quinientos. There are five hundred.
Pago lo demás después de cambiarme un cheque de viajero I'll pay
   the balance after I cash a traveler's check.

¿ **Qué le debo en dólares?** What do I owe you in dollars?
Distribuya esto entre el servicio del hotel. Distribute this among the
hotel service.

Cuban Writer   *José Martí* (1853–95)

Un Cuento [1] de Elefantes

Partidas enteras de gente europea están por Africa cazando elefantes;
y ahora cuentan los libros de una gran cacería, donde eran muchos los
cazadores. Cuentan que iban sentados a la mujeriega [2] en sus sillas de
montar,[3] hablando de la guerra que hacen en el bosque las serpientes al
león, y de una mosca venenosa [4] que les chupa la piel a los bueyes hasta que
se la seca y los mata y de lo lejos [5] que saben tirar la azagaya y la flecha
los cazadores africanos, y en eso estaban, y en calcular cuándo llegarían
a las tierras de Tippu Tib, que siempre tiene muchos colmillos que vender,
cuando salieron de pronto a un claro de esos que hay en Africa en medio
de los bosques, y vieron una manada de elefantes ailá al fondo del claro, unos
durmiendo de pie contra los troncos de los árboles, otros paseando juntos
y meciendo el cuerpo de un lado a otro, otros echados sobre la hierba, con
las patas de atrás estiradas. Les cayeron encima todas las balas de los
cazadores. Los echados se levantaron de un impulso. Se juntaron las
parejas.[6] Los dormidos vinieron trotando donde estaban los demás. Al
pasar junto a la poza, se llenaban de un sorbo la trompa. Gruñían y
tanteaban el aire con la trompa. Todos se pusieron alrededor de su jefe.
Y la caza fué larga: los negros les tiraban lanzas y azagayas y flechas;
los europeos, escondidos en los yerbales,[7] les disparaban de cerca los fusiles;
las hembras huían, despedazando [8] cañaverales como si fueran hierbas de
hilo; los elefantes huían de espaldas, defendiéndose con los colmillos cuando
les venía encima un cazador.

Translation.

A Story of Elephants

*Whole parties of European people are (here and there) in Africa hunting elephants,
and now the books tell of a great hunt in which the hunters were many. They relate
that they went seated woman-fashion on the saddles, speaking of the war waged in the*

[1] **Cuento.** Compare **cuento,** *account, tale,* and **cuenta,** *account, bill.*

[2] **a la mujeriega.** The ending **–iego** (rather uncommon) means *–like,*
mujeriego means *womanlike, womanly,* and also *fond of women.*

[3] **sillas de montar. Silla** means *saddle* as well as *chair.* **Montar** means *to
mount, ride* (horseback).

[4] **mosca venenosa,** *poisonous fly* — here refers to the tsetse fly.

[5] **lo lejos.** The neuter article used before an adverb makes the adverb into
a noun (**lo lejos,** *the distance*); **lo** is often translated *how* (**lo lejos,** *how far*).

[6] **parejas.** A **pareja** is a *pair,* or *couple,* of male and female.

[7] **yerbales,** from **yerba,** usually **hierba,** *herb, grass.*

[8] **despedazando,** from **despedazar,** from **pedazo** *piece,* and **des–,** *dis–*

forest by serpents on the lion, and of a poisonous fly which sucks the hide of oxen until it becomes dry and kills them, and of the long distance the African hunters can send the spear and arrow; and so they were, and calculating when they would arrive in the territories of Tippu Tib, which always has many tusks to sell, when they suddenly came out into a clearing like those there are in Africa among the forests, and they saw a herd of elephants there at the far end of the clearing, some (of them) sleeping standing against the trunks of trees, others walking together and swaying their bodies from side to side, others lying on the grass, with their hind legs stretched out. All the hunters' bullets fell on them. Those lying down got up with one impulse. Pairs rejoined one another. Those (which had been) asleep came trotting where the rest were. As they passed close to the pool, they filled their trunks with one gulp. They grunted and smelled the air with their trumpets. All placed themselves around their leader. And the hunt was prolonged: the Negroes hurled lances and spears and arrows at them; the Europeans, hidden in the grasses, fired their rifles at them from near; the females fled, breaking through cane-fields as if they were slender plants; the elephants fled shoulder to shoulder, defending themselves with their tusks when a hunter came onto them.

§ 4. *Reference List of Noun and Adjective Suffixes (1)* — *José Enrique Rodó: Mirando Jugar un Niño*

REFERENCE LIST OF NOUN AND ADJECTIVE SUFFIXES (1). In the following list, which is full but not complete, the endings that need special attention because they do not closely parallel English endings of like significance are capitalized:

–a (common noun ending; often = *–e*): **forma, idiota, mapa, persona, planeta, agricultura, brigada, causa, dama, disciplina, figura, fortuna, gasolina, isla, rosa.**

–ADA: (1) indicates *capacity*, like *–ful* or *–load:* **cucharada,** *spoonful;* **manada,** *handful;* **mesada,** *month's salary.*

(2) indicates a *group:* **estacada,** *stockade, picket fence* (**estaca,** *stake*); **perrada,** *pack of dogs;* **vacada,** *herd of cows.*

(3), **–AZO:** indicate a *blow or thrust or an act:* **plumada,** *stroke of the pen;* **puñada,** *blow with the fist* (**puño**); **puñalada,** *stab with dagger* (**puñal**); **muchachada,** *childish act;* **balazo,** *bullet wound* (**bala,** *bullet*); **codazo,** *dig with the elbow* (**codo**); **portazo,** *slam of door* (**dar p.,** *to slam the door in one's face*).

(4), **–IDA:** indicate *completed action* (derived from past participles of verbs): **entrada,** *entrance;* **llegada,** *arrival;* **parada,** *stop, halt, parade;* **salida,** *exit, departure.*

–ADO (*–ate*): (1) adj. suffix, from past part., indicating *similarity:*
(a)**naranjado,** *orange-colored;* **serrado,** *serrate*
(**sierra,** *saw*).

(2), **–ATO, –AZGO:** noun suffixes indicating an
office or authority, or *district:* **electorado,** *electorate;*
condado, *county* (**conde,** *count*); **obispado,**
bishopric (**obispo,** *bishop*); **cardenalato,** *cardi-
nalate, –ship;* **hermanazgo,** *brotherhood* (*abstract*);
primazgo, *cousinship* (**primo,** *cousin*).

–ador, –edor, –idor, –or (*–er, –or,*): form nouns indicating the
actor or adjectives indicating *acting* (derived from verbs): **hablador,** *speaker, talker, talkative;* **trabajador,** *worker, hard-working,
industrious;* **comedor,** *eater, diner, dining room* (= **cuarto comedor**);
abridor, *opener;* **actor,** *actor.*

–AJE (*–age*): (1) indicates a *fee:* **carretaje,** *cartage* (**carreta,** *cart*);
garaje (usually improperly spelt *–ge*), *garage;*
portaje, *toll* (**puerta,** *gate*).

(2) forms nouns, often in a *collective* sense: **herraje,**
ironwork (**hierro,** *iron*); **hospedaje,** (*board and*)
lodging (**hospedar,** *to lodge,* from **huésped,** *guest,
lodger*); **potaje,** *thick soup, pottage* (**pote,** *pot*).

–al, –ar (*–al, –ar*) (1): **criminal, mental, social, circular, muscu-
lar, regular.**

–AL, –AR (2): noun suffixes, indicate a *collection* or a *place* where
a thing is found abundantly: **arenal,** *sandy place* (**arena,** *sand*);
chaparral, *region of scrub oaks* (**chaparros**); **dineral,** "*heap of
money*"; **naranjal,** *orange grove;* **olivar,** *olive orchard.*

–ante, –ente: adj. or noun endings (*–ant, –ent, –ing, –er*): **importante, instante** (*adj., n.*), **accidente, negligente; amante,** *loving,
lover;* **teniente,** *having, holding, owning, lieutenant;* **delirante,**
raving, delirious.

–ANZA forms *abstract nouns* from verbs: **matanza,** *slaughter* (**matar,**
to kill); **tardanza,** *delay* (**tardar,** *to delay*); **venganza,** *vengeance*
(**vengar,** *to avenge*).

–astro (*–aster*), *depreciatory:* **camastro,** *wretched bed;* **poetastro,**
poetaster; **hermanastro,** *stepbrother;* **madrastra,** *stepmother.*

–az (*–acious*): **mendaz, pugnaz, rapaz, sagaz, tenaz.**

–ción, –sión, –tión, –ión (*–tion, –sion, –ion*): **nación, misión,
sugestión, religión.**

–cional (*–tional*), etc.: **nacional, provisional, regional.**

–culo, –cula (*–cle*): **círculo. vehículo. partícula.**

–dad, –tad (*–ty, –dom, –ness*): **bondad,** *goodness, bounty;* **maldad,** *badness, wickedness;* **ciudad,** *city;* **libertad,** *liberty, freedom;* **sociedad,** *society.*

–DERO, –DERA: (1) *place* of action: **bañadero,** *bathing place;* **bañadera,** *bathtub;* **matadero,** *slaughterhouse;* **escondedero,** *hiding place* (**esconder,** *to hide*); **paradero,** *stopping place, landing.*

(2) *instrument:* **cerradera** or **–o,** *catch of lock, staple of bolt* (**cerrar,** *to close, lock*); **pasadera** or **–o,** *stepping stone* (**pasar,** *to pass*).

(3) indicate *person engaged in an activity:* **curandero, –a,** *healer* (**curar,** *to heal*); **lavandero,** *laundryman;* **–a,** *laundress, washwoman.*

(4) form adjectives, indicating *fitness* (= *–able*): **casadero,** *marriageable;* **comedero,** *edible, fit to eat;* **pagadero,** *payable;* **valedero,** *valid.*

–DIZO: forms adjectives, indicating *fitness* or *tendency:* **bebedizo,** *drinkable, fit to drink;* **caedizo, movedizo,** *unsteady* (likely to fall or move); **olvidadizo,** *forgetful* (**olvidar,** *to forget*); **quebradizo,** *brittle, fragile, breakable* (**quebrar,** *to break*); **resbaladizo,** *slippery* (**resbalar,** *to slip, slide*).

–DUMBRE: forms *abstract nouns* from adjectives (= *–ness, –ty,* etc.): **certidumbre,** *certainty, certitude* (**cierto,** *certain*); **muchedumbre,** *multitude, crowd;* **pesadumbre,** *sadness* (**pesado,** *heavy*).

–DURA: (1) forms nouns from verbs; ending indicates *action* or *result of action:* **cortadura,** *cutting, cut;* **peinadura,** *combing,* pl. *combings;* **picadura,** *sting,* (insect) *bite;* **quemadura,** *burn.*

(2) added to nouns, indicates a *set:* **botonadura,** *set of buttons;* **dentadura,** *denture.*

READING. No translation is provided with the following piece in order that you may try to work it out for yourself. Notes will supply you with the meanings of words new to you unless the meaning is obvious. Some words are so similar to English words that either you will recognize their meaning at once or you can work out the meaning: **cristal, límpido,** prisma, **manteniéndola** (from **mantener**), firme, **inclinar, graciosa** (*–oso* = *–ous, –ful*), **atento, sonoras, vibrante, agonizar** (*agonize = die*), **prolongó,**

improvisada, motivo, terminada, desigual, bordes, fresca, resonancia, emigrado, diáfano, percusión, suspenso, indeciso, húmedos, pomposa, cercano (adj. from adv. **cerca**), **compañía.**

Take this task slowly and write out your translation sentence by sentence. When you have arrived at as good a literal translation as you can make, rewrite your version in idiomatic, straightforward English. This will be an excellent exercise, which will serve also to test your knowledge of Spanish.

By the way, the extracts from Spanish-American writers given in this lesson and the preceding one are, on the whole, more difficult than those usually used in college entrance examinations.

Uruguayan Writer   *José Enrique Rodó* (1871–1917)

Mirando Jugar un Niño [1]

Jugaba el niño en el jardín de la casa con una copa de cristal, que en el límpido ambiente [2] de la tarde un rayo de sol tornasolaba [3] como un prisma. Manteniéndola, no muy firme, en una mano, traía en la otra un junco,[4] con el que golpeaba [5] acompasadamente [6] en la copa. Después de cada toque,[7] inclinando la graciosa cabeza, quedaba atento, mientras [8] las ondas [9] sonoras, como nacidas de vibrante trino [10] de pájaro,[11] se desprendían [12] del herido cristal y agonizaban en los aires. Prolongó así su improvisada música hasta que, en un arranque [13] de volubilidad,[14] cambió el motivo de su juego,[15] se inclinó a tierra, recogió en el hueco [16] de ambas manos la arena limpia del sendero [17] y la fué vertiendo [18] en la copa hasta llenarla. Terminada esta obra, alisó [19] con primor [20] la arena desigual de los bordes. No

---

[1] The lack of a "personal **a**" before **Niño** implies that the author is not thinking of the boy as an individual but just as "a child."
[2] **ambiente,** atmosphere
[3] **tornasolar,** to make iridescent
[4] **junco,** rush
[5] **golpear,** to beat (**golpe,** blow)
[6] **acompasadamente,** rhythmically (**compás,** measure)
[7] **toque,** touch
[8] **mientras** (usually **m. que**), while
[9] **onda,** wave
[10] **trino,** trill
[11] **pájaro,** bird
[12] **desprenderse de,** to issue from
[13] **arranque,** impulse
[14] **volubilidad,** *not volubility, but* fickleness
[15] **juego,** play
[16] **hueco,** hollow
[17] **sendero,** path
[18] **verter,** to pour
[19] **alisar,** to smoothe
[20] **primor,** dexterity

pasó mucho tiempo sin que quisiera volver a arrancar [1] al cristal su fresca resonancia; pero el cristal, enmudecido,[2] como si hubiera emigrado un alma de su diáfano seno,[3] no respondía más que con un ruido de seca percusión al golpe del junco. El artista tuvo un gesto de enojo [4] para el fracaso [5] de su lira.[6] Hubo de verter una lágrima,[7] mas la dejó en suspenso. Miró, como indeciso, a su alrededor [8]; sus ojos húmedos se detuvieron en una flor muy blanca y pomposa, que a la orilla [9] de un cantero [10] cercano, meciéndose en la rama [11] que más se adelantaba,[12] parecía rehuir [13] la compañía de las hojas, en espera de [14] una mano atrevida.

§ 5. Reference List of Noun and Adjective Suffixes (2) — Illustrative List of Derivatives of Hombre and Tierra — Emilio Castelar: La Lengua Española

REFERENCE LIST OF NOUN AND ADJECTIVE SUFFIXES (2):

–e: common noun and adjective ending: **agente, aire, antropoide, arte, firme, formidable, héroe, posible, simple, tigre.**

–EDA, –EDO: form nouns from basic nouns, indicating *grove, orchard*, etc. [compare –al, –ar (2)]: **arboleda,** *grove* (**árbol,** *tree*); **alameda,** *poplar grove* (**álamo,** *poplar*); **viñedo,** *grape-growing region* (**viña,** *vineyard*).

–EÑO: forms adjectives from nouns or verbs: **aguileño,** *aquiline* (**águila,** *eagle*); **halagüeño,** *alluring, promising, flattering* (**halagar,** *to flatter, allure, coax*); **roqueño,** *rocky* (**roca,** *rock*); **trigueño,** *brunet.*

–EO: forms nouns from verbs ending in –ear (signifying *continued action*): **bombardeo,** *bombardment, shelling* (–ear, *to bombard, shell;* **bomba,** *bomb, shell*); **golpeo,** *beating, pounding* (–ear, *to beat, pound;* **golpe,** *blow*); **rodeo,** *surrounding, turning, round-up,* pl. *beating around the bush* (–ear, *to surround;* **rueda,** *wheel*);

[1] **arrancar a,** to draw out of, wrest from
[2] **enmudecer,** to make dumb (**mudo,** mute)
[3] **seno,** breast, bosom
[4] **enojo,** annoyance
[5] **fracaso,** failure
[6] **lira,** lyre, lyric poem
[7] **lágrima,** tear
[8] **a su alrededor,** about him
[9] **orilla,** margin, border, edge
[10] **cantero,** *probably here* (hard) path
[11] **rama,** (small) branch (**ramo** is branch of tree)
[12] **adelantarse,** to approach
[13] **rehuir,** to flee again
[14] **en espera de,** in wait of (awaiting)

ventaneo, *gazing out of the window, window-flirting* (**-ear, to gaze** *out of the window;* **ventana,** *window*).

-ERO, -ERA: (1) form adjectives from nouns: **florero,** *flowery* (of speech); **guerrero,** *warlike* (**guerra,** *war*); **pasajero,** *passing, transitory;* **petrolero,** *oil* (adj., as in **industria petrolera**).

(2) indicate a *container:* **cartera,** *portfolio* (**carta,** *letter*); **cenicero,** *ash tray* (**cenizas,** *ashes*); **florero,** *flower pot;* **pajarera,** *aviary* (**pájaro,** *bird*); **salero,** *salt cellar;* **sombrero,** *hat* (**sombra,** *shade*).

(3) indicate *owner or person in charge or who acts* (= *-er, -man;* fem. *-woman, wife*): **cartero,** *mailman, postman;* **molinero,** *miller,* *-era, miller's wife* (**molino,** *mill*); **obrero,** *laborer* (**obrar,** *to labor*); **pasajero,** *-a, passenger* (**pasaje,** *passage*); **petrolero,** *-a, oil worker;* **portero,** *porter, janitor, gatekeeper* (**puerta,** *gate*); **ranchero,** *-a, rancher* (**rancho,** *ranch*); **vaquero,** *-a, cowboy, -girl* (**vaca,** *cow*).

(4) indicate *dealer or maker:* **cocinero** *-a, cook* (**cocina,** *kitchen, cooking*); **florero,** *florist;* **florera,** *bower girl or woman, flower-seller* (f.); **joyero,** *jeweler* (**joya,** *jewel*); **librero,** *bookseller;* **sombrerero,** *hatter;* **zapatero,** *shoemaker.*

-ERÍA [derived from **-ero** (4)]: indicates a *collection, shop, or trade:* **cervecería,** *brewery;* **joyería,** *jewelry, j. store, j. business;* **librería,** *bookshop, book trade;* **muchachería,** *crowd of boys or children.*

-EZ, -EZA: form abstract nouns from adjectives (= *-ness, -ty*): **brillantez,** *brightness, brilliance* (**brillante**); **honradez,** *honesty* (**honrado,** *honest;* **honra,** *honor*); **belleza,** *beauty;* **grandeza,** *greatness;* **pureza,** *purity;* **tristeza,** *sadness, sorrow* (**triste,** *sad*).

-ia, -ía: common noun endings: (*-y*) **ceremonia, comedia, democracia, familia, gloria, historia, memoria, cortesía, filosofía, mayoría** (*majority*), **psicología, simpatía, Hungría;** (*-e*) **importancia, experiencia;** (*-ia*) **acacia, amnesia, Asia, histeria;** also note: **copia,** *abundance, copy;* **logia,** *lodge;* **cofradía,** *brotherhood* (relig. org.); **mejoría,** *betterment;* **señoría,** *lordship.*

–ico: adj. or noun ending (*-ic, –ical*): **cómico** (*comic, –al, come-dian*), **físico** (*physical, –cist, physique*), **lógico** (*logical, –cian*), **músico** (*musical, –cian*), **patriótico, político** (*political, –cian*), **público** (adj., n.).

–ica: noun ending (*–ic, –ics*): **aritmética, física, gramática** (*grammar*), **lógica, música, politica** (*politics, policy*), **república.**

–IENTO: forms adjectives from nouns, indicating *resemblance:* **avariento,** *miserly* (**avaro,** *greedy*); **hambriento,** *hungry;* **se-diento,** *thirsty.*

–il, (–ile): **dócil, frágil, reptil, senil, mujeril** (*womanly, –ish*).

–io: common adj. or noun ending: (*–y*) **contrario, ordinario, satisfactorio, misionario, misterio, promontorio, remedio, secretario;** (*–e*) **oficio, palacio, privilegio, servicio;** *also note:* **aluminio,** *alumin(i)um;* **dominio,** *dominion;* **condominio,** *condominium;* **vicario,** *vicarious;* **–ario** may = *–aire:* **con-cesionario, cuestionario, milionario.** (*Also see* –o.)

–ismo (*–ism*): **comunismo, materialismo, patriotismo.**

–ista (*–ist*): **artista, comunista, dentista, egoísta.**

–IZO: indicates a *tendency.* **enfermizo,** *sickly* (**enfermo,** *sick, ill, infirm*); **macizo,** *massive* (**masa,** *mass*); **rojizo,** *reddish.* (Compare **–dizo,** page 244.)

-mento, –miento (*–ment*): **elemento, momento, movimiento, sentimiento; casamiento,** *marriage;* **nacimiento,** *birth.*

-o: common adj. and noun ending: **acto, americano, contacto, disco, líquido, moribundo, mucho, turbulento;** (*–e*). **absoluto, activo, completo, felino, fino, infinito, inmenso, motivo, uso, vestíbulo;** (*–ous*): **ridículo, herbáceo, mis-celáneo, carbonífero, carnívoro;** (*–an*) · **humanitario, subterráneo;** (*–al*): **eterno, nocturno;** (*–um*). **coliseo, museo, geranio, talco;** (*–us*): **aparato, censo, consenso, genio;** indicates *person practicing art or science:* **arqueólogo, astrónomo, filósofo, fotógrafo, geógrafo, psicólogo, teólogo.**

–ÓN: forms nouns from verbs, indicating *result of action:* **apretón,** *squeeze* (*of hand*) (**apretar,** *to tighten, press, squeeze*), **empu-jón,** *push, shove* (**empujar,** *to push*); **presión,** *pressure* (**preso,** past part. of **prender,** *to seize, grasp*); **reventón,** *burst, blowout* (**reventar,** *to burst, blow up or out*).

–ÓN, –ONA: form adjectives or nouns, from nouns or verbs, indicating a *personal trait.* **burlón, –ona,** *mocking, jesting, mocker, joker* (**burla,** *mockery, jest, trick*); **coquetón, –ona,** *flirtatious, flirt,* (m.) *lady-killer* (**coqueta,** *coquette, flirt*); **gruñón,**

–ona, *grumbling, grumbler* (**gruñir**, *to grunt, grumble, growl*);
juguetón, **–ona,** *fond of playing* (**juguete,** *toy*); **preguntón,**
–ona, *inquisitive, nosy, i. person* (**preguntar,** *to ask, inquire*).
(Also augmentative ending; see page 230.)

··**or:** ending of abstract nouns: **clamor, esplendor, horror, verdor**
(*verdure, greenness*). (Also see –**ador,** etc., page 243.)

–**oso** (*–ous, –ful, –ose*): **ambicioso; gracioso,** *graceful, gracious*
(**gracia,** *grace*); **misterioso; odioso,** *hateful, odious* (**odio,**
hate); **cariñoso,** *affectionate* (**cariño,** *affection*); **grandioso;**
verboso; polvoroso, *dusty* (**polvo,** *dust*); **orgulloso,** *proud*
(**orgullo,** *pride*); **verdoso,** *greenish.*

–**sis** (*–sis*): **crisis, metamorfosis, neurosis, psicosis, paréntesis.**

–**tro** (*–ter*): **centro, filtro, metro, ministro, teatro.**

–**tud** (*–tude*): **altitud, magnitud, multitud, solitud.**

–**UDO:** forms adjectives from nouns, indicating *an excessive characteristic*: **barbudo,** *heavily bearded* (**barba,** *beard*); **ceñudo,**
frowning, grim (**ceño,** *frown*); **peludo,** *hairy, shaggy* (**pelo,** *hair,
fur*); **zancudo,** *long-legged, also mosquito* (**zanca,** *shank*).

–**UNO:** forms adjectives from names of species of animals; means
pertaining to (= *–ine*): **caballuno** (*or* **caballar,** *or* **equino**),
equine, of horses, horse (adj.); **ovejuno,** *of sheep, sheep* (adj.)
(**oveja,** *sheep*); **perruno,** *doglike, doggish, dog* (*adj.*); **hom-
bruno,** *mannish.*

–**URA:** forms *abstract nouns* from adjectives: **altura,** *height* (**alto,**
high); **bravura,** *ferocity, bravery* (**bravo,** *fierce, brave*); **hermosura,** *beauty* (**hermoso,** *beautiful*); **hondura,** *depth* (**hondo,**
deep); **locura,** *madness* (**loco,** *mad*).

–**ZÓN:** forms nouns from nouns or verbs: **armazón,** *framework*
(**armar,** *to assemble, put together*); **picazón,** *itch(ing)* (**picar,** *to
sting, bite*); **quemazón,** *conflagration, burning, smarting* (**quemar,**
to burn).

WARNING. Do not try to form Spanish words by adding suffixes
to words you know. A knowledge of Spanish suffixes is extremely
useful for understanding and translating Spanish, but it is not
very useful in translating English into Spanish — there are too
many possibilities. Furthermore, you cannot be sure that the
Spanish derivative word means what it seems to mean; for example,
apartamiento may mean an *apartment,* or it may mean *separation*
or *retirement;* **pomposo** may mean *pompous,* or it may mean *magnificent, splendid,* or *showy:* the fact that **terrón** is derived from

tierra and **-ón** does not prepare you to recognize that a **terrón** may be a lump of sugar.

ILLUSTRATIVE LIST OF DERIVATIVES OF **TIERRA.** The following is an incomplete list of the derivatives of **tierra,** *land, earth, ground,* presented for the sake of showing the wealth of derivative words produced by various suffixes and prefixes:

terraje, terrazgo, land rent
terral, land breeze
terrateniente, landowner
terraza, terrace
terrazo, ground (*of picture*)
terremoto, earthquake
terrenal, earthly
terreno, earthly; terrain, lot, plot
terreo, earthly
terrestre, terrestrial
territorial, territorial
territorio, territory
terrizo, earthen
terrón, clod, lump

terruca, one's native region
aterrar, to bring to the ground (*demolish*), to land (*of plane*)
aterrizar, to land (*of plane*)
aterrizaje, landing (*of plane*)
desenterrar, to dig up, disinter
desterrado, exile (*person*)
desterrar, to exile, banish
destierro, exile, banishment
enterrar, to bury, inter
entierro, burial, interment
soterrar, to bury (*hide*)
subterráneo, subterranean

READING. The translation of the following selection — a free rather than a literal translation — is on page xviii.

Spanish Writer   *Emilio Castelar* (1832–99)

LA LENGUA ESPAÑOLA

De varias y entrelazadas raíces; de múltiples y acordes sonidos; de onomatopeyas tan músicas que abren el sentir a la adivinación de las palabras antes de saberlas; dulce como la melodía más suave y retumbante como el trueno más atronador; enfática hasta el punto de que sólo en ella puede hablarse dignamente de las cosas sobrenaturales y familiar hasta el punto de que ninguna otra le ha sacado ventaja en lo gracioso y en lo picaresco; tan proporcionada en la distribución de las vocales y de las consonantes, que no ha menester ni los ahuecamientos de voz exigidos por ciertos pueblos del Mediodía, ni los redobles de pronunciación exigidos a los labios y a los dientes del Norte; libre en su sintaxis, de tantas combinaciones que cada autor puede procurarse un estilo propio y original sin daño del conjunto; única en su formación, pues sobre el fondo latino y las ramificaciones celtas e iberas ha puesto el germano algunas de sus voces, el griego algunos de sus esmaltes y el hebreo y el árabe tales alicatados y guirnaldas, que la hacen sin duda alguna la lengua más propia, tanto para lo natural como para lo religioso; la lengua que más se presta a los varios tonos y matices de la elocuencia moderna; la lengua que posee mayor copia de palabras, con que responder a la copia de las ideas; verbo de un espíritu que, si ha resplandecido en lo pasado, resplandecerá con luz más clara en lo por venir, puesto que no sólo tendrá este territorio y estas nuestras gentes, sino allende los mares territorios vastísimos y pueblos libres e independientes, unidos con nosotros así por las afinidades de la sangre y de la raza, como por las más íntimas y más espirituales del habla y del pensamiento, cuya virtud nos obligaría ciertamente a continuar en el Viejo y en el Nuevo Mundo una historia nueva, digna de la antigua y gloriosísima historia.

LESSON XV

§ 1. *More about the Articles — The Definite Article*

MORE ABOUT THE ARTICLES. You learned the Spanish articles in Lesson I, and in illustrative sentences, situation material, and readings you have no doubt acquired an awareness of how the articles are used. On the whole, they are used in Spanish as they are in English, but there are a few important differences in usage. In this section and the following one, the rules for the use of the articles will be presented — for review, for reference, and, if necessary, for study.

THE DEFINITE ARTICLE is used:

(1) Just as we use it in English, in referring to a definite person or thing, or to persons or things, that are clearly identified or understood:

El libro está en la mesa en el comedor. The book (*that has been mentioned*) is on the table (*the only table*) in the dining room.

La madre del niño herido lloraba. The mother of the injured boy was weeping.

Los mayas construyeron las pirámides de Yucatán. The Mayans built the pyramids of Yucatan.

La luna está tras de las nubes. The moon is behind the clouds.

(2) Before each noun in a series (as a rule *):

las plumas y los lápices, the pens and pencils
los niños y las niñas, the little boys and girls
el tío y la tía de Manuel, Manuel's uncle and aunt

(3) Before nouns used in a general or representative sense:

La guayaba es una fruta. The guava is a fruit.
El corazón es una máquina. The heart is a machine.
El hombre es mortal. Man is mortal.

---

* In speaking or writing Spanish you need never depart from the rule, but Spanish writers sometimes omit the second or third article if the nouns in series mean more or less the same thing (as **la belleza y gracia de**).

El español no piensa como el inglés. The Spaniard does
not think like the Englishman.

Los perros son más inteligentes que los caballos. Dogs are
more intelligent than horses.

(4) Before abstract nouns:

Para la salud, el sueño es necesario. For health, sleep is
necessary.

La filosofía no la interesa, ni la ciencia tampoco. Philosophy
does not interest her, nor science either.

Hablábamos del matrimonio y del divorcio. We were
talking of marriage and divorce.

¿ Qué son el tiempo y el espacio? What are time and space?

But the article is not used in many common phrases, such as:

**por amor de, en realidad, a decir verdad, hace calor, tengo
sueño, da miedo, no tengo tiempo.**

(5) Before adjectives used as nouns (as in English):

el bueno, the good man; **el malo,** the bad man
los ricos y los pobres, the rich and the poor

(6) Before a verbal noun:

El viajar me encanta. I love traveling.

El leer es buena práctica; el leer alto es mejor. Reading
is good practice; reading aloud is better.

(7) Before most titles:

el presidente Roosevelt; el general Montgomery

(8) Before names of places after a preposition:

a la escuela, to school; **en la iglesia,** in church; **el centro
de la ciudad,** the center of town (but **en casa,** at home;
ir a casa, to go home).

(9) Before names of persons followed by an adjective:

el pobre Tomás; la pequeña Conchita

Or, for special emphasis on the adjective (or noun):

el pobre de Tomás; la pequeña de Conchita

el bueno de mi hermano, my good brother, that good brother
of mine

el embustero de Pepe, that liar Pepe

(10) In place of a possessive pronoun (for clarity or emphasis or politeness):

> **el sombrero de Ud.,** *your* hat
> **la casa de Uds. y la de ellos,** your house and theirs
> **mis opiniones y las opiniones de él,** my opinions and his opinions
> **¿ Cómo está el hermano de Ud.?** How is your brother?

(11) With parts of the body, articles of clothing, and other possessions (where we use the possessive pronoun):

> **Me duelen los pies.** My feet hurt.
> **El pobre ha perdido el ojo.** The poor fellow has lost his eye.
> **Me puse el traje de baño.** I put on my bathing suit.
> **Me robó la pluma fuente.** He stole my fountain pen.

(12) Before the names of the days, months, seasons, and the directions:

> **Envié la carta el lunes.** I sent the letter Monday.
> **Vamos a la playa los domingos.** We go to the beach on Sundays.
> **Estuve aquí en el enero.** I was here in January. (*But:* **Llegué el cinco de enero.** I arrived the fifth of January.)
> **Es el verano ahora en mi país.** It is summer now in my country.
> **Andamos hacia el este.** We are going toward the east.

(13) Before the names of certain continents, countries, states, and cities:

> **la América Central, el Panamá, los Estados Unidos, la Florida, la Habana** (see page 50)

(a) The article must be used if an adjective is used with the name: **el México central; el África del Norte; la España católica**

(b) The article is sometimes used with the name of a country when it is not required; this usually occurs (i) when the name is feminine, (ii) when it is a subject of a verb, (iii) when the country is spoken of as a power: **La Inglaterra era nuestro aliado** (*ally*).

(14) Before names of rivers, seas, oceans, and mountains: **el Misisipí, el Mar Caribe, el Atlántico, el Vesuvio, los Andes.**

(15) Before the names of streets: **la Quinta Avenida, la Calle
Roble.**

(16) Before the names of languages, except after **aprender** and
hablar:

> **El español no es tan difícil como el portugués.** Spanish is
> not as difficult as Portuguese.
>
> **Estoy estudiando el francés.** I am studying French.
>
> **Pero todavía no puedo hablar francés.** But I can't speak
> French yet.

(17) The neuter article **lo** is used with adjectives to give them the
force of nouns:

> **lo difícil,** the difficult thing, what is difficult
>
> **lo más importante,** the most important thing, what is most
> important
>
> **lo venidero,** that which, *or* what, is to come
>
> **lo raro de la cosa,** the strange part of the thing
>
> **lo mío,** that which, *or* what, is mine
>
> **Ud. no sabe lo pesado que es esta maleta.** You don't know
> how heavy this suitcase is.

§ 2. *The Indefinite Article — Omission of the Article*

THE INDEFINITE ARTICLE. The indefinite article is used in Spanish, as it is in English, with a person or thing mentioned for the
first time and not yet identified or individualized:

> **Anoche un hombre entró en una casa cerca de aquí y dió
> muerte a una mujer.** Last night a man entered a house
> near here and killed a woman. *But:* **Creo que la casa
> está en la Calle Quinta.**

OMISSION OF THE ARTICLE: There are some cases in which the
article is omitted in Spanish, where it is used in English. The
following seven cases should be noted.

The article is omitted:

(1) As mentioned in section 1, (4), in various idioms:

> **a decir verdad,** to tell the truth
>
> **con intención de,** with the intention of
>
> **llevar dote,** to bring a dowry
>
> **llevar ventaja a,** to have the advantage of

Extract from a Spanish Newspaper. This selection and those on pages 259 and 261 contain a number of unfamiliar words. Try to read them with the aid of a dictionary.

TOROS

LA NOVILLERIA

«Chiquilín», el novillero cordobés que marcha a la cabeza de los que aspiran a la alternativa

DESPUES del vistazo que en nuestro artículo anterior dimos al escalafón de matadores de toros, justo es que revisemos hoy los principales nombres novilleriles clasificados por el grupo sindical correspondiente para la temporada 1954. Vale la pena por otra parte. Tan escasos de aliciente se presentan los matadores de alternativa que la ansiedad de la afición descansa, sin mucha seguridad por cierto, sobre la vanguardia novilleril, en la que trata de seleccionar tres o cuatro nombres para poner un poco de interés en los festejos que se avecinan.

Comencemos por decir que «Chiquilín» es quien se destaca entre los novilleros a juzgar por la demanda de las Empresas. Sin otras intervenciones en su haber que unas diez novilladas con picadores, el principiante cordobés ha empezado por donde terminó «Manolete»: hospedándose en el hotel Victoria de la capital madrileña. Y aunque esta circunstancia no supone otra cosa que un accidente baladí, la verdad es que «Chiquilín» parece irrumpir en la Fiesta con personalidad y arrestos, esperando foguearse en seis u ocho novilladas de provincias antes de presentarse en Sevilla o Madrid. El cordobés, pues, no ha de ser torero de términos medios. O tomará la alternativa con todos los honores a mediados de la temporada o continuará de matarife en el matadero de Córdoba, siguiendo su antigua profesión.

Pisando los talones a «Chiquilín» marcha también en vanguardia la joven figura de Antonio Borrero, «Chamaco». Quizá tenga más fondo que aquél. Acostumbrado a torear y aun a matar ganado morucho por plazas pueblerinas, llega a la Fiesta convenientemente placeado, como lo demuestran sus dos éxitos recientes en Barcelona. Huelva parece continuar con su racha de toreros. Si «Litri» no vuelve —y es muy posible que vuelva— los onubenses podrán continuar disparando sus cohetes de día de corrida gracias a la aparición de «Chamaco».

From: Madrid

NOVILLERÍA. From novillo, *a young bull*. A novillero is *a fighter of young bulls*, and hence novillería, *the trying out of bullfighters* who have not yet received la alternativa, *the alternative*, which means graduation as a full-fledged matador de toros of the torero who has the honor of killing.

hacer fiesta, to make a holiday
ser cosa de, to be a matter of
ver mundo, to see the world

(2) Before a noun of nationality or occupation following **ser** — if the noun is not modified:

Soy estudiante. I am a student.
Soy norteamericano. I am a North American.
Mi hermano es médico. My brother is a doctor. *But:* **Mi hermano es un muy buen médico.**
Jorge es artista. Jorge, *or* George, is an artist. *But:* **Jorge es un artista comercial.**
¿Es maestra la mujer que habla? Is the woman speaking a teacher?
Antonio es italiano. Antonio is an Italian. *But:* **Antonio es un italiano rubio.**

EXCEPTION:

If a very common adjective precedes the noun:

Jorge es buen artista. Es gran artista. Es mal pintor.

(3) Before an identifying noun in apposition, if it is not modified by an adjective:

mi amigo, médico de Nueva York, my friend, a doctor from New York. *But:* **mi amigo, un médico célebre,** my friend, a famous doctor; *and* **mi amigo, el doctor,** my friend, the doctor (when the man and his profession are known to the person addressed).
Bogotá, capital de Colombia, Bogota, the capital of Colombia.
Colón, descubridor del nuevo mundo, Columbus, the discoverer of the new world.
el coatí, animal de los trópicos americanos, the coati, an animal of the American tropics.

If the modifying adjective identifies (not merely describes) the noun in apposition, the article may be omitted:

Buenos Aires, ciudad principal de Argentina, B.A., the chief city of Argentina.
el Brasil, país más grande de Sudamérica, Brazil, the largest country of South America.

(4) After **o**, *or*, if the following noun explains the one preceding **o** (as in English):

> **Quiero hablar con el director, o gerente.**   I want to speak with the director, or manager.

(5) When a thing is not used in the definite sense, nor in the general, representative sense (as in English):

> **En los trópicos encontramos plantas y animales raros.**   In the tropics we find strange plants and animals.
>
> **Puerto Rico produce, además de azúcar y ron, tabaco, café, plátanos, piñas y otras frutas.**   Puerto Rico produces, besides sugar and rum, tobacco, coffee, bananas, pineapples, and other fruits:

[Compare section 1, (3).]

(6) In many proverbs, for pithiness:

> **A gran arroyo, pasar postrero.**   (In the case of) a great stream, (it is better) to cross last.
>
> **Agua pasada no muele molino.**   Water (that has) passed doesn't turn the mill.
>
> **Pobreza no es vileza.**   Poverty is not a disgrace.

(7) The article at the head of a title of a book, article, etc., may sometimes be omitted, unless the title is very short (not **Nubes** for **Las Nubes**):

> **Gramática de la Lengua Española** (*for* **La Gramática . . .**)
> **Cuento de Elefantes** (*for* **Un Cuento . . .**)

Compare: "*A Short History of England*, by Edward P. Cheney" and "Cheney's *Short History of England*." There is no definite rule on this matter, in English or Spanish.

[See also, in section 1, note on (2).]

§ 3. *SI, IF or WHETHER — Newspaper Items*

SI, IF OR WHETHER.   In the present tense you will have no difficulty putting *if* clauses into Spanish.   The verb following **si** is in the present indicative.   Thus:

> **Si él lo sabe, no importa.**   If he knows it, it doesn't matter.
> **Si son las tres, debo apurarme.**   If it is three o'clock, I must hurry.
> **Venga con nosotros si Ud. quiere.**   Come with us if you wish.

LA ACTUALIDAD EN LA RADIO

Radio Madrid, emisora [1] Central de la Sociedad Española de Radiodifusión [2] ha ampliado el espacio radiofónico en dos horas más de emisión. Desde las ocho de la mañana las antenas de Radio Madrid, abren en el espacio ondas, que llevan a los receptores los variados programas que sostienen el prestigio de la popular emisora.

Los programas musicales más variados, los de puro deleite; los de más fino humor; los que evocan el pasado y comentan el presente ocupan las horas del día hasta la madrugada animando la vida hogareña.

Personalidades del más alto prestigio, artistas eminentes desfilan por estos programas, todos del mayor interés.

Desde las ocho de la mañana hasta la una de la madrugada, Radio Madrid sostiene la atención de los miles de radioyentes, que se recrean con la variedad de los programas que llenan tantas horas sin que decaigan en interés.

Este es el éxito de Radio Madrid.

From: *El Hogar* (1955)

[1] **emisora**, radio station.
[2] **radiodifusión**, broadcasting.

As you remember, the present tense may be used for the future. In the following, the *if* clause refers to future time:

Si tengo tiempo, iré a verla. If I have time, I'll go to see her.

Si no tengo tiempo, será imposible ir. If I do not have time, it will be impossible to go.

There is no difficulty about verbs in the past tense after **si** in such sentences as:

Si él lo sabía, no dijo nada de ello. If he knew it, he said nothing of it.

Si él me llamó, yo no lo sabía. If he called me, I didn't know it.

Si era necesario, yo hablaba español. If it was necessary, I spoke Spanish.

Si he dicho algo indiscreto, lo siento. If I have said anything indiscreet, I am sorry.

Si meaning *whether* may be followed by the indicative, the conditional, or the infinitive. Thus:

No sé si debo ir (o no). I don't know whether I must go (or not).

No sé si iré (o no). I don't know whether I shall go (or not).

Yo no sabía si iría (o no). I didn't know whether I should go (or not). (*Should* does not mean obligation here.)

Yo no sabía si debería ir (o no). I didn't know whether I should, *or* ought to, go (or not).

No sé si ir o quedar. I don't know whether to go or stay.

No sé si ir o no. I don't know whether to go or not.

The *subjunctive* is used after **si** in *contrary-to-fact clauses*, or *suppositions*. If the time referred to is the present, the past subjunctive (either form) is used; if the supposition refers to past time, the past perfect subjunctive is used. The verb used in the conclusion is in the conditional.* Thus:

Si yo fuera (or fuese) Ud., yo no contestaría la carta. If I were you, I'd not answer the letter.

Yo iría a verla si tuviese (or –iera) tiempo. I would go to see her if I had time.

---

* The past subjunctive, **r** form, is sometimes used instead of the conditional in the conclusion, as: **Si yo fuera Ud., yo no contestara** (*for* **contestaría**) **la carta.**

An alternative form sometimes used in place of a clause with **si** is **a** plus infinitive: **A saberlo él** could be used in place of **Si él lo hubiera sabido.** The conclusion is the same in either case.

DALI QUEMA SU FALLA

EN toda España es imposible no hablar de las fallas de Valencia durante estos días. Tomando como centro la festividad de San José, Patrono de los artesanos, los levantinos expresan su alegría de primavera con fuegos, luces y ruido. Más de doscientas bandas llevan la música por delante, a través de las calles de la ciudad del Turia, y los campos ofrecen a la Virgen de los Desamparados el tributo de varios centenares de kilos de flores por las manos de millares de muchachas valencianas. Es una tradición de siglos.

Humeantes todavía las fallas de un año, se empiezan ya las del próximo. Madera, cartón, cera, telas. . . . Materiales sencillos que el artista convertirá en monumentos irónicos, burlescos, con el humor flotando en los gestos de las figuras. En esta semana fallera illuminará también con su fuego, la noche del 19, esta falla de Salvador Dalí, surrealista, pero española, que el perfil de Picasso — parte integrante del grupo — no puede menos de aceptar. El pintor catalán no ha querido estar ausente en las fiestas valencianas, brotes explosivos de la estación a orillas del Mediterráneo.

From: ACTUALIDADES (1955)

FALLA: A bonfire lit in the streets of Valencia on the night of St. Joseph's Eve.

Si yo hubiera (*or* –**iese**) **tenido tiempo, habría ido a verla.**
If I had had time, I'd have gone to see her.
Si él lo hubiese (*or* –**iera**) **sabido, no habría venido.** If he had known it, he would not have come.

The *subjunctive* is also used in a **si** clause to express *improbability*. The past subjunctive is used if the verb in the conclusion is in the conditional. *Should* is used with the English equivalent of the subjunctive verb. Thus:

> **Si yo estuviera** (*or* **–iese**) **muy ocupado, no podría ir.** If I should be very busy, I could not go.

> **Si los Jones me llamasen** (*or* **llamaran**), **él me lo diría.** If the Joneses should call me, he would tell me.

The future subjunctive is used to express improbability if the verb in the conclusion is in the future, but this construction is rarely used in speech:

> **Si yo tuviere tiempo, iré a verla.** If I have time (*which is unlikely*), I'll go to see her.

Emphatic **si.** **Si** may be used with a simple statement with the force of exclamatory *why*, expressing surprise. Thus:

> **Si debe estar borracho.** Why, he must be drunk.
> **Si son las doce.** Why, it's twelve o'clock.

It would be a good idea to glance over the readings from Spanish literature, looking for **si** and the various constructions that follow it.

§ 4. *Weights and Measures — Spanish and Spanish-American Currencies — Extract from George Borrow*, The Bible in Spain, *in English and in Spanish Translation*

WEIGHTS AND MEASURES. If you intend to travel in any of the Spanish-speaking countries, you must acquaint yourself with the vocabulary of weights (**pesos**) and measures (**medidas**). In all these countries the metric system (**el sistema métrico**) is used. Here are the units you should know:

1 kilómetro (0.62, approx. $\frac{3}{5}$, mile) = **1000 metros**

1 metro (39.37 inches, approx. $3\frac{1}{4}$ feet) = **100 centímetros**

1 centímetro (.3937, approx. $\frac{2}{5}$, inch) = **10 milímetros**

1 hectárea (2.47, approx. $2\frac{1}{2}$, acres) = **100 áreas = 10,000 metros cuadrados**

1 kilogramo (2.2 pounds) = **1000 gramos**

1 litro = 1.06 liquid quarts, 0.9 dry quart

100 grados = 180 degrees Fahrenheit:

> **0 C.** = 32 F. (freezing)
> **10 C.** = 50 F.
> **20 C.** = 68 F.
> **30 C.** = 86 F.
> **37 C.** = 98.6 F. (body temp.)
> **100 C.** = 212 F. (boiling)

The names of older units survive, such as **la legua** (about three miles). The following terms correspond roughly to our units, but are not exact equivalents:

pulgada, inch	**el pie,** foot
yarda, yard	**milla,** mile
onza, ounce	**libra,** pound
el galón, gallon	**tonelada,** ton

Adjectives and nouns relating to measurement:

alto, high	**alto, altura,** height; **altitud,** altitude
hondo, profundo, deep	**hondo, profundidad,** depth
largo, long	**largo, longitud, largura,** length
ancho, wide, broad	**ancho, anchura,** width, breadth

Tener with one of the above nouns as object is the usual equivalent of *to be* followed by an adjective:

¿ Qué anchura tiene el río Támesis? How wide is the River Thames?

El Támesis tiene en algunas partes una anchura de media milla. The Thames is in some places half a mile wide.

¿ Qué son las dimensiones de la casa? What are the dimensions of the house?

La casa tiene 15 metros de alto, 17 de largo y 12 de ancho. The house is 15 meters high, 17 long, and 12 wide.

El Himalaya tiene una altura media de casi dos kilómetros y medio. The Himalayas have a mean, *or* average, height of almost two and a half kilometers.

La ciudad de México tiene una altitud de 7800 pies, o 2377 metros. Mexico City has an altitude of 7800 feet, or 2377 meters.

Volamos a una altura de 5000 metros. We are flying at a height of 5000 meters.

SPANISH AND SPANISH-AMERICAN CURRENCIES:

Spain: 1 peseta = 100 céntimos; 1 duro = 5 pesetas

Argentina, Chile, Colombia, Cuba, Mexico: 1 peso = 100 centavos

Uruguay: 1 peso = 100 centésimos

Bolivia: 1 boliviano = 100 centavos

Costa Rica: 1 colón = 100 céntimos

Ecuador: 1 sucre = 100 centavos

Guatemala: 1 quetzal = 100 centavos

Honduras: 1 lempira = 100 centavos

Nicaragua: 1 córdoba = 100 centavos
Panama: 1 balboa = 100 centavos
Paraguay: 1 guaraní = 100 céntimos
Peru: 1 sol = 100 centavos
El Salvador: 1 colón = 100 centavos
Venezuela: 1 bolívar = 100 centavos

Names of former coins remain in use, for example the **real,** which varies in value from country to country. Some old Spanish terms from colonial days are used for various coins and various amounts. For example, in Mexico the 50-centavo piece is called a **tostón.** A large coin, such as the 5-peseta piece in Spain and the peso in Mexico, is often called a **duro.** Wherever you travel, you should ask someone to explain to you the currency and the popular names for various coins or amounts.

There are, of course, Spanish words for foreign coins and amounts, as **dólar, libra** (pound), **chelín** (shilling), **penique** (penny), **franco, marco, lira, rublo,** etc.

Translation from English into Spanish. Much Spanish can be learned by comparing a Spanish version of an English book with the original; for example, Manuel Azaña's translation of George Borrow's famous book, *The Bible in Spain.* Here is Chapter XLII of the original and, beside it, Azaña's version *:

I remained about three weeks in the prison of Madrid, and then left it. If I had possessed any pride, or harboured any rancour against the party who had consigned me to durance, the manner in which I was restored to liberty would no doubt have been highly gratifying to those evil passions; the government having acknowledged by a document transmitted to Sir George, that I had been incarcerated on insufficient grounds, and that no stigma attached itself to me from the imprisonment I had under-	**Unas tres semanas estuve en la cárcel de Madrid, y, al cabo de ese tiempo la dejé. Si yo hubiese sido orgulloso, o abrigado algún rencor contra el partido que me encarceló, el modo como me devolvían la libertad hubiera halagado grandemente esas malas pasiones. El Gobierno, en un documento transmitido a Sir Jorge, reconoció, que me habían detenido sin razón bastante, y que ninguna tacha quedaba sobre mí de resultas de la prisión; se encargaba al**

* Published in the *Colección Granada* (Jiménez-Fraud, Editor, Madrid). The English text is from the best edition (published by John Murray with the Notes and Glossary by Ulick Ralph Burke).

gone; at the same time agreeing to defray all the expenses to which I had been subjected throughout the progress of this affair.

It moreover expressed its willingness to dismiss the individual owing to whose information I had been first arrested, namely, the *corchete* or police officer who had visited me in my apartments in the Calle de Santiago, and behaved himself in the manner which I have described in a former chapter. I declined, however, to avail myself of this condescension of the government, more especially as I was informed that the individual in question had a wife and family, who, if he were disgraced, would be at once reduced to want. I moreover considered that, in what he had done and said, he had probably only obeyed some private orders which he had received; I therefore freely forgave him, and if he does not retain his situation at the present moment, it is certainly no fault of mine.

I likewise refused to accept any compensation for my expenses, which were considerable. It is probable that many persons in my situation would have acted very differently in this respect, and I am far from saying that herein I acted discreetly or laudably; but I was averse to receive money from people such as those of which the Spanish Government was composed, people whom I confess I heartily despised, and I was unwilling to

propio tiempo de pagar todos los gastos que la tramitación del asunto me originó.

Además, se mostró dispuesto a dejar cesante al individuo por cuyos informes me detuvieron, es decir, el *corchete* que me visitó en mi hospedaje de la calle de Santiago y se comportó del modo descrito en uno de los anteriores capítulos. Rehusé, empero, aprovecharme de la condescendencia del Gobierno, más que nada porque me dijeron que el individuo de marras tenía mujer e hijos, y si le dejaban cesante, se quedarían en la miseria. Consideré, además, que en cuanto hizo y dijo se limitó probablemente a obedecer órdenes secretas; le perdoné, pues, sin reservas, y si en el momento presente no conserva su plaza, la culpa, ciertamente, no es mía.

También rehusé aceptar indemnización por mis gastos, que fueron de importancia. Es probable que muchas personas en mi caso hubiesen procedido de muy diferente modo en este punto, y me guardo de afirmar que en ello anduviese yo del todo discreto o acertado. Pero me repugnaba recibir dinero de una gente como la que componía el Gobierno de España, gente a quien, lo confieso, depreciaba yo cordial-

afford them an opportunity of saying that they had imprisoned an Englishman unjustly, and without a cause, he condescended to receive money at their hands. In a word, I confess my own weakness; I was willing that they should continue my debtors, and have little doubt that they had not the slightest objection to remain so: they kept their money, and probably laughed in their sleeves at my want of common sense.

mente, y no quería darle motivo para decir que el inglés a quien habían apresado injustamente y sin proceso, accedía a recibir dinero de sus manos. En una palabra, confieso mi debilidad: deseaba yo que continuasen siendo deudores míos, y estaba seguro de que no opondrían la más leve objeción a continuar siéndolo; se guardaron su dinero y probablemente se rieron para su capote de mi falta de sentido común.

The heaviest loss which resulted from my confinement, and for which no indemnification could be either offered or received, was in the death of my affectionate and faithful Basque Francisco, who, having attended me during the whole time of my imprisonment, caught the pestilential typhus or jail fever, which was then raging in the Cárcel de la Corte, of which he expired within a few days subsequent to my liberation.

La mayor pérdida que me ocasionó el encarcelamiento, y por la que no podía ofrecerse ni recibirse indemnización, fué la muerte de mi afectuoso y fiel Francisco, el vascongado, que por acompañarme durante todo el tiempo que duró mi prisión, cogió el tifus o fiebre carcelaria, que entonces hacía estragos en la cárcel de la Corte, y murió a los pocos días de mi liberación.

§ 5. *Correspondence in Spanish — Some Useful Phrases for Letter Writing — Two Spanish Book Advertisements*

CORRESPONDENCE IN SPANISH. Letter writing is usually more formal and punctilious in Spanish than in English. The dominant rule for English-speaking people is that they should always err on the side of overpoliteness, if err they must. If the following instructions are followed for openings and endings, there need be no great risk in the body of the letter, provided it is kept to simple, direct statements.

The date is written thus: **20 de septiembre de 1957; 1º de enero de 1958.** (The first of the month is always **el primero (1º)**; for other days, just use the number.)

Polite openings:

Muy Señor mío: Dear Sir: **Muy Señores míos:** Gentlemen:

Muy Señores nuestros: Gentlemen: (writing from one firm to another)

Muy Señora mía: Dear Madam:

Distinguida Señorita N.: Dear Miss N.:

Muy estimado Señor N.: Dear Mr. N.:

Muy Señor mío y amigo: ⎱
Distinguido amigo: ⎰ My dear friend: (semiformal)

Mi querido amigo: *or* **Querido amigo:** Dear friend:

Querido don Pablo: *or* **Querido Núñez:** (informal, to a personal friend)

Polite endings:

Su seguro servidor, (abbreviated **S.S.S.,**) Or **De Ud. muy atento y seguro servidor,** (**De Ud. atto. y s.s.,**) Yours very truly,

A moderately familiar ending:

If there has been no previous correspondence:

Se ofrece a Ud., followed by (above the signature) **Afmo. atto. y S.S.,**

If there has been previous correspondence:

Se repite de Ud., followed by **Afmo. atto. y S.S.,** (**Afmo.** stands for **afectísimo,** affectionate.)

Familiar endings:

Saluda a Ud. muy atentamente, su afmo. amigo,
Le saluda su buen amigo, *or* **Le abraza su buen amigo,**

It is usual for one correspondent to refer to another's letter as **la estimada de Ud.**

Some Useful Phrases for Letter Writing:

Tengo el gusto de acusar a Ud. recibo de su carta del 5 de octubre, y en contestación me apresuro a decir que... I have the pleasure of acknowledging receipt of your letter of October 5, and in reply I hasten to say that...

En contestación a su carta del lunes, me apresuro a manifestarle que... In reply to your letter of Monday, I hasten to tell you that...

Muchísimas gracias por su carta del 7 pasado, y ... Many
thanks for your letter of the 7th last, and ...

Permítame Ud. ofrecerle los más sinceros votos por su viaje.
Allow me to offer you my best wishes for your voyage (journey, trip).

**Dándole mil gracias anticipadas por su favor, me repito de
Ud. ...** Thanking you a thousand times in advance for
your favor, I remain ...

THE NEXT STEPS

WHEN YOU HAVE satisfied yourself (and your teacher if you have one) that you have worked through the present course to good effect, your next steps will be to perfect your knowledge and add to it. You can do this in several ways:

Never miss an opportunity of speaking with people whose mother tongue is Spanish.

Listen to radio broadcasts in Spanish. If you have difficulty in finding a regular Spanish program on your radio, write to radio stations in your region until you find a program that you can listen to regularly. If you have a short-wave radio, you will have no difficulty in getting a station that broadcasts from a Spanish-American country. Do not be discouraged if you understand very little at first. Regular listening will bring results.

If you live in a city with a sizable Spanish-speaking population, **buy a Spanish-language newspaper once a week. Try to find a Spanish bookstore, where you can buy books or periodicals.**

Read some books in English about Spain and Spanish America. Read novels written in Spanish.

You must have a good dictionary in order to read Spanish. A good dictionary is necessarily a good-sized dictionary. You might compare dictionaries by looking at *make* in the English-Spanish section and **hacer** in the Spanish-English section. The following are recommended: Holt's *Spanish and English Dictionary*, by E. B. Williams (1955); the "New Velázquez" dictionary (Appleton, rev. ed.); and Appleton's *New English-Spanish and Spanish-English Dictionary*, by Arturo Cuyás, revised and enlarged (1953 ed.). The scholar's final authority is the Dictionary of the Spanish Academy; its definitions are, of course, in Spanish only; it is very conservative and omits many technical terms and words of foreign and popular origin.

If you wish to make a thorough study of the Spanish language, you will find in *A Textbook of Modern Spanish*, by M. M. Ramsey (Holt, rev. ed., 1956), the fullest presentation of Spanish grammar in English, but in some respects it is not up-to-date. For the serious student nothing can replace the *Gramática de la Lengua Española* (an authoritative reference book published for the Spanish Academy by Espasa-Calpe), which is regularly revised.

Armed with a good dictionary, you should read your first Spanish novel. You might well begin with Blasco Ibáñez's **Sangre y**

Arena — first in English (*Blood and Sand*), then in the original Spanish. It is an excellent novel about bullfighting and brings in much about Spanish life in general. Or, if you prefer, you might get, from a bookstore in or near a university, a school edition of **El Sombrero de Tres Picos** or **La Vida de Lazarillo de Tormes**, which will contain a glossary and notes on the difficult words and passages. Pérez Galdós' novel **Doña Perfecta** is interesting and not very difficult; it too can probably be found in a school edition. Reference to articles on Spanish Literature, Mexican Literature, etc., in any encyclopedia will guide you to other important works that would interest you.

In addition to reading Spanish literature, you might find it interesting to read a book in Spanish on some hobby or subject in which you have a special interest. In this way you would at the same time improve your knowledge of Spanish and add to your knowledge of the subject.

The following books in English are recommended for background:

George Borrow, *The Bible in Spain* (Everyman's Library). This book, first published in 1843, is a classic and still very much worth reading.

Richard Ford, *Gatherings from Spain* (Everyman's Library). One of the best books about Spain.

Gerald Brenan, *The Spanish Labyrinth* (economic background to 1936; Cambridge University Press, 2d ed., 1950) and *The Face of Spain* (an account of travels; Farrar, Straus, 1951).

V. S. Pritchett, *The Spanish Temper* (Knopf, 1954). An excellent book based on extensive travels in Spain.

Salvador de Madariaga, *History of Modern Spain* (Praeger, 1958). The same writer's biographies of Bolivar and Cortes are also recommended.

Rafael Altamira, *Spanish Civilization* (abridged translation by J. B. Trend of Altamira's great **Historia de la Civilización Española**).

Hubert Herring, *History of Latin America* (Knopf, 2nd ed. rev., 1961).

Bernal Díaz del Castillo, *The Discovery and Conquest of Mexico* (Farrar, Straus, 1956).

William H. Prescott, *Conquest of Mexico and Conquest of Peru* (Modern Library).

If your special interest is in Spanish America, or perhaps in one of the Spanish-American countries, you still need to have a general knowledge about the history and culture of Spain, the mother country.

A final word: Your present knowledge of Spanish will soon fade away if you do not use it and enlarge it. You have presumably bought this book because of a genuine interest in the Spanish language and Spanish-speaking people. I hope that your interest will persist, for there is immense value in the knowledge of another language and another culture.

APPENDIX

SUPPLEMENTARY READINGS

The readings that follow are examples of contemporary Spanish. Readings I–V were written by the author of this book and were published in the Buenos Aires newspaper *La Prensa*. Reading VI, by Luis Alberto Sánchez, is from the Literary Supplement of *El Nacional*, of Caracas. Grateful acknowledgments are due the editors of the newspapers mentioned.

I. LOS GITANOS [1]

No puedo ver a un gitano o leer algo que se relacione con esta raza extraordinaria sin que se excite mi interés. Es hasta cierto punto un interés romántico, pero en los años últimos se ha cambiado en un interés de investigación, de manera que trato de reunir toda clase de informaciones acerca de esta gente que puede ser encontrada cerca en todas partes. Mi amigo Tschiffely me refería hace poco una anécdota de cómo, en su gran « raid » de Buenos Aires a Wáshington con sus dos caballos criollos Mancha y Gato, cuando se encontraba en las selvas [2] del Ecuador encontró a un grupo de gitanos que se dirigían hacia el sur. Se detuvo y habló con ellos, y su jefe, de repente le preguntó si conocía el camino al Perú, ¡ que estaba a muchos cientos de kilómetros de distancia! El viajero les dió la información pedida y les explicó que, aunque consiguieran cruzar los Andes a pie o a caballo, no debían pretender llevar con ellos sus carromatos [3] a través de aquellas difíciles montañas. « No importa — fué la respuesta del gitano —; lo intentaremos ». Manifestaron a Tschiffely que no tenían intención de permanecer en el Perú. Se proponían llegar más al Sur, a la Argentina, en donde contaban con parientes y muchos amigos. Cuando se enteraron que el jinete [4] no sólo procedía de la Argentina sino que también era muy conocedor de este país, revelaron un gran interés. « ¿ Qué clase de país es ése? — preguntaron —. ¿ Hay allí muchos caballos? ¿ Le gusta al pueblo la música? » Unas hábiles preguntas de Tschiffely le permitieron saber que este grupo de vagabundos venía de los Estados Unidos a través de México y la América Central. Eran representantes típicos de la raza, lo mismo que los que pueden encontrarse en el cercano Oriente, en la Europa Central, en Rusia, en España y en la mayoría de los países del mundo. Pobremente vestidos, con poco o ningún dinero, vitalmente saludab es,[5]

[1] **Los Gitanos,** The Gypsies
[2] **selvas,** forests, jungles
[3] **carromatos,** narrow, tilted carts
[4] **jinete,** horseman
[5] **saludable,** healthy

completamente analfabetos [1] y sin pasaportes ni documentos de identidad,
hablaban su propio lenguaje y confiaban completamente en que su ingenio
les proporcionaría los medios para poder llegar a su lejano destino. Podía
asegurarse de antemano que si no llegaba a gustarles la Argentina, se
marcharían a otra parte; al otro extremo del mundo, si se sentían inclina-
dos a hacerlo. ¿ Cómo podrá ser escrita alguna vez la historia de esta raza?

En la mayoría de los países, la historia de los gitanos es la misma. Es
un « record » de vagancia,[2] de lo picaresco y del fracaso de los gobiernos
para mantenerlos en orden. Tengo ante mí un viejo libro que contiene el
texto de un edicto (de 1792), del emperador José II, respecto a los gitanos
de Transilvania. Se dan en él instrucciones detalladas para el mejora-
miento de estos huraños[3] : deben enseñar religión a sus hijos y enviarlos a
la escuela; deben impedirles que vaguen sucios [4] y medio en cueros [5] por
las calles; todos deben concurrir a las iglesias; deben sujetarse todos a las
costumbres del país, en cuanto a dieta, vestidos y lenguaje; deben cesar de
vestir amplias capas [6] utilizadas para ocultar los artículos robados; ningún gitano debe conservar en su poder un caballo; todos los gitanos deben
trabajar, especialmente en la agricultura. « ¡ Et patatí, patatá! » [7] La
sección final de este edicto imperial declaró ilegal para los gitanos divertirse
haciendo música cuando había trabajo que hacer. ¡ Ay !, los egipcios de
Transilvania, cuando escribo estas líneas, son, en cuanto a métodos de
vida y conducta como lo eran cuando fué concebida dicha ley. Todo país
de Europa podría referir algo similar. En el tiempo de Felipe III de
España, vivía un piadoso doctor Sancho de Moncada, profesor de teología
en la Universidad de Toledo, que publicó un discurso titulado « La expulsión de los gitanos ». Demostró que Fernando e Isabel, por una ley de
1494, habían ordenado la expulsión de estos perniciosos vagabundos; esta
ley fué renovada en 1523, 1528, 1534 y 1560. ¡ Ay ! ¡ Ay ! Todo en vano.
Sabemos que más de doscientos años después — en 1783, para ser exactos
—, Carlos III, dictó otra ley similar, con el mismo propósito, ¡ y con el
mismo resultado ! Los gitanos permanecieron allí y allí continúan todavía
más florecientes que nunca.

Se podría dictar igualmente un cuerpo de legislación para la expulsión
de las moscas.[8]

[1] **analfabeto**, illiterate
[2] **vagancia**, vagrancy
[3] **huraño**, unsociable, shy
[4] **vagar sucios**, to roam, dirty
[5] **medio en cueros**, half in (their) pelts = half-naked
[6] **amplias capas**, roomy capes
[7] **¡ Et patatí, patatá !** (*French*) And so forth, and so on!
[8] **moscas**, flies

II. LITERATURA EN ESPAÑA DURANTE
LA GUERRA DE 1914–18

En cuestiones de literatura y de arte, España no fué un país neutral durante la guerra europea. Los escritores y artistas jóvenes estuvieron muy conscientes de [1] lo que estaba sucediendo en todas partes, en las esferas [2] de su respectivo interés. Se desarrollaron [3] nuevos impulsos creadores, y hombres de una generación más vieja en años pero espiritualmente jóvenes principiaron a absorber algo del acercamiento [4] experimental, investigador y explorador de la juventud. De estos escritores experimentados, los nombres de Unamuno y Azorín serán familiares. Unamuno se hizo viejo en años, pero ¿dónde podríamos encontrar una imaginación más fresca? Intelectualmente, se encuentra tan a la vanguardia como cualquiera de los más jóvenes; y tiene, agregado a [5] su espíritu inquisidor e insubordinado, la sublimidad de San Agustín y la humanidad de Rousseau. Además posee algo de la naturaleza granítica [6] de los vascos, combinado con la fluidez y la potencia de un torrente de montaña. Es uno de los pocos escritores españoles cuyas obras, en traducción, pueden ser apreciadas por el lector inglés que no puede leer el original. En cuanto a Azorín, ese autor encantador, también fué miembro activo de vanguardia, y sus escritos combinan una claridad francesa con una sensualidad y flexibilidad mediterráneas. El humor satírico, natural de Azorín, deleita al lector cuando recae [7] sobre alguna fruslería [8] apartada del tema: la iluminación resultante lleva una evidencia inequívoca de que el autor está familiarizado con el acceso superrealista [9] por medio de la subconsciencia. No hay necesidad de mencionar aquí a Ramón Gómez de la Serna, ese genial y productivo fantasista cuyas obras son tan intensamente españolas que constituyen la desesperación [10] de todos los traductores, y cuya originalidad de visión le coloca automáticamente en todo ultramovimiento [11] que pueda existir o que esté gestándose.

III. ESPAÑOLES Y IRLANDESES

Se me ha ocurrido pensar con frecuencia que el sentido de humorismo [12] de los irlandeses tiene una gran analogía con el de los españoles, y aun me parece que hay algunas buenas razones biológicas para que exista esta

[1] **consciente de,** conscious of
[2] **esfera,** sphere
[3] **desarrollarse,** to evolve, develop, unfold
[4] **acercamiento,** approach
[5] **agregado a,** attached to, in addition to
[6] **granítico, –a,** granite
[7] **recaer,** to fall back
[8] **fruslería,** trifle, tidbit
[9] **acceso superrealista,** surrealist approach
[10] **desesperación,** despair
[11] **en todo ultramovimiento,** in whatever most extreme movement
[12] **sentido de humorismo,** sense of humor

afinidad. Los antropólogos y los geógrafos sostienen la teoría de que los celtíberos y los irlandeses de hace más de dos mil años eran de la misma raza. Según lo que yo tengo leído respecto a ambas, no puedo dudarlo, aunque todavía no se haya llegado a encontrar las pruebas finales que lo demuestren. Los celtíberos fueron el pueblo más guerreador[1] de la península y los que ofrecieron más tenaz resistencia a los romanos. Los irlandeses resistieron a los ingleses aun más obstinadamente. Por la supervivencia[2] de tradiciones en regiones muy apartadas[3] y las pruebas más dignas de fe de nombres de lugares, está demostrado que el elemento céltico existió no sólo en el Norte y el Este de España, sino también en la mayoría del país. Yo mismo, nacido en Irlanda, y celta por parte de padre y madre, me he quedado pasmado[4] a veces al encontrar en España tantas similaridades físicas y psicológicas con mi propia raza. Sobre todo, he podido gustar con placer el humorismo español, a menudo[5] en ocasiones en que mis amigos ingleses no podían descubrir su existencia. La más grande y más sorprendente prueba de tal fracaso puede encontrarse en las traducciones inglesas de « Don Quijote », cuando son obras absolutas de ingleses. ¡ Ah !, la mitad de las veces estos traductores han pasado por alto[6] todo el ingenio y humorismo de Cervantes, y esto jamás es tan sorprendente como en su interpretación de los refranes de Sancho Panza. Fué, según creo, Salvador de Madariaga quien llamó la atención sobre el hecho de que, mientras Don Quijote comienza sus maravillosas aventuras lleno de ilusiones, y hacia su fin demuestra un profundo sentido de la realidad, el desenvolvimiento espiritual de Sancho Panza se desarrolla siguiendo la vía opuesta[7]: éste comienza con un sentido de realismo y termina con ilusión. Cómo estas dos curvas de desenvolvimiento se elevan y caen, y se cruzan en la aventura cuando Sancho embelesa[8] a Dulcinea, es un gráfico psicológico delineado[9] con habilidad incomparable. Las dos cualidades de realismo e ilusión son las cualidades básicas que se pueden encontrar en los irlandeses y los españoles, y en ninguna otra parte están mejor ejemplarizadas que en su humorismo.

Volvamos ahora al lado más iluminado y más brillante, y consideremos unos cuantos ejemplos de este humorismo irlandés característico. Un irlandés que quería aprender español se dirigió a un maestro y le preguntó cuánto le cobraría por sus lecciones. El profesor le dijo diez chelines por la primera y cinco chelines por cada una de las lecciones sucesivas. « Muy bien — replicó el irlandés —; como ya conozco algo del idioma, podemos

---

[1] **guerreador,** warlike
[2] **supervivencia,** survival
[3] **apartado, –a,** separated, different
[4] **pasmado,** astounded (**pasmar,** to astound)
[5] **a menudo,** often (**menudo,** minute, little)
[6] **pasar por alto,** to overlook
[7] **la vía opuesta,** the opposite road, *or* path
[8] **embelesar,** to enchant
[9] **un gráfico psicológico delineado,** a psychological graph drawn

omitir la primera lección y empezaremos con la segunda ». Sancho Panza podría haber dicho eso. En el recinto [1] del Parlamento de Inglaterra, un miembro inglés, contestando una pregunta hecha por un irlandés, dijo: « El asunto es demasiado difícil para que pueda ser considerado ahora; debemos dejar la solución a la posteridad ». Inmediatamente un parlamentario irlandés gritó: « ¿ Qué ha hecho jamás la posteridad para nosotros? » Es ejemplo su humorismo a menudo incoherente, desvariado,[2] desilusionado y, no obstante, respirando alguna esperanza de mejores cosas. « En nuestra lucha con los ingleses — clamaba un patriota irlandés —, ¿ no es tan bueno un irlandés como otro? » « Sí — dijo un aldeano que se encontraba presente —, y aun mejor ». ¿ No recuerda esto el dicho de Cervantes « El hombre es como Dios le hizo y aun peor muchas veces » ? La curiosa y humorística falta de lógica y disgusto del aldeano irlandés está indicada en la siguiente anécdota. Un aldeano pobre ofreció en venta una cacerola [3] vieja, y los hijos le preguntaron por qué se desprendía de [4] ella. « ¡ Ah ! — dijo —. Unicamente para comprar algo que poner en ella ». El disimulo engendrado por temor a sus superiores sociales y al ascendiente de la política inglesa está demostrado por esta otra: Un criado de un hotel irlandés fué enviado a buscar el caballo de un viajero inglés. No sabiendo cuál de los dos caballos que se encontraban en el establo [5] era el que pertenecía al inglés, los ensilló [6] a ambos y los llevó. El viajero señaló a uno como suyo. A lo cual, el irlandés replicó: « Ciertamente, señor, yo ya lo sabía. Pero no estaba seguro de cuál era el que pertenecía al otro caballero ». Esto es burlesco, pero detrás existe la historia de dominación y supresión, acoplada con una cierta fertilidad de expedientes.

IV. EL ARTE DEL TRADUCTOR

El gran traductor es tan raro como el gran artista literario, quizás aun más raro, porque son menos las traducciones realmente grandes que las obras originales de arte. Nadie ha realizado todavía una buena traducción del « Quijote » al inglés, aunque existen varias pasables. Nadie ha traducido bien todavía a Shakespeare al francés: aun Voltaire fracasó en este intento. No obstante, en alemán hay una maravillosa versión del gran poeta inglés, ¡ tan buena que los alemanes reclaman a veces a Shakespeare como gloria propia ! [7] En conjunto, George Bernard Shaw ha sido bien servido por sus traductores, pero éstos han contado con la inestimable ventaja de poder consultarle pidiéndole explicaciones y aclaraciones. El

---

[1] **recinto,** building, hall, precinct
[2] **desvariado,** delirious, disorderly, nonsensical
[3] **cacerola,** saucepan, pot
[4] **desprenderse de,** to get rid of
[5] **establo,** stable
[6] **ensillar,** to saddle (**silla,** saddle)
[7] **como gloria propia,** as (a) glory of their own

traductor que puede acercarse a su autor y tenerlo como colaborador es ciertamente afortunado, y si en tales circunstancias no le hace justicia, podemos censurarle. Pero sólo el cielo puede ayudar al traductor si el autor ha muerto o es inaccessible: aquí es donde tiene que recurrir a la paciencia y al ingenio. Qué tonificador [1] es encontrar una traducción que se lee como el original, especialmente cuando este último es ingenioso o difícil. Tomemos por ejemplo los grandes libros religiosos del mundo. Sin traductores, el cristianismo habría permanecido, posiblemente, siendo una doctrina de segundo orden, limitada al distrito de Galilea. La traducción del hebreo del Antiguo Testamento y del Nuevo Testamento del griego, ambos al latín vulgar, echó los cimientos [2] de la Iglesia católica romana. Y puede asegurarse que si los viejos traductores no hubieran realizado su trabajo en manera supremamente bien, las magníficas ideas, ideales y mensaje de confortación [3] no habrían conseguido una aceptación tan extensa. La Biblia es un soberbio ejemplo de la importancia del traductor sobre los destinos humanos. Es apenas menos importante que las obras de Platón o Aristóteles o los otros filósofos de la antigua Grecia, sin las cuales y sus traducciones no habría surgido la cultura europea que conocemos.

¡ La alegría de traducir ! Sí, puede producir una inmensa alegría la traducción de la obra de un gran escritor. Unicamente un traductor puede apreciar el exquisito placer que existe en producir una versión que sigue fielmente al original, una versión que no sólo conserve el exacto significado e intención del original, sino que también transfiera la atmósfera de un medio [4] al otro. Esto constituye siempre una prueba severa, pero hay una más severa aun: la preservación de la « música » de un original. Hemos tenido un buen ejemplo de esto en la reciente versión de esa obra maestra argentina sobre la vida del gaucho: *Martín Fierro*. El original es uno de mis libros favoritos, porque cuando yo era muchacho conocí las pampas de la Argentina y conocí a los gauchos, y aunque su vida era más civilizada que la pintada en *Martín Fierro*, permanecía aún mucho del espíritu. Por consiguiente, tomé la versión inglesa con cierta vacilación, pero la encontré más que satisfactoria: el ritmo, el lenguaje, la atmósfera permanecen, y lo repasé diciendo para mis adentros que el traductor ha realizado un buen trabajo. Hoy, cuando deseo readquirir algo del espíritu de las pampas y los gauchos, leo el *Martín Fierro* y siempre me maravillo de la proeza de José Hernández. Ha inmortalizado a los gauchos en palabras convincentes. En los recientes años, Inglaterra ha sido afortunada por tener no sólo una excelente traducción de aquel clásico argentino, sino también una versión inglesa de *Tabaré*, la epopeya de Juan Zorrilla de San Martín, traducida por Ralph Walter Huntington, y de la obra brasileña *Ubirajara*, una

---

[1] **tonificador,** tonic, refreshing
[2] **echar los cimientos,** to lay the foundation(s)
[3] **confortación,** consolation
[4] **medio,** medium.

leyenda en verso de los indios tupíes. Los gauchos, el guaraní y el tupí, nombres extraños para los europeos y los ingleses; no obstante, ahora son conocidos entre nosotros. Por ello debemos agradecimiento a aquellos valerosos traductores que han hecho un trabajo con amor, y ésta es la base de toda buena traducción. Debe ser, como lo es en su mayoría, inspirada por el afecto.[1]

V. EL PUEBLO MÁS VIEJO DE EUROPA

Si consideramos la extensión abarcada por [2] su país, es probable que de ninguna raza de pueblo [3] del mundo se haya escrito tanto como se ha escrito respecto de los vascos. Parece que toda persona irresponsable que visita el rinconcito [4] del mundo occupado por los vascos desea contar a sus amigos lo que a aquéllos se refiere, y casi todo turista casual, con una ligera capacidad literaria, siente la urgencia moral de escribir un libro en el que pretende [5] explicar, al resto del globo, lo que es esta raza. Y la cantidad de literatura que se relaciona con los vascos ha llegado a ser tan grande que puede servir de base para hacer un estudio; pero personalmente encuentro que cuanto más leo de esa literatura más confundido [6] quedo, hasta el punto de que he llegado a una situación en la que casi rehuso leer más, consolándome con la reflexión de que jamás me sería posible obtener una idea clara sobre un tema tan vasto. Todo el que ha intentado escribir sobre los vascos comienza asegurando — muy justamente — que la historia no presenta otro problema más difícil que el del origen de esta raza, y los filólogos están todos contestes [7] en que su lenguaje no tiene analogía con ningún otro en el mundo. ¿Por qué, entonces, una persona no experta (tal como yo) habría de preocupar su cerebro con enigmas aparentemente insolubles, cuando aun los expertos más autorizados se ven obligados a admitir que ellos mismos han luchado en vano? ¿Y por qué voy a escribir yo ahora sobre un tema que ofrece semejantes dificultades? Lo que ocurre es que la lectura de un libro me ha permitido aprender respecto a los vascos, en una semana, más que todo lo que el conjunto de los demás libros me enseñó; y este libro tiene la particularidad de estar escrito en inglés por un inglés. Ya no me siento irremisiblemente ignorante acerca de la misteriosa « Euskadi ».[8] El mundo de habla española [9] debe dirigir su atención a una muy excelente obra que está íntimamente relacionada con muchos de sus miembros. *A Book of the Basques* (« Un libro sobre los

---

[1] **afecto,** affection, love
[2] **la extensión abarcada por,** the extent (area) comprised by
[3] **raza de pueblo,** race of people
[4] **rinconcito,** little corner (**rincón,** corner)
[5] **pretender,** to try
[6] **confundir,** to confound, perplex
[7] **estar conteste,** to be agreed
[8] **Euskadi,** *Basque for* the Basque country
[9] **El mundo de habla española,** The Spanish-speaking world

vascos »), por Rodney Gallop, ocupa ahora un lugar no sólo como el mejor libro entre muchos escritos en inglés, sino que, sin la más mínima duda [1] es también el mejor de todos los publicados, en cualquier idioma, sobre este tema. Está deliciosamente ilustrado con fotografías y dibujos hechos por la esposa del autor.

El autor del libro es un joven inglés que ha vivido muchos años en el país vasco y aprendió perfectamente el idioma. Por espacio de muchos años se ocupó Gallop de coleccionar sistemáticamente toda noticia de información auténtica que pudo encontrar, sobre un pueblo que le interesaba intensamente. Ha conducido su método con extremada precaución [2] y ha rechazado todo aquello que no resistiera victoriosamente la más escrupulosa exégesis. [3] Al repasar su libro, resulta agradable ver cuán donosamente se ocupa del trabajo de sus muchos predecesores en este terreno, aceptando esto, rechazando aquello, investigando y pesando cada cosa en la balanza de la razón. Ningún gran hombre le intimida por su autoridad, si la información que busca carece de solidez: ni considera demasiado humilde a un aldeano para ver en él una fuente de evidencia sobre los intrincados puntos relacionados con el dialecto, el folklore, la danza o la música. Rodney Gallop ama a los vascos, los respeta y se muestra extremadamente sensible al espíritu de su país, pero todo esto contribuye sencillamente a crearle más ansias [4] de encontrar la verdad respecto a ellos; no se deja coger nunca por la extravagancia de los entusiastas, limitándose a poner mayor celo en el método científico de su investigación. Como extranjero, los ve con un cierto despego [5] y, quizás, siendo un inglés, este despego es mayor que el que pudiera mostrar un francés o un español. La incomparable ventaja que tiene Gallop sobre todos los escritores (excepto muy pocos) que han estudiado a los vascos, es su profundo conocimiento de su aterrador [6] lenguaje, adquirido en la juventud y perfeccionado durante años de intenso estudio. Esta labor de cariño [7] que ocupa la mayor parte intelectualmente activa de su vida, ha dado por resultado este libro que constituye una bella contribución al saber: obra que puede ayudar a los mismos vascos a comprenderse un poco mejor y, tal vez, a darse cuenta de [8] por qué ellos y su país causarán siempre asombro y admiración en los corazones de cuantos se ponen en contacto con ellos.

[1] **la más mínima duda,** the slightest doubt
[2] **extremada precaución,** extreme care
[3] **exégesis,** exegesis, scholarly interpretation
[4] **ansia,** anxiety, eagerness
[5] **despego,** coolness, impartiality
[6] **aterrador,** terrifying
[7] **labor de cariño,** labor of love (**cariño,** affection)
[8] **darse cuenta de,** to take account of, realize

VI. LAS PELICULAS DE PABLITO CALVO
POR LUIS ALBERTO SÁNCHEZ

Pese a [1] todo cuanto se proclama acerca de las relaciones íntimas entre
España y América, lo cierto es que para ver actuar [2] a Pablito Calvo tuve
que estar en Italia, en 1955, y ahora en Francia, 1957.   Las dos películas
que han hecho famoso al estupendo y cándido niño español se llaman
« Marcelino, pan y vino » y « Mi tío Jacinto » titulada en francés « Le Muchacho ».

El caso de Pablito Calvo es algo especial.   Difiere fundamentalmente
del que los Estados Unidos presentaron años atrás con Shirley Temple.
Esta era una « monada » [3] precoz,[4] que se movía como grande, por lo cual
asombraba a los mayores, al verse caricaturizados por la niña.   En cambio,
Pablito Calvo tiene, como Buster Keaton, la gloria de su aparente impasibilidad.[5]   Es él todo ojos y toda sonrisa.   Y todo desgarbo.[6]   Anda como
quien se arrastra,[7] y corre como quien brinca.[8]   Tiene algo de angelote [9]
y algo de cabrita.[10]   Algo de pollinito nuevo,[11] de ésos que inmortalizó
Juan Ramón Jiménez y otro poco de dulce y sabio bobalicón,[12] cuya gracia
estupenda está en expresarse a despecho de [13] toda traba.[14]

Me atrevo a decir que Pablito Calvo no es sólo un niño prodigio, sino
que presenta una faz renovada [15] del arte escénico, en esa sobriedad ex-
presiva que antes se calificaba de « inglesa » y que aquí posee, además, una
dosis [16] incalculable de graciosa melancolía, o, mejor, de gracia y de
melancolía.

Me asustan [17] los « niños prodigios », pese a la tradición de Mozart.
Estimo más los progresos graduales, sistemáticos.   Mas, en este caso, la
precocidad consiste en . . . la naturalidad.   Pablito Calvo es el actorcito
que nunca desentona,[18] porque nunca se da tono.[19]   Actúa del todo es-
pontáneamente.   Esa es su gloria.   Su servidumbre [20] de mañana, acaso.

[1] pese a, in spite of
[2] actuar, to act
[3] monada, pretty or "cute" child
[4] precoz, precocious
[5] impasibilidad, impassivity
[6] desgarbo, clumsiness, ungainliness
[7] arrastrarse, to crawl, creep
[8] brincar, to leap, jump
[9] angelote, big angel
[10] cabrita, little goat
[11] pollinito nuevo, little newborn donkey
[12] bobalicón, booby, simpleton
[13] a despecho de, in spite of, in defiance of
[14] traba, shackle, bond
[15] faz renovada, renovated face
[16] dosis, dose, amount
[17] asustar, to frighten
[18] desentonar, to be out of tune, i.e., out of place
[19] darse tono, to put on airs
[20] servidumbre, servitude, slavery

« Marcelino, pan y vino » fué la revelación no sólo de Pablito Calvo sino del genio cinematográfico español. « Mi tío Jacinto » es su lado opuesto envés y revés.[1] En la primera, las virtudes; en la segunda, los defectos. Allí, la caballeresca;[2] aquí, la picaresca.[3] La primera trasunta[4] quizá con exageración las calidades. Hasta el Guardia civil resulta con untos de santidad, lo cual resulta excesivo. En la segunda, sólo hay de santo el alma popular, la caridad de todos, la solidaridad humana, frente al vicio vestido siempre de ironía.

Yo no me explico cómo tantas sociedades católicas, tantos grupos de « cultura hispánica », tantos movimientos « tradicionalistas » no han enfilado coordinadamente sus esfuerzos para difundir estas dos estupendas películas. La primera, sobre todo, al paladar[5] de ellos. El héroe es la fe. Porque Pablito Calvo aparece no más que un retacito[6] de la creencia pública, emisario de la fe popular. En la segunda, Pablito es el representativo de una infancia que resiste a la corrupción de la pobreza con su ingenuidad al tope.[7] Un ángel en medio de los demonios.

[1] **es su lado opuesto envés y revés,** is its opposite side, front and back
[2] **la caballeresca,** the chivalrous
[3] **la picaresca,** the picaresque
[4] **trasuntar,** to copy
[5] **paladar,** palate, taste
[6] **retacito,** little piece
[7] **al tope,** at the top, on top

Basic and Supplementary Vocabularies

The Basic Vocabulary that follows consists of 1,470 Spanish words considered essential for the beginner. All of these words or their English equivalents will be found in one or more of the following sources: *Spanish Grammar* by E. V. Greenfield (Barnes and Noble, Inc.); the first thousand words in *A Teacher's Word Book of 20,000 Words* by E. L. Thorndike (Teachers College, Columbia University); the first thousand words in *A Basic Writing Vocabulary* by Ernest Horn (University of Iowa); and the "Basic Words" in *Standard List of Spanish Words and Idioms* by Hayward Keniston (D. C. Heath and Company).

The Basic Vocabulary omits the following classes of words: definite articles; numbers (see pages 31–32); personal and possessive pronouns (see pages 28, 36, 55, 122); and names of days and of months (see page 48).

Any irregularity in a word is indicated either by a page reference or by such indications as the following:

abrir (*p.p.* **abierto**)	means	**abrir** has irregular past participle **abierto**.
acertar (**ie**)	means	the **e** becomes **ie** when accented, as **acierto**.
advertir (**ie, i**)	means	the **e** becomes **ie** or **i**, as **advierto**, **advirtió**.
agradar (**zc**)	means	the **c** becomes **zc** in certain forms, as **agradezco**.
carácter (*m.; pl.* **caracteres**)	means	the accent shifts in the plural.

Orthographic changes in verb stems are not indicated, as they follow definite rules.

The addition of (**se**) to a verb means that it may be used in the active or in the reflexive form with the same translation; **adelantar**(**se**), *to advance*, means: **adelantar**, *to advance* (*put forward*); **adelantarse**, *to advance* (*go forward*). When the reflexive form of a verb may have a different meaning from the active form, you find –**se**, . . .; thus: **acercar**, *to bring near;* –**se** (**a**), *to draw near* (*to*), *approach*, meaning: **acercar**, *to bring near;* **acercarse**, *to draw near, approach;* **acercarse a**, *to draw near to, approach.*

If two or more meanings of a verb are given, the use of *to* indicates that the meaning is not a synonym of the preceding meaning. (Compare the definitions of **aconsejar, acordar,** and **acudir.**)

Past participles are given with verbs if they may have an adjectival meaning not characteristic of past participles, **as acostado** may mean *in bed* or *lying down.*

You will find here and there such space-saving forms as "under(neath)," meaning *under, underneath,* and "cut(ting)," meaning *cut, cutting.* (See **bajo, corte.**)

In idioms the basic word is abbreviated; after **acabar, a. de** means **acabar de.**

Illustrative words in parentheses are not essential to the idiom, as: **a** (**hacerlo yo**), if (I had done it) — only **a** and *if* are the essential parts of the idiom (we might have **a decirlo Ud.,** if you had said it).

Words in italics are explanatory and not to be considered part of the definition. **Arrancar** is defined, first, as "to pull up (by the roots)," which indicates that it may be translated "to pull up" or "to pull up by the roots"; it is also defined as "to start (*suddenly*)" — *suddenly* is explanatory, not part of the translation.

The best way to use this Vocabulary, which is too full for memorizing. is to read and reread it until you become familiar with the words, their meanings — at least the commoner ones (which are given first) — and the idioms in which they occur.

A Supplementary Vocabulary follows the Basic Vocabulary. It is preceded by an explanation and suggestion of how to use it.

BASIC VOCABULARY

a, to, at, by (**al día,** by the day); on (**a pie,** on foot); in (**a este respecto,** in this respect); *placed before personal object (see p. 77);* **al** (*followed by infinitive*), upon; **a** (**hacerlo yo**), if (I had done it)

abajo, *adv.,* down, below, under-(neath), downstairs; **para a.,** downward

abandonar, to abandon, desert, forsake

abrazar, to embrace, clasp, hug

abrir (*p.p.* **abierto**), to open

absoluto, absolute

abuelo, grandfather; **-a,** -mother

aburrir, to bore

acá, (over) here, hither; **para a.,** in this direction

acabar, to finish, end; **a. con,** to put an end to; **a. de** (*foll'd by infinitive*), to have just; **a. por** (*foll'd by infinitive*), to end by, finally to

acaso, perhaps, by chance

acción (*f.*), action, stock, share

acento, accent

aceptar, to accept

acerca de, *prep.,* about, concerning

acercar, to bring near; **-se** (**a**), to draw near (to), approach

acertar (**ie**), to hit the mark, guess right

acompañar, to accompany, go *or* come with

aconsejar, to advise

acordar (**ue**), to bring to agreement, to agree, to remind; **-se de,** to remember

acostar (**ue**), to put to bed, lay down; **-se,** to go to bed, lie down; **-tado,** in bed, lying down

acostumbrar, to accustom, to be accustomed; **-se a,** to get used to

acto, act

actual, present (*of time*)

acudir, to come, hasten, run (to help)

acuerdo, agreement, accord; **de a.,** in agreement, agreed

adelante, forward, ahead; **en a.,** henceforth; **más a.,** further on

además, moreover, furthermore; **a. de,** *prep.,* besides

adentro, *adv.,* inside, within

¡Adiós! Good-by!; *also n.*

adivinar, to guess, divine

admirable, admirable, wonderful

admiración (*f.*), admiration, wonder

admirar, to admire, wonder at; **-se de,** to be surprised at

admitir, to admit

adonde, ¿adónde? = a donde, ¿a dónde?

adorar, to adore, worship

adquirir (*irreg.* = **i** to **ie**), to acquire, get

advertir (**ie, i**), to notice, advise, warn

afán (*m.*), eagerness, zeal (**de,** for)

afecto, affectionate, fond (**a,** of); *n., m.,* affection, love

afición (*f.*), fondness (**a,** for)

afirmar, to affirm, state, to fasten; **-se,** to hold fast

afligir, to afflict; **-se,** to grieve, languish

agitar, to agitate, stir up, to wave; **-se,** to become agitated, to wave, flutter

agradable, agreeable, pleasant

agradar, to be pleasing, please

agradecer (**zc**), to be grateful for, thank for; **-cido,** grateful

agua (**el a.** *but f.*), water; **hacer a.,** to leak

aguardar, to wait for

¡Ah! Oh! Ah!

ahí, there (*near you*); **por ahí,** over there

ahogar(se), to drown, to suffocate, to choke

ahora, now; **a. mismo,** right now;

hasta a., until now, hitherto, thus far; **por a.**, for the present

ahorrar, to save

aire (*m.*), air

ajeno, someone else's, another's, other people's, alien

al = **a** + **el**; *foll'd by infin.*, upon

ala (**el ala** *but f.*), wing, brim (*of hat*)

alabar, to praise

alcanzar, to overtake, reach; **a. a** (*foll'd by infin.*), to manage to, succeed in

alegrar, to gladden; **–se (de)**, to be glad, rejoice (at)

alegre, gay, merry, joyful

alegría, gaiety, merriment, joy

alejar, to remove, to separate, to withdraw; **–se**, to recede, withdraw

algo, something; somewhat; **a. de (nuevo)**, something (new)

alguien, someone, anyone

algun(o), *adj.* (*see pp. 20, 180*), some, any; **alguno**, *pron.*, one, any one, some one, *pl.* some

aliento, breath, courage, encouragement

alimentar, to feed, nourish

alma (**el a.** *but f.*), soul

almorzar (**ue**), to lunch

alrededor, *adv.*, **a. de**, *prep.*, around, about; **–es**, *n.*, *m.*, surroundings, environment

alto, high, tall, loud; *n.*, *m.*, height (**tener . . . de a.**, to be . . . high)

altura, top, height; **tener . . . de a.**, to be . . . high

alumbrar, to illuminate, light up, to give birth; **–se**, to get lit (*tipsy*)

alzar, to raise, lift; **–se**, to rise

allá, (over) there, thither; **a. por**, there in, back in; **más a.**, farther; **más a. de**, beyond; **para a.**, in that direction

allí, there (*in that place*); **por a.**, thereabouts, over there, that way

amable, kind, lovable

amanecer (**zc**), to dawn, get light; **a. en**, to arrive *or* be at dawn, *or* in the morning

amante, loving; *n.*, *mf.*, lover

amar, to love

amargo, bitter; *n.*, *m.*, bitterness

amarillo, *adj.*, *n.*, *m.*, yellow

ambos, both

amenazar, to threaten

amigo, –a, friend

amistad (*f.*), friendship; **hacer amistad(es)**, to make friends; **hacer las a.**, to make up

amo, master, owner, boss; **ama**, mistress, proprietress, boss

amor (*m.*), love, love affair

amoroso, loving, amorous

ancho, wide, broad, loose; *n.*, *m.*, width, breadth (**tener . . . de a.**, to be . . . wide); **a sus anchas**, at ease, freely

andar (*see pp. 154, 182*), to go, walk, (*of machine*) run; **¡Anda!** Go on! (*surprise, incredulity*)

ángel (*m.*), angel

angustia, anguish, distress

animal *n.*, *m.*; *adj.*, animal

animar, to encourage, cheer, animate; **–se**, to cheer up, take heart

ánimo, spirit, courage

anoche, last night

anochecer (**zc**), to get dark, become night (**–ce**, night falls); **a. en**, to arrive at *or* be somewhere at night

ante, *prep.*, before (*of position*), in the presence of

anterior, former, preceding

antes, *adv.*, before (*of time*), formerly sooner, rather; **a. de**, *prep.*, **a. (de) que**, *conj.*, before; **cuanto a.**, as soon as possible

antiguo, ancient, antique, former

anunciar, to announce, to advertise

añadir, to add

año, year; **entrado en años**, elderly; **tener . . . años**, to be . . . years old

apagar, to quench, put out; **–se**, to go out, die out

aparecer (**zc**), to appear, show (up)

apartar, to separate, put aside; **–se**, to withdraw; **–tado**, *n.*, (*P.O.*) box

aparte, *adv., n., m.,* aside

apenas, hardly, scarcely

aplicar, to apply; **–cado,** industrious, studious

apoyar, to support, rest, lean (**en,** on); **–se,** to rest, lean (**en,** on)

aprender (**a**), to learn (to)

apresurar(se), to hasten, hurry (**a,** to); **–rado,** hasty, hurried

apretar (**ie**), to tighten, (com)press, squeeze; **a. a,** to start to (*with haste*); **–tado,** tight

aprovechar, to profit by, take advantage of, avail; **–se de,** to avail oneself of

aquel, –la, *adj.,* that, *pl.* those

aquél, –la, *pron.,* that (one), *pl.* those; the former; he, she, *pl.* they; **aquello** (*neut.*), that

aquí, here (*in this place*); **de a.,** from here, hence; **por a.,** hereabouts, around here, this way

arbol (*m.*), tree, mast, shaft, axle

arder, to burn, to be ardent

ardiente, burning, ardent

arma (**el a.** *but f.*), arm, weapon; **pasar por las a.,** to shoot (*execute*)

armar, to arm, to assemble, mount, to start (*trouble*)

arrancar, to pull up (by the roots), extirpate, wrest, to start (*suddenly*)

arrastrar, to drag, haul; **–se,** to crawl, creep

arreglar, to arrange, regulate, settle

arriba, *adv.,* up, above, upstairs; **para a.,** upward

arrojar, to throw, cast

arte (*m. or f.*), art, craft; **artes y oficios,** arts and crafts; **las bellas a.,** the fine arts

artículo, article, joint

artista (*mf.*), artist

asegurar, to secure, to assure, to insure

así, thus, so; **a. a.,** soso; **a. como,** just as, as soon as; **a. que,** as soon as

asiento, seat, stability, good sense

asistir, to assist, to accompany; **a. a,** to attend, be present at

asomar, to show, appear; **–se** (**a**), to look *or* peep out (of)

asombrar, to shade, to astonish; **–se** (**de**), to be astonished (at)

aspecto, aspect, look

asunto, matter, subject, affair

asustar, to frighten, scare; **–se** (**de**), to be frightened (by)

atar, to tie, bind

atención (*f.*), attention

atender (**ie**), to attend (to), pay attention (**a,** to); **atento** (*irreg. p.p.*), attentive

atrás, *adv.,* back(ward), behind; **a. de,** *prep.,* behind, back of

atravesar (**ie**), to cross; go, walk, *etc.,* across

atreverse (**a**), to dare (to); **–vido,** daring

aumentar(se), to increase

aun (*more emphatic,* **aún**), even, yet, still; **aun cuando,** even if, even though

aunque, (al)though, even if

ausencia, absence

auto, auto, car

autor, –a, author, **–ess**

autoridad (*f.*), authority

avanzar, to advance

ave (**el a.** *but f.*), bird, fowl

averiguar, to verify, ascertain

avisar, to advise

¡ Ay ! Oh ! Ouch !

ayer, yesterday

ayudar, to aid, help, assist

azúcar (*m.*), sugar

azul, blue, azure

bailar, to dance, to spin (*as top*)

baile (*m.*), dance, ball

bajar, to bring (take, let, go, come) down, to get off *or* out (*of a vehicle*)

bajo, low, short; *adv.,* under(neath), below; *prep.,* under (*fig.*)

balcón (*m.*), balcony

banco, bench, bank (*for money*)

bañar, to bathe; **–se,** to b., take a bath

barato, cheap; cheaply; *n., m.,* bargain

barba, beard, chin, whiskers; **en sus b.,** to *or* in his face

bastante, *adj., pron., adv.,* enough

bastar, to be enough (**para, to**); **Basta,** That's enough.

batalla, battle

beber, to drink

belleza, beauty

bello, beautiful

bendecir (*see p. 170*), to bless; **bendito** (*irreg. p.p.*), blessed

besar, to kiss, to touch (*lightly*)

beso, kiss

bien, *adv.,* well; **b. que,** although; **Está b.,** (It's) All right; **más b.,** rather; **no b.,** as soon as; **b.,** *interj.,* Good!; **b.,** *n., m.,* good; (**hombre**) **de b.,** honest (man)

billete (*m.*), bill (*money*), ticket, billet; **b. de ida y vuelta,** round-trip ticket; **b. sencillo,** one-way ticket

blanco, *adj.,* white; *n., m.,* white, target, blank

blando, soft, bland

boca, mouth

boda(s), wedding, nuptials

bolsillo, pocket

bondad (*f.*), goodness

bonito, pretty, nice; *n., m.,* bonito (*fish*)

bosque (*m.*), wood(s), forest

brazo, arm, hand (*laborer*); **de b.,** arm in arm

breve, *adj.,* brief, short

brillante, brilliant, bright; *n., m.,* brilliant (*jewel*)

broma, jest, joke, merriment

buen(o) (*see p. 20*), (*after* **ser**) good, (*after* **estar**) well; **de buenas a primeras,** all at once

burla, jest, fun, trick, mock(ery); **de burlas,** in jest

burlar(se de), to mock

busca, search

buscar, to search, seek, hunt (for); **ir a b.,** to go for

caballero, knight, gentleman

caballo, horse; **a c.,** on horseback

cabello(s), hair (*of head*)

caber (*see p. 158*), to fit *or* go into, have room, to befall; **no cabe duda (de que),** there is no doubt (that)

cabeza, head; **de c.,** head first, headlong, on one's head

cabo, end, rope, cape (*headland*), corporal; **al c.,** at last; **dar c. a,** to finish; **llevar a c.,** to accomplish

cada, each, every; **c. cual,** each (one), every one

caer (*see p. 159*), to fall (down), to befall; **c. de** (**cabeza**), to fall on (one's head); **–se,** to fall down, to become discouraged

café (*m.*), coffee, café

caja, box, case, chest, cash box, safe

calidad (*f.*), quality, *pl.* terms, qualifications; **en** (**su**) **c. de,** in (his) capacity as

caliente, warm; **muy c.,** hot

calma, calm(ness)

calor (*m.*), heat, warmth; **hace c.,** it is warm, hot; **tengo c.,** I am warm, hot

callar, to quiet, make . . . stop talking; **callar(se),** to stop talking, be silent; ¡ **Calla** (*or* **–e**)! Be quiet! You don't tell me!; **callado,** silent

calle (*f.*), street, way

cama, bed

cambiar, to (ex)change; **c. de** (**camisa**), to change (one's shirt)

cambio, (ex)change; **en c.,** on the other hand

caminar, to walk, travel

camino, road, way; **c. real,** highway; **de c.,** on the road *or* way

campana, bell

campesino, farmer

campo, field, country, camp, ground; **c. santo,** cemetery

cansar, to tire, weary; **–se,** to get tired; **–sado,** tired, weary

cantar, to sing; (*fig.*) to squeak, to squeal, to speak

cantidad (*f.*), quantity, amount

canto, singing, song, chant, canto; edge, border, stone

capaz, able, capacious

capital (*m.*), capital (*money*); (*f.*) capital (*city*); *adj.*, main, leading

capitán (*m.*), captain

cara, face

carácter (*m.*; *pl.* **caracteres**), character

carbón (*m.*), coal

carecer (**zc**), to be lacking; **c. de,** to lack

cargar, to load, to carry, to charge, to lean; **c. con,** to carry off *or* away; **—se,** to burden oneself, to cloud up

cargo, loading, load, charge (*keeping, duty; accusation*); **hacerse c. de,** to take into consideration, be aware of

caridad (*f.*), charity

cariño, affection, love (**a,** for)

cariñoso, affectionate

carne (*f.*), flesh, meat; **cobrar carnes,** to put on weight; **echar carnes,** to get fat

caro, dear (*beloved, costly*)

carrera, run(ning), race, course, career; **a la c., de c.,** on the run

carta, letter, chart, charter, bill (*notice*)

casa, house, home; **a c.,** home(ward); **en c.,** at home

casa de correos, post office

casar, to marry (*give in marriage*), to mate, match, blend; **casar(se),** to marry, get married (**con,** to)

casi, almost

caso, case (*event, instance, etc.*); **dado c.,** supposing that; **en c. de que, :. que,** in case; **en todo c.,** at all events; **hacer c. de,** to take note of

castigar, to punish

causa, cause, case (*lawsuit*), trial; **a,** *or* **por, c. de,** because of

causar, to cause

ceder, to yield, to cede, to give out

celebrar, to celebrate, to applaud to be glad of

centro, center

cerca, *adv.*, near; **de c.,** closely, **por aquí c.,** (somewhere) near here; **c. de,** *prep.*, near, nearly, about

cero, zero

cerrar (**ie**), to close, shut, lock, **al c. del día,** at the close of day, **c. con llave,** to lock; **—se,** to close (up), to get cloudy

cesar, to stop, desist (**de,** from)

ciego, blind(ed) (**de,** with, by); **a ciegas,** blindly; **ciego, —a,** blind man, woman

cielo, sky, heaven, ceiling, roof; **a c. raso,** in the open air; **ver el c. abierto,** to see a great opportunity

ciencia, science, knowledge

cierto, (a) certain, sure; **de c., por c.,** certainly, surely; **no por c.,** certainly not; **ser c.,** to be true

cigarro, cigar

circunstancia, circumstance

citar, to make an appointment with, to cite, quote, to summon

ciudad (*f.*), city

claro, clear, bright, light; **a la(s) clara(s),** openly; **claro,** *adv.*, clearly; **¡ Claro !** Sure ! Of course !; *n., m.,* clearing, gap, skylight; **poner en c.,** to make clear; **sacar en c.,** to gather, conclude

clase (*f.*), class, kind

cobrar, to collect, receive, to recover, retrieve, to gain, to charge (*fee*)

cocer (**ue**), to cook, boil, stew

cocina, kitchen, cooking, cuisine

coche (*m.*), coach, carriage, car

coger, to catch, seize, take, to gather

colgar (**ue**), to hang (up)

colocar, to put, place

color (*m.*), color; **c. de (rosa),** (rose-)colored; **de c.,** colored; **so c. de,** under the color of

comedia, comedy, play

comedor, *adj.*, eating, dining; *n.*, eater, diner, *m.* dining room

comenzar (ie), to commence, begin (**a**, to)

comer, to eat, feed, dine, eat dinner; **dar de c. a,** to feed; **comido,** fed, having eaten

comercio, trade, commerce

cometer, to commit

comida, food, meal, dinner, feed; **sobre c.,** after dinner

como, *adv.*, how; *conj.*, as; *prep.*, like; **c. si,** as if

¿cómo? how? what (*did you say*)?; **¿Cómo no?** Of course! Sure!

compañero, –a, companion, comrade

compañía, company

comparar, to compare

complacer (zc), to please; **–se (en),** to take pleasure, delight (in), be pleased (with, to)

completo, complete, full; **por c.,** completely

componer (*see p. 159*), to compose, to compound, to repair, to settle; **–puesto** (*p.p. as n.*), compound

comprar, to buy

comprender, to understand, to comprise

común, common; **por lo c.,** commonly; *n.*, *m.*, **el c. de las gentes,** the general public, the common people

comunicar(se), to communicate

con, with; *before infin.*, by, in spite of; **con que,** and so; **con tal que,** provided that; **con todo,** nevertheless

concebir (i), to conceive

conceder, to concede, grant

concepto, concept(ion), idea, thought, judgment, opinion; **bajo, de,** *or* **por ningún c.,** by no means

conciencia, conscience, consciousness

concluir, to conclude, end

condenar, to condemn, to convict, to sentence, to damn

condición (*f.*), condition, disposition, temper, quality; **a,** *or* **con la, c. de que,** on (the) condition that; **estar en condiciones de,** to be in (a) condition to

conducir (*see p. 166*), to conduct, lead, to drive (*car*); **–se,** to behave

confesar (ie), to confess; **–se,** to confess

confianza, confidence, trust; **de c.,** informal, private

confiar, to confide, entrust, to trust, rely (**en**, in, on)

conforme, (a)like, agreed, acceptable, consistent, OK; **c. a,** consistent with, according to; **c. con,** consistent with, resigned to

confundir, to confound, confuse, to confute; **–se,** to be *or* get confused; *irreg. p.p.* **confuso,** confused

conmigo = con mí, with me

conmover (ue), to move, stir, touch (*emotionally*)

conocer (zc), to know, to meet (*a person*); **–se,** to be acquainted; **–cido,** well-known; *n.*, acquaintance

conocimiento, acquaintance; *sing. or pl.*, knowledge

conque, and so

consecuencia, consequence; **en** *or* **por c.,** consequently

conseguir (i), to get, obtain, to succeed in (*doing it*)

consejo, counsel, advice, council; *pl.* advice

consentir (ie, i), to consent (to), to allow, to spoil, indulge; **–se,** to weaken, get loose, crack; **–tido,** spoiled

conservar, to conserve, keep

consideración (*f.*), consideration

considerar, to consider, show consideration for

consigo = con sí, with himself, *etc.*

consiguiente, consequent; **de** *or* **por c.,** consequently

consistir, to consist (**en**, in, of)

consolar (ue), to comfort

constante, constant, firm

constar, to be clear, obvious; **c. de,** to consist of; **hacer c.,** to make it clear

constituir, to constitute

construir, to build, to construe

consultar, to consult (**con,** with)

contar (**ue**), to count, figure, to tell, relate; **c. con,** to count on; **al contado,** cash

contemplar, to contemplate, study

contener (*see p. 160*), to contain, hold; **–se,** to control oneself, refrain; **–tenido** (*p.p. as n.*), content(s)

contentar, to content, please, satisfy; **–se,** to be satisfied

contento, content(ed), happy; *n., m.,* content(ment)

contestación (*f.*), answer

contestar, to answer

contigo = **con tí,** with you

continuar, to continue

continuo, continuous, continual

contra, against; *n., m.,* contrary, opposite; *f.,* difficulty, contrary; **en c. de,** against

contrario, *adj., n., m.,* contrary; **al c., por el,** *or* **lo, c.,** on the contrary

convencer, to convince; **–se,** to become convinced

convenir (*see* **venir**), to agree (**en,** to), to be convenient, suit; **–se,** to come to an agreement

conversación (*f.*), conversation, talk, intercourse

convertir (**ie, i**), to convert (**en,** into); **–se,** to be converted

convidar, to invite; *p.p. as n.,* (*invited*) guest

copiar, to copy, imitate

corazón (*m.*), heart, core; **de c.,** from the heart, heartily

correctamente, correctly

correo, mail, post office; **casa,** *or* **oficina, de correos,** post office

correr, to run, to race, to draw (*a curtain*); **a más,** *or* **todo, c.,** at top, *or* full, speed; **corre la voz,** it is rumored; **–se,** to run away, out, *or* over, to slide, slip, to become confused

corresponder, to correspond, to c. to, to return (*a favor, etc.*), to come up to (*expectations*)

corriente, current, running, ordinary; *n., f.,* current

cortar, to cut (down, off, out, up); **–se,** to intersect, to be tongue-tied, to chap, to curdle

corte (*m.*), cut(ting), edge; (*f.*), court, courtship; **hacer la c. a,** to court, pay c. to, woo

corto, short, bashful, defective (*as* **c. de oído,** hard of hearing)

cosa, thing; **c. de,** about (*approx.*); **no es gran c.,** it doesn't amount to much; **otra c.,** something else

costa, cost, coast; **a c. de,** at the expense of; **a toda c.,** at any price

costar (**ue**), to cost

costumbre (*f.*), custom

crear, to create

crecer (**zc**), to grow, increase

creer, to believe; **Creo que sí** (**no**), I think so (not); **Ya lo creo,** I should say so, I don't doubt it.

criado, servant; **–a,** s. girl, maid; *also p.p. of* **criar**

criar, to breed, raise, rear

criatura, creature, infant, baby

cristal (*m.*), crystal, glass, pane

cruel, cruel

cruz (*f.*), cross, tail (*of coin*)

cruzar, to cross, place, go, *etc.*, across

cuaderno, notebook

cuadro, square, picture, frame, (*flower*) bed; (**diez pies**) **en c.,** (ten feet) square

cual, (such) as, like; **cada c.,** each one; **el c.,** *etc.,* who, which; **por lo c.,** for which reason

cuál: as in **cuáles buenos, cuáles malos,** some good, some bad

¡**cuál?** which (one)? what?; ¡**cuál** ¹ how !

cualidad (*f.*), quality (*cf.* **calidad**)

cualquier(a) (*pl.* **cualesquier(a);** *see p. 197*), *adj., pron.,* any, anyone

cuando, when; **aun c.,** even though; **c. más,** at best, at the most; **c. menos,** at (the) least; **c. quiera que,** whenever; **de c. en c.,** from time to time

¿ cuándo? when?

cuanto, as much as, as soon as, all (that); **c. antes,** as soon as possible; **c. más,** (all) the more; **en c.,** as soon as; **en c. a,** as for, as regards; **por c.,** for which reason; **unos cuantos,** a few

¿ cuánto? how much? how many?; **¡ cuánto!** how much! how many!

cuarto, fourth; *n., m.,* fourth, quarter, room, quarto; **c. de baño,** bathroom; *f.,* fourth, quarter, quart

cubrir (*p.p.* **cubierto**), to cover; **cubierto,** cover, place at table; **-a,** cover(ing), hood (*of car*), deck (*of ship*)

cuello, neck, collar

cuenta, account, count, bill (*owed*), bead; **caer en la c.,** to catch on; **dar c. de,** to give an account of, report on; **darse c. de,** to realize; **tener en c.,** to take into consideration

cuento, story, account; **sin c.,** countless

cuerpo, body, corps; **c. a c.,** hand to hand

cuestión (*f.*), question

cuidado, care; **con c.,** carefully, anxious; **¡ C. !** (Be) Careful!; **C. con . . .,** Be careful of . . ., Watch out for . . .; **no hay c.,** there is no danger; **tener c.,** to be careful

cuidadoso, careful

cuidar (**de**), to take care of, care for

culpa, fault, guilt, blame; **tener la c.** (**de**), to be to blame (for)

cumplir, to fulfill, keep (*promise*), to reach (*birthday*), to do (*one's duty*); **c. con,** to fulfill; **-se,** to be fulfilled, to expire, be up (*of time*)

cura (*m.*), priest; (*f.*) cure

curar, to cure, heal, to treat; **-se,** to recover; **curar(se) de,** to take care of

curiosidad (*f.*), curiosity

curioso, curious

curso, course

cuyo, whose, of whom, of which

charlar, to talk, chat

chico, little; *n.,* little boy *or* girl

chocolate (*m.*), chocolate

dama, lady

daño, damage, hurt, harm; **hacer d. a,** to hurt, (*of food*) disagree with

dar (*see pp. 154, 188*), to give, to deal, to strike (*the hour*), to wage (*war*), to give in, stretch, give way; *translated variously in many idioms* (*as* **d. fin a,** to finish, **d. golpes a,** to beat, **d. gritos,** to shout, **d. prestado,** to lend); **d. a,** to face, look out on; **d. a conocer,** to make known; **d. a entender,** to let know; **d. a luz,** to give birth; **d. con,** to come across, run into; **d. contra,** to bump into; **d. de sí,** to give (way), stretch; **d. en,** to fall into (*error, habit*), to guess, find out, to hit; **d. por,** to consider as, take for; **d. que pensar,** to give cause for thought; **darse,** to give in, yield, to devote oneself; **d. la(s) mano(s),** to shake hands; **d. por,** to consider oneself as; **d. prisa,** to hurry; **No se me da (nada),** I don't car (at all).

de, of, from; *in various idioms, translated* for, in, on, to, with; **de . . . a,** from . . . to, *but if noun is repeated,* **de . . . en** (**de casa en casa,** from house to house)

debajo, *adv.,* **d. de,** *prep.,* beneath, under(neath)

deber, to owe; (*obligation*) must, ought, should; **d. de,** (*probability*), must; **debido,** owed, owing, due; **deber,** *n., m.,* duty débil, weak, feeble

decidir, to decide; **-se a,** to d. to

decir (*see p. 170*), to say, tell; **d. para
sí,** to say to oneself; **es d.,** that
is (to say); **querer d.,** to mean;
el qué dirán, what people will say;
n., m., saying, language, opinion;
dicho (*p.p.*): **d. y hecho,** no sooner
said than done; **mejor d.,** rather;
n., m., saying, remark

declarar, to declare, state; **-se,** to
declare oneself, state one's opinion

dedicar, to dedicate, devote

dedo, finger, toe

defender (ie), to defend

dejar, to leave, to let, allow, to let
go (of); **d. de,** to fail to, to stop;
-se, to neglect oneself, give up;
dejado, lazy, slovenly, low-spirited

del = de + el

delante, *adv.,* **d. de,** *prep.,* before,
ahead (of), in front (of)

delicado, delicate, fine

demás, other; **lo d.,** the rest (of
it); **los d.,** the others, the rest (of
them); *adv.,* besides

demasiado, too, too much

demonio, demon, devil

demostrar (ue), to demonstrate, show

dentro, *adv.,* **d. de,** *prep.,* inside (of),
within; **a d., por d.,** (on the)
inside; **de d.,** from the inside;
d. de poco, shortly

derecho, right, straight; **a derechas,**
rightly, justly; *n., m.,* right (*privi-
lege*), law, *pl.* duties, dues; *f.,* right
(hand, side); **a la d.,** to *or* on the
right

derramar, to pour (out), spill, shed,
scatter, spread; **-se,** to run over,
overflow, to be scattered

desaparecer(se) (zc), to disappear

descansar(se), to rest

desconocer (zc), not to recognize
or know, to snub, cut; **-cido,**
unknown, unfamiliar; *n.,* stranger

describir, describe

descubrir (*p.p.* **-cubierto**), to uncover, reveal, discover, disclose;

-se, to reveal oneself, to take off
one's hat

descuidar, to neglect, to be careless,
negligent, thoughtless (of); **-se,**
to be careless, *etc.*

desde, from, (*of time*) since; **d.
entonces,** since then; **d. luego,**
immediately; **d. niño,** ever since
I (he) was a child; **d. que,** (ever)
since

desear, to desire, wish

deseo, desire, wish (**de,** for, to)

desesperar, to drive to despair, to
despair, be desperate; **-se,** to
become desperate, despair; **-rado,**
desperate

desgracia, misfortune, disgrace (*loss
of favor*), ungracefulness; **por d.,**
unfortunately

desgraciado, unfortunate

deshacer (*see p. 159*), to undo, to take
apart, to destroy; **-se,** to go *or* fall
to pieces, to dissolve, to be destroyed; **d. de,** to get rid of

desierto, desert(ed), uninhabited; *n.,
m.,* desert, waste, wilderness

despacho, office, dispatch

despedir (*see p. 169*), to dismiss,
discharge (*employee*), to emit, to
see off, bid farewell; **-se de,** to say
good-by to, take leave of, to quit

despertar(se) (ie), to wake (up),
(a)waken; *irreg. p.p.* **despierto,**
awake

después, after(ward, **-s**); **d. de,**
prep., **d. (de) que,** *conj.,* after

destino, fate, destiny, destination,
position (*work*); **con d. a,** bound
for

destruir, to destroy, ruin

detener (*see p. 160*), to stop, detain,
arrest; **-se,** to stop

determinar, to determine, resolve;
-se a, to d. *or* r. to

detrás, *adv.,* **d. de,** *conj.,* behind,
back (of)

devolver (ue) (*p.p.* **-vuelto**), to return,
to bring, give, *or* pay back

día (*m.*), day, daylight; **al d.,** per

day, up to date; **de d.**, by day; **d. de fiesta**, holiday; **d. de huelga**, day off; **Buenos d.**, Good morning; **(mis) d.**, (my) birthday; **ocho d.**, a week; **quince d.**, two weeks; **tener días**, to be old

diablo, devil, deuce; **¡Qué d. . . . !** What the devil . . . !; **¡Cómo diablos . . . !** How the devil . . . !

diario, daily; *n.*, *m.*, newspaper, daily, diary

diccionario, dictionary

dicha, (good) luck

dichoso, lucky, happy

diente (*m.*), tooth, fang, tusk, cog; **Da d. con d.**, His teeth are chattering; **a regaña dientes**, grudgingly, unwillingly; **decir**, *or* **hablar**, **entre dientes**, to mumble, mutter

diferencia, difference; **a d. de**, *prep.*, unlike

diferente, different (**de**, from)

difícil, difficult, hard

dificultad (*f.*), difficulty, trouble

digno, worthy, deserving (**de**, of); suitable, fit(ting) (**de**, for)

diligente, prompt, diligent, swift

dinero, money; **d. contante y sonante**, cash

dios, **-a**, god, **-dess**; **No lo quiera D.**, God forbid; **¡Por D.!** For Heaven's sake!; **Quiera D. . . . , Plegue a D. . . . ,** God grant . . . , Would to God . . . ; **Vaya Ud. con D.**, Farewell.

dirección (*f.*), direction, address, management

dirigir, to direct, to address (*letter*), to manage, to steer; **-se a**, to go to(ward), make one's way to, to address (*person*), to apply to

disgusto, disgust, annoyance, quarrel, sorrow; **a d.**, with disgust

dispensar, to dispense, to excuse, to exempt; **Dispense(me)**, Pardon me.

disponer (*see p. 159*), to dispose, to arrange, prepare; **-se**, to prepare

to, get ready to; *p.p.* **dispuesto**, disposed, ready, handsome; **bien (mal) d.**, feeling well (poorly), favorably (unf.) disposed

disposición (*f.*), disposition, disposal; *pl.*, inclination, preparations; **en d. de**, disposed to

distancia, distance; **a d. (de)**, at a distance (from)

distinguir, to distinguish; **-se de**, to be d'ed from; *irreg. p.p.* **distinto**, distinct, different (**de**, from)

distraer (*see p. 160*), to distract, divert; **-se**, to be distracted, be absent-minded, to enjoy oneself; **-traído**, absent-minded

diverso, diverse, various

divertir (ie, i), to divert, to amuse, entertain; **-se**, to amuse oneself, have a good time; **-tido**, amusing, funny

dividir(se), to divide, separate

divino, divine; *n.*, fortune teller

doblar, to double, to fold, crease, to subdue; **-se**, to bend, to submit, yield

docena, dozen; **a docena(s)**, by the dozen

doctor, **-a**, doctor (*title*); *f.*, doctor's wife

dolor (*m.*), pain, sorrow; **d. de (cabeza)**, (head)ache; **con d.**, in pain

dominar, to dominate, master, control; **-se**, to control oneself

don (*m.*), gift, knack; **don**, **doña**, title (*see p. 83*)

donde, where, at (**d. José**, at José's); **a d.**, **en d.**, where; **de d.**, from which, whence; **por d.**, from where, from which, through which

¿dónde? where?; **¿A d. . . . ?** Where . . . to?; **¿De d. . . . ?** Where . . . from?

doña: *see* **don**

dormir (ue, u), to put to sleep, to sleep; **-se**, to go to sleep; **-mido**, asleep, sleeping

drama (*m.*), play, drama

duda, doubt

dudar, to doubt; **d. de,** to be dubious about

dueño, –a, owner, proprietor, –tress, master, mistress

dulce, sweet; *n., pl.* candy

dulzura, sweetness

durante, during

durar, to last, endure

duro, hard; *n., m., large piece of hard money*

e, and (*used before words beginning with* i– *or* hi–)

echar, to throw, cast, fling, hurl, toss, to throw *or* give off *or* out, to pour, to put, to turn (*key*), to put forth, sprout, to put on, apply, impose, to set (*foot*); **e. a,** to start to; **e. a fondo, e. a pique,** to sink, wreck; **e. a mundo,** to bring forth, create; **e. a perder,** to ruin, spoil; **e. de menos,** to miss; **e. de ver,** to notice; **–se,** to throw oneself, to stretch out

edad (*f.*), age; **de e.,** in age, mature; **e. media,** Middle Ages; **mayor e.,** majority; **mayor de e.,** adult; **menor e.,** minority; **menor de e.,** minor

edificio, building, edifice

educación (*f.*), education, breeding, upbringing

educar, to educate, rear

efecto, effect; *pl.* effects, bills, securities; **en e.,** in effect, in fact, as a matter of fact

¿ Eh ? Eh? Huh?

ejecutar, to execute, perform

ejemplo, example, instance

ejercer, to exercise, exert

ejercicio, exercise, exertion; **hacer e.,** to exercise, drill

ejército, army

elegante, elegant

elegir, to choose, elect; *irreg. p.p.* **electo,** elected, chosen

elevar, to raise, lift

embargo, embargo; **sin e.,** however

empeñar, to pawn, pledge; **–se,** to pledge oneself, to go into debt, to persist (**en,** in), to intercede, to undertake

empeño, pawn, pledge, zeal, determination

empezar (**ie**), to begin, start (**a,** to)

emplear, to employ, use; *p.p. as n.,* employee

emprender, to undertake, to begin

empresa, undertaking, enterprise, firm, company

en, in, into, on, at

enamorar, to inspire love in, to make love to, woo, win the love of; **–se** (**de**), to fall in love (with); **–rado,** in love

encantador, enchanting, charming

encanto, enchantment, charm

encargar, to charge, entrust (**de,** with); **–se de,** to take charge of

encargo, charge, commission

encender (**ie**), to kindle, light; **–se,** to catch fire, burn (**en,** with)

encerrar (**ie**), to shut up, lock up, enclose, to surround

encima, *adv.,* above, on top, overhead, besides; **e. de,** on top of, above; **por e. de,** over

encontrar (**ue**), to find, to meet; **–se,** to find oneself (*be, feel*), to meet, to conflict; **e. con,** to come across *or* upon

enemigo, hostile, opposed (**de,** to); *n.,* enemy

energía, energy

enfermedad (*f.*), illness

enfermo, sick; sick person

enfrente, *adv.,* **e. de,** *prep.,* opposite, in front (of)

engañar, to deceive, cheat, fool, to while away (*time*); **–se,** to be deceived, be mistaken; **–ñado,** deceived, mistaken

enorme, enormous, huge

enseñar, to teach (**a,** to), to show; **–se a,** to get used to

entender (**ie**), to understand; **dar a e.,** to let know, give ... to understand; **e. de,** to be familiar with; **e. en,** to be in charge of, to deal with; **—se,** to be understood; **e. con,** to come to an understanding, have an u., with; *n., m.,* understanding, opinion; **a,** *or* **según, mi e.,** in my opinion

enterar (de), to inform (of), acquaint (with); **—se de,** to find out, learn (about)

entero, entire, whole; **por e.,** entirely; *n., m.,* integer

entonces, then; **desde (aquel) e.,** since then, since that time; **en aquel e., por (aquel) e.,** at that time

entrada, entrance, admission, access, opening, entrée

entrar, to enter; **e. en,** to enter (into); **—se,** to get in (*by stealth or force*)

entre, between, among(st), amid(st); **e. manos,** on hand; **e. nos,** between you and me; **e. tanto,** meanwhile

entregar, to deliver, give up

entretanto, meanwhile

enviar, to send, to ship

envolver (ue; *p.p.* **—vuelto),** to wrap (up), to involve; **—se,** to be *or* get involved

época, epoch

equivocar, to mistake; **—se,** to be mistaken, make a mistake

error (*m.*), error, mistake

escalera, staircase, —way, stair(s), ladder

escapar(se), to escape, run away

escaso, scarce, scant(y), slight

escena, scene, scenery, stage; **poner a e.,** to stage, present

escoger, to choose, select

esconder(se), to hide

escribir (*p.p.* **escrito**), to write; **—se,** to correspond (*exchange letters*), to enroll; **poner por escrito,** to put in writing

escritor, —a, writer

escuchar, to listen (to)

escuela, school

ese, esa, *adj.,* that, *pl.* those

ése, ésa, *pron.,* that (one), *pl.* those; **eso,** that; **eso de,** that affair *or* business of; **E. es,** That's it, That's right; **por e.,** therefore

esfuerzo, effort, endeavor, stress

espacio, space, room

espada, sword, swordfish, swordsman, spade (*card*); *m.,* matador

espalda, shoulder, back, *pl.* back; **por las e. de,** behind one's back

espantar, to frighten *or* scare (away); **—se,** to be *or* get frightened

español, Spanish; *n., m.,* Spaniard, Spanish (*lang.*); *f.,* Sp. girl, woman

especial, special; **en e.,** especially

especie (*f.*), species, kind, case, event, report

espejo, mirror

esperanza, hope

esperar, to hope (for), to expect, to wait (for)

espíritu (*m.*), spirit; **E. Santo,** Holy Ghost

esposo, —a, spouse; —o, husband; —a, wife; —os, husband and wife

esquina, corner

establecer (zc), to establish, found, settle

estación (*f.*), station, season; **e. de gasolina,** filling station

estado, state, condition, estate; **e. mayor (general),** (general) staff; **tomar e.,** to acquire a new status (*as by marrying, becoming a nun, etc.*)

estar (*see pp. 29, 71–74, 76, 130–132*), to be; **e. con,** to be with, to have; **e. en,** to understand, to depend on, to consist in; **e. para,** to be about *or* ready to; **e. por,** to be in favor of, in the notion of; **¿A cuántos estamos?** What date is it?; **Estamos a (diez),** It is the (tenth); **¿Estamos?** Are we agreed?; **estarse,** to stay

este, —a, *adj.,* this, *pl.* these

este (*m.*), east

éste, —a, *pron.,* this (one), the latter, *pl.* these; **esto,** this; **a e.,** hereto;

con e., herewith; **en esto,** at this time; **e. de,** this affair *or* business of; **e. es,** that is; **por e.,** for this reason

estilo, style; **de e. antiguo,** old-fashioned; **por el e.,** of that kind, like that; **y así,** *or* **otras cosas, por el e.,** and so forth

estimar, to estimate, to esteem

estómago, stomach

estrechar, to tighten, to clasp, to constrain; **e. la mano,** to shake hands (**a,** with)

estrecho, narrow, n.-minded, tight, close, stingy; *n., m.,* strait

estrella, star

estudiar, to study

estudio, study, studio

eterno, eternal

evitar, to avoid, shun

exacto, exact, accurate

examen (*m.*), examination

examinar, to examine

excelente, excellent

exclamar, to exclaim

exigir, to demand, exact, require

existencia, existence, living, *pl.* stock (*of store*)

existir, to exist

éxito, outcome, issue, success

experiencia, experience

experimentar, to experience, to experiment

explicar, to explain

exponer (*conj. like* **poner**), to expose, to expound

expresar, to express; *irreg. p.p.* **expreso,** express(ed); *n., m.,* express

expresión (*f.*), expression

extender(se) (**ie**), to extend, stretch out, spread

extensión (*f.*), length, area

extranjero, foreign, –er; **al e., en el e.,** abroad

extrañar, to wonder, be surprised at, to snub, cut; **–se de,** to be surprised at

extraño, strange, –r, foreign, –er

extraordinario, extraordinary

extremo, *adj., n., m.,* extreme, last, furthest, utmost; **con, en,** *or* **por e.,** in the extreme, extremely, to the utmost; **de e. a e.,** from one end to the other

fácil (**de**), easy (to)

falda, skirt, lap, slope, loin

falso, false; **en f.,** falsely

falta, lack, want, fault; **a f. de,** for want of; **hacer f.,** to be needed, lacking, missing, to be missed; **sin f.,** without fail

faltar, to be lacking, be missing, to be needed, to fail; **f. a,** to be untrue to, fail to perform, to offend, to break (*promise*); **f. . . . para,** to be . . . to (**Faltan veinte minutos para la medianoche,** It is twenty minutes to midnight, It will be midnight in twenty minutes); **¡No faltaba más!** That's the last straw!

fama, fame, rumor, reputation; **es f.,** it is rumored

familia, family

famoso, famous

favor (*m.*), favor, compliment; **a f. de,** in behalf of; **Hágame el f. de . . . ,** Please . . .

favorecer (**zc**), to favor

fe (*f.*), faith, –fulness, credence, credit, certificate, testimonial; **a fe,** in truth; **dar fe a,** to attest to, to credit; **de buena (mala) fe,** in good (bad) faith

fecha, date

felicidad (*f.*), happiness, felicity

feliz, happy, fortunate

feo, ugly, bad; *n., m.,* affront

ferrocarril (*m.*), railroad, –way

fiar, to trust, to be surety for, to give bail for, to sell on credit, to confide; **f. en, –se de,** to trust in; **fiado,** on trust; **al f.,** on credit *or* trust; **en f.,** on bail

fiel, faithful (**a,** to); *n., m.,* inspector, pointer (*of scale*)

fiesta, holiday, festival, fiesta, feast;

hacer f., to take *or* make a holiday; **hacer fiestas a,** to make up to, make over (*person*)

figura, figure, shape

figurar, to fashion, shape, represent, to feign; **f. en,** to figure in; **—se,** to imagine (¡ **Figúrese, . . . !** Just imagine, . . . !)

fijar, to fix, to fasten, to affix; **—se en,** to give (all) one's attention to, notice

fijo, fixed, firm, fast

fin (*m.*), end(ing), goal; **a f. de,** in order that; **al f. (y al cabo** *or* **y a la postre), por f.,** at last, finally; **en f.,** lastly, finally, in fine; **sin f.,** endless, without end; **a fines de,** toward the end of

fingir, to pretend, feign

fino, fine

firmar (se), to sign

firme, firm, steady, strong; firmly; *etc.;* **n., m.,** bed (*of road, etc.*); **de f.,** strongly

físico, physical; **n., m.,** physicist, physician, physique; **n., f.,** physics

flor (*f.*), flower, bloom, film, prime; **f. y nata,** flower, cream (*best*), *pl.,* compliments; **a f. de,** flush, level with; **matar en f.,** to nip in the bud

fondo, bottom, (back)ground, basis, fund, foundation, *pl.* funds; **a f.,** thoroughly; **artículo de f.,** editorial; **dar f.,** to cast anchor; **en el f.,** at bottom, basically

forma, form, shape, mold; *pl.* form, figure (*of person*)

formar, to form, shape, frame; **—se,** to take form, shape up, to line up

fortuna, fortune, luck; **por f.,** fortunately

franco, frank, free, open, exempt; **n., m.,** franc

frase (*f.*), phrase

frente (*m.*), front; **de f.,** front (*adj.*); **en f. (de),** opposite, facing, in front (of); **f. a,** facing; **f. a f.,** face to face; **f. por f.,** opposite, facing; **hacer f. a,** to face, resist, oppose; **f., f.,** forehead

fresco, fresh, cool; **estar,** *or* **quedarse, f.,** to get disappointed, get left; **f., n., m.,** coolness, fresh air, fresco; **al f.,** in the open; **hace f.,** it is cool

frío, *adj., n.,* cold; **hace f.,** it is cold; **tengo f.,** I am cold

fruto, fruit (*product, reward*), benefit

fuego, fire; **hacer f. a,** to fire on; **pegar f. a,** to set fire to; **fuegos (artificiales),** fireworks

fuente (*f.*), fount(ain), spring, source; **pluma f.,** fountain pen

fuera, *adv.,* **f. de,** *prep.,* outside (of), out (of); **de f.,** from (the) outside; **f. de sí,** beside oneself; **hacia f.,** toward the outside; **por f.,** on the outside; ¡ **Fuera !** Out ! Get out ! Put him out ! *etc.*

fuerte, strong, bad; *adv.,* strongly, hard, forte; **n., m.,** fort, forte

fuerza, force, strength, power; **a f. de,** by dint of; **a la f., por (la) f.,** by force

fundar, to found, base; **—se en,** to base one's opinion on

futuro, *adj., n.,* future; **en lo f.,** in (the) future

gabán (*m.*), overcoat

gana, appetite, desire, will; **dar gana(s) de,** to make one feel like *or* want to; **No me da la g.,** I don't want to, I don't feel like it; **de buena g.,** willingly, gladly; **de mala g.,** unwillingly; **tener gana(s) de,** to want to, feel like

ganar, to gain, win, earn

gastar, to spend, to waste, to wear (out), to sport (*a luxury*); **—se,** to wear out

gato, —a, cat; **m.,** tomcat, jack (*tool*), pickpocket, petty thief; **g. encerrado,** catch (*trick*); **g. montés,** wildcat; **gata,** she-cat; **a gatas,** on all fours

general, *adj., n., m.,* general; **por lo,** *or* **en, g.,** in general

género, genus, class, kind, gender,

genre, *pl.* goods; **g. humano,** mankind

generoso, generous, noble

genio, genius, temper, spirit; **de buen g.,** good-natured, good-tempered; **de mal g.,** ill-tempered

gente (*f.*), people, folk(s); **g. baja,** lower classes; **g. de paz,** friend(s)

gesto, face (*grimace, expression*), looks, gesture

gloria, glory, bliss

gobernar (**ie**), to govern, to manage, run, steer, drive

gobierno, government, administration, management, control, guidance

golpe (*m.*), blow, stroke, beat, coup; **dar g.,** to create a sensation, cause surprise; **de g.,** suddenly, all at once; **de un g.,** at one stroke; **g. de estado,** coup d'état; **g. de gracia,** coup de grâce; **dar golpes a,** to beat

gordo, fat, big; *n., m.,* fat, fat man, big prize

gozar (**de**), to enjoy; **-se,** to rejoice, take pleasure (**en, in**)

gracia, grace, graciousness, charm, cleverness, wit, joke, favor, *one's* name, *pl.* thanks (**a, to**); **caer en g.,** to please, win the favor of; **de g.,** gratis

gracioso, graceful, gracious, pleasing, witty, funny; *n., m.,* fool (*comedian*); *f.,* comedienne

grado, degree, grade, rank, step; **de g.,** gladly; **de mal g.,** unwillingly, against one's will; **mal de** (**mi**) **g.,** against (**my**) will, to (**my**) regret

gran(de) (*see p. 21*), great, large, big; **en g.,** on a large scale; **g.,** *n., m.,* great man, grandee

grato, pleasing, gratifying; **su grata,** your favor (*letter*)

grave, grave (*serious*)

gritar, to shout, cry out, scream

grito, cry, shout, scream; **poner el g. en el cielo,** to cry to heaven, howl

grupo, group

guapo, good-looking, handsome, dashing; *n., m.,* gallant

guardar, to guard, watch over, keep, observe (*form, respect, etc.*); **-se de,** to guard against

guerra, war, -fare; **dar g.,** to annoy; **en g.** (**con**), at war (with)

guiar, to guide, steer

gustar, to taste, try, to please, to like; [**Me gusta(n)** ..., I like...; **Me gusta(n) más** ..., I prefer...; **Como Ud. guste,** As you please, *or* like]; **g. de,** to like, enjoy; **g. en,** to take pleasure in

gusto, pleasure, taste, liking; **a g.,** at one's pleasure, to one's taste; **de buen** (**mal**) **g.,** in good (bad) taste; **Mucho g.,** Pleased to meet you; **Tanto g.** (...), So glad (to ...), It's such a pleasure (to ...).

haber (*see pp. 74, 132*), to have (*aux.*), to get (hold of), catch; **h. de,** to have to, to be to (**he de,** I am to); **He aquí** ..., Here is ...; (**diez años**) **ha,** (ten years) ago; **bien haya,** welcome; **¡ Mal haya !** Confound it !; **hay,** there is, there are; **hay que,** one must, it is necessary to; **No hay de que,** Don't mention it, You're welcome; **¿Qué hay?** What's the matter ?; **habérselas con,** to deal with, have it out with

habitación (*f.*), dwelling, abode, habitation, room

habitante (*mf.*), inhabitant, dweller

habitar, to inhabit, live in

hablar, to speak, talk; **-se,** to be on speaking terms

hacer (*see p. 159*), to make, to do, to suppose, think, to matter, to have (*require to*), to act, behave, to be (*of weather, temp. — see p. 186*); *variously translated in many idioms* (*as* **h. agua,** to leak, **h. caso de,** to pay attention to, take note of,

h. frente a, to face); **h. con,** to provide, furnish, supply with, to match; **h. de,** to act as, play; **h. por** *or* **para,** to try to; **h. que,** to pretend, to have (*require*); **hace,** ago (*see p. 186*); **hace ... que** (*of time*): *see p. 186;* **hecho,** made, ready-made, done, like; **h. y derecho,** real, true; **mal h.,** wrong; **hacerse,** to become, to move (*oneself*), to pretend to be; **h. a,** to become accustomed to; **se me hace ...,** it seems ... to me

hacia, toward(s)

hacienda, (*large*) farm, ranch, plantation, estate, treasury

hallar, to find; **–se,** to find oneself (*be*)

hambre (el h. *but f.*), hunger; **tener h.,** to be hungry (**de,** for)

hasta, *prep.,* until, till, up *or* down to, as far as; **H. luego,** So long, See you soon; **H. mañana,** See you tomorrow; **h. no más,** to the utmost; **h.,** *adv.,* even; **h. que,** *conj.,* until

hecho, fact, act, deed; **de h.,** in fact, really, in earnest; *p.p. of* **hacer** (*see* **hacer**)

herir (ie, i), to wound, injure

hermano, brother; **–a,** sister; **–os,** brothers, brother(s) and sister(s)

hermoso, beautiful

hermosura, beauty

hierro, iron, brand; **de h.,** iron (*adj.*)

hijo, son, child, junior; **–a,** daughter; **–os,** sons, children

hilo, thread, wire, string

historia, history, story

hoja, leaf, blade, sheet (*of paper*), foil

¡Hola! Hey! Ahoy! Hello!

hombre (*m.*), man

hombro, shoulder; **arrimar el h.,** to lend a hand, to put one's shoulder to the wheel; **echar al h.,** to shoulder

hondo, deep; *n., m.,* depth; **tener ... de h.,** to be ... deep

honor (*m.*), honor

honrar, to honor; **–rado,** honest, honorable

hora, hour, time (*of day*) (**de,** to); **¿Qué h. es? ¿Qué horas son?** What time is it?; *adv.* = **ahora**

horrible, horrible

hotel (*m.*), hotel

hoy, today, now; **h. (en) día,** today, nowadays

huerta, (vegetable) garden

hueso, bone; **la** *or* **el sin h.,** the tongue

huésped, **–a,** guest, host, **–ess**

huevo, egg

huir (*see p. 169*), to flee (**de,** from)

humano, human

humilde, humble, meek

humo, smoke, fume, *pl.* airs

humor (*m.*), humor, temper, mood; **buen h.,** good humor *or* nature; **de buen (mal) h.,** in a good (bad) humor

idea, idea

ideal, *adj., n., m.,* ideal

iglesia, church

ignorar, to be ignorant of, not to know (of), to ignore

igual, equal, alike, same, even, equable; **i. que,** equal to, the same as; (**Me) es i.,** It is all the same to (me); *n., m.,* equal; **al** *or* **por i.,** equally

ilusión (*f.*), illusion, (day)dream

imagen (*f.*), image

imaginación (*f.*), imagination

imaginar, to imagine; **imagínese,** just imagine, just think

imitar, to imitate

impedir (i), to impede, hinder, prevent; **i. que,** to hinder *or* prevent from

imperio, empire, rule

imponer (*see* **poner**), to impose, lay (**a,** on, upon), to acquaint; **impuesto,** *p.p. as n.,* tax, impost; **i. sobre ventas,** income tax

importancia, importance

importante, important

importar, to be important, matter, to be worth, cost, to import; **No (me) importa,** It doesn't matter to, *or* concern, (me).

imposible, impossible

impresión (*f.*), impress(ion), stamp, print(ing)

imprimir (*p.p.* **-preso**), to print, to impress, stamp; **impresos,** printed matter

inclinar(se), to incline, lean, tilt, bend, bow, to induce; **–se a,** to be inclined to

indicar, to indicate, show, point out

infeliz, unhappy, unfortunate

infinito, *adj., n., m.,* infinite

inmediato, adjacent, adjoining, immediate

inmenso, immense

inocente, innocent

inquieto, restless, uneasy, nervous

insistir, to insist (**en,** on)

inspirar, to inspire; **–se para,** to be inspired to

instante (*m.*), instant, moment; **al i.,** right away; **por instantes,** every moment

inteligencia, intelligence

inteligente, able, intelligent

intención (*f.*), purpose, intention (**de,** of. to), viciousness, malice; **segunda i.,** double meaning

interés (*m.*), interest (**en, por,** in)

interesante, interesting

interesar, to interest, to affect; **–se por,** to be interested in

interior, interior, inner, inside, domestic (*national*); **ropa i.,** underclothes; *n., m.,* interior, inside, *pl.* insides, innards

interrumpir, to interrupt

íntimo, intimate, in(ner)most

inútil, useless

investigar, investigate

invierno, winter, rainy season

invitar, to invite (**a,** to)

ir (*see pp. 170, 182*), to go; to affect, concern; to bet; to be, do (*well*

or badly); to leave (*subtraction:* **De 4 a 7 van 3**); *sometimes used instead of* **estar** *before p.p.* (**voy satisfecho,** I am satisfied); *before pres. part.,* to be (**–ing**) (**voy aprendiendo,** I am learning); **ir a,** to go to, to be going to, to bet on; **Eso no me va ni me viene,** That doesn't concern me in the least; **vamos,** let's go; **¡ Vamos ! ¡ Vaya !** Go on ! (*surprise, incredulity*); **¡ Vaya un(a) . . .!** What a . . .!; **Vaya Ud. con Dios,** Farewell; **irse,** to go (away), to be (**–ing**) (**se va mejorando,** he is improving), to get out of control (**se me fueron los pies,** my feet slipped; **se me iban los ojos,** my eyes were popping out); **¿ Cómo se va a . . .?** How does one get to . . .?

isla, island, isle

izquierdo, left, left-handed, crooked; *n., f.,* left (hand, side); **a la i.,** on *or* to the left

jamás, never, not ever; **nunca j.,** never again; **por siempre j.,** for ever and ever

jardín (*m.*), (flower) garden

jefe (*m.*), chief, boss, officer

joven, young; *n., mf.,* young person, y. man, y. woman; **los jóvenes,** (the) y. men, y. people, the y.

juego, play, game, sport, gambling, set (*of objects*), suite, gear; **entrar en j.,** to come into play; **hacer j.,** to match; **j. de azar** *or* **suerte,** game of chance; **j. de palabras,** play on words; **j. limpio,** fair play

juez (*m.*), judge, justice; **ser (buen) j. en,** to be a (good) judge of

jugar (**ue**), to play, sport, to gamble, wager, to move, wield, to match; **j. a (tenis),** to play (tennis)

juicio, judgment, trial, wits, senses, mind; **a mi j.,** in my judgment

juntar, to join, bring together, assemble, gather; **–se,** to join (together), come together, unite, meet, gather, assemble; **j. con,** to join with, associate (oneself) with

junto, joined, *pl.* together; *adv.,* near (at hand), together, close; **j. a,** next to, beside; **j. con,** together with; **en j.,** in all, together

jurar(se), to swear, take an oath (**sobre,** on)

justicia, justice

justo, just, exact

juventud (*f.*), youth, –fulness

juzgar, to judge

labio, lip

lado, side; **al l. de,** to the side of, beside; **a un l.,** to one side, aside; **de l.,** sideways, askance; **por otro l.,** on the other hand; **por un l.,** on one side; **por todos l.,** on all sides

lágrima, tear

lanzar, to throw, cast, fling, hurl, to launch, to evict

largo, long; **a lo l.,** lengthwise, at a distance; **a lo l. de,** along, the length of; *adv.,* largely; **¡ L. !** Get out ! Go away ! Beat it !; *n., m.,* length, largo; **tener . . . de l.,** to be . . . long

lástima, pity; **Da l.,** It is pitiful; **Es l.,** It's a pity, It's too bad.

lavar(se), to wash, to launder, to wash away *or* off

lección (*f.*), lesson, reading

leche (*f.*), milk

leer, to read

lejano, *adj.,* distant, far

lejos, *adv.,* far (**de,** from); **a lo l.,** in the distance, far away *or* off; **de**(**sde**) **l.,** from afar; *n., m.,* perspective, *pl.* background

lengua, tongue, language

lentamente, slowly

letra, letter (*of alphabet, of credit*), hand-(writing), print, type; **a la l., al pie de la l.,** literally, verbatim; **l. de cambio,** draft, bill of exchange; **l. de molde,** print

levantar, to raise, lift, to start; **–se,** to rise, to get up, to stand (up)

leve, light, slight

ley (*f.*), law, standard, quality

libertad (*f.*), liberty

librar, to free, pass (*sentence*), **to** open (*battle*); **–se de,** to escape from, to get rid of

libre, free, unoccupied, available

librero, bookseller

libro, book

ligero, light, slight, swift, nimble, flighty; **l. de cascos,** scatterbrained; **a la ligera,** lightly; *adv.,* swiftly

límite (*m.*), limit, bound, –ary

limpiar, to clean (off, up), cleanse; **–se,** to clean oneself

limpio, clean, clear (*neat*); **en l.,** clearly; **poner en l.,** to make a clean copy of, rewrite; **sacar en l.,** to gather (*conclude*)

lindo, pretty, neat, nice

línea, line

lista (*f.*), list, bill of fare

loco, mad, crazy (**de,** with); **l. de atar,** fit to be tied; **l. rematado,** stark mad; *n.,* crazy person, madman, –woman

locura, madness, folly

lograr, to obtain, attain, gain, win, achieve, to succeed in

lucir (**zc**), to shine, glow, to sport, show off; **–se,** to shine (*be brilliant, successful, etc.*)

lucha, struggle, strife, wrestling; **l. libre,** free-for-all

luego, soon, next, presently; **desde l.,** right away, at once, of course; **Hasta l.,** So long, See you soon; **l. que,** right after, as soon as

lugar (*m.*), place, spot, room; **en l. de,** in place of, instead of; **en primer l.,** in the first place; **tener l.,** to take place

luna, moon, glass plate, lens; **l. de miel,** honeymoon; **media l.,** half moon

luz (*f.*), light, daylight, window,

pl. spangles, lights (*knowledge*), culture; **dar a l.,** to give birth (to), to publish; **sacar a l.,** to publish; **salir a l.,** to come out, be published; **entre dos luces,** at dawn *or* twilight; **traje de luces,** *bullfighter's costume*

llamar, to call, name, to knock, ring (*at door*), to attract; **—se,** to be called *or* named (**¿Cómo se llama Ud.?** What is your name?)

llave (*f.*), key, wrench, faucet, tap; **cerrar con ll., echar ll. a,** to lock; **ll. inglesa,** monkey wrench

llegada, arrival

llegar, to arrive, come, to reach, to bring near; **ll. a,** to come to, reach (to); **ll. a ser,** to come to be, become; **no ll. a,** not to come to; **—se,** to approach, draw near

llenar, to fill (out, up), stuff (**de,** with), to fulfill, to satisfy; **—se,** to stuff oneself, to fill up, to get fed up

lleno, full; **de ll.,** fully, completely; *n., m.,* full, fulness

llevar, to carry, bear, take (away), to wear, to lead, to have spent (*time*), to beat *or* keep (*time, step*), to keep (*books*); (*aux., for* **haber**) to have; **ll. . . . años a,** to be . . . years older than; **ll. a cabo,** to carry out, accomplish; **ll. lo mejor (peor),** to get the best (worst) of it; **—se,** to carry away, off; **ll. bien (mal) con,** to get along well (badly) with

llorar, to cry, weep (over), bewail

llover, rain

madera, wood, timber, lumber

madre (*f.*), mother, matrix, channel, bed (*of river*); **m. de leche,** wet nurse; **m. política,** mother-in-law; *adj.,* mother

maestro, *adj.,* master, —ly; *n.,* master, teacher

magnífico, magnificent, splendid

maíz (*m.*), corn

mal, *adv.,* badly, poorly, wrong(ly), ill; **de m. en peor,** from bad to worse; **m. de (su) grado,** against (his) will; **¡M. haya!** Confound (it)!; **m. hecho,** badly done, wrong (**malhecho,** deformed); *n., m.,* evil, ill(ness), wrong, trouble (*illness*), harm; **m. de la tierra,** homesickness; **m. de ojo,** evil eye; *adj.: see* **mal(o)**

maldecir (*see p. 170*), to curse, damn, to defame; *irreg. p.p.* **maldito,** (ac)cursed, damned

mal(o) (*see p. 20*), bad, evil, ill, wicked; **estar m. de . . .,** to be sick at . . ., have a sore . . .; **lo m.,** the bad thing, the trouble, the worst of it; **de malas,** unlucky, with evil intent; **por malas o por buenas,** by hook or crook

mandar, to command, order, to send, to have (*something done*), to be in command, be the boss, to leave (*will*); **—se,** to be up and about, (*of rooms*) to communicate

manera, manner, way, style; **a (la) m. de,** in the style, *or* fashion, of; **de csta (esa) m.,** in this (that) way; **de m. de,** so as to; **de m. que,** so that; **de ninguna m.,** by no means, in no way, under no circumstances; **en gran m.,** in large measure, greatly; **sobre m.,** exceedingly

manifestar (ie), to manifest, show, to declare

mano (*f.*), hand, paw, foot (*of animal*); coat (*of paint, etc.*); **a la m.,** at hand; **a m.,** by hand; **bajo m.,** underhandedly; **dar la m.,** to shake hands with; **m. de gato,** make-up, editorial work; **m. de obra,** labor; **venir a las m.,** to come to blows; **darse la(s) mano(s),** to shake hands

mantener (*see* **tener**), to maintain, keep; **—se,** to support oneself; **m. en,** to stick, *or* keep, to

mañana, morning; **de la m.,** of *or* in the morning; **de,** *or* **por la, m.,** in the morning; **m. por la m.,** tomorrow morning; **pasado m.,** day after tomorrow

mantequilla, butter

mapa (*m.*), map

máquina, machine, engine; **m. de escribir,** typewriter

mar (*mf.*) sea, tide; **la m. de,** a lot of; **m. de fondo,** swell; **m. en leche,** calm sea

maravilla, marvel, wonder; **a m., a las mil m.,** marvelously

marcar, to mark

marcha, march, progress, functioning; **ponerse en m.,** to start (out); **sobre la m.,** at once

marchar, to march, go, to progress, to run (*function*); **–se,** to go away

marido, husband

mas, but

más, *adj.,* more, most; **a lo m.,** at most; *pron.,* more, most; **a m. de,** besides (*prep.*); **de m.,** over, extra, besides; **por m. que,** however much; *adv.,* more, most, –er (*as:* **m. grande,** bigger, **m. tarde,** later), –est (*as:* **el m. rico,** the richest), over, besides, rather; **el que m. y el que menos,** every single one; **m. bien,** rather; **m. de,** more than, over (*see p. 23*); **nada m.,** no more, nothing else; **no m. que** *or* **de,** no more than, not over, only (*see p. 23*); **no ... m.,** not ... again; *prep., n.,* plus

matar, to kill, to quench, to harass, worry, bother; **a mata caballo,** at breakneck speed; **un mátalas callando,** a sly dog

materia, matter, material, subject matter

material, *adj., n., m.,* material, equipment

matrimonio, matrimony, married couple

mayor, *adj.,* greater, –est, larger, –est, older, –est, senior, of age, adult, grown, major, high (*mass*); **m. edad,** majority (*age*); *n., m.,* major, chief, *pl.* elders, forefathers; **(al) por m.,** wholesale; **m. de edad,** adult

medianoche (*f.*), midnight

médico, medical; *n., m.,* doctor; *f.,* (woman) doctor, doctor's wife

medida, measure, –ment, standard, gauge, moderation; **a m. de,** according to; **a m. que,** according as, as

medio, (a) half, half a(n), middle, mean; **(las dos) y m.,** half past (two); **a medias,** by halves, fifty-fifty; *n., m.,* half, middle, midst, medium, *pl.* means; **de por m.,** (in) between; **–a,** *n.,* mean, *pl.* stockings; *adv.,* half

mediodía (*m.*), noon, midday

medir (i), to measure; **–se,** to be moderate, restrain oneself

mejor, *adj.,* better, best; **el m. día,** some fine day; **lo m.,** the best (thing); **a lo m.,** unexpectedly; *adv.,* better, best, rather; **m. dicho,** rather; **tanto m.,** so much the better

memoria, memory, souvenir, memorial, memorandum, report, *pl.* regards, memoirs; **de m.,** from memory, by heart; **hacer m. de,** to remember, to make a note of; **traer a la m.,** to bring to mind

menor, *adj.,* less, –er, least, small, –er, –est, younger, –est, minor; **m. edad,** minority (*age*); *n., m.,* minor; **m. de edad,** minor; **(al) por m.,** retail

menos, *adj., pron.,* less, least, fewer, –est (**de, que,** than); **al m., a** *or* **por lo m.,** at (the) least; **a m. (de) que,** unless; *adv.,* less, least; **de m.,** less, missing; **echar de m.,** to miss; *prep.,* less, except, but, minus; *n.,* minus (*sign*)

mentir (ie), to lie; **¡Miento!** I'm wrong!

mentira, lie; **¡M.!** It's a lie!; **Parece m.,** It's incredible.

menudo, minute, (very) small; *n.,*
m., small change, *pl.* entrails;
a m., often; **por m.,** in detail

merced (*f.*), mercy, grace, favor;
grant; **a la m. de,** at the mercy of;
a m. de, at the expense of; **m. a,**
thanks to; **Vuestra M.,** Your
Grace, Your Honor

merecer (**zc**), to deserve, to be
deserving; **m. en bien de,** to
deserve well of

mérito, merit, worth

mes (*m.*), month, month's pay; **al m.,**
by the month

mesa, table, mesa, plateau, board
(*directors*)

meter, to put *or* stick in, insert, to
make, create, cause; **m. en,** to
put, stick, get into, to involve in;
—se, to butt in, involve oneself, introduce oneself, get (**en,** into), to become, turn; **m. a,** to set oneself up as

mezclar, to mix, mingle; **—se,** to mix,
mingle, take part

miedo, fear; **dar m.,** to frighten;
tener m. (de, a), to be afraid (of)

mientras, while; **m. más,** the more;
m. que, while, as *or* so long as;
m. tanto, meanwhile

milagro, miracle; **No es m.,** No
wonder.

militar, military; *n., m.,* military
man, soldier; *v.,* to serve in the
army, to be militant, to militate

mina, mine

minuto, *n.,* minute

mirada, look, glance, gaze

mirar, to look (at), gaze (at), to
regard, to watch; **m. a,** to look
out upon, overlook, face, to look
after, look out for; **m. bien,** to
think highly of, to approve; **m.
mal,** to disapprove of, dislike;
m. por, to look after *or* out for;
mirado, thoughtful, regarded

misa, mass; **m. de gallo,** midnight
mass; **m. mayor,** high mass

miseria, misery, poverty, miserliness,
pittance

mismo, same (**que,** as), very; **lo m.,**
the same (thing); **Lo m. da,** It is
all the same, It makes no difference;
lo m. que, the same as; **por lo m.,**
for the same reason; *intensive pron.;*
myself, himself, *etc.;* **ahora m.,**
right now

misterio, mystery

misterioso, mysterious

mitad (*f.*), half, middle; **mi cara
m.,** my better half; **por la m.,**
in the middle, in two

modelo, model

moderno, modern

modesto, modest

modo, mode, way, manner, means;
mood (*of verb*); **de este (ese) m.,**
in this (that) way; **a(l) m. de,** in
the manner of; **del mismo m. que,**
in the same way as *or* that; **de m.
de,** so as to; **de m. que,** so that;
and so; **de todos modos,** at any
rate

molestar, to bother, annoy, trouble

momento, moment; **al m.,** in a
moment *or* minute

montaña, mountain

montar, to mount, to ride, to assemble, to cock (*gun*); **m. a,** to
amount to

monte (*m.*), mount(ain), wood(s);
forest; **m. bajo,** scrub; **m. de
piedad,** pawnshop

moral, moral; *n., f.,* morality, ethics,
morale; *m.,* mulberry tree

morir (**ue, u;** *p.p.* **muerto**), to die
(**de,** of, from, with); **¡Muera...!**
Down with...!; **haber muerto,**
to have died, to have killed; **—se,**
to be dying

mortal, mortal, deadly; *n., m.,* mortal

mostrar (**ue**), to show

motivo, motive, reason; **con m. de,**
by reason of, on the occasion of;
de ningún m., on no account

mover(**se**) (**ue**), to move

movimiento, movement, move, motion

mozo, young, youthful, single; *n.;*

m., youth, young fellow, boy, lad, servant, porter, waiter; **buen m.**, good-looking boy, handsome youth; **–a**, (young) girl, maid, servant (girl); **buena m.**, good-looking girl

muchacho, boy, child; **–a**, girl; **–os**, boys, children, boys and girls

mucho, *adj.*, much, a great deal of, (*of time*) long, *pl.* many; *pron.*, much, *pl.* many; **con m.**, by far; **ni con m.**, not by a long shot, far from it; **no ha m.**, not long ago; **por m. que**, no matter how much; *adv.*, much, a great deal, a long time, long, (*to work*) hard; **ni m. menos**, nor anything like it

mudar, to change, to move, to moult; **m. de**, to change (*clothes, one's mind, etc.*); **–se**, to change (*oneself*), to change (one's clothes), to move (*to new address*)

mueble, movable; *n.*, *f.*, piece of furniture, *pl.* furniture

muerte (*f.*), death; **a (la) m., de m.**, to the death, mortal

mujer (*f.*), woman, wife

mundo, world, society; **hombre de m.**, man of the world; **tener (mucho) m.**, to know the world; **todo el m.**, everybody

música, music, band; **músico**, musical, musician

muy, very, quite a

nacer (**zc**), to be born, to sprout, to spring, rise; **–se**, to sprout, to rip (*at seam*); **nacido**, born, living; *n.*, *m.*, living being, sprout, boil

nación (*f.*), nation; **de nación**, by nationality

nada, nothing, not anything, naught, nonentity; **De n.**, Don't mention it, It's nothing; **n. de (nuevo)**, nothing (new); **n. de eso**, none of that; **n. más**, no more; **no . . . por n.**, under no circumstances; **n.**, *adv.*, not at all

nadie, no one

naranja, orange

nariz (*f.*), nose, *pl.* nostrils

natural, natural; *adj.*, *n.*, native

naturaleza, nature; **n. muerta**, still life

necesario, necessary

necesidad (*f.*), necessity, need

necesitar, to need

negar (**ie**), to deny, to refuse, to forbid; **–se a**, to refuse to

negocio, business, transaction, *pl.* business; **de n.**, on business

negro, *adj.*, *n.*, black, Negro; *n., f.* Negress, sweetheart

nevar (**ei**), snow

ni, neither, nor, and not, not even; **ni . . . ni**, neither . . . nor; **ni siquiera**, not even

ningun(o), *adj.*, no, not any; *pron.*; not one, none

niño, (little) boy, child; **–a**, (little) girl; **–os**, (little) boys, children, boys and girls

no, no, not

noble, *adj.*, *n.*, noble

noche (*f.*), night, evening; **de la n.** **a la mañana**, overnight; **de n.**, at *or* by night; **esta n.**, tonight; **por la n.**, at *or* in the night; **Buenas n.**, Good evening, Good night.

nombrar, to name, to nominate, to appoint

nombre (*m.*), name, noun; **n. bautismal, n. de pila**, Christian name; **n. y apellido**, full name

norte (*m.*), north, n. wind, guiding star, guide; **del n.**, northern

nota, note, grade (*on exam.*)

notable, notable, remarkable

notar, to note, notice

noticia, notice, (piece of) news, *pl.* news

novedad (*f.*), novelty, newness, change; *pl.* news; **sin n.**, just the same, as usual

novio, fiancé, lover, (bride)groom; **–a**, fiancée, sweetheart, bride; **–os**, sweethearts, bride and groom

nube (*f.*), cloud; **por las n.**, to the clouds, sky high

nuevo, new, novel; **de n.,** anew, again

número, number, numeral

nunca, never, not ever; **mejor que n.,** better than ever; **n. jamás,** never again

o, or; **o . . . o,** either . . . or

obedecer (zc), to obey

objeto, object

obligación (*f.*), obligation

obligar, to obligate, to oblige

obra, work, deed, action; **o. de romanos,** tremendous job; **poner por o.,** to start to work on

o(b)scuro, dark, obscure; **a o(b)scuras,** in the dark

observación (*f.*), observation

observar, to observe, watch, notice, to remark

obtener (*see p. 160*), to obtain

ocasión (*f.*), occasion, opportunity

ocultar, to hide

ocupar, to occupy, to employ, to disturb, to concern; **—se de,** to busy oneself with, attend to; **—pado,** busy, occupied

ocurrir, to occur, happen; **o. a,** to have recourse to; **—se a,** to occur to; **se (me) ocurre,** it occurs to (me)

oeste (*m.*), west

ofender, to offend; **—se,** to be offended, get angry

oficial, official; *n.* (*f.* **—ala**), officer, official

oficina, office

oficio, trade, occupation, office; **de o.,** by trade, officially

ofrecer (zc), to offer; **—se,** to volunteer, to occur; **o. a,** to offer to

¡Oh! Oh!

oído, hearing, (inner) ear; **al o.,** in one's ear; **de o.,** by ear; **dar oídos a,** to listen to

oír (*see p. 166*), to hear; **o. decir,** to hear it said; **¡Oye!** Hey!; **¡Oiga(n)!** Listen!

ojo, eye, hole, keyhole, spring (*water*),

span (*of bridge*), attention; **avivar el o.,** to look sharp; **¡Ojo!** Notice!; **a los o. de,** in the eyes of; **a o. cerrados,** blindly; **a ojos vistas,** in plain sight; **en un abrir y cerrar de ojos,** in the twinkling of an eye; **mirar con buenos (malos) o.,** to look upon favorably (unfavorably); **saltar a los o.,** to be obvious

oler (huelo), to smell, scent, sniff; **o. a,** to smell of *or* like

olvidar, to forget; **—se,** to forget (**me olvido, se me olvida,** I forget)

operación (*f.*), operation, (*chem.*) process

opinión (*f.*), opinion

oponer (*see p. 159*), to oppose, to face; **—se a,** to oppose, to object to; **opuesto,** opposed, opposite, contrary

oportunidad (*f.*), chance, opportunity

oración (*f.*), prayer, sentence, oration; **parte de la o.,** part of speech

orden (*m.*), order (*system, class, peace, architectural*); **en o.,** in order; **por su o.,** in its turn; (*f.*), order (*command, instruction, brotherhood*); **a la o.,** to (the) order; **o. del día,** order of the day; **a sus órdenes,** at your service (*a formula used in introductions*)

ordenar, to arrange, to order, to ordain

ordinario, ordinary, common; *n.; m.;* daily household expense, everyday food, regular mail delivery, ordinary (*eccles.*); **de o.,** ordinarily

oreja, (outer) ear; **descubrir,** *or* **enseñar, la o.,** to give oneself away; **ver las o. al lobo,** to find oneself in danger (*of attack*)

orilla, border, edge, bank, shore

oro, gold

otoño, autumn, fall

otro, *adj., pron.,* (an)other (**one**)

paciencia, patience

padecer (zc), to suffer

padre (*m.*), father, sire, *pl.* fathers, parents; **p. de pila,** godfather; **p. nuestro,** Lord's Prayer

pagar, to pay (back, for), repay; **p. el pato,** to be the goat; **pagarlas,** to pay for it (*error, sin*)

página, page

país (*m.*), country; **del p.,** domestic

pájaro, bird

palabra, word; **de p.,** by word of mouth; **llevar la p.,** to be the spokesman; **tener la p.,** to have the floor

palacio, palace

pálido, pale, pallid

palo, tree, pole, stick, blow (*with stick*), mast, suit (*of cards*), pale; **dar (de) palos,** to cudgel, thrash

pan (*m.*), bread, loaf, cake (*of soap*)

paño, cloth, spot (*discoloration*), *pl.* clothes, robes; **p. menores,** underclothes

pañuelo, handkerchief

papel (*m.*), paper, piece of paper, role, foil; **hacer p.,** to play a part; **p. de seda,** tissue paper; **p. higiénico,** toilet paper; **p. moneda,** paper money; **p. para la máquina,** typewriter paper; **p. secante,** blotting paper, blotter; **p. sellado,** official paper; **p. viejo,** waste paper

par, equal, even; *n., m. or f.,* pair, brace, par, peer; **a la p.,** at par, equally; **de p. en p.,** wide open; **ír a la p.,** to share equally; **un** (*not* una) **p. de,** a pair of

para, for, in order to, to, toward(s); **estar p.,** to be about to; **p. acá,** in this direction; **p. allá,** in that direction; **p. con,** toward(s); **p. entre los dos,** between the two of us; **p. eso,** for that (matter); **p. que,** in order that, so that; **¿P. qué?** What for?; **p. siempre,** forever; **tengo p. mí,** it is my opinion

parar, to stop, to bet, to fix, place; **p. en,** to end up as *or* in; **p. mientes en,** to put one's mind to, consider carefully; **venir a p. a,** to come to, arrive at; **–se,** to stop, come to a stop, halt, to stand up; **parado,** stopped, standing (still); **bien (mal) p.,** in good (bad) condition

parecer (zc), to seem, appear; **a lo que parece,** to judge by, *or* to all, appearances, as it seems, as things look; **(me) parece que,** it seems to (me) that, (I) think that; **¿Qué le parece?** How does it look to you?; **–se,** to look alike; **–se a,** to resemble; **parecer,** *n., m.,* opinion, appearance; **al p.,** apparently; **por el bien p.,** for the sake of appearances; **parecido a,** resembling; **bien (mal) p.,** good-(bad-)looking; **–o,** *n.;* resemblance

pared (*f.*), wall

pariente, –a, relative, relation

parte (*f.*), part, share, party, side, message, notice; **dar p. (de),** to inform (of); **de** *or* **por (mi) p.,** on (my) part, in (my) behalf, for (me); **de** *or* **por p. de,** on the part of, in the name of, in behalf of, for; **hacer de su p.,** to do one's part *or* share; **la mayor p. de,** most of; **no ser p. en,** not to be a party to; **en** *or* **por todas p.,** everywhere, on all sides

particular, particular, private; *n., m.,* particular, private person; **en p.,** privately

partida, departure, item, entry, certificate, party (*expedition, band*), game, lot, shipment; **mala p., p. serrana,** dirty trick; **p. de campo,** picnic

partido, (*polit.*) party, advantage, odds, handicap; **hacer p. con,** to join (*in a game*); **sacar p. de,** to derive benefit(s) from, to turn to advantage; **tomar p.,** to join

partir, to part, divide, split, crack, to depart; **a p. de,** beginning with; **p. de,** to leave from, start from

pasado, *p.p., adj.,* past, last (*week, etc.*), stale, spoiled, out of style; **p. mañana,** day after tomorrow; *n., m.,* past

pasar, to pass, go, come, to cross, to go past *or* beyond, to carry, take, to smuggle, to happen, to give (*a disease*), to pass through, suffer, experience, to surpass, to review, rehearse, to pass away, to pass (*not play*), to pass (*be acceptable*); **p. de largo,** to pass by; **p. en claro,** to pass over, omit; **p. lista,** to call the roll; **p. por,** to pass as, by, *or* through; **p. por alto,** to pass over, overlook; **p. por las armas,** to shoot (*execute*); **p. sin,** to do without; **¿Cómo lo pasa Ud.?** How are you doing? *or* getting along?; **¿Qué (le) pasa?** What's the matter (with him, you)?; **Pase adelante,** Come in; **Ya pasó,** It's over; **ir pasando,** to be (just) getting along, to make out; **—se,** to pass (away), to spoil, get stale, to outdo oneself, to go too far, to leak; **p. a,** to go over to; **p. de,** to be too; **se (me) pasó,** (I) forgot; *see* pasado

asear, to take for a walk; **pasear(se),** to take a walk *or* ride

paseo, walk, ride, drive, outing, promenade; **dar un p.,** to take a walk; **echar, enviar,** *or* **mandar a p.,** to send one on his way (*dismiss*); **ir de p.,** to go for a walk

pasión (*f.*), passion (**por,** for)

paso, pace, step, passage, incident, rate; **al p. que,** at the time when; **ceder el p. a,** to make way for; **dar un p.,** to take a step; **de p.,** by the way, in passing; **mal p.,** trouble, "fix"; **p. a p.,** step by step; **p. doble,** two-step; **salir del p.,** to get out of it; **a dos pasos de,** a few steps away from; **paso,** *adv.,* softly, low

patio, courtyard, patio

patria, fatherland

paz (*f.*), peace; **en p.,** at *or* in peace, even, square; **gente de p.,** friend(s); **hacer las paces con,** to make peace with

pecho, breast, chest, bosom, (*fig.*) heart, courage; **echarse a pechos, tomar a pecho(s),** to take to heart

pedazo, piece

pedir (*see p. 168*), to ask (for), beg, to order; **a p. de boca,** just as one would wish, to perfection; **p. prestado,** to borrow

pegar, to stick, glue, fasten, post, to sew on, fasten on, to give, deal, to beat, to set (*fire*), to go, pass, do (*be acceptable*), to close (*the eyes*); **p. con,** to go (*harmonize*) with; **—se,** to stick (**a,** to)

peligro, danger, risk

peligroso, dangerous

pelo, hair, fur, down, coat, fiber, hairspring; **contra p.,** the wrong way; **en p.,** bareback; **hacerse el p.,** to have one's hair cut; **no tener p. de,** to be not at all; **tomar el p. a,** to pull (one's) leg, kid; **venir a p.,** to be just right; **tener pelos,** to be tough (*difficult*)

pena, penalty, pain, sorrow, trouble, effort; **valer la p.,** to be worth while

penetrar (en), to penetrate (into)

pensamiento, thought

pensar (ie), to think, to intend; **p. de** *or* **en,** to think about, of; **el día menos pensado,** when you least expect it

peor, *adj., adv.,* worse, worst; **de p. en p.,** worse and worse; **tanto p.,** so much the worse

pequeño, little; **en p.,** in short, in miniature, on a small scale; *n.,* little one

perder (ie), to lose, to waste, to miss, to ruin, spoil; **p. de vista,** to lose sight of; **p. los estribos,** to lose control of oneself; **—se,** to be *or* get lost, to ruin oneself, be ruined *or* spoiled

perdón (*m.*), pardon, forgiveness; **Con p.,** Pardon (me), Excuse me.

perdonar, to pardon, forgive, excuse, to overlook

perfecto, perfect

periódico, periodical; *n., m.,* periodical, newspaper

permanecer (**zc**), to remain

permiso, permission, permit; **Con p.,** Excuse me.

permitir, to permit

pero, *conj.,* but

perro, dog; **p. de aguas** *or* **lanas,** poodle; **p. dogo,** bulldog; **–a,** bitch

perseguir (i), to pursue, to persecute

persona, person

personaje (*m.*), personage, character

pertenecer (**zc**), to pertain, belong

pesado, heavy, deep, tiresome, dull, slow

pesar, to weigh; (**Me**) **pesa** (**de**), (I) regret; **mal que le pese,** whether you, *or* he, like(s) it or not; **pese a quien pese,** whether anybody likes it or not; *n., m.,* grief, sorrow, regret; **a p. de,** in spite of; **a p.** (**mío**), in spite of (me); *see* **pesado**

peseta, peseta

peso, weight, peso; **caerse de su p.,** to be self-evident; **p. específico,** specific gravity

picar, to prick, puncture, to sting, bite, nibble, peck, to chop up, to spur, to smart, itch, to pique; **–se,** to be *or* get angry, to be moth-eaten, to sour, go stale, to begin to rot *or* (*of teeth*) decay, to become choppy

pícaro, rogue, rascal; roguish, rascally

pico, beak, bill, point, pick(ax), spout, peak, corner, small amount (*remaining*), (*slang*) mouth; **callar el p.,** to hold one's tongue; **p. de oro,** silver-tongued orator; **tener mucho p.,** to be a great talker; **y p.,** and some (*a little over*)

pie (*m.*), foot, base, leg (*of furniture*): stand, sediment, motive, reason, cue; **al p. de,** at the foot of, near; **al p. de la letra,** to the letter; **a p.,** on foot; **a p. firme,** firmly; **dar p.,** to give reason; **de a p.,** foot (*adj.*); **de** *or* **en p.,** on foot, standing; **echar p. a,** to set foot on; **en p. de guerra,** on a war footing; **p. de amigo,** prop; **p. de cabra,** crowbar; **ponerse de p.,** to stand (up); **de pies a cabeza,** from head to foot; **ni pies ni cabeza,** head nor tail; **Se** (**me**) **fueron los p.,** (My) feet slipped.

piedra, stone, rock; **p. angular,** cornerstone; **p. viva,** solid rock

piel (*f.*), skin, hide, pelt, fur; **p. de gallina,** goose flesh

pierna, leg; **a p. suelta** *or* **tendida,** soundly, tranquilly; **en piernas,** barelegged

pieza, piece, room

pintar, to paint; **p. de** (**azul**), to paint (blue)

pintura, picture, painting

piso, floor, story, tread; **p. bajo,** ground floor

placer (*see p. 175*), to please; *n.; m.,* pleasure

planta, plant, (*floor*) plan, sole (*of foot*)

plata, silver, plate, (*slang*) money

plato, plate, dish

plaza, plaza, square, room, space; **p. de armas,** parade ground; **p. de toros,** bull ring; **sentar p.** to enlist

pluma, feather, plume, pen; **p. fuente,** fountain pen

población (*f.*), population, town

pobre, poor; **¡P. de** (**mí**)! Poor (me) !; *n.,* poor person, poor man (woman), poor fellow (girl)

poco, *adj.,* little, small, short (*of time*), *pl.* few; *adv.,* little, not very; **p. a p.,** little by little; **p. más o menos,** more or less; *pron., n.,* little (bit), little while; **a p.,** shortly after(wards); **por p.,** almost; **ser**

para p., not to amount to much; **tener en p.,** not to think much of; **un p. de,** a little

poder (*see p. 159*), can, may; **a más no p.,** to the extent of one's ability; **no p. con,** not to be able to deal with, *or* stand; **no p. más,** to be able to do no more; **no puedo menos de,** I can do no less than; **puede que,** it may be that; **poder,** *n., m.,* power

poderoso, powerful

poeta (*m.*), poet

político, political, polite; *n., m.,* politician; *f.,* politics, policy, politeness

polvo, dust, powder, pinch, *pl.* (face) powder; **p. dentífrico,** tooth powder

poner (*see p. 159*), to put, place, set, to put on, to turn on, to cause to be, make, to lay (*egg*), to suppose, to impose, to bet, to put down; **p. casa,** to set up housekeeping; **p. de** *or* **por,** to call (*a bad name*); **p. por escrito,** to put in writing; **p. por obra,** to carry out; **—se,** to become, to put on; **p. a,** to start to; **bien (mal) puesto,** well (poorly) dressed; **puesto que,** *conj.,* since

por, by, for, through, about, for the sake of, on account of, by way of, to be (*foll'd by infin.*), however; **p. entre,** among, amidst; **p. eso,** therefore

porque, because

porvenir (*m.*), future

poseer, to possess, to be a master of (*an art or subject*)

posesión (*f.*), possession

posible, possible, *pl.* assets, wealth; **en lo p.,** so far as possible

posición (*f.*), position, status

práctica (*f.*), practice, exercise

precio, price, worth; **poner a p.,** to put a price on

precioso, precious

preciso, necessary, precise

preferir (**ie, i**), to prefer

pregunta, question; **hacer una p.,** to ask a question

preguntar, to ask

prenda, pawn, pledge, garment, jewel (*person*), *pl.* forfeits, gifts (*talents*); **p. de vestir,** article of clothing; **en prenda(s),** as security

preparar, to make *or* get ready; **—se (a),** to prepare (to)

presencia, presence, appearance; **p. de ánimo,** p. of mind

presentar, to present (with), to introduce; **—se,** to appear, to volunteer

presente, *adj.,* present; **hacer p.,** to call attention to; **lo p.,** the present; **tener p.,** to bear in mind; *n., m.,* present (*gift, time*); **al** *or* **de p.,** at present

presidente, —a, president, chairman; *also, f.,* president's wife

prestar, to lend, give (*aid*), pay (*attention*), to stretch; **—se,** to lend oneself; **dar prestado,** to lend; **pedir p.,** to borrow; **tomar p.,** to borrow

pretender, to ask for, try to get, to try, to aspire to

primavera, spring, flowered silk, primrose

primer(o), first, prime; **de p. instancia,** in the first place; **p. dama,** leading lady; **p. galán,** lead; **p. enseñanza,** primary education; **p. fila,** front rank; **p. materias,** raw materials; **de buenas a primeras,** all at once; **de primera,** prime, high-grade; **primero,** *adv.,* first, sooner, rather

primo, first, prime; *n.,* cousin, boob; **p. carnal** *or* **hermano(—a),** first cousin

principal, main, renowned; *n.; m.* principal (*money*), head, ground floor

príncipe (*m.*), prince; **edición p.,** first edition; **autores p.,** old masters

principio, beginning, principle; **al**

p., at first; **a principios de,** at the first *or* beginning of

prisa, haste, speed; **a** *or* **de p.,** in a hurry, promptly; **a toda p.,** at full speed; **correr p.,** to be urgent; **darse p.,** to hurry; **estar de p., tener p.,** to be in a hurry

privar, to deprive, to prohibit, to "fire," to have pull, to prevail, be in vogue; **–se,** to deprive oneself; *p.p.,* private

probar (ue), to test, try, sample, to prove, to suit, agree with

proceder, to proceed; *n., m.,* procedure, behavior, action

procurar, to try, to procure

producir (*see p. 166*), to produce

profundo, profound, deep; *n., m.,* deep

prometer, to promise, give promise, bid fair; **–se,** to fully expect, to become engaged; **–tido,** promised, engaged, *n.,* fiancé(e); **–o,** promise

pronto, prompt, ready, quick; *adv.,* soon, promptly; **de p.,** suddenly; *n., m.,* sudden impulse; **al p.,** at first, on impulse; **por el p.,** for the present

pronunciar, to pronounce, deliver (*speech*)

propio, proper, own; **amor p.,** self-esteem; *n., m.,* messenger

proponer (*see p. 159*), to propose, to propound; **–se a,** to propose to

proporcionar, to proportion, to provide, furnish

propósito, purpose, intent(ion); **a p.,** to the purpose, apropos, by the way; **de p.,** on purpose; **fuera de p.,** not to the purpose

protestar, to protest

provincia, province

próximo, nearest, next

proyecto, project, plan; *adj.,* projected

prueba, test, trial, proof, evidence; **a p. de (fuego),** (fire)proof

publicar, to publish

público, *adj., n., m.,* public

puebio, people, town

puerta, door, gate **(de, to); a p. cerrada,** behind closed doors; **p. excusada** *or* **falsa,** side *or* back door

puerto, port, harbor, haven, (*mtn.*) pass

pues, *adv.,* well, then; **p. bien,** well then, very well; **p. no,** but no, no indeed; **p. sí,** yes indeed; **p. (que),** *conj.,* since, because

puesto, post, position, stand; *p.p.* of **poner** (*q.v.*)

punto, point, dot, period, nib, sight (*of gun*), stitch; **al p.,** immediately; **a p.,** on the dot; **a p. de,** on the point of; **a p. fijo,** definitely; **de todo p.,** at every point, absolutely; **en p.,** on the dot; **hasta cierto p.,** to a certain extent; **p. menos,** a bit less; **p. y coma,** semicolon; **trabajo de p.,** knitting; **dos p.,** colon (:)

puro, pure, sheer; **de p.,** perfectly; *n., m.,* cigar

que, *conj.,* that, as, since, for, because, than, may, let, why (*exclam.*), but; **a q.,** I bet; **para q.,** in order that; **por . . . q.,** no matter how; **q. . . . q. no,** whether . . . or not; **¡Q. sí!** Yes (indeed)!; **¡Q. no!** No (indeed)!; **Creo (Digo) q. sí (no),** I think (say) so (not, no); **(si) yo q. Ud.,** if I were you

que, *rel. pron.,* that, which, who; whom

¿qué? what? how?; **¿a q.?** **¿para q.?** what for?; **¿por q.?** why?; **¿Q. tal . . . ?** How is (are) . . . ?; **¿Q. tal?** How are you?; **¡Qué . . . !** What (a) . . . !; **¡Pues q.!** What do you think!; **¡Q. de . . . !** How much . . . ! How many . . . !; **¡Q. . . . tan . . . !** What a . . . !; **sin q. ni para q.,** without any reason

quedar, to stay, be left; **q. bien (mal),** to do well (badly); **q. en,** to agree on *or* to; **q. por,** to remain to be, to go to; (**Me**) **queda . . . ,** (I) have . . . left; ¿ **En qué quedamos?** What have we decided on? What do you say?; **–se,** to stay, to find oneself, be, get; **q. con,** to keep

quejarse, to complain, moan, grumble; **q. de,** to complain of, bewail, lament

quemar, to burn (up), be burning hot, scorch; **–se,** to burn (up), be *or* get hot, get warm (*near*)

querer (*see p. 159*), to want, wish, be willing, to try, to love, to be about to, look like (*rain, etc.*); **no q.,** to be unwilling to, refuse to; **q. decir,** to mean; **q. más,** to like better, want more, prefer; **sin q.,** unwillingly; **como quiera,** in any way, however; **cuando quiera,** whenever; **donde quiera,** wherever, anywhere; **querido,** beloved, dear; **querer,** *n., m.,* love, wish, will

quien, who, whom, he who, *etc.,* one who; ¿ **quién?** who(m)?

quitar, to take away, off, *or* out, remove, to subtract, to take away from, to prevent from; **–se,** to take off; **q. de,** to get rid of, free oneself from

quizá(s), perhaps

rama, branch, bough; **andarse por las r.,** to beat about the bush

rápido, swift; *adj., n., m.,* express

raro, rare, strange; **r. vez,** rarely

rato, while, (short) time; **de r. en r.,** from time to time

rayo, ray, flash (of lightning), spoke

raza, race, breed, crack, split; **de r.,** purebred, pedigreed

razón (*f.*), reason, right, account, ratio; **a r. de,** at the rate of; **dar la r. a,** to agree with; **en r. a** *or* **de,** as regards; **ponerse en r.,** to be reasonable; **por r. de,** on account of; **tener r.,** to be right

real, real, royal; *n., m.,* camp, fair grounds, real (*coin or amount varying in value from 10 to 25 centavos*); **alzar** *or* **levantar el r.,** to break camp; **sentar el r.,** to (en)camp

realidad (*f.*), reality

realizar, to fulfill, carry out, **to** turn into cash

recibir, to receive; **–se de,** to graduate as, to be qualified as

recién, recently

recobrar, to recover, regain; **–se,** to recover (one's health), to recoup one's losses

recoger, to pick (up), gather, collect, to shrink, shorten, to shelter; **–se,** to take shelter, withdraw, retire

reconocer (**zc**), to recognize, **to** reconnoiter

recordar (**ue**), to remember, **to** remind of

recorrer, to go over, travel, to look over, to overhaul

recuerdo, recollection, remembrance, keepsake, *pl.* regards

recurso, recourse, *pl.* resources

redondo, round; **en r.,** all around

reducir (*see p. 166*), to reduce, lower; **–se,** to reduce, to retrench, to be reduced

referir (**ie, i**), to refer, to tell, relate; **–se a,** to refer to

regalar, to give, present, to regale, treat, entertain; **–se,** to indulge oneself, live well

regalo, gift, gratification, delicacy, comfort, luxury

regañar, to scold

región (*f.*), region

regla, rule, ruler

regresar, to return

regular, regular, ordinary; **por lo r.,** regularly; *v.,* to regulate

reina, queen

reír (*see p. 169*), to laugh (at); **–se,** to laugh, to split, tear; **r. de,** to laugh at

relación (*f.*), relation, account

religioso, *adj., n., m.,* religious

reloj (*m.*), clock, watch; **r. de arena,**

hourglass; **r. de sol,** sundial; **r. de pulsera,** wrist watch; **r. despertador,** alarm clock

remedio, remedy, help

rendir (i), to subdue, to surrender, to render, to produce, yield; **–se,** to surrender, to be exhausted, worn out; **–dido,** tired out

renunciar, to renounce, give up, to resign, to waive, to retire; **r. a,** to renounce

reñir (i), to quarrel, fight, to scold

reparar, to repair, to restore, to make up for, to notice, to parry; **r. en,** to observe

repartir, to divide (up), distribute

repente: de r., suddenly

repetir (i), to repeat, to copy, (*law*) to claim

replicar, to reply

representar, to represent, to present, act (*play, role*)

reservar, to reserve, keep back

resistir, to resist, to endure, stand; **r. a,** to resist; **–se,** to resist

resolución (*f.*), resolution, solution, decision; **en r.,** in short

resolver (ue; *p.p.* **resuelto**), to resolve (on), to solve, to decide (on), to dissolve; **–se a,** to resolve to; *p.p.,* resolute

respecto: a este (ese) r., in this (that) respect; **(con) r. a,** with respect to, in regard to

respetar, to respect

respeto, respect, honor; **de r.,** spare, extra; **faltar al r. a,** to be lacking in respect to

respirar, to breathe, to catch one's breath

responder, to reply, to correspond; **r. por,** to answer for

respuesta, reply

resto, rest, remainder, *pl.* remains

resultado, result; *p.p. of* **resultar**

resultar, to result, turn out

retirar, to withdraw, remove; **r. a,** to take away from; **–se,** to withdraw, retire

retrato, portrait, picture

reunir, to unite, join, to gather, collect; **–se,** to unite, meet, assemble

revolver (ue; *p.p.* **revuelto**), to revolve, turn (over), stir

rey (*m.*), king; **(el día de) los Reyes,** Epiphany, Twelfth-day

rezar, to pray, to say, to read

rico, rich

ridículo, ridiculous

rincón (*m.*), nook, corner

río, river; **r. abajo,** downstream; **r. arriba,** upstream

riqueza, riches, richness

risa, laugh(ter), smile; **morirse de r.,** to die laughing

robar, to rob, steal (from)

rodear, to surround, to round up, to go around, to beat about the bush

rodilla, knee; **a media r.,** on one knee; **de rodillas,** on one's knees

rogar (ue), to beg, pray

rojo, red, red hot; *n., m.,* red

romper (*p.p.* **roto**), to break, burst, tear (open), shatter, to open; **r. a,** to break out into, start to; **r. con,** to break with

ropa, clothes; **a quema r.,** at close range, unexpectedly; **r. blanca,** linen; **r. interior,** underclothes

rosa, rose, rosette, red spot; **r. de los vientos,** mariner's compass

rostro, countenance, beak

rubio, *adj., n.,* blond, fair

ruido, noise, report

saber (*see p. 160*), to know (how), to find out, to taste (a, of); **a s.,** to wit, namely; **un no sé qué de,** a certain; **y no sé que más,** and goodness knows what else; **sabido,** known, learned, well-read, well-informed; *n., m.,* knowledge, learning; **según mi leal s. y entender,** to the best of my knowledge

sabio, wise, learned; **wise man;** scholar

sacar, to extract, to bring, draw, drag, pull, take, *etc.*, out, to withdraw, to get (out), derive, to win, to take (*a picture*); **s. a luz,** to bring out, mention, publish; **s. de sus casillas** *or* **de madre,** to exasperate, make one lose his temper; **s. en claro** *or* **limpio, to gather,** make out, conclude

sacudir, to shake (off, out), to beat (*as rug*)

sala, hall, parlor, drawing room, room (*as* **s. de espera,** waiting room, **s. de recibo,** reception r.)

salida, departure, exit, outlet, outcome, outlay, sally

salir (*see p. 166*), to go *or* come out, leave, (*of sun*) to rise, to sail, to come up, sprout, to turn *or* come out; **s. a,** to open upon, to look like (*a parent*), to come *or* amount to; **s. bien,** to come out well, succeed; **s. con,** to come out with, get (*what one wants*)

saltar, to jump, leap (out, over), to burst forth *or* out, gush, to break, crack; **s. a la vista** *or* **los ojos,** to be obvious

salud (*f.*), **health**

saludar, to greet

salvar, to save, to avoid, dodge, clear; leap; **–se,** to save oneself, escape

sangre (*f.*), blood; **a s. caliente (fría)** in hot (cold) blood; **a s. y fuego,** by fire and sword; **s. fría,** coolness of mind

sano, healthy, sound, healthful, sane; **s. y salvo,** safe and sound

santo, holy, simple (*naïve*); **s. varón,** simpleton; **santo, –a,** saint; *m.,* saint's day, birthday, password; **s. y seña,** password; **San(to),** **Santa,** St.

satisfacción (*f.*), satisfaction

satisfacer (*conj. like* **hacer**), to satisfy

seco, dry, dried (up), (*of leaves*) dead, curt, cold (*unemotional*), (*of pain*) dull; **en s.,** dry

secreto, *adj., n., m.,* secret; **s. a voces,** open secret

sed (*f.*), thirst (**de,** for); **tener s.,** to be thirsty

seda, silk; **como una s.,** as smooth as silk, smoothly; **de s.,** silk(en); **ser (como) una s.,** to be very amiable *or* reasonable

seguida: de s., in succession; **en s.,** immediately, right away; **en s. que,** the moment that, as soon as

seguir (i), to follow, to go *or* keep on; **–se,** to follow, ensue

según, according to, as; **s., s. y como, s. y conforme,** just as, it *or* that depends

segundo, *adj.,* second, favorable; **de s. mano,** second-hand; **s. intención,** double meaning; *n.; m.,* second; **sin s.,** unequaled

seguro, secure, sure, dependable; **s. de,** sure of; **s. de que,** sure that; *n., m.,* assurance, insurance; **de s.,** surely, assuredly; **en** *or* **sobre s.,** in safety; **s. contra (incendio),** (fire) insurance; **s. sobre (la vida)** (life) insurance

semana, week, week's pay *or* wages; **a la s.,** by the week; **entre s.,** (during the) week (*excluding week end*)

semejante, like, such a; *n., m.,* like, kind

sencillo, simple, plain, single, naïve, one-way, thin, light; *n., m.,* (small) change

sentar (ie), to seat, to set (up), to fit; **s. bien,** to fit well, become, to agree with, to set well; **s. mal,** to fit badly, to disagree with; **–se,** to sit down, to settle (down); **sentado,** seated, sitting (down); **dar por s.,** to take for granted

sentido, felt, sensitive, touchy; *n., m.,* sense, feeling, meaning, consciousness; **perder el s.,** to lose consciousness; **sin s.,** senseless

sentimiento, feeling, sentiment, sensitivity, sorrow, regret

sentir (ie, i), to feel, sense, to feel sorry, regret; **sin s.**, without knowing it; **–se**, to feel, to feel bad, to be resentful, to start to crack, give way, *etc.; see* **sentido**

seña, sign, signal, password; *pl.* address, (*personal*) description, signs, evidence

señal (*f.*), sign, signal, mark(er), bookmark, trace, down payment; **en s. de**, as a token of

señalar, to mark, brand, to point (out), indicate, to signal; **–se**, to distinguish oneself

señor (*m.*), lord, master, mister, gentleman, sir; *pl. as title:* Mr. and Mrs., Messrs.

señora, lady, madam, Mrs., wife

señorita, young lady, Miss

separar, to separate, divide; **–se**, to separate, part; **s. de**, to part, withdraw, *or* go away from

ser (*see pp.* 29, 71), to be; **a no s. que**, unless; **con s.**, in spite of being, although (he, *etc.*) is; **con s. que**, in spite of the fact that; **Eso es**, That's right; **es que**, the fact is that; **¿Qué ha sido de ...?** What has become of ...?; **sea como sea, fuera (fuese) como fuera (fuese)**, be that as it may; **Érase que se era ...**, Once upon a time ....

sereno, serene, calm, (*of sky*) clear; *n., m.*, night watchman, dew

serio, serious, sincere, businesslike; **en s.**, seriously

servicio, service; **al s. de**, in the s. of

servidor, –a, servant; **Quedo de Ud.,** *or* **Su, atento y seguro s.,** Yours very truly

servir (i), to serve, to do (*be satisfactory*); **s. de**, to serve as; **s. para**, to be (good) for, to do for; **–se**, to serve oneself; **s. de**, to make use of; **Sírvase ...**, Please ....

si, if, whether; *gives emphasis to exclamations and may be tr'd* why;

si bien, although; **si no**, if not; otherwise

si, (*music*) si

sí, *adv.*, yes; do, does, did, *etc.* (**Él no baila, pero yo sí,** He doesn't dance, but I do)

siempre, always, ever; **lo de s.**, the same old story; **para** *or* **por s.** (**jamás**), forever (and ever); **s. que,** provided (that)

siglo, century, age, world

significar, to signify, mean

siguiente, following, next

silencio, silence

silla, chair, saddle

simple, simple, simple-minded

sin, *prep.*, **s. que**, *conj.*, without

sino (*see p.* 57), but, only, if not; **s. que,** but

siquiera, *adv.*, even

sistema (*m.*), system

sitio, place, site, siege; **en el s.;** on the spot (*of killing, dying*)

situación (*f.*), situation

sobrar, to exceed, surpass, to be too much, be left over *or* extra

sobre, (up)on, over, above; **s. comida**, after dinner; **s. manera,** exceedingly, excessively; **s. sí**, on guard, in control of oneself; *n., m.;* envelope, (*sender's*) address

sobrino, nephew; **–a**, niece

sociedad (*f.*), society, corporation; **s. anónima**, corporation (S.A., Inc.)

sol (*m.*), sun, (*music*) sol, *Peruvian coin;* **al s.**, in the sun; **al ponerse el s.**, at sunset; **al salir el s.**, at sunrise; **hacer s.**, to be sunny

soldado, soldier; **s. de a caballo,** cavalryman; **s. de a pie**, foot soldier; **s. raso**, private (soldier); *p.p. of* **soldar**, to weld

soler (ue), to be accustomed *or* wont, be in the habit of, to usually

solicitar, to solicit, apply for, ask for, to attract

solo, alone, only, single; **a solas**, alone, unaided; **a (mis) s.**, by (my)self; *n., m.*, solo

sólo, *adv.*, only, solely

soltar (ue), to untie, to let go (of), to loose(n), to let out, to utter, to deal; **—se,** to be *or* get loose, to free oneself *or* itself, to come off *or* out; **s. a,** to break *or* burst out (*crying, etc.*)

sombra, shade, shadow; **a la s.,** in the shade, in jail; **tener buena s.,** to be liked; **tener mala s.,** to be disliked *or* feared

sombrero, hat

sonar (ue), to sound, make a noise, to ring, to blow (*nose*); **—se,** to blow one's nose

sonido, sound

sonreír(se) (i), to smile (**de,** at)

sonrisa, smile

soñar (ue), to dream (**con, en,** of); **s. despierto,** to daydream

sordo, deaf, still, muffled, dull

sorprender, to surprise; **—se de,** to be surprised at

sorpresa, surprise

sospechar, to suspect; **s. de,** to be suspicious of

sostener (*see p. 160*), to sustain, support; *p.p. as n., m.,* sharp (*note, sign*)

suave, soft, gentle, mellow, suave

subir, to rise, come *or* go up, to climb (up), to raise, bring *or* put up; **s. a,** to rise, *etc.*, to, to amount to, to get into *or* onto (*vehicle*), to mount (*horse*); **—se,** to rise, *etc.*; **s. a la cabeza,** to go to one's head

suceder, to happen; **suceda lo que sucediere,** come what may; **s. a,** to succeed, follow, to inherit from

suceso, event

suelo, ground, soil, floor, bottom, hoof; **medir el s.,** to fall flat

sueño, sleep, —iness, dream; **echar un s.,** to take a nap; **tener s.,** to be sleepy; **en sueños,** dreaming, sleeping

suerte (*f.*), fate, chance, luck, lot, sort, trick; **de s. que,** in such a way that, so that, and so; **por s.,** by chance; **tener s.,** to be lucky; **echar suertes,** to cast *or* draw lots

sufrir, to suffer

sujeto, *adj.*, subject, liable; *n., m.,* subject, person, fellow

suma, sum, addition; **en s.,** to sum up, in short

superior, superior, higher; *n., m.,* superior

suplicar, to entreat, beg

suponer (*see p. 159*), to suppose; **por supuesto,** of course

sur (*m.*), south

suspirar, to sigh; **s. por,** to long for

suspiro, sigh

tal, *adj.*, such (a); **el t. (N.),** that fellow (N.); **un t.,** a certain; **t. cual,** such as, one or another; *pron.*, such a thing, such a person *or* man; **con t. que,** provided (that); **t. para cual,** two of a kind; *adv.*, so; **t. cual,** soso; **¿Qué t.?** How goes it? Hello.

también, also, too

tampoco, (*answer to question*) No (*nor I either, not that either, etc.*); **ni ... t.,** nor *or* not ... either

tan, so, as, such a; *n., m.,* bang

tanto, *adj., pron.,* so *or* as much *or* many; **algún t.,** somewhat, a little; **al** *or* **por el t., t. por t.,** at the same price; **a t.,** to such a degree *or* extent; **en t. (que),** until, while, as long as; **entre** *or* **mientras t.,** meanwhile; **No es para t.,** It's not so bad; **otro t.,** another such, as much more; **por (lo) t.,** for that *or* which reason, therefore, wherefore; **y tantos,** and some, odd; *n., m.,* certain amount, point (*of game*), counter; **al t. de,** familiar with, well informed about; *adv.*, so much, so hard; **t. (A) como (B),** (A) as well as (B), both (A) and (B); **t. cuanto,** a little, somewhat; **t. mejor (peor),** so much the better (worse); **t. que,** as much as, so much that

tapar, to cover (up), to stop *or* plug (up)

tardar(se), to delay, be late, to take long; **a más t.,** at the latest

tarde, late, too late; **de t. en t.,** now and then, once in a while; **t., mal y nunca,** late and badly; **t. o temprano,** sooner or later; **t. piache,** altogether too late; **Para luego es t.,** Soon it will be too late; **Ya es t.,** It's too late; *n.*, *f.*, afternoon; **de** *or* **por la t.,** in the afternoon; **Buenas t.,** Good afternoon.

teatro, theater

techo, roof, ceiling

temblar (ie), to tremble, quake

temer, to fear, be afraid

temor (*m.*), fear

temprano, early, too early; **tarde o t.,** sooner or later

tender (ie), to extend, to stretch, spread, *or* lay out, to hold out, to lay (down), to tend; —**se,** to stretch out

tener (*see p. 160*), to have, hold; **t. a,** *or* **en, menos,** not to think much of, to hold lightly; **t. . . . años,** to be . . . years old; **t. calor, frío, hambre, miedo, sed, sueño,** to be hot, cold, hungry, afraid, thirsty, sleepy; **t. . . . de alto, ancho, largo,** to be . . . high, wide, long; **t. en mucho (poco),** to hold in high (low) regard; **t. para sí,** to believe, hold; **t. por,** to consider, regard, *or* take as; **t. que,** to have to; **¿Qué tiene (N.)?** What's the matter with (N.)?; **no tenerlas todas consigo,** to be uneasy; —**se,** to hold on, to hold oneself, stop; **t. a,** to hold on to, to stick to; **t. con,** to have it out with

tercer(o), third; *n.*, *m.*, third party; mediator, umpire, go-between

terminar(se), to end, finish; **t. de (comer),** to finish (eating)

término, end(ing), term; **t. medio,** average; **por t. m.,** on the a.; **en buenos términos,** in plain language

terreno, earthly; *n.*, *m.*, ground, land, terrain, piece of land, lot, plot

terrible, terrible

tesoro, treasure

tiempo, time, tempo, tense, weather, season; **andando el t.,** as time goes, *or* went, on; **a su t.,** in due time, at the right time; **a t.,** in *or* on time, timely; **con t.,** in time; **¿cuánto t.?** how long?; **engañar, hacer, matar,** *or* **pasar, el t.,** to kill time; **mucho (poco) t.,** a long (short) time; **t. de,** time to

tienda, tent, store, shop

tierno, tender

tierra, earth, land, ground; **dar en t. con, echar** *or* **poner por t.,** to bring down, overthrow; **echar t. a,** to bury; **irse** *or* **venirse a t.,** to fall down, collapse

tío, uncle; **t. vivo,** merry-go-round; **tía,** aunt; **tíos,** uncles, uncle(s) and aunt(s)

tipo, type, character; **t. de cambio,** rate of exchange

tirar, to throw, cast, hurl, fling, pitch, *etc.*, away *or* off, to shoot, fire, to deal, to draw, to print, to turn; **t. a,** to tend to, to turn to, to aspire to; **t. de,** to pull (on); —**se a,** to throw oneself into

título, title, heading, caption, headline

tocar, to touch, to play (*music, instrument*), to knock, to ring, to belong, pertain, concern, to be one's turn, to fall to one's lot

todavía, still, even, yet; **t. no,** not yet

todo, *adj.*, all, whole, *pl.* all, every (**todos los días,** every day); **t. aquel,** *or* **el, que,** everyone that; **t. aquello que,** everything that; **todos los que,** all who, all (those) that; **todo,** *pron.*, *n.*, *m.*, all, whole, *pl.* all, everybody; **ante t.,** first of all; **con t. (y t.),** in spite of everything, nevertheless; **del t.,** wholly;

en t. y por t., completely; **en un t.,** as a whole; *adv.,* wholly

tomar, to take, to drink, to eat, to acquire (*habit*), to gather (*strength*), *and variously in other idioms;* **t. por,** to turn to, to follow (*direction, road*); ¡ **Toma !** You don't say !; **tomarla con,** to have a row with, to tangle with; **–se,** to rust; **t. con = tomarla con**

tono, tone, tune; **a t. con,** in tune with; **darse t.,** to put on airs; **de buen (mal) t.,** in good (bad) taste; **gente del buen t.,** smart people

tonto, foolish, stupid; *n.,* fool

torcer (ue), to twist, to wind, to bend, to turn, to sprain, to distort; **–se,** to turn (sour)

torre (*f.*), tower, turret

total, *adj., n., m.,* total, sum

trabajar, to work; **t. mucho,** to work hard; **t. por,** to work *or* struggle to

trabajo, work; *pl.* hardships; **t. de manos,** handiwork

traer (*see p. 160*), to bring, carry, to bring (about), to draw, attract, to wear, to bring in, cite; **t. a,** to bring into *or* to; **t. consigo,** to have with one, to bring *or* carry with it; **–se (bien, mal),** to dress, to carry oneself (well, badly)

traje (*m.*), dress, suit, costume; **t. de baño,** bathing suit; **t. de ceremonia** *or* **etiqueta,** evening dress, full dress, dress suit; **t. de luces,** bullfighter's costume; **t. de montar,** riding habit; **t. serio,** formal dress; **baile de trajes,** costume ball

tranquilo, tranquil, quiet, peaceful

tras, *prep.,* behind, after, beyond, besides; **t. de = tras;** *n., m.,* behind, rear; thump, whack, sock (*sound of blow*)

trasladar, to (re)move, shift, transfer, to translate

tratar, to treat, to deal; **t. acerca de,** to deal with, discuss; **t. con,** to deal with; **t. de,** to try to, to address as, to call (*accuse of being*), to treat of; **t. en,** to deal in; **–se,** to behave, to live (*well, badly*); **t. de,** to be a matter *or* question of

trato, treatment, usage, behavior, trade, business, deal, form of address, (*personal*) relations; **gente de t.,** tradespeople; **tener buen t.,** to be pleasant, agreeable, nice

través (*m.*), crossbeam, –piece, traverse, slant, bias, reverse (*misfortune*); **a(l) t., de t.,** crosswise; **al t. de,** across; **dar al t. con,** to waste, ruin

tren (*m.*), train, equipment, following, pomp

trigo, wheat

triste, sad, sorrowful, dismal

tristeza, sadness, sorrow

triunfo, triumph, trump

tropezar (ie), to stumble; **t. con,** to stumble onto, run into

turbar, to disturb, upset; **–se,** to be *or* get upset, disturbed

u, or (*used before words beginning with* **o–** *or* **ho–**)

último, last, latest, latter, farthest, utmost, ultimate; **por u.,** at last, finally, lastly; **a últimos de,** toward the end of

único, only, unique

unión (*f.*), union, joining, junction

unir(se), to unite, join

un(o), a(n), one, *pl.* some; **de uno en uno, u. a u., u. por u.,** one by one, one after another, one at a time; **todo es uno,** it is all the same; **uno a otro,** each other; **unos a otros,** one another; **uno con otro,** on the average; **uno que otro,** one or another, a few; **uno y otro,** both of them; **unos cuantos,** some few; **a una,** at once, with one accord; **de una,** at once; **la una,** one o'clock; **una y no más,** once is enough

universidad (*f.*), university

usar, to use, to wear, to be accustomed to, to usually; **u. de,** to make use of

uso, use, usage, custom, habit; **a(l) u.,** according to usage

útil, useful; *n., m., pl.,* utensils; tools, equipment

vacaciones (*f. pl.*), vacation

vacío, empty, vacant; *n., m.,* void, vacancy, vacuum, hole, gap, *etc.*

valer (*see p. 160*), to be worth, to avail, to be worth while, to be valid, to protect; **hacer v.,** to avail oneself of, to assert (*one's rights*); **v. la pena,** to be worth while; **v. por,** to be worth; **más vale,** better, it is *or* would be better; **Válga(me) Dios,** God bless *or* help (me); **valerse,** to help *or* protect oneself, take care of oneself; **v. de,** to avail oneself of; **valer,** *n., m.,* value, worth

valiente, valiant, brave, vigorous, fine, great; *n., m.,* brave man, bully

valor (*m.*), worth, valor, nerve, validity, import(ance), *pl.* securities

vano, vain; **en v.,** in vain

vapor (*m.*), vapor, steam, fume, mist, steamer; **con v.,** steaming; **de v.,** steam (**máquina de v.,** steam engine)

variar, to vary

vario, varied, changeable; *pl.* various, several

vaso, glass, vase, vessel; **v. de noche,** chamber pot

vecino, neighbor, –ing

velar, to watch (over), to be *or* stay awake, to work at night, to veil; **v. por,** to watch over

vencer, to defeat, overcome, to win, to fall due, mature

vender, to sell, to sell out, betray; **–se,** to be sold, be for sale, sell, to sell oneself; **v. caro,** to be expensive, to hide oneself (*be seen rarely*)

venir (*see p. 171*), to come; **en lo por v.,** in time to come, hereafter; **v. a,** to come to, to be able to,

succeed in, to end by, to finally **v. a menos,** to decline, decay, worsen; **v. bien,** to grow well; **v. bien a,** to become, be becoming to, to fit well; **v. (bien) en,** to agree on *or* to, *also* **v. en,** to decide on, to obtain; **v. mal,** to be unbecoming, not to fit; **¿A qué viene eso?** What has that to do with it? What's that for?; **Eso no me va ni me viene,** That does not concern me in the least; **que viene,** coming; **venga lo que viniere,** come what may; **bien venido,** welcome; **–se,** to come (along), to work (*ferment*); **v. abajo** *or* **al suelo,** to come *or* fall down, collapse, fail

ventana, window; **v. de la nariz,** nostril

ver (*see p. 160*), to see, to try (*a case*); **A** *or* **Hasta más v.,** I'll be seeing you, See you soon, So long; **A v.** Let's see; **de v.,** to be seen; **hacer v.,** to make see, to show; **no poder v. a,** not to be able to stand (*a person*); **ser de v.,** to be worth seeing, to be seen; **tener que v. con,** to have to do with; **v. de,** to try to; **v. en,** to look *or* see into, see about; **Allá veremos,** We shall see; **visto** (*p.p.*), seen, evident, clear; **bien v.,** approved, proper; **mal v.,** disapproved, improper; **por lo v.,** apparently; **v. bueno (V°B°),** OK; **v. que,** considering that, since; **verse,** to see oneself, to find oneself, be, to be seen, to be conspicuous *or* obvious, to (go to) see each other; **v. con,** to see, interview, have a talk with; **Ya se ve,** Of course, Obviously; **ver,** *n., m.,* seeing, sight, appearance; **a mi v.,** as I see it

verano, summer, dry season

veras: de v., in truth, really, in earnest

verdad (*f.*), truth; **¿V.?** Is that true *or* so? Isn't that so?; **a la**

v., de v., en v., in truth, truly, really; **Bien es v. . . . , Verdad es que . . . ,** It is true that . . . ; **¿(no es) v.?** am I not? isn't it? weren't you? haven't they, *etc.;* **v. de Perogrullo,** platitude; **decir cuatro verdades,** to give a piece of one's mind

verdadero, true, real, actual

verde, green, youthful, off-color, "dirty"; *n., m.,* green

vergüenza, shame, modesty, shyness; **dar v.,** to make ashamed; **sacar a la v.,** to put to shame; **tener v. (de),** to be ashamed (to)

verso, verse, line, stanza

vestido, dress, clothing, costume; **v. de ceremonia** *or* **etiqueta, v. serio,** evening *or* full dress

vestir (i), to dress, clothe, to wear; **–se,** to dress (oneself), wear; **vestir(se) de,** to dress in, wear

vez *(f.),* time *(occasion, turn), pl.* duties, offices; **una v.,** once, **dos v.,** twice, **tres v.,** thrice, three times, *etc.;* **a la v.,** at a, one, *or* the same time; **a la v. que,** at the time that; **alguna v.,** sometime, ever; **algunas veces,** sometimes; **a (su) v.,** in (his) turn; **a veces,** at times; **cada vez (que),** each *or* every time (that); **cada vez más (alto),** (high)er and (high)er; **de una v.,** once and for all, at one blow, *etc.;* **de v. en cuando,** from time to time; **en v. de,** instead of; **hacer las v. de,** to perform the duties of, act as; **muchas v.,** many times, often; **otra v.,** another time, again; **rara(s) v.,** rarely, seldom; **tal v.,** maybe; **tantas v.,** so many times, so often; **una que otra v.,** at one time or another

vía, way, road, route, track, gauge, process, canal *(of body);* **v. de agua,** leak; **v. férrea,** railway

viajar, to travel

viaje *(m.),* trip, voyage, water supply; **hacer un v.,** to take a trip

viajero, traveler

vicio, vice, (bad) habit, perversity; naughtiness; **de v.,** from habit, habitually

víctima, victim

vida, life, living; **de (por) v.,** for life; **En la** *or* **mi v. . . . ,** Never in my life . . . ; **hacer v.,** to live together; **hacer** *or* **llevar una v. . . . ,** to lead a . . . life; **mi v., v. mía, v.,** dearest; **v. airada,** gay *(loose)* life; **v. ancha,** easy *or* loose life; **v. y milagros de,** life of *(a disreputable person);* **tener siete v.,** to have nine lives

viejo, old, former, old man; **–a,** old woman; **–os,** old people

viento, wind, scent; **v. en popa,** before the wind, full steam ahead, swimmingly

vino, wine; **tomarse del v.,** to get drunk

virgen, *adj., n., f.,* virgin

virtud *(f.),* virtue

visita, visit, call, visitor, caller, company, inspection

visitar, to visit, call on, to inspect, search

vista, sight, view, appearance, look, trial; **a la v.,** at, in, *or* on sight; **a la simple v., a primera v.,** at first sight; **a v. de,** in the presence of; **a v. de ojos,** with one's own eyes; **de v.,** by sight; **echar la v. a,** to set one's eyes on; **echar una v. a,** to keep an eye on; **en v. de,** in view of; **estar a la v.,** to be obvious; **hacer la v. gorda,** to wink at, overlook *(intentionally);* **Hasta la v.,** I'll be seeing you; Au revoir; **perder de v.,** to lose sight of; **perderse de v.,** to disappear; **saltar a la v.,** to be obvious; **v. cansada,** farsightedness; **v. baja** *or* **corta,** nearsightedness

viuda, widow; **–o, –er**

vivir, to live; **v. de,** to live by *or* on; **¿Quién vive?** Who goes there?;

¡**Viva** (...)! Hurrah (for ...)! Long live ...!; *n., m.,* living, life

vivo, alive, living, lively, vivid, (*of flesh*) raw, (*of rock*) solid; *n., m.,* living person, piping, border, mange

volar (ue), to fly, soar, to blow up

voluntad (*f.*), will, good will

volver (ue; *p.p.* **vuelto**), to turn (over, up, upside down), to return, come back, give back, to drive, make (*crazy, etc.*); **v. a,** to turn to, to ... again; **v. en sí,** to come to (oneself); **–se,** to turn, to become, go (*mad*)

voz (*f.*), voice, sound, rumor, word; *pl.* cries, shouts; **a media v.,** in a whisper; **a una v.,** with one voice, unanimously; **a v. en cuello** *or* **grito,** at the top of one's voice; **corre la v.,** it is said *or* rumored; **en v. alta,** aloud; **en v. baja,** in a low tone; **v. común,** general opinion; **a voces,** shouting; **dar voces,** to shout, cry out, scream; **pedir a voces,** to clamor, *or* cry aloud, for

vuelta, turn(ing), revolution, return, reverse, whipping, spanking, frill, change (*money*), walk, somersault; **a la v.,** on one's return, round the corner, on the back, over; **a (la) v. de,** within (*a certain time*); **a v. de,** about; **a vueltas de,** besides; **dar la v. a,** to walk *or* go around; **dar una v.,** to take a walk, to turn; **dar vueltas,** to pace to and fro, to go *or* look here and there; **de v.,** on returning, back

y, and

ya, already, now, right away; *often merely adds emphasis, as:* **Ya lo creo,** I believe it, Of course, I should say so!; **¡Ya voy!** I'm coming!; **¡Ya!** Yes!; **¡Pues ya!** Yes indeed! Of course!; **ya no,** no longer; **ya que,** since; **ya ... ya,** now ... now, whether ... or

zapato, shoe; **zapatos papales, z. de goma,** overshoes

SUPPLEMENTARY VOCABULARY

The Supplementary Vocabulary consists of more or less common Spanish words very useful to the reader or traveler. Of 1,337 words in this list, 1,060 words or their English equivalents will be found in one or more of the following sources: *Spanish Grammar* by E. V. Greenfield (Barnes and Noble, Inc.); the first thousand words in *A Teacher's Word Book of 20,000 Words* by E. L. Thorndike (Teachers College, Columbia University); the first thousand words in *A Basic Writing Vocabulary* by Ernest Horn (University of Iowa); and the "Useful Words" and "Derivatives" in *Standard List of Spanish Words and Idioms* by Hayward Keniston (D. C. Heath and Company). The author has included 277 words which are not in these sources but which he has found most helpful during many years of teaching foreign languages to adults.

The Supplementary Vocabulary omits words which are similar or alike in form and meaning to English words — such words as **accidente, actividad, americano, aplauso, aventura, calmar, clasificar.** (But **prevención,** for example, is not omitted — because it means *foresight, preparation, prejudice* as well as *prevention*.) Also omitted are geographical adjective-nouns (see pages 50–51, 225–226) and adverbs in **–mente.**

After you feel that you are familiar with all the words in the Basic Vocabulary, you should begin to study the words in this Supplementary Vocabulary. Study them a few at a time — say, half the a's, or all the b's, or the i's, j's, and k's. Look each word up in the dictionary, even if you believe that you know it or understand it at sight. Read through the list now and then, refreshing your memory of the words you do not remember well.

abastecer, abeja, abertura, abogado, aborrecer, abrazo, abreviar, abrigar, abrigo, acariciar, aceite, aceituna, acera, acero, acierto, aclarar, acoger, acometer, acomodar, acompañamiento, acontecer, acontecimiento, acorazado, actitud, actualidad, adelanto, ademán, adoptar, adormecer, adorno, aduana, advertencia, aéreo, aeropuerto, afecto, afeitar, aficionado, aficionarse, afortunado, afuera, agente, agradecimiento, agrado, agregar, aguacero, aguantar, agudo, aguja, agujero, ahorro, aislar, ajustar, alabanza, alcalde, alcance, alcoba, aldea, alentar, alfiler, alfombra, alfombrilla, algodón, alhaja, aliado, alimento, aliviar, alivio, almacén, almidón, almohada, almuerzo, alquilar, alquiler, alterar, altivez, altivo, ¡ Alto !, alumno, amabilidad, amargura, amarillento, amenaza, americana (*coat*), amistoso, amueblar, anciano, anchura, andén, ángulo, angustiar, anillo, ansia, ansiedad, ansioso, anteayer, anteojos;

323

antigüedad, antojarse, anual, anuncio, apacible, aparato, apariencia, apasionado, apellido, aplaudir, apoderarse, aposento, apoyo, apreciar, aprecio; aprisa, aprobar, aproximarse, apuntar, apurar, apuro, arado, araña, arco; arena, arranque, arreglo, arrepentirse, arriesgar, arrodillarse, arroyo, arroz, arruinar, asado, asar, asamblea, asentar, asociar, asombro, asombroso, aspereza, áspero, atacar, ataque, atormentar, atraer, atrasado, atrevimiento, aumento, ausente, autobús, automóvil, autorizar, auxiliar, auxilio, avena, avenida, aventurar, aventurero, avergonzar, avión, aviso, ayuda

bahía, bailarina, baja, bala, balde, bandeja, bandera, banquete, baño, baraja, barbaridad, barbarie, bárbaro, barco, basar, bastón, batir, baúl, bebida, bendición, beneficio, bestia, biblioteca, bicicleta, bienestar; bif– or bistec, –tek, or –té; blancura, bobo, bocado, bola, bolsa, bomba, bondadoso, borde, borrar, bota, bote, botella, botica, boticario, botón, bravo, bravura, brillar, brillo, brindar, brotar, buenaventura, buey, bulto, buque, burlón, butaca, buzón

caballería, cabellera, cabra, cacao, cadena, caída, cajón, calcetín, caldera; caldo, calentar, calentura, cálido, calleja, cámara, camarero, camarote, camión; camisa, campanilla, campaña, campesino, canción, cancha, cansancio, cantina; cantor, caña, cañón, capa, capítulo, capricho, caprichoso, carbón, cárcel, carga; caricia, carnero, carnicería, carretera, carro, carruaje, cartel, cartera, cartero; cartón, casamiento, castigo, castillo, casualidad, caucho, caudal, caza, cazador; cazar, cebolla, cegar, célebre, celeste, celo, celoso, cena, cenar, cenicera, ceniza; centenar, ceñir, cepillo, cera, cercano, cerdo, cerilla, cerradura, cerro, cerveza, cesta, cesto, cifra, cigarrillo, cima, cine, cinta, cinto, cintura, cinturón, circular (*v.*), círculo, cita, ciudadano, claridad, clavar, clavo, clima, cobrador, cobre; cocido, cocinera(–o), cochero, cochino, cola, colegio, cólera, colérico, colina; colocación, colorado, colorido, comandante, comerciante, comestible, cómico (*n.*), comienzo, comodidad, cómodo, compadecer, comparación, composición; compra, comprador, comprensión, comprometer, compromiso, conde, condesa; conductor, conformar, conjunto, conquista, conquistar, consagrar, consejero; consentimiento, conservador, constancia, consuelo, consulta, contrariar; contribución, conveniencia, conveniente, convite, copa, copia, corbata, corcho; cordel, cordón, corona, coronar, corredor, corregir, correspondiente, corrida; cortés, cortesano, cortesía, cortina, cosecha, coser, creciente, creencia, crema; cría, crianza, cruce, cuadrado, cuadrar, cuan, cuán, cuartel, cuchara, cucharada; cucharita, cuchillo, cuerda, cuerno, cuero, culpar, cultivo, culto, cumpleaños; cumplimiento, cuñado(–a), curación

chaleco, chaqueta, charla, chícharo, chiste, chistoso, chocar, chófer, choque

dama, dañar, datos, debilidad, debilitar, décimo, defensor, delantal, delantero; deleitoso, delgado, delicadeza, delicia, delito, dependiente, deporte, derrota, derrotar, desagradable, desagradar, desahogarse, desarrollar, desarrollo; desatar, desayunarse, desayuno, descanso, descargar, descomponer, desconfianza, desconfiar, descubrimiento, descuido, desdichado, desembarcar, desempeñar, desengañar, desengaño, desenvolver, deseoso, desigual, deslizar, desmayar; desmayo, desnudar, desnudo, despacio, despachar, despedida, despreciar; desprecio, desterrar, destinar, detalle, deuda, dibujar, dibujo, dictadura, dictar;

diferenciar, dignarse, diligencia, diosa, diputado, disculpa, disculpar, discurrir, discutir, disfrutar, disgustar, disimular, disparar, disparate, disponible, doblar, doble, doler, doloroso, dominio, doncella, dorar, dormitorio, dorso, dramaturgo, ducha, dudoso, duelo, dureza

edificar, efectivo, efectuar, eje, ejecutivo, ejemplar, ejercitar, embarcarse, embarque, emperador, empleo, empréstito, empujar, encaminar, encantar, encuentro, endosar, enérgico, enfadar, enfado, enfermera(-o), enfriar, engaño, engañoso, enlace, enlazar, enojar, enojo, ensalada, enseñanza, ensueño, entendimiento, enterrar, entierro, entrañas, entretener, entusiasmar, envidia, envidiar, envidioso, equipaje, equipo, equivocación, errar, escala, escalón, escandalizar, escándalo, escandaloso, escasez, escenario, esclavitud, esclavizar, esclavo, escoba, escribano, escritorio, escritura, escultor, escultura, esforzarse, espanto, espantoso, esparcir, espectáculo, espectador, espeso, esponja, establecimiento, estacionarse, estampilla, estancia, estanciero, estaño, estatua, estimular, estorbar, estropear, estudiante, estufa, exceptuar, excusado, explicación, extrañeza, extremar

fábrica, fabricación, fabricante, fabricar, fábula, facilitar, factura, falsedad, faro, fiebre, fiero, fila, filo, final (n.), firma, firmeza, flaco, flaqueza, flojo, florecer, floresta, florido, flota, flotar, fonda, formal, fortaleza, forzar, forzoso, fósforo, franqueza, frescura, frijol, frito, fruta, fulano, fumador, fumar, función, funcionar, fundamento, fusil

gabinete, galleta, gallina, gallo, ganadería, ganado, ganancia, garantir, garganta, gasto, genial, gerente, girar, giro, gobernador, goce, golfo, golondrina, golpear, gorra, gota, gozo, gozoso, graduar, gramática, grandeza, grano, gris, grosero, grueso, guante, guerrero, guía, gustoso

hábil, habilidad, hábito, habla, hablador, hambriento, harina, harto, helado, helar, hembra, heredar, heredero, herencia, herida, herramiento, hielo, hierba, hilar, hilera, hinchar, historiador, hogar, hoguera, honra, honradez, honroso, horario, horizonte, hormiga, hueco, huelga, huerto, huida, humedad, humedecer, húmedo, humillar, hundir

ida, idioma, igualar, igualdad, ilustre, impermeable, imponente, importe, imprenta, incapaz, incendio, incluir, incomodar, inconveniente (n.), increíble, indigno, industria, inesperado, infame, influir, informe, ingeniero, ingenio, ingrato, instancia, instantáneo (n.), instruir, intentar, intento, intimar, intimidad, ira, iracundo

jabón, jamón, jugador, juguete, junta, juramento

kilo(grama), kilómetro, kiosco

labor, labrador, labrar, labriego, ladrillo, ladrón, lago, laguna, lámpara, lana, lance, lanza, lápiz, lastimar, lata, latón, lavandera, lavandería, lazo, leal, lealtad, lector, lectura, lecho, lechuga, legua, legumbre, lenguaje, lento, león, letrero, libertador, libertar, libra, librería, ligereza, lima, limpiabotas, limpieza, liso, listo, litro, lodo, lucero, lúcido, luchar, lujo, lumbre llama, llano, llanta, llanura, lloroso, lluvia

macho, majestuoso, maldad, maldición, maleta, malsano, mancha, manchar. mandato, mando, manejar, manga, manojo, manso, manta, manteca, manzana, maravilloso, marca, marina, marinero, marino, martillo, masa, máscara, matador, mayoría, mecanógrafo, mejilla, mejorar, mensaje, mente, mentiroso, mercado, mercancía, merecimiento, meseta, método, metro, mezcla, miel, miembro, milagroso, milla, mineral, mínimo, ministerio, ministro, mira, moda, modista, mojar, moler, molestia, molesto, molinero, molino, moneda, mono, montón, morder, moreno, mosca, mostrador, móvil, muchedumbre, mudanza, mudo, muestra, multa, músculo, museo, muslo

nacimiento, nadar, naipe, naranja, naranjo, nave, navidad, neblina, necedad, necio, nervio, nido, niebla, nieto(–a), nieve, niñez, nobleza, novela, noveno, nublado, nudo, nuez

obrar, obrero, o(b)scurecer, o(b)scuridad, obstante, occidental, occidente, ocioso, octavo, oculto, ocurrencia, odiar, odio, odioso, ofensa, oficina, oficinista, ola, óleo, olor, oloroso, olvido, onda, operar, opinar, óptimo, orar, orgullo, orgulloso, orquesta, osar, oveja

pacífico, paga, pago, paisaje, paisano, paja, paliza, paloma, panadería, panadero, pantalón, papa, paquete, parabrisas, paracaídas, paracaidista, parada, paraguas, pardo, pareja, parque, participar, partidario, pasaje, pasajero, pascua, pasillo, pasta, pastel, pata, patata, patinar, patrón(–a), pecado, pecador, pecar, peinar, peine, pelar, pelear, película, pelota, penoso, pensador, pensativo, pensión, pera, pérdida, pereza, perezoso, periodista, período, perla, permanencia, persecución, perteneciente, pescado, pescador, pescar, pez, pintor, pintoresco, pisar, piscina, pista, placa, planchar, plantar, plátano, plática, platicar, platillo, playa, plazo, plegar, plomo, poblar, pobreza, poesía, policía, pólvora, polvoroso, pollo, poquito, portal, portátil, porte, portero, posada, postre, potencia, pozo, practicar, práctico, preciar, precisar, precisión, predicar, premio, prender, prensa, preocupación, preocupar, presenciar, preso, préstamo, presto, presumir, pretensión, prevención, prevenir, principiar, prisión, procedimiento, profesar, profesor, profundidad, progreso, promesa, propiedad, propina, proseguir, proteger, provecho, proyectar, puente, puerco, pulga, pulgada, pulmón, punta, puntapié, pureza

quebrantar, quebrar, queja, queso, química(–o), quinto

rabia, rabiar, rabioso, radiodifusión, raíz, ramo, rancho, rapidez, raso, ratón, raya, rayar, razonable, reacción, realización, recado, recibo, reclamar, recomendar, reconocimiento, recreo, rechazar, red, rededor, refrescarse, refresco, registrar, registro, regocijo, regreso, rehusar, reinado, reinar, reino, relámpago, remitente, remitir, renovar, renta, reparo, reparto, repentino, repollo, reponer, reposar, representación, representante, requerir, reserva, resfriado, resfriarse, resignarse, resonar, respetuoso, retiro, retratar, retrete, reunión, revelación, revelar, reventar, revés, revista, ribera, riesgo, risueño, ritmo, rodar, rosado, rueda, ruego, ruidoso sábana, sabiduría, sabor, sacacorchos, sacerdote, saco, sagrado, sal, salado, salchicha, –chón, salón, salsa, salto, saludable, saludo, salvador, salvaje, salvo, sangriento, santidad, sartén, sastre, sastrería, secar, seda, seguridad, selva, sellar, sello, semblante, semblar, semejanza, semejar, semilla, sencillez, senda, sendero, seno, sensible, señorío, señorito, séptimo, sepultar, sepultura, servidumbre, servilleta, seso, sexto, sierra, silbar, silbido, sillón, simpático, situado, soberano, sobra, sobretodo, socio, socorro, soledad, solicitud, soltero, sombrilla, sombrío, someter, son, sonoro, soñoliento, sopa, soplar, sospecha, sospechar, sospechoso, suavizar, súbito, sucesivo, sucio, sudar, sudor, suegro, sueldo, suelto, sufrimiento, sujetar, sumar, superficie, surgir, surtido, surtir, suspender, suspenso, susto

tabla, talón, talonario, talle, tamaño, tanque, tapa, tardanza, tarea, tarifa, tarjeta, taza, té, teatral, tejado, tela, telón, temblor, tembloroso, temerario, temeridad, temeroso, temible, temporada, temporal, tenedor, teniente, ternera, ternura, terremoto, testigo, tieso, tijeras, tinta, tinto, tirano, tiro, titular, toalla, tocante, tonelada, tontería, toque, torear, torero, torno, torpe, tortilla, tos, toser, tostada, trabajador, traducción, traducir, tragar, traición, traidor, transporte, tranvía, trapo, tratamiento, trazar, trepar, tribunal, triunfar, tronar, tronco, tropa, tropiezo, trozo, trueno, turbio

unido, uña, utilidad, uva

vaca, vacilar, vagar, vago, vagón, valentía, valeroso, valle, varón, vasija, vecindad, vejez, vela, velo, vencedor, veneno, venganza, vengar, venida, venta, ventaja, ventanilla, verdura, vergonzoso, vidrio, votar, voto, vuelo, vulgar, vulgo

yerno, yodo

zanahoria, zapata, zapatería, zapatilla, zarzuela, zorro, zumo

INDEX

(An asterisk is placed before each entry that appears in the text as "Situation Material.")

A (personal), 77; (preposition) 62, 93, 260n.; see **Al**

Absolute superlative, 25

Abstract nouns, 253

Accents and accent marks, 3, 13, 17, 31, 74, 212n.

*Accounts, paying, 240

−**Acho**, 231

−**Ada**, 242–243

Address, forms of, 83; see Personal titles

Adjectival phrases, 209

Adjective endings similar in English and Spanish, 46

Adjectives, 19–21, 23; agreement with nouns, 19; not capitalized, 17; comparison, 22–26; compound, 209–211; in compound words, 204; demonstrative, 54; geographical, 50, 224–226; that lose −o before a noun, 20; of nationality, 17, 19, 50, 224–226; as nouns, 24, 253; position, 19, 21, 25, 80, 81, 205; as pronouns, 37; similar in English and Spanish, 46; superlative of, 25; verbs formed from, 214; see Articles, Suffixes

−**Ado**, 242–243

Adverbs, 59–61; from adjectives, 60; in compound adjectives, 209; invariable, 60; position, 60, 81

Age, telling, 42

Agreement: of adjectives and nouns, 19; of articles and nouns, 11

*Air travel, 98

−**Aje**, 243

−**Ajo**, 231

Al, 11

−**Al**, 243

Algo, 181

Alguien, 181

Alguno, 180, 182

Alphabet, Spanish, 3, 15

Andar, 154, 182

Any in Spanish, 180–182

−**Anza**, 243

Apposition, nouns in, 257

−**Ar**, 243

−**Ar** verbs, 69, 75–77, 126, 152–154; 213

Argüir, 169

Articles, 11–12; definite, 252–255; indefinite, 255; neuter, 11, 255; omission of, 255–258

Asir, 166

−**Ato**, 243

Augmentatives, 230, 236, 239; see −**Azo**, etc.

*Automobile: see Motoring

Auxiliary verbs, 70, 73, 131; see **Estar, Haber**

−**Azgo**, 243

−**Azo**, 230, 242

*Baggage, 101

*Barbershop and hairdresser's, at the, 206

*Bathroom, the, 141

*Bed, going to, 146

*Bills: see Paying accounts

*Boarding house, 127–129

Books about Spain and Spanish America, 270

*Breakfast, 171

*Bullfight, at the, 211

Caer, 159

Capitalization, 17, **212n.**

Cardinal numbers, 31

Cerrar, 152

Cien(to), 32

−**Cillo**, 235

*Cinema, the, 236

Cities and towns, **15**

−**Cito**, 235

*Clothing; laundry and cleaning, 226

Commands, 195; negative, 194; *see* Imperative, Requests

Comparison of adjectives, 22–26

Compound adjectives, 209–211

Compound nouns, 204–206

Compound tenses, 74, 93, 133; *see* **Haber**

Compounds of irregular verbs, 149

Con, 28n., 63

Conditional mood, 121, 260–262; *see* **Si**

Conditions: *see* Conditional . . ., **Si**

Conducir, 166

Conjugation: full c. of **comprar, vender, vivir** in simple tenses, 110–112; *see* –**Ar** verbs, *etc.,* **Estar, Haber,** Irregular verbs, Mood, Tense, Voice

Conjunctions, 56–58; followed by subjunctive, 197

Conocer, 97, 157

Consonants, pronunciation of, 5–8, 16

Continuous tenses, 73, 76, 131, 133, 141

Contractions, 13

Contrary-to-fact conditions, suppositions, wishes, 117, 198, 260

Correspondence, 266–269

Costar, 153

Countries, names of, 15, 50, 225, 254

Currencies, 263

*Customs, the, 112

Dar, 144, 154, 188

Dates, 33, 48, 73, 266

Days of the week, 14, 17, 48, 254

De, 63, 93; see **Del**

Deber, 95

Decir, 170

Declension: of nouns, 11–13; *see* Agreement, Pronouns

Defective verbs, 175

Definite article, 11, 252–255; omission of, 255–258

Del, 11

Demonstrative adjectives and pronouns, 54

*Dentist, the, 220

–**Dera,** 244

Derivatives: *see* Augmentatives, *etc.;* Suffixes, **Tierra,** Word-building

–**Dero,** 244

Desde, 64

Desire, subjunctive to express, 195, 198

*Desserts, 199; *see* Eating

Dictionary, 186, 270

Diminutives, 234–236, 239; *see* –**Cillo,** *etc.*

*Dinner, 183; *see* Eating

Diphthongs, 4, 17

Direct and indirect object pronouns, 27–29, 30, 69, 79; *see* Reflexive pronouns

–**Dizo,** 244

*Doctor and dentist, 220–221

Don, doña, 83

Dormir, 168

Double letters, 16, 18, **44**

*Drinking, 154–156

–**Dumbre,** 244

–**Dura,** 244

E, 57

*Eating, 161–163, 171, 177, 183, **191;** 199

Echar, 189

–**Eda, –edo,** 246

En, 64

Endings: of letters, 267; similar English and Spanish word e., 45; *see* Augmentatives, Conjugation, Declension, Diminutives, Gender, Pejoratives, Plurals, Suffixes

–**Eño,** 246

–**Eo,** 246

–**Er** verbs, 69, 92–93, 126, 152–154, 157, 158–160

–**Ería,** 247

–**Ero, –era,** 247

Estar, 29–30, 71–74, 76, 93; full conjugation of, 130–132

Exclamations and exclamation marks, 17, 41, 58, 262

Exhortations, subjunctive to express, 195

–**Ez, –eza,** 247

Family names, 84; *see* Personal names, Relationships

Fear, subjunctive to express, 195

Females: *see* **Hembra**, Males . . .

*Food: *see* Eating

Fruits, 15

*Fruits, 191; *see* Eating

Future perfect tense, 74

Future tense, 133, 149, 260, 262

Gender of nouns, 11, 14–16, 218–220, 223; *see* Agreement

Geographical nouns and adjectives, 15, 17, 19, 50–52, 224–226, 254, 257

*Getting up, 135–136

*Going to bed, 146

Gran(de), 21

Greetings, 22; *see* Salutations

*Greetings, 96

Gustar, 77

Haber, 70, 74, 93, 101, **132**

Hacer, 159, 186–188

Hacia, 64

*Hairdresser's, at the, 206

Hasta, 64

Hay, 72n., 101

Hembra, 223

Hope, subjunctive to express, 195

*Hotel and boarding house, 127–129

Hour: *see* Time of day

Huir, 169

–Ida, 242

Idioms, 134, 185–191, **283**

–Iento, 248

If in Spanish: *see* **Si**

–Illo, 235

Imperative mood, 99, 195; *see* Requests

Imperfect tense, 71

Impersonal expressions, 43, 73, 176; followed by subjunctive, 198

Improbability, subjunctive to express, 261–262

Indefinite article, 11, 255–258

Indicative mood, 116; *see* Conjugation

Indirect object pronouns, 27, 30

Indirect questions or statements, 196

Infinitives, 69, 93–95, 260; used as nouns, 96, 253

Intensive pronouns, 145

Interjections, 58; *see* Exclamations

Interrogative pronouns, 41

Introductions, 85

Invariable adverbs, reference list of, 60

Ir, 101, 144, 170, 182

–Ir verbs, 69, 92, 126, 157, 166–171

Irregular past participles, 173–175

Irregular verbs, 147–149, 152–154, 157–160, 166–171; *see* **Andar**, *etc.*

–Ito, 235, 239

–Izo, 248

Jamás, 67, 68

Jugar, 154

Languages, names of, 16, 50, 224–226, 255

*Laundry and cleaning, 226

Let, Spanish equivalents of, 100, 195

Letters: *see* Alphabet, Capitalization, Correspondence, Double letters

Lo, 11, 255

Lucir, 157

*Lunch, 177; *see* Eating

Llevar, 189

Macho, 223

Males and females, words for, 218–220, 223–224; *see* Gender

Mas, más, 57

*Meals: *see* Eating

Measurement, 34, 262; *see* Weights

*Meats, 177; *see* Eating

–Mente, 60

*Menu, Spanish, 162; *see* Eating

Mil, millón, 32

Mismo, 56

*Money and exchange, 123–**124**

Months, 15, 17, 48, 254

Mood: *see* Conditional, *etc.*

*Motoring, 231

Mountains, 15, 254

Mover, 153

*Moving pictures: *see* **Cinema**

Nacer, 175

Nada, 67, 68, 181

Nadie, 66, 68, 181

Names: see Geographical names, Personal names

Nationality, nouns and adjectives of, 15, 17, 19, 50, 224–226, 254, 257

Negative commands, 194

Negative words and expressions, 29, 57, 66–68, 194, 196; position, 29, 67, 81; see **No,** etc.

Neuter article, 11, 255

Ni, 57, 67

Nicknames, 239

Ninguno, 67, 180, **182**

No, 29, 66–68, 81

None in Spanish, 180–182

Nouns: abstract, 253; adjectives as; 24; in apposition, 257; compound, 204–206; in compound adjectives, 209; gender of, 11, 14–16, 218–220, 223; infinitives as, 96; noun phrases, 205; plurals of, 12; in series, 252; similar in English and Spanish, 45–47; verbal, 96, 253; verbs derived from, 213; see Agreement, Declension, Endings, Nationality, Suffixes, Word-building, Word order

Numbers: cardinal, 31, 34; ordinal; 33

Nunca, 67, 68

Occupations, 73, 86, **257**

Oceans, 15, 254

Oír, 166

Omission: of article, 255–258; of subject pronoun, 122

–Ón, 230, 248–249

Orthographic accent, 31

Orthographic changes in verbs, 126; 148, 149, 153, 154, 169

Orthographic changes when suffix is added, 229

Orthographic differences between words similar in English and Spanish, 44

–Ote, 231

Para and **por,** 65, 93, 104–107

Participles: see Past participles, Present participles

Passive voice, 73, 138–141

Past definite tense, 72, 149

Past participles, 70, 74, 93, 149; irregular, 173–175

Past perfect tense, 74

*Paying accounts, 240

Pedir, 168

Pejoratives, 231; see **–Acho,** etc.

Pero, 57

Personal a, 77

Personal names, 12, 72, 83, 253; diminutives, 235; see Nicknames, Personal titles

Personal pronouns, 21, 27–29; omission of subject pronouns, 122; position, 30, 79–80; see Direct and indirect object pronouns, Possessive pronouns, Reflexive pronouns, **Tú . . .**

Personal titles, 83–87, 219, 253; see **Don, San**(to), **Tú, Ud.**

*Photography, 215

Placer, 175, 198

*Plane: see Air travel

Plurals of nouns, 12

Poder, 98, 159

Polite expressions, 85, 100; 267; see Greetings, Requests

Poner, 159, 190

Por: see **Para** and **Por**

Position: see Adjectives, Adverbs, Negative words, Personal pronouns, Word order

Possessive pronouns, 36, 254

*Post office, at the, 149

Prefixes, 17, 44, 214

Prepositions, 62–66; compound, 66; in compound nouns, 205; simple, 62

Present participle, 73

Present perfect tense, 70; see Compound tenses

Present tense, 69, 133, 258

Professions: see Occupations

Progressive forms of verbs, 73, 76, 131, 133, 141

Pronouns: see Adjectives, Demonstrative . . ., Intensive . . ., Interrogative . . ., Personal pronouns, Possessive . . ., Reflexive . . ., Relative . . .

Pronunciation, 3–8, 16
Proverbs, 258
Punctuation, 17

Quantitative expressions, 35; *see* Numbers
Querer, 122, 159, 198
Questions and question marks, 17, 29, 82; indirect questions, 196; *see* Interrogative pronouns
–Quiera, words ending in, 197

Radio programs in Spanish, 53, 203, 270
*Railway station, at the, 113
Reference books, 270, 283
Reflexive pronouns, 28, 55, 144; *see* Reflexive verbs
Reflexive verbs, 55, 141, 143–145
Regional names and nicknames, 51
Relationships, personal, 73, 85
Relative pronouns, 39–41, 197
Requests, 100, 117, 194
*Restaurant: *see* Eating
Rivers, 15, 254

Saber, 97, 160
Salir, 166
Salutations in letters, **267**
San(to), 21
*Sea travel, 107
Seas, 15, 254
Según, 66
Sentir, 167
Señor, –a, –ita, 83
Sequence of tenses, **198**
Ser, 29, 71–74, 138
Sex: *see* Gender
Si, 258–262
Simple tenses, 75, 92, 110–112
Sobre (prep.), 66
Soler, 175
Some in Spanish, 180–182
Spanish-American pronunciation, 7
*Spanish menu, 162: *see* Eating
Streets, 255
Stress, 3; *see* Accents . . .
Su, clarifying phrases after, 37
Subject pronouns: omission of, 122; *see* Personal pronouns

Subjunctive mood, 100, 116–119, 131, 193–198, 260–262; *see* Conjugation
Suffixes, noun and adjective, 242–244, 246–249; *see* Augmentatives, Diminutives, Pejoratives
Superlative of adjectives, 25; absolute s., 25
*Supper, 183; *see* Eating
Suppositions, contrary-to-fact, 198, 260; *see* Conditional mood
Syllables, 18

Tampoco, 67, 68
*Taxis, 118
Telling age, 42
Tener, 70, 135, 160, 263
Tense: *see* Present tense, *etc.*, Compound . . ., Continuous . . ., Progressive . . ., Sequence . . ., Simple
*Theater and cinema, 236
Thinking in Spanish, 26, 102
Tierra, illustrative list of derivatives of, 250
Time of day, 49, 73
Titles: of books, 258; *see* Personal titles
Traer, 160
*Travel: *see* Air . . ., Motoring, Railway . . ., Sea . . ., Taxis
Trees, 15
Triphthongs, 5
Tú and **vosotros,** 28, 36, 84, 122

U, 57
–Ucho, –uco, 231
Ud., 21, 28, 122
–Udo, 249
–Uelo, 235
Uncertainty, subjunctive to express, 196, 197
Uno, compounds of, 32
–Uno, 249
–Ura, 249

Valer, 160
*Vegetables, 191; *see* Eating
Venir, 171
Ver, 144, 160
Verb endings similar in English and Spanish, 46

Verbal nouns, 96, 253

Verbs: in compound nouns, 204; formed from adjectives, 214; formed from nouns, 214; not followed by prepositions, 95; orthographic changes, 126; similar in English and Spanish, 46; *see* Conjugation, Defective . . ., Impersonal . . .

¡Viva! 101

Vocabularies: basic, 283–322; supplementary, 323–327; *see* Dictionary, Word-building

Voice, 138; *see* Passive voice

Vowels, pronunciation of, 3–5, 17

Weather, 176

Weights and measures, 262

Whether in Spanish; *see* Si

Wishes, subjunctive to express, 195, 198

Word-building by derivatives, 229–231, 234–236, 239

Word order, 25, 79–82; *see* Adjectives: position, *etc.*

Words alike or similar in English and Spanish, 44–47

–Zón, 249

–Zuelo, 236